Wallace Stevens

AND THE

Limits of Reading and Writing

Wallace Stevens

AND THE

Limits of Reading and Writing

Bart Eeckhout

University of Missouri Press

COLUMBIA AND LONDON

Library of Congress Cataloging-in-Publication Data

Eeckhout, Bart, 1964–
Wallace Stevens and the limits of reading and writing / Bart Eeckhout.
p.   cm.
Includes bibliographical references and index.
ISBN 0-8262-1427-4
1. Stevens, Wallace, 1879–1955—Criticism and interpretation.   I. Title.
PS3537.T4753 Z627 2003
811'.52—dc21
2002028990

♾™ This paper meets the requirements of the
American National Standard for Permanence of Paper
for Printed Library Materials, Z39.48, 1984.

Designer: Stephanie Foley
Typesetter: Bookcomp, Inc.
Printer and binder: Thomson-Shore, Inc.
Typeface: Goudy

For permissions, see page 303.

To my parents

Contents

Acknowledgments

THIS BOOK HAS BEEN so long in the making that I have incurred a great many debts in the process. It gives me particular pleasure to be able to repay them here, if only symbolically and briefly. My major institutional supporters of the past fifteen years should come first: the English Department and Research Council at Ghent University in Belgium, the Belgian National Research Council (NFWO), the Flemish Ministry of Education, the Flemish Research Council (FWO-Vlaanderen), the Belgian American Educational Foundation, Columbia University and Fordham University in New York, and the Fulbright Commission. The collective confidence of these institutions in me has been much greater than my self-confidence could ever hope to be, and I thank them for it.

To Kries Versluys, who supervised the dissertation out of which this book grew, I am grateful for more than just the perceptiveness of his intellectual feedback and the exhilarating brilliance of his stylistic advice: I also owe him for his unstinting trust and support, his generosity of spirit, the contagiousness of his love of New York, and his—and his family's—personal friendship.

I consider myself lucky to be able to extend such thanks for professional help and personal sympathy to many other people in my immediate academic environment: to all members of the English Department in Ghent (including some no longer there), to several colleagues in other departments (especially the Teacher Training, Architectural, and Comp Lit departments), and to the members of the Ghent Urban Studies Team (GUST), who have made my life in recent years socially and intellectually much more rewarding. These colleagues and friends, together with my Columbia pals (who conceived Eden on Morningside, as Wallace Stevens predicted) and my sometime colleagues at Flemish Public Radio, have been largely responsible for tiding me over during the past fifteen years of mostly uncertain prospects.

I am grateful to Gert Buelens, Anne Marie Musschoot, and Jean-Pierre Vander Motten for their comments on my dissertation, which helped me in revising it for publication. This applies to John Serio as well, but in his case I am happy to add an extra word of appreciation for introducing me to the world of international Stevensians, first by cutting a special deal for me in becoming a member of the Wallace Stevens Society, then by asking me to write several book reviews for *The Wallace Stevens Journal*, and most recently by inviting me to act as a guest editor of the twenty-fifth anniversary issue of this wonderful journal. As a letter writer on my behalf, too, whether in support of applications or to negotiate permissions fees, he has been indefatigable.

At the University of Missouri Press, it has been a great pleasure working with my editors, Clair Willcox and Jane Lago, and my wonderfully meticulous and helpful copyeditor, Gary Kass. I am much indebted to the press's enthusiasm for my book and for its patience in awaiting the final manuscript, as well as for the praise and intellectual challenges provided by my two anonymous readers' reports. I am sure the quality of my work has profited from so much careful and concerted attention.

In one of my more pedantic moments, I am known to have coined a Barthesian variant on Descartes by writing: *J'ai des amis donc je suis*. I still stand by this idea, if not by the pedantry, and can only hope to repay the debt I owe to my friends (mentioned and unmentioned) by my daily companionship and torrent of e-mails. My parents, brother, sister-in-law, and three fantastic nephews, finally, know how important they are to me and I need not court sentimentality in expressing my love for them.

Abbreviations

Wallace Stevens's works are cited as follows:

CP   *The Collected Poems of Wallace Stevens*. New York: Alfred A. Knopf, 1954.

L   *Letters of Wallace Stevens*. Ed. Holly Stevens. New York: Alfred A. Knopf, 1966.

NA   *The Necessary Angel: Essays on Reality and the Imagination*. New York: Vintage Books, 1951.

OP   *Opus Posthumous*. Revised, Enlarged, and Corrected Edition. Ed. Milton J. Bates. New York: Alfred A. Knopf, 1989.

OP 1957   *Opus Posthumous*. Ed. Samuel French Morse. New York: Alfred A. Knopf, 1957.

PEM   *The Palm at the End of the Mind: Selected Poems and a Play by Wallace Stevens*. Ed. Holly Stevens. New York: Alfred A. Knopf, 1971.

SP   *Souvenirs and Prophecies: The Young Wallace Stevens*. By Holly Stevens (includes Stevens's letters and journals). New York: Alfred A. Knopf, 1977.

Wallace Stevens

AND THE

Limits of Reading
and Writing

Introduction

An Impossible Possible Philosophers' Poetry

> If you say on the hautboy man is not enough,
> Can never stand as god, is ever wrong
> In the end, however naked, tall, there is still
> The impossible possible philosophers' man,
> The man who has had the time to think enough,
> The central man, the human globe, responsive
> As a mirror with a voice, the man of glass,
> Who in a million diamonds sums us up.
> ~Wallace Stevens, "Asides on the Oboe"

THE POETRY OF WALLACE STEVENS is full of limits and questions of liminality. At the most straightforward, thematic level, this is immediately obvious from a wealth of liminal scenes: whether it is twenty men crossing a bridge into a village, a blackbird marking the edge of one of many circles, flocks of pigeons winging their way down into darkness, the latest freed man sitting at the edge of his bed, one of the limits of reality presenting itself in Oley, an old philosopher on the threshold of heaven, or the palm at the end of the mind on the edge of space, we come across limits and liminal situations at every point throughout the collected poetry. This thematic focus is further enhanced by Stevens's well-attested predilection for the most archetypical binary divisions, such as day and night, sun and moon, sea and earth (or sea and sky, earth and sky), summer and winter (or their transitions, spring and fall), matter and mind, or reality and the imagination. The ubiquity of such poetically pedigreed oppositions in his work may even count as an important reason for his relatively smooth assimilation into the poetic canon, whose traditional topoi he so inventively and extensively developed as to

1

become their twentieth-century American master. Questions of liminality and demarcation, moreover, inform not only Stevens's subject matter, but also his diverse ways of enacting and realizing those subjects at a more formal and aesthetic level. After all, few other poets of his day and age have so consistently explored the question of what it means to begin and end a poem (or a stanza, or indeed a single line). Few have so humorously walked the thin line that separates sense from nonsense. And few have so variously and unpredictably tapped the delimiting effects of titles, the slippery connections enabled by syntax, or the manifold opportunities for registering shifts and discontinuities in tone and voice.

Stevens criticism, as we might expect, has often followed up this interest in liminality. Critics with a penchant for poststructuralist theories have been eager to analyze Stevens's poetry for its ability to elucidate or enact the difficult and shifting (so-called "undecidable" and "aporetic") relationships between inside and outside, center and margin, world and self, signifier and signified, content and form. Deconstructionist critics in particular—who will often, characteristically, start by denouncing the delimiting quality of the very label—have been nothing if not concerned with questions of limits and the instabilities of binary systems of opposition. In the words of Rodolphe Gasché, one of the principal spokesmen for the movement, Derridean deconstruction has shown a marked interest in how "[t]he outside of the text is precisely that which *in* the text makes self-reflection possible and at the same time limits it. . . . [F]ar from being an operation *in the limits* of the text, deconstruction proceeds *from and at the limit* of the text."[1]

Because of this topical focus, both the poetry and the critical interpretations of Wallace Stevens promise to extend our appreciation—conceptually as well as aesthetically—of the intrinsic finitude of our human condition. This is true not only in the more banal sense: the fact that we are all troubled and challenged by limits every day, from trying to arrive in time and finding a parking space to exhausting our energies in writing prefaces to books. This daily rhythm of humdrum limits often merely numbs, exasperates, or entertains us. Every so often, however, it finds itself disrupted or punctuated by a confrontation with the larger realities of our intrinsic human finitude: the watersheds that are those of giving birth, enjoying love, fighting sickness, dealing with loss, facing death. These are the kinds of experiences we very much bring with us whenever we read poetry, expecting to find in compacted

1. Rodolphe Gasché, *Inventions of Difference: On Jacques Derrida*, 28.

and augmented form some of the million diamonds that sum us up. They are experiences, moreover, with which we are never truly finished. The finitude of our human condition is such that it requires the flexibility of constant rethinking, since every new experience has the potential to rearrange our perceptions. This applies to the small scale of individual lives as well as to the vaster and grander scale of intellectual history.

With respect to the latter, it has been argued that some of the most influential Western philosophies and religions have in fact developed oddly lopsided views of the ways in which the reality of limits "determines" us and our worlds. (The verb *determine*, through its etymological root of *terminus*, itself conjures up the image of a stone or post marking a border.) Although such claims can be made only in the most sweeping and provisional of terms, they are nonetheless worth formulating: throughout the history of Western philosophy and religion there runs a deeply hostile streak that would picture human finitude only, or very largely, in negative terms. This is the claim made by the German existential phenomenologist Rudolf Boehm, whose ambitious analysis of the crisis of modernity in *Kritik der Grundlagen des Zeitalters* (Critique of the foundations of our time) provides the distant and much-deflected impetus to the present study.[2] Fears of the ultimate and absolute limit of death in a premodern world in which health hazards and natural catastrophes were much less easily contained than they are today and material well-being was at a much higher premium (at least compared to the modern West) have spawned world views—from Platonism to Christianity, to take only the most influential examples—that have tended to equate the notion of human finitude above all with lack, vulnerability, disease, fall, or shortcoming. One of the first thinkers to have countered this long-standing negative emphasis was Immanuel Kant, who conjured up the simple image of a bird in flight:

2. The starting point of Boehm's critique (which was shaped by his wartime experience as a young man in Berlin and his training in Heideggerian and Husserlian phenomenology) is the observation that we live in the age of science, and the hypothesis that his book tries to substantiate is that the fundamental crisis of our age is directly related to the type of knowledge advocated by modern science, which is a type of knowledge governed by the ideal of objectivity. Boehm traces the origins of this ideal back to Aristotle's writings, in particular to the idealization of "theoria" as a pure knowledge pursued entirely for its own sake, without any external practical goal. He demonstrates how this ideal is paradoxically still motivated by a wish for freedom, for a godlike existence, and for immortality, and argues that it betrays a basic inability to accept human mortality for what it is. The ideal of "theoria," so the argument goes, is informed by a basically negative view of the finitude of our human condition. It is an ideal that prefers the certainty of unimportant exact knowledge to the uncertainties of important inexact knowledge (like those offered by poetry).

The light pigeon, when it flies freely through the air, whose resistance it feels, might begin to entertain the notion that flying would be still easier in a vacuum. Thus, Plato too left the world of the senses behind, since it imposes such narrow restrictions on the mind, and ventured beyond, on the wings of ideas, in the empty space of pure reason. He did not notice that he failed to cover any distance through his efforts, for he had no resistance to cling to or to exert his forces upon so as to move reason from its place.[3]

Arguably, Kant was one of the first modern philosophers to demonstrate how the finitude of our human existence—the fact that we are all embodied, sensuous, vulnerable, mortal beings—does not merely *limit* reality (and our perception of it): it *realizes* reality (and our perception of it) *by limiting it*. Limitations, in other words, should not be viewed as essentially negative, as ever so many constrictions and privations, but as the necessary and productive conditions for human existence. They *produce* even as they *restrict* our fates, and they do so irrespective of the powerlessness we may feel over and against the radical contingency and absurdity of those fates. The phrase "constitutive constraint," coined by Judith Butler in a completely different context,[4] may be borrowed here to remind us that limits may be regarded as at once enabling and constraining, liberating and oppressive, inextricably a nexus of inclusion and exclusion, of possibility and impossibility. In ways that are alternatively or even simultaneously fascinating and frustrating, Wallace Stevens's poetry may be seen to reflect this awareness. With his deeply felt humanistic project of offering an alternative to traditional religions and ontological thinking, Stevens was a poet who appeared to be aesthetically and intellectually obsessed with the establishment of limits and with the satisfactions and disappointments afforded by the intrinsic finitude of our condition.

"Finding better questions to ask," writes philosopher and cognitive scientist Daniel C. Dennett, "and breaking old habits and traditions of asking, is a very difficult part of the grand human project of understanding ourselves and our world."[5] If the question of how we are conditioned by limits appears to be one of the "better" questions to ask in the epistemological and ethical realms of philosophy and religion, this is not automatically the case also in the more performative and aesthetic world of poetry. In philosophy, at least,

3. Quoted in Rudolf Boehm, *Kritiek der grondslagen van onze tijd,* 273 (my translation).
4. Judith Butler, *Bodies That Matter: On the Discursive Limits of "Sex,"* xi.
5. Daniel C. Dennett, *Kinds of Minds: Toward an Understanding of Consciousness,* vii.

the question may be addressed in direct confrontation with theoretical and ideological texts that have shaped our thinking and discourse on the subject. Genealogical traces of a philosophy of finitude may be found from Kant, Fichte, and Feuerbach, to Nietzsche and Marx, and down to the twentieth-century phenomenologists Husserl, Heidegger, and Merleau-Ponty.[6] In an American context, the names of the pragmatists Emerson, James, Dewey, Rorty, and Fish are easily added to such a list. Yet for all the influence such thinkers have undeniably exerted "outside" philosophy, and specifically on literary writers (a group to which some of them, characteristically, *also* belonged), the difficulty of finding the right questions to ask of poetry in this context remains considerable. The genre of poetry does not integrate itself unproblematically with philosophical metanarratives and conceptual critiques, even though the confrontation with human limits has traditionally been no less urgent to poets than to philosophers. How, we should wonder, does one avoid lapsing into a treatment of poetry as a mere literary kitchen maid that is hired to dust off and polish a number of philosophical tenets? How, indeed, does one determine the limits of the analytical activity of criticism in this context?

As Richard Rorty warns us, "the natural tendency of professionalization and academicization is to favor a talent for analysis and problem-solving over imagination, to replace enthusiasm with dry, sardonic knowingness," but we should not cave in too readily to "the latest attempt by knowing philosophers to gain supremacy over inspired poets." Simon Critchley confirms: "From the perspective of a philosopher, like myself, it is distressing to see how much theoreticism (whether formalist or historicist) abounds in discussions of literature, where we are offered *réchauffé* versions of rather stale philosophical dishes." We had better continue to be wary, then, of importing external theories into literary criticism if these theories do not promise or prove to enrich our comprehension of literary texts. "Poetry," says Critchley, "needs a philosophy that needs poetry."[7] When the subject of this book, Wallace Stevens, engaged in some modest lobbying for the institution of a poetry chair at Princeton University (the year was 1940), he famously argued that "it must be an odd civilization in which poetry is not the equal of philosophy" (*L* 378). It must be a no less odd civilization in which poetry critics feel called upon to plead *against* this equality.

6. See Willy Coolsaet, translator's introduction to *Kritiek der grondslagen van onze tijd*, 14.
7. Richard Rorty, "The Inspirational Value of Great Works of Literature," 14, 16; Simon Critchley, "The ancient quarrel," 26.

Stevens's lifelong agonistic relationship with philosophy, however, may at least be taken to point to a shared interest that in its own way sheds light on the nature and function of limits, in life as in art. The very attention bestowed by Stevens on liminal issues suggests a "topical" compatibility with philosophy. This study, it should be stated at the outset, presupposes this compatibility. It relies, more particularly, on the remarkable productivity that Stevens's poetry has demonstrated on the many occasions when it was presented in the philosophical contexts of phenomenology (especially during the sixties), deconstruction (roughly from the mid-seventies through the eighties), and American pragmatism (most spectacularly and copiously in the nineties)—three traditions in which the question of human limits is often implicitly or explicitly posed. Stevens is without doubt the one Anglo-modernist poet whose work has been most worried from a philosophical perspective, even if it was T. S. Eliot who actually received the most extended academic training in philosophy. This is true even today, after almost two decades of concerted critical attempts (many of them impressive and invaluable) to historicize and deidealize our understanding of Stevens's work. One recent example among several comes from Gyorgyi Voros, who in her ecologically inspired study of Stevens returns to the poet's affinity with phenomenology. Quoting the following definition by the French phenomenologist Pierre Thévenaz, Voros indeed manages to come close to sketching the most general intellectual framework for interpreting Stevens's poetry: "phenomenology is neither a science of objects nor a science of subject," writes Thévenaz; "it is a science of *experience*. It does not concentrate exclusively on either the objects of experience or on the subject of experience, but on the point of contact where being and consciousness meet. It is, therefore, a study of consciousness *as intentional*, as directed towards objects, as living in an intentionally constituted world."[8]

Such analogies between a particular brand of philosophy and a highly unique body of poetry should nevertheless be seen for what they are: general meeting-points from which a critic may set off. They provide a set of angles, perspectives, and directions, but are not in themselves sufficient to generate valid readings of the poems under discussion. And so the question remains: How can a topicalization of finitude be adapted to Stevens's poetry *without losing the poetry*? How, indeed, can general philosophical questions be deflected into questions that may be fruitfully asked of these very specific poems? The questions, it would seem, ultimately have to surface from within;

8. Quoted in Gyorgyi Voros, *Notations of the Wild: Ecology in the Poetry of Wallace Stevens*, 12.

they have to be questions about limits that Stevens's poetry itself wants to raise. And they have to be questions that a critic—or rather, this particular critic—feels up to addressing. Take, for example, the aspect of the *embodiedness* of our human condition. While it is theoretically no doubt possible to investigate Stevens's attitudes in this respect, the topic seems to me also likely to leave us shortchanged and frustrated. The body in Stevens's poetry is almost exclusively represented as a site of pleasure—primarily visual, secondarily aural—and rarely as a site of pain. (Pain in Stevens is almost wholly mental; it is a matter of solitude and despair.) Apart from registering sensual delights, moreover, his texts refer to the physical or corporeal only in highly indirect ways: above all, through the unaccountable cycles of vitality and exhaustion that are any lyric poet's (certainly Stevens's) constantly implied subject.

Other essential aspects of our human finitude do not readily invite critical appropriation either. One crucial limit that is undeniably all over the works is that of death and mortality. Stevens's is, after all, an unusual oeuvre in that it was largely composed by a man between the ages of fifty-five and seventy-five who for much of the time had health problems (so much so that, ironically for an insurance man, he found himself unable to take out a life insurance policy). Yet the topic of mortality appears to me unwieldy by virtue of its omnipresence, and too much in danger of inviting moralistic platitudes and cloying personal testimonies to be addressed in scholarly prose. Something similar applies to the limits of desire in this poet's work: here the topic is not only unwieldy, but also highly elusive and demanding. The question of the constrictive/productive limits of desire in Stevens's poetry is no doubt a major one that should be addressed head-on some day—and not only from the usual Freudian and Lacanian angles, or simply in a sexual context. Frank Lentricchia's critique of Stevens's economic status, in *Ariel and the Police*, offers one useful, if partial, inroad into the problem. It could be combined with Douglas Mao's recent analysis of the bemusing affective relationship with objects entertained by Stevens, whom Mao calls "the century's great poet of desire," as well as with a discussion of the phenomenon of "humanistic narcissism" developed by Rudolf Boehm and the romantic individualization ethic underlying the birth of consumerism, which both speak to Stevens's recurrent idealization of, and basking in, a kind of autotelic, self-sufficient desire.[9]

9. Frank Lentricchia, *Ariel and the Police: Michel Foucault, William James, Wallace Stevens, and Modernist Quartet*; Douglas Mao, *Solid Objects: Modernism and the Test of Production*, 258; Rudolf Boehm, *Ideologie en ervaring: materialen voor een ideologiekritiek op fenomenologische*

The present study, by contrast, grew out of questions that were more certain to be rewarding (though I was still pleasurably uncertain as to the precise nature of those rewards). It started with an attempt to recast the threadbare, but still crucial, Stevensian reality-imagination debate in more epistemologically inspired terms: as a topicalization of the limits of perception, thought, and language. As I undertook the attempt, however, a second major issue surfaced, which had to be dealt with beforehand. The issue is familiar to all critical readers of Stevens, since any interpreter of his poems is quickly and acutely made aware that one cannot legitimately address the limits of writing explored by Stevens *in* his poetry without first addressing the limits of *reading* his poetry. After all, this is a poetry so rife with possibilities for interpretation, a poetry that has already been interpreted so variously and contradictorily, that it becomes necessary first of all to address the question of limits to its signifying potential. Thus, the present study is divided into two equal parts, respectively called "The Limits of Appropriation and Contextualization" and "The Limits of Perception, Thought, and Language."

In the case of a writer like Stevens, an exploration of the "limits" of reading and writing is not possible without first emphasizing the deep ambiguities and ambivalences of his perspective. For Stevens's poetry is more than simply obsessed with staging liminal scenes and scenarios: it is also preoccupied with the limitations of the very effort to establish fixed limits. His work is generated out of the tension between possibility and impossibility, between finitude and infinitude. It is the work of an "impossible possible philosophers' man" as envisaged in "Asides on the Oboe" (CP 250). Rather than fix boundaries, Stevens tries to bring boundaries into focus, only to insist, in one and the same gesture, on the various ways in which these boundaries continue to define one another dynamically—not as fixed territories, but as competing if necessary ways to articulate certain complexities in a variety of experiences. My analysis in the following pages is thus infused by a strong interest in those situations—often temporal and transitional in nature—where limits are hard to set or tend to be traversed even as they are being determined. Limits often liberate, but the resulting liberty is not so easily limited when we move into the world of art, where the proverbial goal-orientedness of work and reason is constantly mixed up with the self-sufficient or indirect gratifications of play and imagination. Nor are limits

LUDICITY

---

grondslag, 22–23. For the birth of consumerism, see Peter Corrigan, *The Sociology of Consumption: An Introduction*, 9–16.

easily set in the world of reading. The activity of reading is to a considerable extent a dislocating and dislodging activity that involves a subjection, by the readerly subject, both *of* and *to* the text. We are read by literary texts as much as we read them. We do not only assimilate texts, they also assimilate us. "Reading," suggests Richard Poirier, "ought to get down ultimately to a struggle between what you want to make of a text and what it wants to make of itself and of you." This may be "a lonely discipline that makes no great claims for itself,"[10] but it is also one of the two most important disciplines we have at our disposal—along with conversation—for opening our minds to other forms of thinking and feeling and other objects of experience and contemplation.

One of the reasons why the following study is so strongly soaked in the words of others—not only Stevens's seductively quotable lines, but also the comments of his many critics and the language of several other writers and thinkers—is that this dialogical approach seems to me to constitute the most productive way of delimiting topics and working them out. As Bertolt Brecht once remarked about Lenin: "He thought inside other heads, and in his own head, too, others were thinking. That is real thinking."[11] Lenin may no longer be our favorite paragon of sound thinking, but the description is still apt. Certainly as readers we are a clearinghouse of thoughts, and in the case of thoughts prompted by a Stevensian sort of poetry, we had better not strive to shut the doors and foreclose traffic too soon.

A similar wish to open up rather than foreclose underlies my approach to the handful of poems that will be my focus of attention. As I argue in the conclusion to the first half of this book, Stevens's work continues to elicit further readings because of the simple fact that in his case any *close* reading serves to preclude a *closed* reading. Although I will linger on certain emblematic poems, working incrementally through a multitude of earlier critical voices while staying as close as possible to the fine points of the text, my reading procedure depends fundamentally on affirming the productive tension between the delineation and dissemination of meanings. It should not, in other words, be confused with the New Critical ideology of "close reading," which was an ideology of unity, organicism, and isolation of the poetic artifact from its historical context that has since been rightly discredited. In this respect, I find myself sympathizing with J. Hillis Miller in his preface to a collection of his essays, *Tropes, Parables, Performatives*:

10. Richard Poirier, *Poetry and Pragmatism*, 167, 193.
11. Bertolt Brecht, "Notizen zur Philosophie 1929–1941," 166 (my translation).

those essays, Miller writes, are kept together by an "irresistible penchant for 'close-reading' of individual texts" that should not, in his opinion, be viewed as " 'an inheritance from the New Criticism.' It springs rather from an initial and persistent fascination with local strangenesses in literary language." There is still much to be said for Miller's conviction that "[c]lose reading is the only way to get into any proximity to that 'other' to which the works of any author seem to give access."[12] And determining, encircling, and clarifying the irreducibly "other" remains precisely what all attempts at setting limits strives to facilitate.

12. J. Hillis Miller, preface to *Tropes, Parables, Performatives: Essays on Twentieth-Century Literature*, vii-viii.

Part One

The Limits of Appropriation and Contextualization

∽

It can never be satisfied, the mind, never.

~Wallace Stevens, "The Well Dressed Man with a Beard"

Chapter 1

Reading Stevens

READING STEVENS, as a literary critic, can no longer be done without confronting the existence of the full-blown critical industry that has sprung up in the poet's wake. Any critical reflection upon the act of reading this poet must be undertaken against the historical backdrop of a burgeoning Stevens criticism and the myriad ways in which this massive body of criticism has opened up and delimited interpretations of the poetry. To be able to address the limits that shape, produce, and constrict the reading of Stevens's poetry, I must first synoptically retrace the history of Stevens criticism.[1] In its roughest and most panoramic outline, that history is characterized by diffidence and deferral. The much-debated slowness and hesitancy with which Stevens's poetic career got off to a start was reiterated by his critics, who were equally slow and hesitant to respond to his poetry and attest to its stature and overall seriousness of purpose: appreciation for his earliest book, *Harmonium* (1923), became widespread only in the forties, by which time the poet himself had long passed on to other increasingly intractable and resistant compositions. The so-called middle and late Stevens—the poet from the mid-thirties through the mid-fifties producing the larger part of his literary output—in turn came to be widely admired only after the publication of the

1. Versions of this history have been written more than once and at various stages of its development: see especially Joseph N. Riddel, "The Contours of Stevens Criticism" and "Wallace Stevens"; Doris L. Eder, "A Review of Stevens Criticism to Date"; Abbie F. Willard, *Wallace Stevens: The Poet and His Critics*; Steven Gould Axelrod and Helen Deese, "Wallace Stevens: The Critical Reception"; Melita Schaum, *Wallace Stevens and the Critical Schools*; and the theoretically and sociologically most instructive study so far, John Timberman Newcomb's *Wallace Stevens and Literary Canons*. For an annotated secondary bibliography of Stevens criticism through 1990, see John N. Serio, *Wallace Stevens: An Annotated Secondary Bibliography*.

Collected Poems (1954), and especially posthumously, in the sixties. By that time, however, the diffidence—and, frequently, downright dismissiveness—of early book reviewers, who were overcome by the difficulty of getting a secure grasp on this playfully elusive and abstruse writer, was shed, and academia took matters in hand.

In the boom years of educational democratization—the sixties—few better goals were available to talented graduate students with a penchant for poetry than to decipher the works of Wallace Stevens. For this was a writer who was arguably not only the most enigmatic and sophisticated American poet on record, but also a prime candidate for contesting the critical hegemony of T. S. Eliot, as well as for wresting poetry free from the stranglehold of New Critical dogmas and establishing a new field of critical and literary theory.[2] A spate of articles, dissertations, and books on the poet flowed over America (though not over the British Isles).[3] Such an avalanche was, in fact, as John Timberman Newcomb demonstrates, "unmatched in the history of twentieth-century American literature scholarship."[4] Up-and-coming critics of great acumen and steadily growing renown took it upon themselves to tackle the poetry, especially in its middle to late phases. All were working at approximately the same time, and so could afford to feel like pioneers

2. Frank Lentricchia, *After the New Criticism*, 30–31; Newcomb, *Literary Canons*, chap. 6.

3. As far as Stevens's long-standing lack of success with British poetry critics is concerned, Frank Kermode was the proverbial exception that proved the rule. Indeed, although Kermode today occupies a solidly central position as a critical éminence grise, sitting on the editorial board of such intellectual institutions as the *London Review of Books*, it should not be forgotten that this native of the Isle of Man was once deemed a maverick living on the margins of British academic culture, where, as a self-styled "sort of one-man diaspora" (quoted in Michael Wood, "A Sort of Nobody," 11), he has never felt entirely at home. The fate of Stevens among the British has been studied by George S. Lensing ("Wallace Stevens in England"), as well as, more recently, Carolyn Masel ("Stevens and England: A Difficult Crossing") and the Irish critic Lee Margaret Jenkins (*Wallace Stevens: Rage for Order*, 1–6). It is too early to tell whether the appearance of Jenkins's book, almost in tandem with Tony Sharpe's biography (*Wallace Stevens: A Literary Life*), may be taken to herald a belated surge in academic interest in Ireland and Great Britain.

4. Newcomb, *Literary Canons*, 203. The first book-length study of Stevens, William Van O'Connor's *The Shaping Spirit*, appeared in 1950. Stevens criticism made a quantum leap in 1954, the year before the poet's death, when at least forty-four articles, reviews, and briefer statements appeared and the first three dissertations were written. It saw another stepping up of efforts in the sixties, with an annual harvest of one or more books and between five and thirteen dissertations (see Serio, *Annotated Secondary Bibliography*). Newcomb gives us the telling facts that "between 1960 and 1966 there were 27 dissertations completed on Stevens at 21 American universities, by far the largest number on an American modernist poet during those years. In contrast, Eliot was the main subject of 15 dissertations completed during the same years; Pound 11; Aiken and Williams 5 each; Robinson, MacLeish, Jeffers, and Crane 4 each; Frost only 1; and Moore none" (*Literary Canons*, 205).

and trailblazers, the first to land upon magical soil and explore the Ultima Thule of poetry. The upshot of so much critical groundbreaking was twofold. Stevens in almost no time entered the canon and became a staple ingredient of the modernist curriculum that was being established in the postwar years (and that, for better or worse, substantially continues to be with us). And a publishing industry sprang up on his now closely mapped and marked-out textual soil.

A collection of previously unpublished poems, plays, aphorisms, and prose had already been published, shortly after the poet's death, under the stylistically appropriate, hybridly Latinate title *Opus Posthumous*. By the midsixties, this supplementary treasure trove was followed by a concordance to the poems and a hefty selection from the poet's lavishly self-explanatory and just as lavishly mystifying letters, edited by his daughter Holly Stevens, whose professional role in the establishment of a family member's canonical centrality in American poetry has been matched only by the industry of T. S. Eliot's widow, Valerie Eliot. In the seventies, *The Wallace Stevens Journal* was founded, and in the same decade Holly Stevens edited her father's early journals and letters as *Souvenirs and Prophecies* (thereby enabling less speculative studies of Stevens's long literary gestation) and made an enormous amount of material available to researchers by selling her father's literary archive and most of his remaining library to the prestigious Huntington Library in San Marino, California.[5] This academic institutionalization in turn sparked off further investigations, including, in due course, several biographical studies of one of the most unpromising and unrewarding subjects in this respect. In the eighties, the institutionalizing buzz did not show any signs of slowing down: the Critical Heritage Series devoted one of its collections to the historical reception of Stevens's work; the correspondence with José Rodríguez Feo was collected in a volume titled *Secretaries of the Moon*; *Opus Posthumous* was revised, enlarged, and corrected; and a handsome facsimile edition of

5. The price of $225,000 paid by the Huntington Library in 1975 (Peter A. Brazeau, *Parts of a World: Wallace Stevens Remembered*, 26) offered a telling token of Stevens's soaring cultural capital at the time, as did the fact that a number of bibliophilic editions of his works was immediately put on display in the main exhibition hall, "where they [kept] the company of the Ellesmere *Canterbury Tales* and two First Folios of Shakespeare" (Milton J. Bates, "Stevens' Books at the Huntington: An Annotated Checklist," 23). A second purchase of several hundred books and journals belonging to Stevens's amply provided library was made in 1990 (for details, see Robert Moynihan, "Checklist: Second Purchase, Wallace Stevens Collection, Huntington Library"). Stevens's posthumous net worth has continued to multiply over the years: in the spring of 1999, for instance, a copy of *Harmonium* was sold at Christie's for $14,500.

the poet's commonplace book, *Sur Plusieurs Beaux Sujets*, was published—no doubt more as a token rival to the successful facsimile of T. S. Eliot's *The Waste Land* than for reasons of intrinsic critical importance. By the end of the nineties, to top it all, Stevens's poetry and prose were finally awarded the most canonizing laurel of all: inclusion in the prestigious Library of America series of "Literary Classics of the United States."

When the eighties drew to a close and books and articles on Stevens numbered nearly two thousand, the point was already reached where some of the poet's greatest and most enduring champions were beginning to shudder in the face of a tentacularly growing, no longer individually digestible, academic industry.[6] Thus, Frank Kermode in his 1989 preface to a reprint of *Wallace Stevens*, his pathbreaking study of 1960, appeared haunted by the immense loss we would suffer "if Stevens were to be driven into some enclosure where only the Ph.D.'s and their instructors were deemed capable of dealing with his thought." And a few years before, in 1985, sketching a short *status quaestionis* that openly voiced sadness and distrust, Harold Bloom had wondered whether Stevens's poems had not become "so many statues in the formal parks of our university culture . . . Have we made him too into Literature? Do we need now to defend him against ourselves?"[7] The strictures of both Kermode and Bloom were understandable enough. Nevertheless, the fact that they were sounded by members of the academic establishment—even if two of the most unwilling members, who preferred to picture themselves as antiestablishmentarians—only serves to underline that Stevens, for better or worse, had become an almost exclusively academic poet. At least from my personal, severely restricted vantage point within academe and outside the United States, there seem to be very few indications that Stevens is being read much outside undergraduate dorms, graduate seminars, or professorial offices.[8] And despite Kermode's and Bloom's wistful sighs and

---

6. The impossibility of individual digestion is beautifully illustrated by the fact that even the indefatigable editor of *The Wallace Stevens Journal*, John N. Serio, in drawing up his annotated secondary bibliography of Stevens, had to call upon the help of a onetime coauthor, Roger Labbe, and two research assistants.

7. Frank Kermode, preface to 1989 edition of *Wallace Stevens*, xviii; Harold Bloom, introduction to *Wallace Stevens*, 2.

8. The fact that traces of Stevens in Hartford, Connecticut, his home for nearly four decades, have been almost entirely erased is partial evidence of the low profile he has in the eyes of the general public. (A few initiatives in Hartford do counter this trend, such as the annual Wallace Stevens Memorial Poetry Reading in Elizabeth Park and the annual Wallace Stevens Birthday Bash at the public library.) Even the unavoidable omnipresence of his poetry in literary undergraduate classes in some senses constitutes a limit-case, judging from

the severely diminished marketability of monographs in the world of American university presses, Stevens criticism kept on expanding in the nineties at more or less the same pace set in the previous decade, with some four to five books appearing every year in addition to a few dozen articles and ten dissertations on average.

More than ever, then, to read this poet, as a literary critic, is to read him through the lenses of others—to familiarize and confront oneself with the multiple ways in which his work has been framed and configured. And viewed as a whole, the most striking feature of Stevens criticism, after all these years, is surely its extreme disparity: the extraordinary pluralism of perspectives it has deployed for explicating the poetry. This has made the act of reading Stevens from yet another critical-theoretical or philosophical angle seem like an increasingly futile, dissatisfying exercise that is more and more subject to the law of diminishing returns. One of the more fruitful questions to ask of Stevens's poetry today is rather: Why is it that this poetry has lent itself so well to professionalized academic appropriation—and of such diversity to boot? Or, in Melita Schaum's words, how is it that "Stevens' works remain texts around which criticism engages in its recurrent revolutions, a literary *arena*—as that word denotes 'a clearing for struggle, conflict, play'—in which major critical assumptions continue to be determined and debated"?[9]

To attempt an answer to this question, we should begin by recalling that no other major American modernist was as much given to writing poetry about poetry as Wallace Stevens. It should not come as a surprise, therefore, to see that one of the principal ways in which his work can still speak to us, after all the expert critical scrutiny to which it has been submitted, is by contributing to the exercise of marking out and recollecting some of the major functions and possibilities of modernist poetry itself, in particular as these functions and possibilities find themselves construed, implicitly or explicitly, by literature's most devoted professional advocates. The question of

---

the testimonies of various contributors to John N. Serio and B. J. Leggett's *Teaching Wallace Stevens*, some of whom argue that it is possible to teach Yeats and even Gertrude Stein but not Stevens (Jacqueline Vaught Brogan, "Introducing Wallace Stevens: Or, the Sheerly Playful and the Display of Theory in Stevens's Poetry," 51), that his "quirkiness makes him one of the toughest poets of the twentieth century to teach in college classrooms" (Alison Rieke, "Wallace Stevens in the Classroom: 'More Truly and More Strange,'" 130), and that teaching him is as fickle as "teaching about the weather" (Joan Richardson, "Learning Stevens's Language: The Will & the Weather," 140).

9. Schaum, *Critical Schools*, xvi.

the remarkable productivity of Stevens's work in terms of the critical atten-
tion it has received is thus also the question of which poetic ideologies that
work has historically served to buttress. This suggests that we should start
by acknowledging the enormous importance of readers in the interpretive
process. If Stevens's poetry has given rise to an extraordinary wealth of inter-
pretations, it is not itself to be credited in any simple and direct causal sense
for these effects. Meanings, we should recall, are produced by readers first and
foremost, and to a large extent the historical diversity of critical perspectives
on Stevens is a function of the "distinction drive" and coveting of "symbolic
capital" that motivate the competition among "interpretive communities"
(to borrow the relevant terms from Pierre Bourdieu and Stanley Fish).

At the same time, however, this emphasis on the reader can never be the
complete story. The construction of textual meanings, generally speaking, is
not to be understood with respect to the reader alone: it is to a certain extent
also "shaped" or "enabled" by the object of analysis (even if we understand
this textual "object," as many nowadays do, in nonessentialist terms). In
other words, the choice of texts that academically competing critics make
to develop their new interpretations is not a matter of sheer indifference.
Or in the case under discussion: the diversity of critical perspectives that
has been developed to analyze Stevens's poetry must have been called forth,
at least to some degree, by the poetry itself. Even if readers, as Fish insists,
are always involved in the production of texts, and even if texts have no
independent objectivity outside the reading process, it is still the case that
texts play their own specific role in this reading process by "channeling"
responses to them. And although this "channeling" may not happen in any
inevitable, deterministic way that allows us to ascertain objective textual
facts and detect simple interpretive causalities, it nevertheless operates in
indirectly limiting (at once constraining and liberating) ways that in the
case of intentionally polysemous literary works like Stevens's are all the more
tantalizing for *not* being objectifiable. Textual meanings are not simply or
singularly produced by readers: they arise from an encounter between readers
and texts. In this encounter, we should be willing to grant, Stevens's poetry
exerts its own enabling and disabling forces on the interpretive process. If
it were not to do so, interpretations would never be interpretations *of* texts,
and the meanings submitted by critics to their "interpretive communities"
would only be, in the final analysis, self-generated.

Once we accept that the remarkable critical productivity of Stevens's
work may be explained at least in part by referring to specific features of that

work, we are still left with a variety of possible angles to be explored. One angle that clearly no longer satisfies is that of trying to define the essence of what used to be called "literariness." To attempt such a definition to-day would only amount to flogging a dead horse. We know how, in Robert Weimann's words, "the dualism and, even, opposition between poetic language and nonpoetic language constituted the most comprehensively important area of agreement between Russian formalism, Anglo-American New Criticism, and the dominating current in structuralist poetics." But this agreement has been shattered in a postmodern era that has effectively debunked facile oppositions between "high" and "low" cultural practices and become more sensitive to multiplicity, contamination, and hybridization at the expense of gestures of totalization and essentialization—gestures to which Stevens himself was often averse. The supposed existence of a definable literariness or "poeticity," always ultimately ideological in inspiration, has not stood the test of critical scrutiny. "The formalist criterion of poeticity or literariness," says Owen Miller, "has been challenged by speech-act theory and post-Saussurian linguistics with the result that the notion of literature as linguistically autonomous or functionally distinct from other forms of verbal utterance has eroded and, with it, the whole liberal conception of poetic language as a cultural mode of knowledge and value."[10] This may be a too comfortably absolutist way of formulating relativist principles, but the fact remains that the autonomistic view of poetic language—often enough historically accompanied by a self-serving sanctification of the poet's numinous task as a cultural shaman—is not about to be resurrected today. Arguments about the value of reading, in particular the value of reading complex and dense poetry, are equally available within a more relativistic world view that remains skeptical of both the metaphysics of definition and the ideological inflation of elitist art-making.

A much better way of addressing the question of the diversity of Stevens's critical afterlife is by historicizing the sociological and ideological conditions that shaped this afterlife. Such a historicizing project has already been mounted—more than satisfactorily—by Newcomb in his diachronic analysis of the critical reception history and canonization process of Stevens's poetry, *Wallace Stevens and Literary Canons* (1992). Newcomb's study, nevertheless, stands in need of a complement. Its historicist take on the subject is itself one-sided in papering over any possible *intrinsic* qualities of

10. Robert Weimann, "Textual Identity and Relationship: A Metacritical Excursion into History," 279; Owen Miller, preface to *Identity of the Literary Text*, viii.

Stevens's work for the purpose of presenting the *extrinsic* contexts that led up to the inclusion of that work in the canon of American poetry.[11] Not only do we need to trace the ideological frames and "institutional practices, processes, and discourses" that have historically conditioned responses *to* Stevens's poetry,[12] we should also keep circumscribing the qualities of the poetry *itself* as these qualities *interacted with* those institutional practices, processes, and discourses. Both forms of analysis—the one more broadly literary-sociological, the other more narrowly literary-critical—are dialectically related, even if Newcomb's contribution is the more innovative and, after decades of dehistoricized, vacuum-packed interpretations of the poetry, the more timely one.

Steering clear of a radically externalizing historicist approach while not dissociating myself from the need to historicize, my attempt to get a purchase on the question of Stevens's fertility and disseminating potential for literary criticism must be aware also of a second form of contamination or overlap. For the attempt cannot be made without acknowledging in one and the same gesture the *aesthetic* qualities of Stevens's poetry. If the poetry has prompted so many critics to produce such a spate of commentaries, this must automatically and to a large extent be a function also of its artistic mastery. The problem with "artistic mastery" and "aesthetic qualities," however, is that they are more easily acknowledged than defined and identified. Both concepts have become vexed and much-maligned categories in contemporary cultural theory, and many who have contested them have in fact come close to wishing them away. Yet some such concept as "the artistic" or "the aesthetic," no matter how question-begging and resistant to rational discourse, continues to answer to a phenomenal reality, to an irreducible "skreaking and skrittering residuum" of which Stevens's own "Autumn Refrain," in one of several available readings, tangentially yet stubbornly speaks (CP 160). As Stevens's most famously and adamantly aestheticist critic, Helen Vendler, argues:

> It is impossible . . . to name a single set of defining characteristics that will discriminate an aesthetic object from one that does not exert aesthetic power, but that is no reason to deny the existence of aesthetic power and aesthetic response. Though aesthetic response is culturally conditioned, and tastes differ even among those within a single culture, nevertheless the phenomenon of

11. See also Barbara M. Fisher, review of *Wallace Stevens and Literary Canons*, 106.
12. Newcomb, *Literary Canons*, 4.

aesthetic response always remains selective. Nobody finds everything beautiful. And no other category ("the rhetorically complex," "the philosophically interesting," "the overdetermined," "the well structured" and so on) can be usefully substituted for the category "the aesthetic."[13]

Provocatively, Vendler has even gone so far as to plead against training students "to identify and discuss things that are irrelevant to the competence of a piece of art,"[14] but this is to risk turning the tables too radically; it threatens to erect a barrier between certain aspects of the literary artifact—general ideas and their concrete aesthetic embodiment/performance, or, more simply, content and form—that are in actual fact heavily entangled and mutually enriching. To the extent that the category of the aesthetic tends to be associated with effects produced above all at a stylistic and formal level, the ensuing inquiry into the critical productivity of Stevens's poetry moves beyond such a category to spread out into a more idealistic realm of analysis. The three major productive characteristics of Stevens's poetry that I will delineate in the following chapters are not easily styled aesthetic qualities in a traditional sense. They are too critically deflected by an interest in larger, more theoretically and philosophically colored questions than those Vendler prefers to address in the locally analytic "art criticism" she considers to be the aptest response to lyric poetry. At the same time and for analogous reasons, my exercise is distinguished from Daniel R. Schwarz's attempt to list all the characteristics that might be held to differentiate Stevens's poetry from that of other major poets and thus to constitute his poetic uniqueness.[15] Attempts of this sort are too much in danger of maintaining some of the impossible distinctions on which the earlier quests for literariness and poeticity were seen to rest.

It should be repeated, finally, that the question of the limits of reading Stevens is not imposed from the outside by some extraneous theoretical concern, but ultimately derives from the problematic character of reading (and writing about the experience of reading) this particular poet. "More than any other major figure," suggests Schwarz, "Stevens restructured our concept of what it means to read."[16] Certainly his poetry provides one of the more salient examples for supporting the claim that what have come

---

13. Helen Vendler, *The Music of What Happens: Poems, Poets, Critics*, 1–2.
14. Helen Vendler, "Wallace Stevens: Teaching the Anthology Pieces," 4.
15. Daniel R. Schwarz, *Narrative and Representation in the Poetry of Wallace Stevens*, 23–25.
16. Ibid., 14.

to be called "postmodern" literary theories are often enough more chronologically than antagonistically "post." For these theories, with their shift to the reader's role in the communicative process—a shift that is styled no less than a "change of paradigm" by Umberto Eco[17]—can still be seen as the self-reflective critical products or effects of one strand within the self-reflective high modernism that preceded them. It is not in postmodern critical obsessions with self-reflectivity or fashionable invitations to interpretive freedom from which the first part of this study springs, but rather Stevens's own texts as they compel the reader to develop a more than usual degree of self-consciousness about the act of reading. Stevens's metapoetry demands and engenders its own type of metareader. It actively prompts or begs us to study the question of its appropriability and possibilities for contextualization. And lest this question appear too cerebral, we might recall that such prompting or begging is of more than theoretical importance: it engages us in many senses, including that of doubling the poet's self-styled task—the task, that is, of recording the mind in the act of finding what will suffice.

17. Umberto Eco, *The Limits of Interpretation*, 45.

Chapter 2

It Must Resist the Intelligence
Almost Successfully

"Is THE PRUDENTIAL Seer of Hartford only the most eloquent elaborator of our way of life, the Grand Defender of our sanctified evasions, our privileged status as the secular clergy of a society we cannot serve, let alone save?"[1] The tone and style of this question immediately bespeak its author, for they are vintage Harold Bloom; yet the topic and gist of the question are much more exceptional and surprising for Stevens's most formidable and awe-inspiring critic. As a rule, Bloom is not given to worrying over the social and political relevance of his critical activities—quite to the contrary: he likes to flaunt them as an entirely personal and subjective affair more frequently grounded in gnostic and visionary than in any worldly interests.[2] It is all the more telling, therefore, that even this critic should be unable to repress doubts both about Stevens's proverbial evasiveness and the seductiveness of such evasiveness to critics with a perch in the ivory towers of academia. A few lines before the excerpt just quoted, Bloom dons one of his favorite robes—

---

1. Bloom, introduction to *Wallace Stevens*, 2.
2. In an interview given around the same time (the mid-eighties) he made the above comment about Stevens, Bloom taunted his opponents by asking rhetorically: "Since I am convinced that literary criticism is a purely personal activity, that it has exactly the same status as lyric poetry or narrative writing, why should I care about the response to it, one way or the other? Praise or blame, alike, is beside the point" (interview by Imre Salusinszky, 49). Bloom has remained true to this principle even in the face of mounting opposition from an increasingly politicized critical industry: in his more recent end-of-the-millennium defense of the Western Canon, he continues to show himself, in Denis Donoghue's words, as "a convinced philosophic idealist" whose primary interest lies in "ego psychology" and in "the egotistical sublime" ("The Book of Genius: Harold Bloom's agon and the uses of great literature," 3).

that of the prophet—only to come down surprisingly hard on the twentieth-century American poet perhaps most dear to him: "Someone will rise to ask the hard question: How many qualifications can you get into a single poem and still have a poem?"[3] We need not push matters to such a rhetorical point of crisis to be able to concur with Bloom that the poetic recording and enacting of well-nigh endless qualifications are one of Stevens's most conspicuous and characteristic trademarks.

The tradition of underlining this characteristic of his work (and of wrestling with its desirability) goes at least as far back as Marianne Moore's early sympathetic engagement with the poetry.[4] Within the era of professional academic appropriation, the young Helen Vendler was quick to signal the central importance of Stevens's qualifications: not only did the phenomenon explicitly inspire one of her first articles, "The Qualified Assertions of Wallace Stevens," but it was also at the root of her award-winning book of 1969, On Extended Wings: Wallace Stevens' Longer Poems (in particular its first chapter, "The Pensive Man: The Pensive Style"). Vendler's critical success, which launched her on a distinguished career as one of the four or five major Stevens scholars and, later still, as the nation's most influential poetry critic overall, was clearly due in part to her touching a nerve. To this day, exploring Stevens's poetry continues to be synonymous with riding the lip of a sometimes dizzying maelstrom that precludes any critically reassuring arrival at determinate conclusions. Northrop Frye, when asked about Stevens's prestige among so many leading critics, simply attributed it to the fact that "there is no point of closure in his mind." Yet another preeminent Stevens connoisseur, J. Hillis Miller, sums up decades of familiarity with the experience of reading this particular poet by emphasizing that "Stevens's poetry is full of surprises and discontinuities, both from poem to poem and within a given poem. The reader soon learns that it is impossible to predict just what is going to come next. What comes next often does not seem to follow logically or according to any other discernible form of continuity from what has come before. An extreme mental and emotional agility is therefore demanded of the reader of Stevens."[5]

Evasions, seemingly endless qualifications, an absence of closure, discontinuity in thought and feeling, short circuits of logic and expectation: these

---

3. Bloom, introduction to Wallace Stevens, 1–2.
4. Robin Gail Schulze, The Web of Friendship: Marianne Moore and Wallace Stevens, 115.
5. Northrop Frye, interview by Imre Salusinszky, 35; J. Hillis Miller, "William Carlos Williams and Wallace Stevens," 987.

are some of the most frequently observed hallmarks of Stevens's art. One of the main reasons why this poetry has been so welcome to critics and so inviting of commentary in a post-New Critical era is that it is not a poetry of unified, well-rounded *products* so much as a poetry of continual *process*. Both the writing and the reading processes of a Stevens poem were and are to a large extent unpredictable, elusive, and uncontainable. Stevens's most eloquent (though also shrewdly evasive) explanation of the improvisational and uncontainable processes of his compositional method occurs in "The Irrational Element in Poetry," where he writes that

> just as the choice of subject is unpredictable at the outset, so its development, after it has been chosen, is unpredictable. One is always writing about two things at the same time in poetry and it is this that produces the tension characteristic of poetry. One is the true subject and the other is the poetry of the subject. The difficulty of sticking to the true subject, when it is the poetry of the subject that is paramount in one's mind, need only be mentioned to be understood. In a poet who makes the true subject paramount and who merely embellishes it, the subject is constant and the development orderly. If the poetry of the subject is paramount, the true subject is not constant nor its development orderly. (*OP* 227)

Understandably, then, critics have been able to enlist Stevens's poetry in an antiteleological, pragmatist project that attaches most value to concepts like contingency and transitionality, or they have found fit to construct his writings with reference to the idea of a "radical provisionality."[6] Others have been fascinated by related notions like "evanescence" (J. Hillis Miller, for instance, from his earliest phenomenological analyses in *Poets of Reality* right through to his later deconstructive period), or have remarked upon the fact that "if [Stevens] has a dogma, it is the dogma of the shadowy, the ephemeral, the barely perceived, the iridescent." In her general introduction to Stevens's poetry, Janet McCann even points to the work's growing popularity among physicists and critics interested in chaos theory.[7]

6. For pragmatist readings, see especially Richard Poirier, *The Renewal of Literature: Emersonian Reflections* and *Poetry and Pragmatism*; Margaret Dickie, *Lyric Contingencies: Emily Dickinson and Wallace Stevens*; Thomas C. Grey, *The Wallace Stevens Case: Law and the Practice of Poetry*; Anca Rosu, *The Metaphysics of Sound in Wallace Stevens*; Patricia Rae, *The Practical Muse: Pragmatist Poetics in Hulme, Pound, and Stevens*; and Jonathan Levin, *The Poetics of Transition: Emerson, Pragmatism, & American Literary Modernism*. For the notion of "radical provisionality," see George Bornstein, *Transformations of Romanticism in Yeats, Eliot, and Stevens*, and Schulze, *Web of Friendship*.

7. Helen Vendler, *On Extended Wings: Wallace Stevens' Longer Poems*, 35; Janet McCann, *Wallace Stevens Revisited: "The Celestial Possible*," 143.

As the quotation from "The Irrational Element in Poetry" suggests, much of Stevens's elusiveness derives from a persistent postromantic distrust of rationalism (associated, in the manner of so many modernist artists, with the dominance of positivistic science, industrialization, urbanization, and bureaucracy that defined modernity in the early twentieth century). This distrust found its most salient expression in the point-blank dictum that "[p]oetry must be irrational" (OP 188), and its artistic origins have been traced back alternatively (or cumulatively) to Stevens's romantic and symbolist poetic predecessors, to the writings of such vitalistic and skeptical thinkers as Ralph Waldo Emerson, William James, George Santayana, Friedrich Nietzsche, and Henri Bergson, and to a lifelong interest in the formal experiments of modernist painting and music. Especially in recent years, historicist critics have done much to help us understand the subtle twists and turns that Stevens's belief in provisional and "irrational" improvisation underwent as it strove to respond to various, more or less dramatic, changes in the sociopolitical climate. The fact that so many of these influences have been patiently uncovered and so many of the historical vicissitudes of this poet's growth so painstakingly reconstructed, has undoubtedly contributed greatly to our understanding of the poems, but it does not therefore mean that interpretations of the poetry have somehow been securely anchored or that the reading process has been halted. It is a measure of Stevens's artistic success that he continues to remain ahead of almost all his readers, no matter how armed these readers come with all the cumbersome and pedantic paraphernalia of scholarship. His is a poetry about which no critical consensus can ever be achieved.

One of Stevens's most frequently quoted aphorisms proclaims that "[p]oetry must resist the intelligence almost successfully" (OP 197). Although critics are agreed that this remark constitutes a crucial poetic credo, it has seldom received the careful attention it deserves. Only Eleanor Cook has sufficiently lingered over it to observe that "[w]e do not always give enough emphasis to the word 'almost.' (As if Stevens ever supposed the intelligence did not have a vital role in reading poetry.) Nor do we give enough thought to the word 'intelligence.' For it is not the intelligence alone that gives meaning to poems, any more than the intelligence alone gives meaning in general."[8] Interestingly, Stevens seems to have grappled with the formulation of his tenet more than Cook was able to know at the time

8. Eleanor Cook, Poetry, Word-Play, and Word-War in Wallace Stevens, 4.

she made her observations. As an editorial endnote in the revised edition of *Opus Posthumous* shows (*OP* 326), what Stevens originally jotted down in his collection of aphorisms, *Adagia*—*pace* Cook's parenthetical disclaimer—ran quite simply: "Poetry must resist the intelligence successfully." This, no doubt, was the easier, comfortably provocative, and dogmatical statement to make. But being an inveterate qualifier, Stevens apparently thought better of his first impulse and inserted that treacherous little modifier "almost." Cook was right, then, to emphasize the importance of Stevens's inconspicuous little adverb, though not to deny the process of doubt leading up to it.

In fact, the importance of the little insertion increases as we look at the second occurrence of Stevens's premise—for he was sufficiently charmed with his trouvaille to recycle it—in the first two lines of "Man Carrying Thing" (*CP* 350–51). A remarkable poem in its own right, "Man Carrying Thing" is nevertheless almost invariably referred to only because of its eye-catching opening statement, which tends to be simply wrenched from its context.[9] Yet one should not fail to observe how the opening lines function within the overall narrative of the text. After all, Stevens wrote the poem, in 1945, in direct response to his Ceylon correspondent Leonard van Geyzel's request that he explain "the genuine difficulty that arises out of the enigmatic quality that is so essential a part of the satisfaction that a good poem gives."[10] After stating, in a delicately timed enjambment, that "The poem must resist the intelligence / Almost successfully," Stevens proceeds by first giving an "Illustration" (of a "brune figure" at dusk too vague to identify, as if resisting the intelligence were merely the natural corollary of mimetically recording semiobscure sense impressions), then by swerving into an extended, almost self-hypnotizing parenthesis about the relation between parts and whole or primary and secondary senses, until he winds up shockingly with

> A horror of thoughts that suddenly are real.
>
> We must endure our thoughts all night, until
> The bright obvious stands motionless in cold.
>   (*CP* 351)

---

9. The two most important exceptions to this rule of neglect are B. J. Leggett's extensive analysis—based on a comparative study of Charles Maurron's *Aesthetics and Psychology*—in his *Wallace Stevens and Poetic Theory: Conceiving the Supreme Fiction*, 110–19; and George S. Lensing's recent commentary in *Wallace Stevens and the Seasons*, 150–52.

10. Leonard van Geyzel's words quoted in Alan Filreis, *Wallace Stevens and the Actual World*, 186.

This surprising ending reflects back on the poem's opening claim in more ways than one. It bestows, first of all, a specific *affective* value on the earlier word "intelligence," which can no longer be supposed to refer neutrally to any rational capacity or thought process whatsoever but must be understood now to involve, at least in part, a "horror of thoughts" that desperately needs to be staved off.[11] What is more, because of the long conspicuous parenthesis, the opening and ending of this short lyric seem to form a direct, overarching connection, so that the entire text, despite its typically wayward course meandering through a series of qualifications, may be summed up by one embracing statement: "The poem must resist the intelligence / Almost successfully . . . until / The bright obvious stands motionless in cold." Such a reading only underscores the importance of the word "almost": at the end of the day (or, in this case, the nightmarish night), some "bright obvious" will come forth. Something "obvious" suggests, from one point of view, something clearly understood (even if we are made to pause and wonder about the possible disparity between visible obviousness and rational intelligence), which means that if Stevens wants the intelligence to be resisted, he does not want it to be ultimately defeated. In one of several possible readings, he continues to long for the serendipity of *some* sort of intelligence, even if (and perhaps because) it will be hard to come by, and even if the wish that it stand "motionless in cold" may be at once heartfelt and, as Tony Sharpe suggests, an unnerving prefiguration of death.[12] Ambivalence is not merely one in a whole series of characteristics of Stevens's writings: in its densest and most complex instantiations, it is itself responsible for resisting the intelligence almost successfully.

Rather than say that "Man Carrying Thing" is "finally unintelligible," as Alison Rieke does, I would argue that it illustrates the necessity of patiently weighing each word in Stevens's claim that poetry should resist the intelligence almost successfully.[13] We should not overlook, first of all, the need for *resistance*. To resist is not to cancel or destroy, nor to deny or elide. "Resistance is the opposite of escape," wrote Stevens in "The Irrational Element

---

11. One of the valuable guidelines distilled by Helen Vendler from years of reading experience is "never [to] trust beginnings in Stevens; the emotional heart of a lyric by Stevens is likely to be found in the middle of the poem" (*Wallace Stevens: Words Chosen Out of Desire*, 44). In this case, the "horror of thoughts" breaking out toward the end of the text turns out to be the emotional center of gravity from which the preceding, seemingly dispassionate meditations acquire their force and feeling.

12. Sharpe, *Wallace Stevens*, 176.

13. Rieke, "Wallace Stevens in the Classroom," 136.

in Poetry" (OP 230), and the sociopolitical context of the Depression era in which he made that statement can only convince us of the seriousness of his observation. One critic, Janet McCann, even opened her book-length study by announcing that "Wallace Stevens's poetry is about resistance." And Melita Schaum calls Stevens's concept of resistance at once "personal, poetic, and political."[14] Certainly it found multiple forms of expression, both in and outside the writing of poetry. Stevens's social habit of reserve to the point of bluntness and his unwillingness to ingratiate himself are notorious and well-attested, as are the hurdles he liked to raise to the interpretation of his own work in his correspondence. Stevens's most common attitude was in many ways a tough-minded one. Professionally, this was an asset: as a corporate lawyer with far-reaching responsibilities he developed a skeptical, casuistic mind that interiorized resistance. But at home, too, in the contemplative quiet of his reading chair, he was given to more than an occasional spell of recalcitrance. His private library contained not only such items as Artur Schnabel's tellingly entitled *Music and the Line of Most Resistance*, it also displayed "the habits of a dialectical reader. . . . A perusal of Stevens' own comments in the marginalia of the Huntington's first purchase shows that he usually marked to refute, only secondarily to assimilate, and almost never to imitate. His stance before a text was dialectical: he questioned everything and rejected more than he accepted."[15]

This resisting mind is everywhere on display in the poetry, which, at its best, fascinates precisely because of the tension it enacts between intelligible thoughts and a counterforce that is constantly in the process of undercutting or resisting intelligibility. One major reason why critics are pulled back to the same poems over and over again is that these texts leave them spellbound by giving them a sense of being on the verge of understanding something momentous—a sense that in its own insistent, promising way can be highly pleasurable and addictive. Much of this addictive pleasure derives from what Stevens himself called "a laborious element, which, when it is exercised, is not only a labor but a consummation as well" (NA 165). It involves the taking of interpretive risks, a facing up to the risk of opacity that itself both engenders and endangers—which is to say, limits—Stevens's poetry.

Probably the most striking way in which Stevens continues to resist our intelligence is by inverting our most deeply entrenched patterns of expectation.

14. McCann, *Wallace Stevens Revisited*, ix; Melita Schaum, "Lyric Resistance: Views of the Political in the Poetics of Wallace Stevens and H. D.," 202.
15. Moynihan, "Checklist," 76.

He is a master of the topsy-turvy who likes to short-circuit the neural chan-
nels by which our brain, through the repetitions of learning in infancy, has
been structured. In an interview, Northrop Frye formulated this feature of
Stevens's poetry with special reference to the fourth and final section of
"Peter Quince at the Clavier" (CP 91–92). "You're never quite sure just
what you are hearing," Frye noted. "You said a moment ago that Derrida is
perhaps the first non-Platonic critic; well, when you read a poem of Stevens
saying 'beauty is momentary in the mind . . . but in the flesh it is immortal,'
people just blink. That's not what he's supposed to say. He's supposed to say
it's momentary in the flesh, but it's immortal in the mind."[16]

Stevens rarely gives us what he is supposed to say according to the pro-
tocols of "common sense." His is a poetry of sense-making, of making new
sense. He appears to have been fully aware of what Wolfgang Iser calls "one
of the important findings of psycholinguistics—namely, the fact that all
linguistic utterances are accompanied by the 'expectation of meaningful-
ness.'"[17] He knew that his feats of topsy-turvydom, however counterintu-
itive, would eventually be brought to signify by the reader. "It is necessary to
propose an enigma to the mind. The mind always proposes a solution," he
observed (OP 194). The *meaning* of his texts, he realized, existed where the
noun in English, derived from a verb, suggests that it does: in an ongoing
temporal process of mean-ing. No doubt, there are other ways of producing
great art—by inventing images that strike us, say, by their exceptional clar-
ity, their immediately elucidating power, their strong emotional impact—
but they do not produce the sort of art to which one always feels a strong urge
to return. Stevens's art is at the opposite end of the imaginative spectrum—
that of the Big Tease.

But we have not exhausted Stevens's formula yet. We need to come back
to the question of "intelligence." To Stevens, the call to resist the intel-
ligence was certainly also a call to make room for other types of readerly
response, in particular those governed by the imagination, the feelings, and
the musical seductions of language. His early explanation, in a letter, of
"Domination of Black" (CP 8–9) is famous in this respect: "I am sorry that
a poem of this sort has to contain any ideas at all, because its sole purpose
is to fill the mind with the images & sounds that it contains. A mind that
examines such a poem for its prose contents gets absolutely nothing from

16. Frye, interview, 36.
17. Wolfgang Iser, "Feigning in Fiction," 222.

it. You are supposed to get heavens full of the colors and full of sounds, and you are supposed to feel as you would feel if you actually got all this" (L 251). Several years later, in a letter to another correspondent, Stevens again argued that "poetry must limit itself in respect to intelligence. There is a point at which intelligence destroys poetry" (L 305). And toward the end of his life, in a letter to Barbara Church, he remained loyal to this principle when noting (about Santayana's swerve from poetry to philosophy): "It is difficult for a man whose whole life is thought to continue as a poet. The reason (like the law, which is only a form of the reason) is a jealous mistress" (L 761). Not surprisingly, then, Stevens was occasionally willing to go so far as to deny any relevance at all to the aspect of meaning in his writing. "A poem need not have a meaning," he claimed, "and like most things in nature often does not have" (OP 201). Again, historicizing analyses have helped us realize how such defenses of an organically naturalizing and radically aestheticizing poetic ideology were more common at the earlier stages of his career, specifically in the days of Harmonium, when his poetry was more clearly and more happily rooted in a postsymbolist, consciously avant-garde tradition of art for art's sake. But the conviction that poetry should be so much more than a mere matter of posing conundrums to the intelligence remained with him throughout his career. After all, as one of his lesser-known epigrams contends: "One reads poetry with one's nerves" (OP 189).

Apart from wanting to clear space for the imagination, feelings, and the titillations and tintinnabula of verbal music in the writing and reception of poetry, Stevens was obviously also motivated by a recurrent and deep distrust of the potential of the rational mind to satisfy. In "Of Mere Being"—a poem that taps so well into the critical nostalgia for teleological narratives that it is presented time and again as Stevens's final text, though it is really of uncertain date—he observes: "You know then that it is not the reason / That makes us happy or unhappy" (OP 141). It is not the reason, nor the intelligence, that ultimately procure satisfaction—unless satisfaction is precisely to be found in artfully resisting these. Stevens, early and late, was obsessed with the fundamental dissatisfactions of his mind's innate restlessness. "It can never be satisfied, the mind, never," he sighs at the conclusion of "The Well Dressed Man with a Beard" (CP 247), and in his Adagia he explained why this should be so: "We never arrive intellectually. But emotionally we arrive constantly (as in poetry, happiness, high mountains, vistas)" (OP 198). As "Man Carrying Thing" also demonstrates, Stevens was frequently haunted by the oppressive horrors of spinning thoughts, or by what Emerson famously called the real "Fall of Man": the fall into consciousness. William W. Bevis shows how he tried to defend himself, at various points throughout his life, against this fall by mobilizing a Buddhist-like "no-mind," but that this state was not easily reached and often came at a premium.[18] Just as often, his mind would remain caught in its endless vortex, and we have the poetry to bear witness to this.

The insatiable quality of Stevens's mind points to the great subject of desire in his work, a subject that has been treated from highly diverse angles and with very different biases by such critics as Helen Vendler, Frank Lentricchia, Barbara M. Fisher, Margaret Dickie, and George S. Lensing, but that still—perhaps by its very nature—often eludes us.[19] "The reason can give nothing at all / Like the response to desire," Stevens wrote in "Dezembrum" (CP 218), and in "The Irrational Element in Poetry" he invited us to see how "the desire for literature is the desire for life. The incessant desire for freedom in literature or in any of the arts is a desire for freedom in life" (OP 231). He was particularly prone to deferring satisfactions and gratifications, so that he could linger in desire itself—that "sumptuous Destitution," as Emily Dickinson called it. The wish to resist the intelligence almost successfully, then, was in some deep sense frequently also the wish to inject his poetry with desire, and the wish to transplant this desire onto his readers and critics. In Alain Suberchicot's formulation, Stevens's "figures of instability find their origin and finality in the exercise of a freedom—that of not responding to the analyzer, while of course having captured his desire."[20]

The effects on criticism of Stevens's almost successful resistance to the intelligence have been various. Many of them will surface in the course of this study, but two of the more general ones should be specified in advance. The first effect is that Stevens has been a most welcome poet for critics with a preference for formal over content-oriented analysis. The case of Helen Vendler, half-mockingly crowned the "Queen of Formalism" by Frank Lentricchia, is again exemplary.[21] A staunch Leavisite by training,

18. Ralph Waldo Emerson, "Experience," 487; William W. Bevis, *Mind of Winter: Wallace Stevens, Meditation, and Literature*.

19. Vendler, *Words Chosen Out of Desire*; Lentricchia, *Ariel and the Police* and *Modernist Quartet*; Barbara M. Fisher, *Wallace Stevens: The Intensest Rendezvous*; Dickie, *Lyric Contingencies*; and Lensing, *Seasons*.

20. Emily Dickinson, *The Poems of Emily Dickinson*, 3:952; Alain Suberchicot, *Treize façons de regarder Wallace Stevens: Une écriture de la présence*, 202 (my translation).

21. Lentricchia, *Ariel and the Police*, 204.

Vendler opened her first major study, *On Extended Wings*, by pitting against each other the two poetries identified by Stevens as the poetry of the idea and the poetry of the words, and argued that Stevens is more profitably served by studying the latter. Others, like Marie Borroff, Eleanor Cook, and Beverly Maeder, have followed suit, and these principally formalist and aestheticist critics have collectively demonstrated how rewarding the close scrutiny of Stevens's complex and many-layered style can be—how indeed "[t]he pleasure of exegetical sleuthing is unlimited for anyone who wants to pick apart grammatical constructions, mine etymologies, or exploit the secondary denotations of words given in the *Oxford English Dictionary* (as Stevens reportedly did)."[22]

The second effect of Stevens's credo and practice, however, has turned out to be even more important: it has to do with the unusual degree to which critics of his poetry have been interpretively enfranchised. Recalling his own experience of reading La Fontaine, Stevens testified to being pleased by "a play of thought, some trophy that we ourselves gather, some meaning that we ourselves supply" (*NA* 109). A similar play of supplying meanings is what he actively sought to set off in his own readers. Frank Doggett and Dorothy Emerson have probably coined the aptest phrase for this textual dynamic by calling Stevens a poet of "a realizable possibility." The wealth of realizable possibility, needless to say, is to a great extent the result of rhetorically brilliant manipulation by Stevens, which is responsible for an at times dazzling overdetermination. But it is also the uncontainable textual effect of a compositional practice that allows latent meanings to proliferate beyond the control of authorial intentions. It is this irreducible excess of signification, this boiling cocktail of authorial and textual intentions, that helps to explain why Steven Gould Axelrod and Helen Deese were able to simultaneously praise and damn Milton Bates's 1985 study of Stevens, *Wallace Stevens: A Mythology of Self*, as "a beautifully researched, commonsensical portrait of Stevens—with all the strengths and weaknesses that commonsense understandings usually possess."[23] Indeed, commonsensical readings of Stevens, desirable and satisfactory as they are as correctives to the frivolousness and pretentiousness of some of the more freewheeling interpretations that have been bandied about, nevertheless have their own

---

22. Beverly Maeder, *Wallace Stevens' Experimental Language: The Lion in the Lute*, 4.
23. Frank Doggett and Dorothy Emerson, "A Primer of Possibility for 'The Auroras of Autumn,'" 53; Axelrod and Deese, "Critical Reception," 18.

limitations, and can do the poetry a disservice by suppressing the exciting mental fertility and freedom it is able to spark in its readers.

To some readers, evidently, the liberty extended by Stevens's poetry can be frightening and unsettling. But others have made it a central argument in their defense of the value of reading literature. One such explicit appropriation of Stevens's liberating resistance to the intelligence is to be found in two of Richard Poirier's books, *The Renewal of Literature* and *Poetry and Pragmatism*, where a case is made for the idea (recently taken up by Jonathan Levin) that to read literature is to learn to live in transition, to remain inside the process of thinking, to resist security of meaning, and to dissolve the self. "We do not go to literature to become better citizens or even wiser persons," according to Poirier, "but to discover how to move, to act, to work in ways that are still and forever mysteriously creative." Such a stance, in his opinion, forms the essence of a pragmatic American tradition that started with Emerson, ran through William James, and found its best twentieth-century representatives in Frost and Stevens. Writers in this tradition argue for "the virtue and necessity of vagueness."[24] That Stevens stands as an epitome of this tradition is one more telling indication of how far he managed to go in his poetic attempts at resisting the intelligence almost successfully.

24. Poirier, *Renewal of Literature*, 44, and *Poetry and Pragmatism*, 139.

Chapter 3

It Must Be Served like Sukiyaki

"SUKIYAKI IS A STEW whose every element can be known and recognized, since it is made in front of you, on your table, without interruption while you are eating it." Roland Barthes, the most famous gourmet of sign systems, appreciated this Japanese dish especially because he saw in it a system whereby

> everything is the ornament of another ornament: first of all because on the table, on the tray, food is never anything but a collection of fragments, none of which appears privileged by an order of ingestion; to eat is not to respect a menu (an itinerary of dishes), but to select, with a light touch of the chopsticks, sometimes one color, sometimes another, depending on a kind of inspiration which appears in its slowness as the detached, indirect accompaniment of the conversation . . . [1]

Eulogistic improvisations of this kind are typical of the "later" Barthes of the seventies, with his attempts at advocating a value-free hedonism that could break the sociopolitical hegemony of French bourgeois values. What he liked about eating sukiyaki he equally liked about reading: both should ideally be steered by the appetites, whims, needs, or tastes of the moment. In an interview dating from the same years, he pointed out the implications of this reading strategy for literary criticism: "[I]f you think of the way in which the human sciences think, conceptualize, formalize, verbalize—it becomes clear that they are absolutely not acclimated to thinking about discontinuity: they are still dominated by the superego of continuity, a superego of evolution, history, filiation, etc."[2]

1. Roland Barthes, *Empire of Signs*, 19, 22.
2. Roland Barthes, "Interview: A Conversation with Roland Barthes," 132.

Barthes's ideology of the seventies need not be followed through to its more questionable extremes of irresponsibility and narcissism for one to argue that the drift of his thinking may shed some light on both the writing practice and the critical appropriations of Stevens. Like Barthes, the American gourmet Stevens was principally interested in the *saveur* of *savoir*. His intellectual dances were in one respect, as we have seen, simply ploys for mobilizing and circulating desire. Samuel French Morse quotes the poet looking back in the year of his death and observing that "it did not matter that his work remained 'indefinite,' that it had 'not got anywhere' philosophically. 'What we all need,' he said in the spring of 1955, 'is to find that in which we can be easily fecund.'" Such fecundity for Stevens was more easily found in the disguised refraction of personal moods and feelings than in "getting anywhere philosophically." When J. Hillis Miller underlines the need for an "extreme mental and emotional agility" in reading Stevens, it is especially the second type of agility, we should realize, that is the more problematic of the two.[3] For this is a poetry pervaded not only by intellectual but also by strong affective discontinuities, and not just from one lyric poem to the next but also within short and seemingly close-knit texts. Moreover—and here lies another endlessly teasing quality of the work—the readability of Stevens's emotional seismograms is made especially difficult by the fact that fault lines tend to run underground: as a rule, emotions do not glisten on, nor are they allowed to erupt from, the textual surface.

Both personal and poetological reasons underlie the general absence of emotional directness in Stevens. At the personal level, we know this was a writer with a massively repressive psyche, full of defense mechanisms, many of which derived from his having been inculcated in the nineteenth-century patriarchal and Puritan-Calvinist middle-class values of social and professional solidity and moral and emotional self-restraint. (To be sure, Stevens was also capable of the most lucid flashes of insight into the workings of such repressions and self-disciplines. But these more often resulted in the distancing ploy of third-person narratives and metapoetic theorizations than in any spontaneous outcries.) That his upbringing should have been so effective is in turn largely explicable by a more genetically conditioned streak in his temperament. There is ample biographical evidence to show that Stevens, much like his father, was a particularly reticent and private man who did not

---

3. Samuel French Morse, "A Sense of the Place," 24; J. Hillis Miller, "Williams and Stevens," 987.

wear his heart on his sleeve. He described his taciturnity as "straight out of Holland" (*L* 422) and his daughter Holly was later to call reticence simply "a family trait."[4] We need only remind ourselves of Stevens's odd-man-out attitude in the avant-garde circles he frequented in New York, and how in those years he developed a publication policy of "hard-to-get reticence,"[5] to understand that this taciturnity stretched back to the earliest years of his literary gestation. As the years went by, moreover, and the reaching of old age went hand in hand with the disappointments of a failed love life and a diminution of sexual drive, Stevens showed himself more than commonly apt to cast a cold, inquisitive eye on his own more passionate feelings. We cannot really be surprised, therefore, that no less a scholar than Richard Ellmann, after bringing to bear his biographer's expertise upon Stevens, felt forced to admit partial defeat because of his subject's constant "struggles to suppress the merely personal" (*L* 413), even in his love letters to his future wife, Elsie, and in his journal.[6]

With such a mutually reinforcing nexus of temperamental and cultural-educational conditions, Stevens could naturally be expected to willingly submit and contribute to the poetological beliefs of his day, in particular to the (post)symbolist and early avant-garde modernist beliefs in the relative objectivity and autonomy of the literary artifact.[7] Thus, personal and poetological factors combined in him to prompt a repeated insistence on the impersonality of poetry. "Poetry is not personal," he jotted down as one of the first entries in his *Adagia* (*OP* 186), and he symptomatically felt the need to repeat the same idea, almost verbatim, not long afterwards: "Poetry is not a personal matter" (*OP* 189). In their introduction to the published correspondence with José Rodríguez Feo, the editors, Beverly Coyle and Alan Filreis, were able to claim that Stevens's young Cuban friend "was almost alone in sensing that to know Stevens personally was to know his poetry and vice versa." And several critics have judiciously observed that the modernist tenet of poetic impersonality popularized by T. S. Eliot in his prose writings more often found its embodiment in Stevens's poetry—despite the latter's considerable dislike of his emigrated colleague—than in Eliot's own works,

---

4. Barbara M. Fisher, "Recollecting Holly," 211.

5. Newcomb, *Literary Canons*, 30.

6. Richard Ellmann, "How Wallace Stevens Saw Himself," 151. How much of Stevens's suppression of the personal should be attributed to Elsie's later censorship (she excised pages from the journals, and held back or destroyed personal letters) has been a critical bone of contention for years and is likely to remain so forever.

7. See Milton J. Bates, *Wallace Stevens: A Mythology of Self,* 91–92.

where the writer's personality and ideology are frequently enough only too plainly displayed.[8]

Personal secrecy and concealment are essential strategies of Stevens's art. In *Wallace Stevens: Words Chosen Out of Desire*, Helen Vendler devotes an entire chapter to the topic of secrecy, arguing that "many of Stevens' strategies for freshness and originality are strategies of concealment, chiefly concealment of the lyric 'I.' " Charles-Maurice de Talleyrand's hyperbolic suggestion that "[l]anguage was invented so that people could conceal their thoughts from each other"[9]—an idea that has since found support from serious cognitive-evolutionary scientists—would no doubt have struck a responsive chord with this poet, especially if Talleyrand's "thoughts" were replaced by the even more vulnerable "emotions." After all, this was a poet who could protest against "the poetry of X" (his antagonist's name itself characteristically concealed) because its author was "an obstruction, a man / Too exactly himself," rather than "an artificial man // At a distance, a secondary expositor," and who could proceed to advise his opponent (indirectly, to be sure):

> Tell X that speech is not dirty silence
> Clarified. It is silence made still dirtier.
> ("The Creations of Sound," CP 310–11)

Stevens often suppressed his more spontaneous affections by displacing them to quasi-theoretical reasonings, self-consciously artificial symbols, fantastic characters, and descriptions of places and the weather, but what is more important than any of these displacements is the way in which he made silence still dirtier by working on his tone and voice. Both these poetic features—tone and voice—sound notoriously suspect in critical prose,

---

8. Beverly Coyle and Alan Filreis, introduction to *Secretaries of the Moon: The Letters of Wallace Stevens & José Rodríguez Feo*, 11. George S. Lensing writes that "Stevens was a stubbornly private person, and his poems in one sense are far more impersonal than those of T. S. Eliot, who championed that stance" (*Wallace Stevens: A Poet's Growth*, ix). An excellent investigation into the discrepancy between Eliot's theory and his poetic practice is to be found in James Longenbach, "Hart Crane and T. S. Eliot: Poets in the Sacred Grove." With the publication by Christopher Ricks of Eliot's juvenilia (*Inventions of the March Hare: Poems 1909–1917 by T. S. Eliot*), further evidence has been produced of Eliot's inclination toward writing psychograms of an at times "intimidating candour" (Helen Vendler, "Writhing and Crawling and Leaping and Darting and Flattening and Stretching," 8).

9. Vendler, *Words Chosen Out of Desire*, 44; Talleyrand quoted in Dennett, *Kinds of Minds*, 119.

partly because they lend themselves so uneasily to academic protocols of falsification and partly because they invite a language that all too readily restores the metaphysics of phonocentrism. Yet in Stevens's case they are of the essence. If there is one field in which Stevens criticism—for all its undeniably high standards in general—continues to be hard pressed to catch up with its subject and develop the necessary sensibility and analytical tools, it is that of tone and voice. Often it proves much easier to make Stevens's words *signify* (meanings) than to let them *express* (feelings). Stevens's natural reticence and emotional reserve prompted forms of expression that strike us as unusually indirect, unclearly shifting, and tonally insecure. His poems, as Daniel R. Schwarz argues, "contain many voices":

> Even when we hear an "I," is not the omniscient voice present as an ironic second character in a duet with the speaker? Do we not at times implicitly and explicitly respond to the dramatization of a listener as another character— even while raising the possibility that voice, listeners and characters are different versions of the same self? At times, it is helpful to think that Stevens dramatizes different versions of the same self; at other times, we think we hear a ventriloquistic voice wearing many masks. But from yet another perspective, we may find it helpful in reading Stevens to abandon the concept of a consistent persona and to admit the possibility of hearing multiple—and at times contradictory and cacophonous—voices, as if they were intersecting planes on the order of a Cubist collage or diverse motifs in a symphony.[10]

Schwarz does a fine job of confusing us, and he is right to do so, for the problem of tone and voice in this poetry comes in various multiply entangled guises. We could point, for instance, to Stevens's notoriously destabilizing tactic of littering his texts with laconic questions whose literalness and seriousness are highly uncertain.[11] We could talk of the recurrent compositional strategy whereby he flattens his tone so much that he winds up speaking in what might be called—borrowing a term from the French— the "middle voice." Vendler sees this strategy at work especially in the late poetry, where "tonelessness" is to her "the ultimate lyric risk" taken by the poet.[12] In such cases we are often left at sea, wondering about a plethora of tonal possibilities: Is the poet reigning in more sanguine feelings, mocking himself by way of the most refined irony, being icily detached, or perhaps

---

10. Schwarz, *Narrative and Representation*, 7.
11. Suberchicot, *Treize façons*, 79.
12. Vendler, *Words Chosen Out of Desire*, 15.

ambivalently wavering about what exactly it is that he should feel? And how are we to disentangle this blankness of tone, this atonality, from a seemingly diametrically opposed writing tactic whereby Stevens is able to produce a rich tonal polyphony? At those moments, he refuses to speak in the single voice traditionally associated with lyric poetry, suggesting instead the super-imposition of several irreconcilable voices. Not infrequently, for instance, his most visionary, solemn, and ecstatic tone is accompanied by a burlesque, frivolous, mannered, or tinkling overtone that creates a modernist disso-nance and opens the poem to the indeterminacies of irony. In this sense, Stevens's work has obvious affinities with much late-romantic and postro-mantic music. (We might note that he took an interest in Gustav Mahler long before that composer's music was popularized in the sixties.) Melita Schaum's paraphrase of an early review by Edna Lou Walton catches such musical affinities particularly well. "Stevens," argued Walton, "explores the difficult simultaneity of all emotions."[13]

In some respects, then, Stevens belongs with those major modernist po-ets who give the lie to Bakhtin's downgrading of poetry "in the narrow sense." In *The Dialogic Imagination*, Bakhtin classifies such narrowly de-fined (lyric) poetry as basically monologic and puristic, a genre that en-lists language in the service of the poet's unitary and self-contained voice and develops a discourse that does not allow any contradictions, conflicts, or doubts to enter the language itself.[14] Both Gerald Bruns and Marjorie Perloff have invoked this theory to oppose Stevens's supposedly monologic poetry (what Perloff calls the "straight lyric") to the novelistic collage of voices in the Eliot-Pound tradition, but this antagonization has been rightly and persuasively contested by, among others, Schaum, Alain Suberchicot, and M. Keith Booker. Booker in particular convincingly demonstrates that "Stevens' poetry does consistently deny that there can ever be a single priv-ileged voice to which all other voices must pay obeisance," and that what

13. Schaum, *Critical Schools*, 55.
14. M. M. Bakhtin, *The Dialogic Imagination: Four Essays*, 284–88. In setting up his hierar-chical difference between the genres of novel and poetry "in the narrow sense," Bakhtin did not, however, blind himself to an irreducible difference *within* both genres as traditionally conceived: at one point, for instance, he subsumes Heine's lyric work under the category of the novelistic, and at another takes Tolstoy's prose to be monologic (see also Judith Still and Michael Worton, introduction to *Intertextuality: Theories and Practices*, 15). For the ar-gument that Bakhtin's venom was "directed more at certain formalist ways of reading poetry than at poetry itself," see M. Keith Booker, "'A War between the Mind and Sky': Bakhtin and Poetry, Stevens and Politics," 72.

Stevens practiced was a type of " 'serial' polyphony."[15] Stevens's poetry is full of its own Bakhtinian heteroglossia: not that of pasting together and recycling sundry quotations from a variety of sociolinguistic environments, as his close poetic friend Marianne Moore was wont to do,[16] but that of concocting a highly hybridized language that jumbles diction from incompatible registers, that "compound[s] the imagination's Latin with / The lingua franca et jocundissima" (CP 397), and that can propound: "Natives of poverty, children of malheur, / The gaiety of language is our seigneur" (CP 322).

This is not to suggest, of course, that Bakhtin's characterization of the novel—the genre he pits against lyric poetry—as revolutionary and carnivalistic can simply be borrowed for Stevens. Insofar as Stevens's poetry is dialogic, too, the dialogue occurs less with other people and their alien voices ("other socio-ideological languages," in Bakhtin's words,[17] or the language of the Other, as we would call it today) than with a multiplicity of *inner* voices (although, again, these are necessarily inflected and tainted by the socio-ideological languages of the Other). Yet it is a measure of Stevens's artistic modernity that he constantly questioned the unity of the speaking subject, drew the reader's attention to the tangle of discourses out of which this subject is composed, and sought to expand the domain of lyricism through the inclusion of formerly excluded voices, such as the comic, the absurd, the disinterested, and the technocratic. His well-known journal entries in which he proclaims that "my opinions generally change even while I am in the act of expressing them" and "[t]here is a perfect rout of characters in every man—and every man is like an actor's trunk, full of strange creatures, new & old" (SP 165–66) bespeak an early sense of inner fragmentation and multiplicity that he went on to explore even as new modernist strategies, in painting and literature alike, developed around him. As Margaret Dickie argues, Stevens was strongly given "to disrupt notions of a coherent and continuous identity" and to disturb "the integrity of the lyric speaker."[18]

The remarkable result of both the indeterminacy and overdetermination of voice that characterize Stevens's poetry is a tonal undecidability that

---

15. Gerald L. Bruns, "Stevens without Epistemology," 29–32; Marjorie Perloff, "Revolving in Crystal: The Supreme Fiction and the Impasse of Modernist Lyric," 61; Schaum, "Lyric Resistance," 192; Suberchicot, *Treize façons*, 89–110, 173–94; Booker, " 'War between the Mind and Sky,' " 75, 80.

16. See Gert Morreel, " 'Cycloid Inclusiveness': The Striated Heteroglossia of Marianne Moore's 'Marriage.' "

17. Bakhtin, *Dialogic Imagination*, 287.

18. Dickie, *Lyric Contingencies*, 10, 76.

leaves critics with an extraordinary freedom to project their own emotions and personalities onto the text. The relative eagerness to exploit this freedom has certainly not been diminished by the postwar economic and institutional conditions of production for literary critics in the United States: in a competitive, capitalist academic context, rhetorical self-assurance, the construction and arrogation of authority, and the art of self-promotion tend to be much rewarded—and not just figuratively or symbolically. In the case of Stevens, the poet's voice has thus been turned regularly into a sound box for the assertion of the critic's voice. Indeed, Stevens criticism has been full of a privileging of certain expressions, ideas, lines, and poems as being more true to the poet's "inner nature," "temperament," "attitude," or "beliefs" than others. The critics' own respective agendas (spoken or unspoken) are in those cases almost always presented as equally important as or more important than a nuanced reconstruction of Stevens's views and feelings.

In her later work on Stevens, Vendler performs a type of recuperation by persistently trying to salvage the traditional qualities of the lyric poet. She offers a number of psychological and emotional readings framed by the more perennial existential themes of life and death, love and loss, solitude and desire, and passion and misery, and defensively argues that "Stevens' poetry is a poetry of feeling pressed to an extreme: the pressure itself produces the compression and condensation of the work."[19] In her opinion, the poetry is as emotionally forceful and as humanly moving as any other major poet's, and we are only deluded into believing otherwise because of its many repressive and distancing ploys. Vendler's claim, however, persuasively and elegantly argued with respect to particular texts, by its very insistence proves how problematic it is to determine the affective value of much of this poetry. For it is striking, to say the least, how often her readings are contradicted by those of other, no less sensitive, critics, precisely on the basis of different conjectures about tone and voice. Conflicts, disparities, and incompatibilities of this sort demonstrate how Stevens's violently fluctuating moods and multiple ambivalences, on the one hand, and the openness of his tonally undecidable passages, on the other, manage to speak to critics of radically different temperaments. Richard Wilbur, one of Stevens's most gifted and suave poetic descendants, exults at "the versatile energy with which [Stevens] faced the aesthetic challenge of every mood, place, and weather," and this versatility, extended to a wider range of phenomena that

19. Vendler, *Words Chosen Out of Desire*, 53.

energized him, has shown the astonishing capacity to confirm a great many readerly inclinations: from the hedonistic to the ascetic; from the skeptical, secular, and humanistic to the essentially religious; from the joyfully vital to the bleakly miserable and exhausted; from the insecurely wavering to the brashly assertive; from the expansionistic to the minimalistic; from the irresistibly and boisterously humorous to the forbiddingly and aridly abstruse; from the iconoclastic to the contemplative; from the outrageously fantastic to the accurately realistic; from the centralistic to the eccentric. Clearly, it is not without reason that John Timberman Newcomb speaks of a "chameleonic quality" in Stevens's poetry. And even Vendler has to admit that "Stevens is so many-sided, and has attracted such different sorts of readers" that "he is variously represented by different commentators."[20] More than any other canonical Anglo-modernist poet, Stevens has spawned binarisms, and one major reason for this, as the above list illustrates, is that he was himself a highly divided figure who was able to dramatize his own inner contradictions.

A poet who is able to accommodate such a wide range of prominent critical personalities, extending from the muscular quondam Marxist Frank Lentricchia to the graciously self-surrendering Richard Poirier, from the linguistically sophisticated and lucid J. Hillis Miller to the unassuming ironist Frank Kermode, and from the hieratic and furrow-browed Freudian/Nietzschean Harold Bloom to the strong-willed aestheticist Helen Vendler, must be a marvel of flexibility, especially since just about every critic on this list would single out Stevens as his or her favorite twentieth-century poet. Such flexible appropriability could be possible only if the tone of Stevens's poetry is a matter of conjecture and is able to contain an exceptional gamut of overtones. Hence the analogy with Barthes's culinary image of sukiyaki, for that image can be made to apply not only to Stevens's own variously invested compositional habits, but also to the reading habits of his critics, who can pick and choose from his poetry in accordance with their own moods, temperaments, dispositions, whims, tastes, and appetites, "depending on a kind of inspiration which appears," in Barthes's words, "as the detached, indirect accompaniment of the conversation" which all critics are eager to keep going.

---

20. Richard Wilbur, "From Key West, Florida," 140; Newcomb, *Literary Canons*, 105, 174; Helen Vendler, "Wallace Stevens" in *The Columbia History of American Poetry*, 378.

Chapter 4

It Must Be Intertextualized

IN THE COURSE OF AN INTERVIEW, Edward Said once pointed to some of the limits of the category of the aesthetic as an independent subject for criticism: "Nobody would deny that there is a literary quality to, say, an ode by Keats or a poem by Stevens; but is that interesting in and of itself, past one's enchantment and one's enjoyment of it? Maybe it's enough just to enjoy it, but if one wants to talk about it, I think one can increase one's enjoyment by *connecting* it to other things" (emphasis added).[1] For Said, of course, the most enjoyable and stimulating connections are those that manage to link up the text to the world and the critic—thus building the triad that figures as the title of one of his influential books. But another valid option is, quite simply, to bring together different texts—to juxtapose, say, an ode by Keats *and* a poem by Stevens. Some writers invite this reading strategy more than others. One extreme instance, I would argue, is that of Wallace Stevens, whose poems are rarely discussed independently, without being yoked to other texts and writers. It is no coincidence that one of this poet's most frequently quoted aphorisms is: "Things are because of interrelations or interactions" (*OP* 189).

We need only glance at the 1951 lecture "A Collect of Philosophy," delivered both at the University of Chicago and at the City College of New York (hence aimed at exactly the right sort of audience to plant the seeds of an academic industry that would canonize the poet in decades to come), to realize how the practice in Stevens criticism of connecting the poet to other writers—and of engaging, even, in a bit of name-dropping—takes its cue from the poet himself. For in the course of a mere fourteen pages, Stevens

---

1. Edward W. Said, interview by Imre Salusinszky, 141.

manages to flash the following names (most of them illustrious, a few of his day and age, all male): Jean Wahl, Giordano Bruno, Victor Hugo, Plato, Nietzsche, Bergson, Leibniz, Russell, Jowett, William James, Santayana, Lucretius, Milton, Pope, Wordsworth, Hegel, Socrates, Paul Weiss, Aristotle, St. Francis, St. Bonaventure, St. Thomas Aquinas, Descartes, Spinoza, Kant, Locke, Schopenhauer, Berkeley, Whitehead, Shelley, Rogers, Samuel Alexander, Husserl, Pascal, Vico, Lequier, Malebranche, Traherne, Novalis, Fichte, Hölderlin, Blake, Mallarmé, Jean Paulhan, Planck, Louis de Broglie, du Bellay, Alain, and André George (OP 267–80). Critics cannot be held entirely responsible, under these circumstances, for having in turn developed the habit of crossing Stevens's ideas with those of other writers. Here is a second forbidding, albeit necessarily selective, list, this time of philosophers and thinkers whose ideas and theories have been drawn upon in more than perfunctory and tangential ways to elucidate Stevens's poetry: Kant, Schopenhauer, Hegel, Kierkegaard, Emerson, Nietzsche, William James, Santayana, Bergson, Bakhtin, Husserl, Heidegger, Sartre, Wittgenstein, Freud, Jung, Lacan, Levinas, Derrida, de Man, Rorty, Deleuze, Cixous, and Irigaray.[2] From a more strictly literary perspective, moreover, Stevens has been compared with, and played out against, almost every major poet writing in English from the romantics down to the modernists, as well as a sizable number of preromantic and postmodernist poets.[3]

2. See esp., in the bibliography, Michael Beehler for Kant; Adams for Schopenhauer; Jennifer Bates and Butler for Hegel; Anthony Whiting for Hegel and Kierkegaard; Hertz, Levin, and Poirier for Emerson; Leggett for Nietzsche; Grey, Hassan, Levin, and Lentricchia's later books for William James; Kermode's early Stevens book, Lentricchia's 1994 book, and Sawaya for Santayana; Quirk for Bergson; Booker for Bakhtin; Naylor for Husserl; Bové and Kermode's 1980 essay for Heidegger; Hines for Husserl and Heidegger; Mao for Sartre; Altieri's 1985 essay for Wittgenstein; Dale and Fisher for Freud; Brogan's 1988 essay and Doggett and Emerson's 1989 essay for Jung; Baeten for Lacan; Beehler's 1994 essay for Levinas; Argyros, Kronick, Parker, Suberchicot, Beehler's book, J. Hillis Miller's 1986 essay, and Riddel's work from the seventies and eighties for Derrida; J. Hillis Miller's 1985 works for de Man; Suberchicot for Rorty; Shaviro for Deleuze; and Springer for Cixous and Irigaray. Doggett's book, Leggett's first book, and Leonard and Wharton cover several of these names at once. Needless to add, almost all of the names also pop up in Harold Bloom's interpretations, but Bloom's case will be discussed later in this chapter. It should be pointed out, finally, that this is a list of individual names only, and does not include crossings with bodies of theoretical ideas such as Zen Buddhism (see Bevis and Tompkins).

3. The beginning of this massive literary linkage (itself an indispensable factor in the process of canonization) may be dated in 1940 with the appearance of an issue of The Harvard Advocate devoted to Stevens (Newcomb, Literary Canons, 122–25). Given the number, omnipresence, and mixed occurrence of literary crossings in Stevens criticism, it would be a pointless and impracticable exercise to offer another rundown. The most frequent literary

Surely, the most conspicuous aspect of Stevens criticism is its almost end-less habit of crossing the poems with outside texts. Stevens's is a poetry that so patently and consciously inscribes itself in literary as well as philosoph-ical traditions—from which it borrows terms, themes, topoi, images, and conventions (often, as Eleanor Cook insists, "in compact, elliptical, even enigmatic ways")[4]—that it continuously calls for prosthetic enhancement through comparison and juxtaposition. In 1990, Joseph N. Riddel, with the help of a few more dizzying enumerations, rightly observed that

> Stevens is an exceptional instance among American modernists in being *the* poet who has served as an exemplary model for almost every mode and theory of literary criticism from the 1950's to the present, even when these theo-ries were sharply contradictory and mutually exclusionary. How, indeed, I ask myself, can the same poet be subsumed, perhaps sublated, by so many diverse and, in some cases, tautological critical positions—New Critical formalism, historicism, the criticism of consciousness, psychoanalytical theory, various linguistic theories, rhetoric and the new rhetoric, deconstruction and other so-called poststructuralisms, the new historicism, and even, recently, by fem-inist criticism and a certain Marxism—or how could his poetry be identified, classified, and read in the context of so many period styles or poetic move-ments—Renaissance meditative poetry, Romanticism, post-Romanticism, symbolism, postsymbolism, modernism, post-modernism, even surrealism?[5]

While *literary* traditions are of course commonly confronted by poets—all the more so in the case of high modernists, whose anxious awareness of belatedness and agonistic quest for originality are two of their most defining

---

names figuring in such a list would probably be, before the romantics, Shakespeare; among the romantics, Wordsworth, Keats, Shelley, Tennyson, Emerson again, and Whitman; among the symbolists and postsymbolists, Baudelaire, Mallarmé, and Valéry; among Stevens's modernist contemporaries, Eliot, Williams, Frost, and Moore; and, among his descendants, Ashbery, Ammons, and Adrienne Rich.

4. Eleanor Cook, "Wallace Stevens and the King James Bible," 129.

5. Joseph N. Riddel, "Postscript '90," 286–87. That the multiplicity of interpretive frame-works used to analyze Stevens's work is indeed, as Riddel contends, "exceptional" among Anglo-modernist poets, and not simply a function of readers projecting the newest critical fashion onto a random textual victim, is illustrated by Lee Margaret Jenkins when she writes: "Whether or not it is convincing to look at Stevens in relation to postmodernism, it is the case that Stevens' poetry has been the subject of postmodern literary criticism, as it has been the subject of almost all of the twentieth-century literary schools: Yeats, in contrast, successively fails to be the vehicle for successive waves of literary theory, with the obvious exception of the New Criticism . . . to the extent that postmodern versions of Yeats are few and far between" (*Rage for Order*, 179).

characteristics—it is Stevens's connection to *philosophical* traditions (loosely defined) that has proved most spectacularly fruitful. Frank Kermode beautifully sums up Stevens's treacherously seductive qualities in this respect: "He's not a philosopher, and people who take him seriously as a philosopher obviously make a mistake, but he has a kind of peripheral awareness of the important issues in philosophy, which is more impressive in a poet than actually getting down and working them out."[6] In the early years of Stevens criticism, the poet's embryonic philosophical aperçus were often tested for their consistency and coherence. Thus, people like Northrop Frye, Frank Doggett, and J. Hillis Miller (in his early and influential phenomenological study, *Poets of Reality*) inaugurated what could be called the genre of bouquet criticism—the sort of criticism that picks and arranges particular words and lines from various poems with an eye toward recomposing the basic philosophical strands of Stevens's ideas and theories. This device was over the years copied by many critics, who, by judiciously choosing excerpts and some of the more striking aphorisms, proved able to enlist Stevens in the service of almost any philosophical (especially epistemological) theory.

Surprisingly perhaps, Stevens's most emblematic, not to say symptomatic, critic may well be Harold Bloom—despite the willfully and wistfully idiosyncratic packaging that has put off many Stevens lovers. For Bloom embodies, *à outrance*, the theoretical and intertextual comments so widely triggered by this poetry. Indeed, Bloom's own theoretical slant as a critic is known to derive as much from a long-standing fascination and profound acquaintance with Stevens's poetry as from the influence of such oedipal father figures as Emerson, Nietzsche, Freud, W. Jackson Bate, and Paul de Man. Bloom's own inclination illustrates how easily Stevens's teasing ideas stand midwife to vaster theoretical structures. It is not for nothing that the first part—the groundwork—of his theoretical tetralogy of the mid-seventies, *The Anxiety of Influence,* is shot through with unmarked, subcutaneous quotations from Stevens. What is more, one of the major elements of the theory expounded in that book, Bloom's highly personal brand of intertextuality, seems to have its roots in (among others) Stevens himself—specifically in the poet who wondered: "How has the human spirit ever survived the terrific literature with which it has had to contend?" (*OP* 194). Stevens's often vigorously suppressed allusions to, and echoes of, the works of predecessors have found

---

6. Frank Kermode, interview by Imre Salusinszky, 115.

in Bloom a mischievously disobeying, almost perversely receptive audience. The fact that Bloom has sometimes pushed the envelope and scandalized readers with the quixotic eccentricity and virile violence with which he has performed his intertextual readings matters less than the fact that he has also gone a long way toward legitimating the interpretation of Stevens's poetry in terms of repressed influences. Stevens's own notorious dismissiveness, exemplified by his assuring José Rodríguez Feo that he did not read a single line of poetry and chose to do so as "a way of defeating people who look only for echoes and influences" (*L* 575), makes the critical quest only more tantalizing. Not writing in any plainly allusive style, he has in fact caused intertextualizing readers to keep on establishing connections for a much longer time than either Eliot or Pound managed to do with their straightforward collages of quotations.

Bloom's copious intertextualizations of Stevens—like those of any other critic—can be seen as a particular way of contextualizing the poetry. They thus point to a wider debate that needs some elucidation. In traditional literary theory, the categories of intertext and context are often kept apart, with the latter referring principally to the biographical-historical and sociological conditions of texts. Yet if we want to get a clearer view of the critical practice of cross-pollinating Stevens, we need to understand how the two categories are in fact inseparably entangled. One way of looking at this entanglement is to examine the following excerpt from Jacques Derrida's much-quoted essay "Signature Event Context"—an excerpt in which the emphasis lies on the theoretical limitlessness of contexts:

> This is the possibility on which I wish to insist: the possibility of extraction and of citational grafting which belongs to the structure of every mark . . . Every sign, linguistic or nonlinguistic, spoken or written (in the usual sense of this opposition), as a small or large unity, can be *cited*, put between quotation marks; thereby it can break with every given context, and engender infinitely new contexts in an absolutely nonsaturable fashion. This does not suppose that the mark is valid outside its context, but on the contrary that there are only contexts without any center of absolute anchoring. This citationality, duplication, or duplicity, this iterability of the mark is not an accident or an anomaly, but is that (normal/abnormal) without which a mark could no longer even have a so-called "normal" functioning.[7]

7. Jacques Derrida, "Signature Event Context," 320–21.

What Derrida establishes in this passage is the *necessary condition* for any mark or sign to be able to function and thus to exist: it must be iterable and reconfigurable, extricable and reemployable in different contexts. The act of contextualization is thus a potentially endless, "nonsaturable" one whose limits are set by the performer (in the case of a text, the reader). At the same time, however, Derrida points out the *sufficient reason* for the operativeness of any mark or sign: only through a delimited context can a mark or sign acquire meaning and hence come to be, for neither mark nor sign have any existence outside a signifying practice. He does no more, in fact, than deny the possibility of an "absolute anchoring" of a mark (or text) in its context(s). He does not, in other words, dispute the possibility of some or other anchoring that is *relative to* the circumstances of production. He merely skirts the issue; or, as Umberto Eco says: "Derrida—in order to stress nonobvious truths—disregards very obvious truths that nobody can reasonably pass over in silence."[8]

This theoretically unresolvable but phenomenologically crucial tension between necessary condition and sufficient reason, which is relevant to any discussion of writing and to the production of meaning in general, is of particular importance to the practical study of a poet like Stevens, in whose work we find few internal authorizations for directing the establishment of a text's contexts, while some such establishment is yet always necessary for the production of meaning. Ordinarily, an immense range of constraints can be brought to bear upon signs. For practical, daily purposes of communication, texts ("spoken or written") seek to enforce their contextual limits as cogently as possible, so as to avoid unnecessary or unwelcome ambiguity. Most of the time, we talk and write to inform other people, and be informed by them, about what it is that we precisely think, feel, and want. But such painstakingly achieved strictness of delimitation diminishes as texts become less immediately goal-oriented and meanings more uncertain. This is especially true of the postsymbolist and experimental modernist kind of poetry developed by Stevens: the determination of contexts becomes ever more fickle as texts become denser, more elliptical and fragmented, less directly and mimetically referential, and less personally addressed to a specific interlocutor or audience. Viewed from this perspective, a good many of Stevens's poems move close to the opposite pole from ordinary, practical texts (or

8. Eco, *Limits of Interpretation*, 36.

so the illusionism of art would have it, for the paradoxical aim usually re-mains one of the greatest signifying accuracy). The historical contexts these poems provide are so spare and effaced, the diction so shot through with abstractions and incongruities, and the climaxes frequently marked by such an aphoristic—that is, widely applicable and reappropriable—ring that the texts become contextualizable in an unusually high number of ways. More even than is the case with much modernist prose, where at least internal contexts and concrete external references tend to be elaborated, Stevens's words, phrases, and ideas actively invite the sort of extraction and grafting to which all signs are theoretically open.[9] Critics are constantly tempted to frame Stevens by mining other writers who could help elucidate, or at least provide an enriching foil to, his texts. That they should come up primarily with literary and philosophical intertexts in this process is a function both of their own academic expertise and of the fact that such were the texts that Stevens himself, as a voracious reader, consciously or unconsciously recycled in his poetry.

As said, the numerous contexts drawn upon to interpret Stevens's po-etry have been mostly, though by no means exclusively, those of still other texts.[10] And today the name for the institutionalized reading practice where-by texts are related to one another is, of course, intertextuality. It is a shibbo-leth of poststructuralist theorists, but nevertheless is a notoriously dangerous concept to set to work. Word formations with "textuality" are particularly prone to promiscuity, as Vladimir Nabokov's biographer, Brian Boyd, il-lustrates by subtitling an article on Joyce and Nabokov "Intertextuality,

9. J. Hillis Miller's contrasting of Stevens and William Carlos Williams with respect to the possibility of grafting further texts onto their work is appropriate and revelatory. Miller observes that Stevens is "especially open to academic criticism. My fascination with and admiration for William Carlos Williams is exactly the reverse: that Williams is so resistant to intellectualizing. He is a very great poet, but difficult for somebody trained in abstractions. I can deal with ideas, and the thing itself, and so on—no problem—but what do you say about 'The Red Wheelbarrow' or about a poem that just describes a sycamore tree?" (interview by Imre Salusinszky, 233).

10. The most fruitful possibility of crossing Stevens with nontextual media has been with modern painting: see especially Glen G. MacLeod, *Wallace Stevens and Company: The Har-monium Years, 1913–1923*, and *Wallace Stevens and Modern Art: From the Armory Show to Abstract Expressionism*; Charles Altieri, *Painterly Abstraction in Modernist American Poetry: The Contemporaneity of Modernism*; Jacqueline Vaught Brogan, *Part of the Climate: American Cubist Poetry*; and Daniel R. Schwarz, *Reconfiguring Modernism: Explorations in the Relationship between Modern Art and Modern Literature*. The place of biographical-historical and socio-logical contextualizations in the reading of Stevens will be addressed in my conclusion to Part One.

Intratextuality, Supratextuality, Infratextuality, Extratextuality and Auto-textuality in Modernist and Prepostmodernist Narrative Discourse," adding in a footnote that the list is itself an elaboration of Maurice Couturier's notion of "transtextuality."[11] None of these other textualities, however, have become nearly as widespread as "intertextuality," and it may be useful to look at how an understanding of the latter concept affects our appreciation of the limits of reading Stevens's work.

B. J. Leggett goes a long way toward expounding relevant questions about intertextuality in the theoretical opening chapter of his *Early Stevens: The Nietzschean Intertext*. He sets out by analyzing Bloom's variety of intertextuality, only to find that Bloom constantly muddles source study and intertextual free play, pushing the tension between these methods to an extreme without signaling that he is doing so. Leggett points up the limits of both methods—the positivistic philological source study of those he calls "Socratic" or "canny" critics as well as the playful crossing with other texts of their "Apollonian/Dionysian" or "uncanny" colleagues: "If the uncanny critics must necessarily be blind to history, to anything outside the act of reading texts that links Nietzsche [or any other writer] and Stevens, then their counterparts require a blindness to the problematical nature of sources and of the act of reading itself."[12]

The uncanny critics—for whom J. Hillis Miller in his pyrotechnical reading of "The Rock" serves as a model—implicitly or explicitly deny influence studies any legitimacy and discount the significance of biographically and historically identifiable intrusions, while canny critics, who try to establish the precise extent of other writers' influence on Stevens—most prominently among them, Milton J. Bates—engage in a project that is "threatened by the inability to escape textuality, the inability to enter a world of cause and effect where the relationship between text and source can be established." In the specific case of "the permutations of the term *Nietzschean* as applied to Stevens in the last two decades," Leggett runs down the many disparate functions this label has actually, if not always consciously, served:

> According to the perspective we adopt, we may say that Stevens is a Nietzschean poet because he exemplifies qualities we associate with Nietzsche, because he has been a frequent subject of critics who are themselves influenced by Nietzsche's theories of language, because his poetry may be glossed

11. Brian Boyd, "Words, Works and Worlds in Joyce and Nabokov."
12. B. J. Leggett, *Early Stevens: The Nietzschean Intertext*, 13.

usefully with passages from Nietzsche, because his concepts, ideas, and tropes parallel Nietzsche's in striking ways, because certain of his assumptions, values, themes, images have their source in Nietzsche, because his concepts and figures are generally identified with Nietzsche even if Stevens acquired them elsewhere—there are presumably a number of other possible combinations and nuances.[13]

The whole notion of intertextuality is so slippery that, according to Owen Miller, another student of the phenomenon, "[t]he current vogue it enjoys in literary studies stems precisely from [its] provisionary and unstable status."[14] What we are left with, after much theoretical give and take, especially among poststructuralist theorists, may be little more than a few metaphors of empowerment, expedience, and enrichment: "Intertextual connections might *strengthen* one interpretation over another, *help* articulate a particular interpretation which intratextual features fail adequately to support, *add*, in short, to the potential polysemy of the text, while, at the same time, suggesting heuristic *strategies* on how to deal with it" (emphases added).[15] In the final analysis, intertextuality may be nothing more than a phenomenon of "informational associationism" that does not allow any specific, practical rules to be deduced from an overall theory of the workings of signification. It may be little else than a receptive strategy that has been territorialized by an academic literary-theoretical profession somewhat corporativistically in search of a discipline to call its own.[16] Yet the heuristic legitimacy of drawing on outside texts as a signifying practice, irrespective of whether or not those texts actually inspired (even *could* have inspired) the poet in the act of writing, is undeniable. The precise *value* of establishing textual connections, however, can only lie in the performance itself, much as the acceptability of particular textual links ultimately resides in their appeal to the members of the interpretive community to which they are being submitted. Beyond the act of crossing texts, little more can be done than to signal a sufficiently self-reflective awareness of the specific nature of one's reading praxis—as either tending toward source study or else toward a freer cross-fertilization—and to vary in types of performance. Such a mixed method also offers the best results with Stevens, in whose case neither a strictly

13. Ibid., 14, 18–19.
14. Owen Miller, "Intertextual Identity," 19.
15. Ibid., 32.
16. Benjamin Biebuyck and Jürgen Pieters, "Enkele bedenkingen bij het begrip 'interteks-tualiteit,'" 29, 33. "Informational associationism" is my translation.

deterministic philological geneticism nor a free-floating associative praxis in and of itself manages to do justice to the complex dynamics of reading set off by his writings.

One particularly characteristic and conspicuous type of intertextualization in the critical appropriation of Stevens's work, finally, deserves special attention. For nothing tells critics to restrict the outside texts they choose to poetry and prose composed by *other* writers. Indeed, one would be hard pressed to think of another poet whose oeuvre is so easily and automatically read as one gigantic network, as one big text (in the etymological sense of the word, a weaving) or one large ecosystem (in the formulation of Gyorgyi Voros). James Longenbach refers to this quality as the "seductive wholeness of Stevens's oeuvre."[17] Longenbach's phrase is certainly apt for a poet who, having called his first volume *Harmonium* (thereby proffering an index of his wish to harmonize the variegated poems living under the same umbrella), toyed at the end of his life with the idea of calling his collected poems *The Whole of Harmonium*, in spite of the fact that he was a poet who, early and late, tended to resist the inclination toward totalization.[18] On the face of it, Stevens could seem very little preoccupied with the interrelationship among his own compositions. There is much evidence to show that he was not only given to deprecating his earlier work, but also repeatedly strove to actively forget what he had written—witness the amazing carelessness with which he at times treated his poems once he had finished them and sent them out to magazines and publishers. Harriet Monroe, who as the publishing godmother of American modernist poetry was peculiarly well placed to make comparisons, recalled that "of all the poets I have ever met, Stevens is the most indifferent as to the fate of his works after they have emerged from his mind."[19] But this indifference was partly a pose and partly a defense mechanism. Moreover, the blotting out of finished poems was to Stevens an important way of wiping the slate clean so as to allow a rewriting of earlier texts that promised freshness and novelty. It was a symptom of his deeply rooted originality neurosis, his wish to write a poetry that was "constantly new" (*L* 277).

Stevens's mind-set was clearly such that he kept mulling and lingering over the same issues. He originally wanted to call his first volume *The Grand*

17. Voros, *Notations of the Wild*, 19; James Longenbach, "The Idea of Disorder at Key West," 95.
18. Schulze, *Web of Friendship*, 41, 198.
19. Quoted in Lensing, *Poet's Growth*, 265–66.

Poem: Preliminary Minutiae, thereby announcing from the outset a wish to integrate his still-to-evolve writing career, and there is a wide critical consensus that he found his congenital compositorial style in "The Man with the Blue Guitar," a cycle that playfully develops thirty-three perspectives on his favorite binarism: imagination and reality.[20] The upshot of so much interconnectedness is that a good many of the intertextual crossings performed on Stevens's poems occur from *within* the collected works themselves, thus helping to disrupt the traditional New Critical boundary of the well-rounded single lyric. "One of the most rewarding experiences in reading Stevens," according to Srikanth Reddy, "is the moment when several poems coalesce into a 'poem-group,' in which various lyrics point toward one another thematically, logically, or through allusion. In such poem-groups, less pressure is placed on the endings of individual lyrics, as no single text bears the full burden of resolving itself; rather, each poem can simply gesture toward one of its companions." There is to Stevens—and, as a result, also to his critics—a sort of constant echolalia, and it may be linked again to the subject of desire in his work. As Margaret Dickie argues, Stevens's projection of a "man-hero" as "he that of repetition is most master" (CP 406) is deceptive to the extent that repetition is precisely "what cannot be mastered. Repetition is desire and desire repetition."[21]

Although most intertextualizing readings from within Stevens's oeuvre have understandably shaded into a type of genetic criticism—with the poet pictured as "the late romantic master of the hypercyclical,"[22] the ceaseless, conscious rewriter of a handful of central or archetypical lines or poems—it should not be forgotten that the arrow of time may also be reversed and that

---

20. The (probably unintended) analogy with Beethoven's thirty-three Diabelli Variations reminds us of Stevens's not-so-negligible affinity with the musical form of the variation. Angus Fletcher argues that "[t]he governing rhetorical figure in Stevens is a figure equivalent to musical variations" (foreword to *Wallace Stevens: The Intensest Rendezvous*, xi), and both Northrop Frye and Barbara Holmes have devoted entire essays or chapters to the influence of the musical form of theme and variations on Stevens's writing praxis. In Michael O. Stegman's discography of Stevens's phonograph record collection, the Diabelli Variations are included in a set of complete Beethoven sonatas recorded by Artur Schnabel, along with sixteen other works in the genre, not all of them obvious buys, like compositions by Arensky, Dohnanyi, Dukas, Pierne, and Reger. Stevens's choice of subject in "Two Tales of Liadoff" (CP 346–47) and his choice of dedicatee in "More Poems for Liadoff"—a set of twelve poems (CP 360–70) originally published in *Quarterly Review of Literature*—is equally significant, since the little-known Russian composer Anatole Liadoff (or Lyadov) was above all a specialist in variations (Schulze, *Web of Friendship*, 167).

21. Srikanth Reddy, "'As He Starts the Human Tale': Strategies of Closure in Wallace Stevens," 16; Dickie, *Lyric Contingencies*, 86.

22. Fletcher, foreword, ix.

it has repeatedly proved possible to shed light on an early poem through the lens of a much later one. This process is further enhanced by the remarkable phenomenon that in Stevens's case, as Alain Suberchicot notes, "one has the impression that, as soon as the oeuvre begins, it is already finished. . . . [F]or those who are in the habit of grasping in all literary works a gradation or an internal growth, he launches a defiance to analysis. . . . This absence of signs of a beginning, and this refusal of the literary quest, are a form of so-phistication proper to Stevens."[23] If intertextual reading practices are always potentially a two-way process, this applies with a vengeance to an inter-Stevens reading. Reading this poet can make one realize, with particular force, how meaning is produced both backwards and forwards, or, as Harold Bloom would say, both metaleptically and proleptically. The meaning of a poem can never be found at a specific textual site, and Stevens's work drives this home with particular insistence. His poetry constantly invites us to de-velop meanings in difference, afloat in time, incessantly emerging between texts and their intertexts/contexts. Stevens's "endlessly elaborating" poems (CP 486) are in some sense veritable hypertexts *avant la lettre*.

23. Suberchicot, *Treize façons*, 15–16 (my translation).

Chapter 5

It Must Be Made of Snow
A Case Study

THERE ARE SEVERAL GOOD REASONS for embarking upon an extended case study at this point. Not the least of these is the need to keep up a constant skepsis about the potentially sweeping, leveling, or streamlining character of synthesis and generalization, especially in the case of a poet for whom the resistance to totalization and the cultivation of qualifications and nuances were supposedly of the utmost importance. To avoid the pitfalls both of paraphrastic truism and of a critical narrative that cuts itself loose from its textual base, my preceding synthetical arguments should be supplemented by some form of analytical work. For it is only by tracing the possibilities of a particular reading that one can acquire a felt sense of the problematic and complex dynamics of reading this poetry and that one can experience how multiple the tracks offered by Stevens's poetry really are. Concomitantly, it is only by attending to concrete texts that one can critically reenact some of the primary pleasures of reading Stevens: the pleasures of following trails and of being overwhelmed by their proliferation, the delight of juggling with words and ideas, of framing them—or of getting lost in the far and deep textual woods.

A great many rewarding poems could be chosen to serve as a case in point, but I have four strategic reasons for turning to "The Snow Man." First of all, the poem is by most critics taken to constitute something of a cynosure or keystone in Stevens's oeuvre and thus provides ample opportunity for illustrating the potential for intertextual ramification within the poet's own works. Secondly, it is a poem that has received so much critical attention that the diversity of possibilities for reading Stevens can be more sharply etched on the basis of its critical reception than would be the case with

56

less central texts. Thirdly, it happens to be a widely loved poem—and this not only among professional Stevensians, judging from the high frequency with which it is anthologized and the fact that an allusion to it can pop up in a classical-music magazine—which in terms of aesthetic economy means that it allows us to identify some of the best qualities in Stevens's writing. (Alison Rieke even complains that the poem "perhaps goes down *too* easily with students," partly because of its relative closeness to Robert Frost.)[1] And finally, it is an early poem, not yet as abstruse as the poetry of the late forties, where strongly divergent appropriations can be the all-too-obvious outcome of a text's stylistic condensation and metaphorical imperviousness.

The specific signifying and appropriative potential of "The Snow Man" may best be demonstrated, it appears, by distinguishing between a formal, a tonal, a thematic, and an intertextual level. These four levels will be the structuring categories of the ensuing case study. Needless to add, however, they constantly interact and such a fourfold division is no more than a critical expedient in which categorial boundaries are nothing if not porous. Form, for example, can and should never be discussed without a minimal involvement of (thematic) content. And it would be downright Procrustean to offer a formal or thematic reading of the poem without allowing oneself an occasional comparison with other writers, or without establishing links to other Stevensian texts: such associative intertextual reflexes are, as a framing device, a natural part of the critic's methodological repertoire.

To be of real use, also, my case study must attempt to steer a middle course between documentation and personal appropriation. Its purpose cannot simply be to document all existing interpretations of the poem, since that would be both practically unfeasible and theoretically suspicious. This case study would itself fall prey to the worst sort of objectivism that would force me to treat compelling and convincing readings on the same level as sloppy and misguided ones. Nor could the arguments made in the previous chapters be advanced, deepened, or complicated if I were to stick to a supposedly neutral description. Interpretive decisions always have to be taken, and they are of necessity subjective. In this sense, I will need to appropriate the poem in my own turn, like any other critic. Yet the primary emphasis cannot fall on personal conviction either, since the purpose of this case study is not to come up with a single, well-rounded interpretation of my own (supposing that were possible), but to follow the various possible tracks for interpretation laid out

---

1. For the allusion in a magazine, see Bryce Morrison, review of *Debussy: Complete Piano Works*; Rieke, "Wallace Stevens in the Classroom," 131.

by the text. The main purpose of the exercise, in other words, is to display the text's signifying potential (as evidenced by its critical reception) and to show both the constrictions and productivities constituting that potential.

For easier reference, let me first reprint the text:

The Snow Man

One must have a mind of winter
To regard the frost and the boughs
Of the pine-trees crusted with snow;

And have been cold a long time
To behold the junipers shagged with ice,
The spruces rough in the distant glitter

Of the January sun; and not to think
Of any misery in the sound of the wind,
In the sound of a few leaves,

Which is the sound of the land
Full of the same wind
That is blowing in the same bare place

For the listener, who listens in the snow,
And, nothing himself, beholds
Nothing that is not there and the nothing that is.

(CP 9–10)

I. FORMAL APPROPRIATIONS

The Contiguity of Syntax

The most eye-catching formal characteristic of "The Snow Man" is undoubtedly its syntax—the fact that its fifteen lines are cast in a single sentence. To Geoffrey H. Hartman, this fact bespeaks Stevens's wish to "[catch] consciousness in the act."[2] Hartman's formulation is carefully worded, echoing as it does another famous short lyric by Stevens, "Of Modern Poetry." It will be remembered how this second, explicitly programmatic, poem unrolls

---

2. Geoffrey H. Hartman, "The Poet's Politics," 256.

between two of Stevens's more typical phrases: the first of these proposes, as a working hypothesis, "The poem of the mind in the act of finding / What will suffice" (*CP* 239), and the final phrase retroactively sums up the preceding poetological experiment as "The poem of the act of the mind" (*CP* 240). This concluding proposition is so appropriate to the whole of Stevens's oeuvre that it was also one of the first to catch on: it was borrowed (in clipped form) as the title of one of the earliest and still most interesting collections of critical essays on the poet, Roy Harvey Pearce and J. Hillis Miller's 1965 *The Act of the Mind*. Given this centrality of "the act of the mind" in Stevens's work overall, it does not prove hard to let the single, meandering period that trickles down the five tercets of "The Snow Man"—that "periphrastic striptease," as William W. Bevis wittily calls it[3]—take on an emblematic character. The sentence easily serves as a *pars pro toto* for Stevens's overall syntactic habits and, more specifically, for his continuous endeavors to present thinking *in statu nascendi*, his wish to let his thoughts roam and amble, twist and turn within the tracks laid out by his verse. (And the word "verse," as this poet knew too well, etymologically goes back to the metaphor of plowing.)[4]

Stevens's single sentence also offers a particularly felicitous illustration of his wish to resist the intelligence almost successfully, for its very grammatical construction has been the object of critical controversy. According to David H. Hesla, the poem is almost universally misread by critics as a hypothetical proposition in the form "if . . . then . . ." "The crux of the poem," he writes, "lies in the relation of 'and not to think' with what goes before." There is a sliding movement between the poem's two halves (hinging on the semicolon that splits line 7 into two hemistichs). Strictly speaking, as Hesla demonstrates, the beginning of the poem's second half cannot be read as implicative or imperative in meaning; it can only be read as inferential. Accordingly, the poem "does not tell us what one must have or do or be

3. Bevis, *Mind of Winter*, 24.
4. Roger Gilbert, in a highly enjoyable study, enlists Stevens among those poets who write what he calls "walk poems"—poems composed while walking and hence resembling "a brief excursion directed toward no practical goal but undertaken purely for the pleasures of movement, reflection, and aesthetic perception" (*Walks in the World: Representation and Experience in Modern American Poetry*, 3). In this respect, the biographical fact that Stevens was a lifelong hiker, who in his younger days went for long weekend rambles up to forty-two miles and later in life composed much of his poetry while walking to and from his Hartford office, is worth recalling. To Bevis, this ambulatory or peripatetic habit was even conducive to the special sort of meditative experience characteristic of so much of his work, including, in particular, "The Snow Man" (*Mind of Winter*, 7, 88, 218–27).

in order not to think of any misery. It says, rather, that from the fact that someone does not or cannot think of any misery in the sound of the wind it can be inferred that the person has a mind of winter."[5] Ingeniously, Hesla proceeds to interpret the rest of the poem as saying, rather phenomenologically and in a most un-Cartesian manner, that one cannot look at a bleak winter landscape without thinking of misery, that the experience of things is naturally invested with feelings. But to propose this interpretation he must, first of all, ignore the poem's shift from beholding to hearing; secondly, he must read the listener's becoming "nothing himself" as really saying that the listener is becoming "no thing himself"; and thirdly, he must interpret "the nothing that is" with which the poem concludes as simply standing in for the earlier "misery." In other words, he has to perform a few critical gestures that (a) are strangely counterintuitive, (b) blatantly contradict Stevens's own paraphrase of the poem (about which more in a moment), and (c) fail to account for the poem's opening lines as well as for Stevens's decision to arrange the poem the way he did—an arrangement more like the dislocation of a shoulder in Hesla's reading than the seductively progressing bemusement it seems to offer to most readers.

All in all, Hesla's principal, unintended merit has been to show how the poem's syntax is so organized as to disrupt any easy intelligence and open up various heuristic possibilities. When Hartman observes that the entire sentence "in fulfilling itself, also cancels itself out,"[6] his observation does more, in fact, than simply describe the poem's eventual arrival at three nothings: it also sums up some of the logical-syntactic workings of the text. The transition between the poem's two halves is sufficiently elusive to set critics wondering, for instance, about an "effect of blurring distinctions between, on the one side, the human perceptions allowed in lines one to the middle of seven, and, on the other, the perceptions thereafter ascribed to the snow man."[7] And blurring distinctions is, of course, a well-tried method for resisting the intelligence.

Since Stevens pushes his periodic style and "principle of apposition"[8] to such an extreme, he opens up a more general critical route as well. The conspicuousness of his idiosyncratic stylistic device almost begs comparison with the habits of fellow modernist artists—mostly, though not exclusively,

5. David H. Hesla, "Singing in Chaos: Wallace Stevens and Three or Four Ideas," 242, 249–50.
6. Hartman, "Poet's Politics," 256.
7. Poirier, *Renewal of Literature*, 219.
8. George S. Lensing, "Stevens's Prosody," 114.

literary. As a staunch advocate for extending the literary critic's reach by including analogies from the fine arts, Helen Vendler talks of "a syntactic version of the series of receding planes with which we are familiar in painting." But such loose analogies are inevitably less productive than the possibilities for comparative contextualization at a more literary level. In the early thirties, in the first ambitious critical article on the poet, R. P. Blackmur usefully contrasted Stevens's style to that of T. S. Eliot, in particular the Eliot of *The Waste Land* who attempted to shore fragments against his ruin. More than sixty years later, A. Walton Litz would come to argue, on the basis of such contrasts, that "the 'difficulty' of modern poetry . . . varies from writer to writer; unlike the poets of a more unified period, we have to learn to read the moderns one by one, gradually habituating ourselves to the unique difficulties of each poet."[9] Indeed, few starker syntactic-stylistic contrasts within the overarching category of Anglo-modernist poetry present themselves than the one between the radical juxtapositions of the early Eliot and the endless flow of modulations and qualifications in Stevens. Where Eliot, at some deep level, longed to erect a textual temple out of distinct building blocks, Stevens favored weaving a web of complications, leading the mind into a textual labyrinth. "After all," the older poet remarked in 1950, "Eliot and I are dead opposites and I have been doing about everything that he would not be likely to do" (*L* 677).[10]

9. Vendler, *Words Chosen Out of Desire*, 48–49; R. P. Blackmur, "Examples of Wallace Stevens," 233–41; A. Walton Litz, " 'Compass and Curriculum': Teaching Stevens among the Moderns," 235.

10. That the (always also ideologically informed) syntactic-stylistic contrast may be worked out with respect to Ezra Pound as well is only too apparent from Hugh Kenner's sanctification of the latter in *The Pound Era*. When Kenner—to whom the work of Stevens evinced no more than "an Edward Lear poetic, pushed toward all limits" (517)—talks of an "American preference for denotation over etymology, for the cut term over association and the channelled path" (404), the oppositional terms against which he defines American (i.e., Poundian) poetry are obviously Stevensian traits. It is not for nothing that Harold Bloom, spurred by his usual vituperative animosity toward Eliot and certainly Pound ("as good a poet as Edmund Waller" [interview, 72]), countered Kenner's famous title by positing a "Stevens Era" (*Wallace Stevens: The Poems of Our Climate*, 152). The opposition between Pound and Stevens has been polarized most explicitly by Marjorie Perloff, who developed the questionable dichotomies of "fact vs. invention, form vs. content, outwardness vs. inwardness, the political vs. the personal, the historical epic vs. the lyric" (as summarized by Newcomb, *Literary Canons*, 10) only to "promote the Pound Era as a politically progressive version of modernism" (ibid.). Against this, Newcomb convincingly argues that "[t]he gap between Stevens and Pound, if it can be said to exist, is a function of the conditions of postwar criticism, is neither intrinsic nor necessarily permanent, and does not explain the essential questions of modernism" (ibid., 12–13).

The contrast may be profitably pursued in less metaphorical and more the-oretical terms as well: in the language of structuralist linguistics, for instance, the early Eliot's characteristic style may be qualified as basically paradig-matic, whereas Stevens's style shows itself to be excessively syntagmatic.[11] Such an opposition is especially momentous for what it helps to say about Stevens, since to write syntagmatically is to stake everything on a potentially endless capacity—and need—for contextualization. It is to move contigu-ously, to tie text to text, to be suspended in an ongoing process of deferral and differing (hence to become popular among deconstructionists). Stevens's very syntax, it could be argued, is largely responsible for the critical dis-semination his poetry has produced. This becomes all the more apparent if we restyle the opposition between the paradigmatic and the syntagmatic in still other, more philosophical terms, as one between the spatial and the temporal. J. Hillis Miller was one of the first to focus on Stevens's consistent attempts to "match the mobility of the moment" and represent "the flowing of time."[12] Pace Vendler's spatial analogy with the planes of painting (them-selves presented dynamically, and thus temporally, as "receding"), Stevens's poetry—even in the act of stabilizing itself to a single point (which is para-doxically also a nonpoint) in space, as it seems to be doing toward the end of "The Snow Man"—primarily reflects and records the ongoing temporal dynamics of thought.

Thus, before you know it, the slippery descent down the hypotactic step-ladder of "The Snow Man" brings more than just the nothing of absence it claims to wind up with. It simultaneously carries in its wake a necessary presence: the presence of that background only against which it can acquire meaning, of those narratives that frame Stevens's conspicuous syntactic act. In this respect, the paradox with which the poem concludes at the referential level finds a displaced sort of formal counterpart, for the unfocusing-focusing stasis expressed at the end of the text is undercut by the floating temporality of the syntax that leads up to it. Any illusion of a final arrival at the end of the poem, whether intellectually or emotionally, is subverted by the textual

11. In Ihab Hassan's terms, this would qualify Eliot as a modernist and Stevens as a post-modernist, since Hassan sees paradigm, hypotaxis, and metaphor as characteristic of mod-ernism and syntagm, parataxis, and metonymy typical of postmodernism ("The Culture of Postmodernism," 124). The syntagmatic, we might add, is also the axis of desire, for desire (at least in Lacanian theory) operates metonymically. Strategies of contiguity, furthermore, are preponderant in Stevens's work not only through his elongated syntax, but also through his frequent alliterative habit, which is sometimes even expanded into a principle of orga-nization, as in "The Comedian as the Letter C."

12. J. Hillis Miller, Poets of Reality: Six Twentieth-Century Writers, 270, 272.

history that precedes it, and readers soon realize they are not likely to be able to bring their interpretations of the poem quite round; more likely they will want to return to the text. This is what Stanley Fish suggests when writing that "the act of revising has as its object not merely a syntactic structure, but the structure of the reader's understanding. That is, each time we revise or reanalyze ['The Snow Man'], what changes is not only our understanding of the syntax but our understanding of what is required to regard the frost and the junipers; and the shape of that change is a complicating of what it means to 'have a mind of winter.' "[13]

The Widening Circles of Diction

Although Litz rightly points to the "simplicity of the diction" in this poem—especially in view of Stevens's notorious indulgence in a finicky fastidiousness and his habit of writing a poetry where, as George S. Lensing notes, "diction constantly highlights itself"[14]—the words appear nevertheless shrewdly chosen and resonate more amply than they seem to do at first sight. This is most strikingly true of the poetic/biblical word *behold:* not only is the word sufficiently remarkable in its own right to set off associative ruminations on the ironical status of *holding* (containment) and even *wholeness* in the case of an agent and an object that are both defined as "nothing"; it is also sufficiently overlaid with semantic connotations to suggest feelings of wonder, maybe even to carry an overtone of apocalyptic revelation.[15] Moreover, the word can be felt to function in more overtly formalist ways as well—that is, visually and acoustically. For it may be argued (inconclusively

13. Stanley Fish, *Is There a Text in This Class? The Authority of Interpretive Communities*, 256.

14. A. Walton Litz, *Introspective Voyager: The Poetic Development of Wallace Stevens*, 100; Lensing, "Stevens's Prosody," 113.

15. The pivotal line in "From the Journal of Crispin," "Crispin beholds and Crispin is made new" (OP 48; reworked into the past tense in "The Comedian as the Letter C" [CP 30]), does not only play a mischievous variation on the line "Behold, I make all things new" from the Book of Revelation (Cook, "King James Bible," 129), but also directly associates the act of beholding with the experience of rejuvenation. Interestingly, "The Snow Man" was written in the months immediately before Stevens started work on his epical rite of passage, so that it may have paved the way for Crispin's adventures (Joan Richardson, *Wallace Stevens: The Early Years, 1879–1923*, 516). In the poem under discussion, Susan B. Weston also hears a pun on embrace ("be-hold") (*Wallace Stevens: An Introduction to the Poetry*, 8), and Harold Bloom pits the verb against *regard*, which figures earlier in the text: to him, *regard* introduces a trope of "ethos" while *behold* commences a trope of "pathos" (*Poems of Our Climate*, 58).

and speculatively, to be sure) that Stevens plays on the symbol and the letter *o* in *behold*, as well as on the sounds it represents. Several critics have observed how the poet strives to attain a *zero* degree of consciousness in his text, but only Eleanor Cook has begun to exploit the full potential of the image of zero by linking it to eye and ear. Taking her cue from the poem's final lines, she embroiders: "Letters on the page give the lie to the last two lines as simple description though not as paradox or trope. This paradox is an old one, inherent also in the mathematical concept of zero and in the letter O . . . And we should not forget the acoustic sounds of O, and its visual shape, since a snowman is made of three O's. (The letter and number and shape of O seem to go to extremes, for its other associations are just the opposite of nothing; they are of plenitude.)"[16]

Cook's remarks may sound like tangential improvisations, yet their interpretive fertility cannot be denied. If we look at the number of key words in the poem that contain the letter *o*, we find that we might almost reconstruct the entire narrative from the verbal string *one frost boughs snow cold long behold rough not sound blowing snow nothing beholds nothing not nothing*. Bringing the words with an *o* together like this allows us to hear more clearly the pervasive assonantal echo of *snow-cold-blowing-behold*, acting almost like a ritualistic mantra in yoga.[17] Both visual and acoustical effects are noteworthy because they sensuously support the poem's ideas. Cook's playing off of inside against outside and of nothingness against plenitude is well-considered. For an *o* is also a circle, and this in turn opens up a vast cyclorama of significations. Suddenly, and despite the ostensible unallusiveness of its plain style, "The Snow Man" evinces a potential for intertextual interaction with Emerson's "Circles," one of the central essays of American Transcendentalism, or with Derridean meditations on topics like the parergon, the relationship between inside and outside, or the circum-scription of the "identical" and the "proper."

The play with *o* is finally also extendable to the only typographical oddity of the poem: its title. For this is not a poem about a snowman but about a

---

16. Cook, *Poetry, Word-Play, and Word-War,* 49.

17. The fact that the mantra *om* in Eastern philosophies is chanted to invoke the whole cosmos and its creative principle nicely supports Bevis's detailed reading of the poem as evincing a meditative, near-Buddhist sensibility. The overall musicality of "The Snow Man" is in no doubt: by 1992 the poem had been set to music by at least five composers, thus ceding only to four other poems in the Stevens canon: "Thirteen Ways of Looking at a Blackbird" (set by fifteen composers), "Peter Quince at the Clavier" (eight composers), and "Of Mere Being" and "The Man with the Blue Guitar" (both seven) (Michael O. Stegman, "Checklist of Musical Compositions Relating to Stevens").

metaphorical man of snow, with the phrase written on the analogy of an "iron man." Stevens was too much of an *O.E.D.* addict not to know that ever since its first appearance in English in 1827, the word for denoting a manlike figure sculpted in snow is spelled as either "snowman" or "snow-man," but never as two separate words. His deliberate splitting of the word helps us question the degree to which the speaker (or is it merely the listener in the snow?) retains his humanity, as traditionally conceived, at the end of the poem. In Cook's witty, elliptical formulation, the poem asks: "Who am I? A snow man. Am I? No man."[18] Had this poem been written by e. e. cummings, it might have been called something like "the s-NO-w man." But a typographical trick of that sort could only have horrified Stevens for being so obtrusively and unmysteriously explicit: this is a writer who de-tested "poetry pretending to be contemporaneous because of typographical queerness" (*L* 326).

If we can agree that the title wants us to distinguish between a snow man and an ordinary snowman, we are nevertheless in one and the same gesture made to ponder alternative perspectives for interpretation. What if the title *had* been "The Snowman"? Then a different reading would open up, one in which the first four stanzas simply refer to an actual snowman; only in the fifth and final stanza would a listener (arguably the poet) enter the scene to empathize with the nothing that is there: the snowman. We are left to wonder: Are we actually meant to picture a snowman as part of the scenery and does any of the description refer to it? Or has the sight of a snowman only been the anecdotal starting point for the poet to picture himself as a man of snow? Anne Ferry taps into this unresolvable confusion by arguing that the poem

> present[s] "Man" in an aspect at once ridiculous and archetypal, by conjuring up the image of a cheery, childish, perishable artifact, the snowman, and also an elemental, mythic being, the man of snow (who might be compared with "The man of autumn" of "Secret Man" in Stevens's *Opus Posthumous*). In the poem the snowman is immediately dissolved while the man of snow emerges gradually. The process is recorded grammatically as the "One," who opens the poem-sentence guardedly regarding, disappears into the other-than-humanly personal "listener" who, "nothing himself," is receptive to "Nothing that is not there and the nothing that is." Although the grammar of the sentence makes no dramatic interchange between speaker and hearer, "the listener"

18. Cook, *Poetry, Word-Play, and Word-War*, 50.

obliquely allows the possibility of our representation with the poet in the generic man of snow.[19]

In other words, the precise status of all possible participants in the poem—the snowman, the listener, the speaker, the man of snow, the writer, the reader—is left unclear by Stevens. Boundaries melt as we read this poem, feel personally involved, and start groping for our own ways of making sense.

II. TONAL APPROPRIATIONS

Given my earlier observations in Chapter 3, it will come as no surprise to see that one particularly problematic feature of "The Snow Man"—a feature suspended somewhere in the twilight zone between form and content—is its tone. The only safe, verifiable observation that can be made is that Stevens makes conspicuous use of repetition in the second half of the poem. Vendler underscores this by rewriting the lines and italicizing (almost) all the words that are repeated:

> *the sound of the wind*
> *the sound of* a few leaves
> *the sound of the* land
>   full of the *same wind*
>   that is blowing in the *same* bare place
>   for the *listener,* who *listens* in the snow
>   and, *nothing* himself, beholds
>   *nothing that is* not there
>   and the *nothing that is.*[20]

Yet Vendler also proffers an interpretation: she talks of a "deadly repetition," which is in fact to make a strong statement about the tone of the text. Most readers would agree that the repetitions serve some incantatory purpose (as they are wont to do, in poetry as much as in liturgy) and that they may be felt to reinforce a sense of freezing and numbing, or else that they may be taken to reflect an emptying of language, a sense of "the monotonous opaqueness of

19. Anne Ferry, *The Title to the Poem*, 102–3.
20. Helen Vendler, "Stevens and Keats' 'To Autumn,'" 188.

the wind's speechless voice"[21]—all of which seems appropriate to the experience of turning into a snow man in a windswept landscape. But beyond this it becomes much harder to determine the precise affective quality of Stevens's tone, to assess his exact emotional investment, especially as the poem builds up toward its final climax. (Should we call it an anticlimax? Is the category of the climactic at all to the point?) The result of this relative undecidability is that "The Snow Man" has been appropriated in radically divergent ways, with readings ranging from the "numb stoic endurance" found by Vendler, through the "pleasure" of "self-dissolution" detected by Richard Poirier, or even "a sense of power and plenitude" in Richard A. Macksey's commentary, to a perception that is either "appalled" or "not without humor" in Hesla's and Frank Lentricchia's respective opinions. Bevis, the only critic to have grafted an entire book onto the poem, feels that the problem indeed rests with the poem's elusive tone—"that the poem's difficulty springs not from its statement but from its tone, the emotions associated with the utterance."[22] Bevis provides one major hypothesis for this tonal insecurity and the critical diversity of opinion it has spawned: the presence in Stevens of a thoroughly meditative streak—a characteristic also noted in this context, though without being pursued, by R. P. Blackmur and Eleanor Cook.[23] This meditative tendency must itself be seen as an important factor in Stevens's earlier-noted poetic dogma of impersonality—a dogma that is adhered to in the poem from the very first word, only to be pushed further and further as the text progresses and the generic "One" finds itself displaced by an entirely dissociated third-person "listener."

Clearly, "The Snow Man" offers a choice example of Stevens's ability to level his tone until the reader is left with a wide range of overtones, free to invest those emotions which happen to square best with his or her mood or temperament. Even if this range is not unlimited—we cannot think of the speaker's voice as either hysterical or orgastically exultant without lapsing into absurdity and bad faith—and even if some interpretations are obviously more compelling than others, no critic will ever be able to prevent the flatness of the tone from being variously brought to life by different readers.

21. Maeder, *Experimental Language*, 103.

22. Vendler, "Wallace Stevens" in *Voices & Visions: The Poet in America*, 151; Poirier, *Renewal of Literature*, 218, 212; Richard A. Macksey, "The Climates of Wallace Stevens," 200; Hesla, "Singing in Chaos," 251; Frank Lentricchia, *The Gaiety of Language: An Essay on the Radical Poetics of W. B. Yeats and Wallace Stevens*, 156; Bevis, *Mind of Winter*, 25.

23. Blackmur, "Examples of Wallace Stevens," 237; Cook, *Poetry, Word-Play, and Word-War*, 47.

Bevis, for one, may be on to a momentous aspect of Stevens's art when claiming that "the kind of detachment that colors some of Stevens' subjects, structures, and syntax (colors them white) is simply foreign to our critical awareness and vocabulary,"[24] but to demonstrate this critical alienation is not to take away the cultural contradictions inherent in the production and reception of "The Snow Man": no matter how intuitively Eastern in some of his sensibilities Stevens may have been, he was and remains a westerner writing for westerners. And within this Western context, "The Snow Man" continues to be a score that can be emotionally interpreted almost ad libitum.

III. THEMATIC APPROPRIATIONS

The Insufficiency of Authorial Intentions

"I shall explain The Snow Man as an example of the necessity of identifying oneself with reality in order to understand it and enjoy it" (L 464). This is the only explanatory comment on record by Stevens himself, and it provides a fine instance of the treacherousness inherent in reducing the meaning of texts to a reformulation of the author's intentions. To be sure, Stevens's gloss supports those critics who argue that " 'The Snow Man' is not a poem of negation, as has often been claimed, but an affirmation of primary reality." A more provocative and interventionist critic like Harold Bloom, however, has not felt hampered by any of this. On the contrary, he defiantly throws down the gauntlet at all those who "follow Stevens by seeing the poem as a *celebration* of the Freudian reality principle" when it should be clear that "[t]he worst reading possible . . . is the canonical one we received from Stevens himself."[25]

The critical conflict dramatized by these clashing views is not incidental but structural: it is part of a paradigm that is analyzed by B. J. Leggett with particular reference to Stevens's comments on Nietzsche. In the case of those comments, too, critical responses have covered the whole spectrum, from an unquestioning, at times naive, acceptance of everything Stevens said as honest and lucid testimony all the way down to a wholesale dismissal (once more by Bloom) of the poet's observations as so many repressions resulting

24. Bevis, *Mind of Winter*, 6.
25. Litz, *Introspective Voyager*, 100; Bloom, *Poems of Our Climate*, 53, 63.

from an anxiety of influence. The most responsible, though hardly the easiest, option for a critic is to steer a middle course between these extremes. Following Pierre Macherey, Leggett believes that "the *meaning* of [any comment by Stevens] is neither in what it explicitly says nor in what it cannot say in order to say something. The meaning . . . is in the tension between the two."[26]

Even if there is no demonstrable need to embrace Bloom's strong-willed and hyperbolically radical dissent from Stevens's own explanation of "The Snow Man," it should nevertheless be clear that some suspicion is in order. For one thing, the comment was made in 1944, twenty-three years after "The Snow Man" was first published. It is the remark, therefore, of an altered poet who may well have been retrojecting a later attitude toward reality onto his own earlier text.[27] Moreover, one should attend with circumspection both to the way Stevens formulates his remark and to what he fails to say. The bemusing and somewhat affected introductory clause "I shall explain" could be taken to express hesitancy and tentativeness, the more so since we can notice similar instances of diffidence in the very same letter in which the gloss occurs. The letter was a response to a series of questions from Hi Simons; asked to elucidate another early poem, "The Curtains in the House of the Metaphysician" (*CP* 62), Stevens merely answers in the most slapdash manner: "I suppose this was written at a time when I felt strongly that poems were things in themselves" (*L* 463). Apart from signaling a possible grain of uncertainty, both comments may additionally be taken to evince Stevens's defensiveness about being called upon to clarify his own work. "I shall explain" may just be a polite way of saying: "Here you have my two cents' worth, for all I care." Indeed, it is striking, to say the least, how concise the replies to Simons's questions are. Stevens cannot stand accused of excessive generosity in offering such heavily reductive answers and leaving so much unsaid.

The overall interpretive usefulness of the *explications de texte* that are scattered around in Stevens's letters is worth lingering over at this point, because

26. Leggett, *Early Stevens*, 48.
27. There is a similar risk involved in tying the poem to a much earlier biographical anecdote, as Joan Richardson does when digging up a passage from a 1907 letter by Stevens to his then-fiancée and future wife, Elsie Viola Kachel, in which he records an exhilarating outing in the New York snow (see *SP* 173 and Richardson, *Early Years*, 250–51). The time lag of nearly fourteen years between the supposed originary event and the poem's date of publication and probable composition should of itself be enough to kindle critical suspicion. Richardson's hypothesis is also weakened by the fact that as a poem "The Snow Man" in no way seems to depend on an anecdotal referent.

those explanations play a primary role in the attribution of meaning to, and the contextualization of, so many of the poems. On the one hand, there is no disputing the fact that every so often Stevens proved graciously prepared to discuss his own work with his correspondents, irrespective of whether or not he personally knew these correspondents, and that he was quite willing to provide confidential clarifications—with the one proviso that they not be used in print.[28] Because of this willingness, which was probably strengthened by the fact that Stevens "found it much easier to relax on paper than in person,"[29] we have at our disposal a small treasure trove of comments on the poetry, the existence of which has certainly aided the understanding and abetted the critical appropriation of difficult and dense passages and texts. John Timberman Newcomb lists some of the first reactions to the *Letters*, illustrating the hyperbolic one-upmanship to which this publication prompted people like Stanley Kunitz, who hailed "the most extensive commentary that any major poet has ever provided on his own work," and Richard Howard, who managed to up the ante by claiming to find in the book "the most consistent meditation any poet in any language has ever put in writing on the sense of his own work."[30] That the publication of *Letters of Wallace Stevens*, as Newcomb argues, has played a principal role in the establishment of Stevens's canonical status and the promotion of Stevens criticism is undeniable.

On the other hand, we would just as clearly be amiss to welcome the poet's self-explanations in any naive sense. Frank Doggett and Dorothy Emerson have rightly pointed up that "Stevens' remarks about his poems have an air of latent disclosure. Even when most significant, they are oblique, laconic, and offer limitations more often than information."[31] Doggett and Emerson warn us that the comments are often as much in need of close scrutiny as the poems themselves—a warning that has also been sounded with respect to another traditional aid in reading this poet: his poetic-theoretical prose essays collected in *The Necessary Angel* and *Opus Posthumous*.

---

28. See Stevens's closing remark to L. W. Payne Jr. after having answered a number of questions on his poems: "Please destroy these notes. I don't mind your saying what I have said here. But I don't want you to quote me. No more explanations" (L 252). Or the conclusion to a similar letter to Hi Simons: "These notes are for your personal use. They are not to be quoted" (L 350).

29. Sharpe, *Wallace Stevens*, 25.

30. Quoted in Newcomb, *Literary Canons*, 239.

31. Frank Doggett and Dorothy Emerson, "About Stevens' Comments on Several Poems," 26.

Any attempt at determining the authorial intention of Stevens's poems has to be undertaken with the utmost skepsis, then, even in those cases where the poet himself appears to be reaching out a hand to us. In fact, the metaphor here is treacherous, for Stevens did not likely have future readers of a volume of selected letters in mind when addressing his correspondents, so that he cannot be held to have simply "reached out" a posthumous "hand" to his later critics. His comments were always part of a personal dialogue—with all the individually tailored psychological strategies this may on each occasion have entailed. Since only one side of the correspondence tends to be available, these strategies are often hard to reconstruct. Thanks to Alan Filreis's diligent historical research, we do know a few things about Hi Simons, the addressee of the letter quoted above, but again they happen to be things that work against any simple, unquestioning acceptance of Stevens's self-explication. Filreis calls Simons not only "suggestible," but also a critic with a tendency to ask "reductive questions" about poems and a philosophical bent in interpreting them.[32] According to Filreis, Stevens after a while

> realized he was explicating his poem[s] for a critic who had a great deal invested in authorial intentions. Simons was . . . mired in the critical biography he would never finish, an all-consuming "'life's work.'" Because it took him "an inordinate amount of time to analyze" Stevens's poems, the critic came to depend greatly—sometimes emotionally—on the poet's explications. "It is always difficult for me to acknowledge the letters you send me," Simons once wrote, "because, to confess the literal truth, I get so excited over them that I don't sleep."

Filreis suggests that the "intention-oriented Simons" and the "fluid Stevens" may not have been a perfect match.[33] Certainly the evidence collected by him seems to lend support to the possibility that Stevens's paraphrase of "The Snow Man" was the reaction of a horse twitching its tail against a parasitical fly, that it really came down to an offhand, almost throwaway gesture.

Apart from the static noise produced by the fact that Stevens's comment was aimed at an apparently incompatible addressee, there are always the more general ploys and quirks of the poet's conscious and unconscious drives

---

32. Alan Filreis, *Modernism from Right to Left: Wallace Stevens, the Thirties, & Literary Radicalism*, 100, 161; Filreis, *Actual World*, 180.
33. Filreis, *Actual World*, 171.

to be reckoned with as well. Stevens, it bears repeating, was a defensive and retentive man who did not wear his heart on his sleeve. Comments on his own writing, consequently, cannot as a rule be looked upon as inno- cently spontaneous. In addition, we have seen how deeply committed as a poet he was to the literary value of suggestion, opacity, enigma, and resis- tance. It is unlikely, therefore, that he would have suddenly ironed out all possible cruxes and solved all riddles simply to please and assuage a reader who happened to feel flabbergasted. Part of him sounded a strong echo to contemporary New Critical protests against the heresy of paraphrase. An- other letter to Simons opens significantly with the remark: "A long time ago I made up my mind not to explain things, because most people have so little appreciation of poetry that once a poem has been explained it has been destroyed: that is to say, they are no longer able to seize the poem" (L 346). And Peter Brazeau's oral biography of Stevens simply abounds with recollections of a poet unwilling to say much or anything about his work. Lensing's formulation of Stevens's deeply conflicted ambivalence, then, is spot-on: "No poet ever disparaged more and indulged more in the practice of self-commentary than did Stevens."[34] And so far we have been talking only about Stevens's *conscious* motives for not providing unequivocal illumi- nations; there are of course always *unconscious* interferences, too—various repressive mechanisms at work both in the act of composing and of com- menting post-factum.

A work of art, as Stevens knew, is produced under the aegis of excess. Most artists would not even be motivated to buckle down to the demand- ing work of writing, composing, painting, or sculpting unless they expected their intentions to be exceeded by both the act and the result. This is, in a term from speech act theory, the essentially *performative* quality of art- making, which is responsible for the unpredictability of results as much as for their limited, provisional sufficiency and the recurrent need to start all over again and perform something anew. The act of writing, notes Maurice Merleau-Ponty in one example, "is no longer (if ever it was) tantamount to enunciating what one has conceived. It is to work with an instrument that at times gives more, at times less than what one has put in, and this is only the consequence of a series of paradoxes that turn the writer's job into an exhausting and interminable task."[35] Conversely, any artistic end product would be robbed of its dynamic value or interest if it could afterwards be

34. Lensing, *Poet's Growth*, 268.
35. Quoted in Suberchicot, *Treize façons*, 53 (own translation).

recuperated entirely by a reconstruction of the intentional processes that gave rise to it. Jonathan Culler's analogy between the plight of criticism and that of the Freudian talking cure offers an instructive illustration in this respect. "The discovery of the unconscious," claims Culler,

> is in some ways a threat to notions of a person's identity. . . . The unconscious is not to be thought of simply as something belonging to the patient that is disclosed and interpreted by the psychoanalyst's metalanguage; it emerges in the dramas that analyst and analysand find themselves playing out. . . . [T]ransference, which Freud called a "factor of undreamt-of importance," complicates the picture considerably, by disrupting the relation of mastery and problematizing the notion of identity. Analyst and patient get caught up in stories or scenarios—displaced repetitions in which the unconscious emerges. It is no longer quite clear whose stories these are, yet it is in this playing of roles that cures seem to be effected.
>
> Like the analyst, the literary critic is generally thought to be in a position of mastery and exteriority: outside the discourse he explains, interprets, and judges. But we discover transferential relationships here too.[36]

As a highly self-conscious metapoet, Stevens was fully aware of the difficulty of mastering his texts and sometimes testified to his own relative incomprehension of what it was that he had exactly meant to say. He could return to his own poems as to those of a stranger, at a loss to grasp his original intentions. His niece, Jane McFarland Wilson, later recalled a discussion with her uncle about some of the *Harmonium* poems, in the course of which she asked him: "Is this what you meant?" To which Uncle Wallace gave the point-blank reply: "Well, I might have meant that at one time. I don't know what I meant now."[37] It was especially at such moments of interpretive discomfiture that Stevens was quick to anticipate a certain vein of poststructuralism—quick, that is, to waive his property rights on the meaning of his texts, to insist that the author never be authoritarian about his own writings, and that, as soon as a work is published, it and its meaning become the reader's.[38] In 1940, he chided Simons for staking everything on

36. Jonathan Culler, introduction to *The Identity of the Literary Text*, 9–10.
37. Brazeau, *Parts of a World*, 269.
38. I use the term poststructuralism in this context not because poststructuralist theoreticians have a patent on ideas of the sort expressed by Stevens—other modernists like Eliot professed similar notions, and in certain New Critical quarters analogical ideas gave rise to a deprecation of the "intentional fallacy" (W. K. Wimsatt and Monroe C. Beardsley, "The Intentional Fallacy")—but because the idea of "the alienability of characters, of signifiers, from

writerly intentions: "I think that the critic is under obligation to base his remarks on what he has before him. It is not a question of what an author meant to say but of what he has said. In the case of a competent critic the author may well have a great deal to find out about himself and his work. This goes to the extent of saying that it would be legitimate for a critic to make statements respecting the purpose of an author's work that were altogether contrary to the intentions of the author" (L 346). Restricting meanings was to Stevens far less desirable than proliferating them, as he explained to his business associate and friend, Stevens T. Mason: "Some one said not long ago that a poem consists of all the constructions that can be placed upon it. Its measure is the variety of constructions that can be placed upon it: the variety of meanings that can be found in it."[39]

In today's literary-theoretical context, it is probably Umberto Eco's views on the limits of authorial intentions that are most germane to Stevens's own attitude. In recent years, Eco has sought to situate the meaning of a literary text somewhere beyond the *intentio auctoris* and the *intentio lectoris,* in a twilight region that opens itself up to theory with considerable difficulty: that of the *intentio operis.*[40] He draws the following useful distinction:

> When I speak with a friend I am interested in detecting the intention of the speaker, and when I receive a letter from a friend I am interested in realizing what the writer wanted to say. In this sense I feel perplexed when I read the *jeu de massacre* performed by Derrida upon a text signed by John Searle [in Derrida's "Limited Inc."]. . . . There is a case, however, where I feel sympathetic with many reader-oriented theories. When a text is put in the bottle—and this happens not only with poetry or narrative but also with *The Critique of Pure Reason*—that is, when a text is produced not for a single addressee but for a community of readers—the author knows that he or she will be interpreted not according to his or her intentions but according to a complex strategy of interactions which also involves the readers, along with their competence in language as a social treasury.

Eco accordingly believes that in those cases where an author has responded to interpretations of his work by clarifying his intentions, "the response . . .

---

any signifying intention" (Lee Edelman, *Homographesis: Essays in Gay Literary and Cultural Theory,* 127) has been foregrounded most prominently and expanded upon most conspicuously by poststructuralists, and is today most readily associated with them.

39. Quoted in George S. Lensing, "Wallace Stevens and Stevens T. Mason: An Epistolary Exchange on Poetic Meaning," 36.

40. Eco, *Limits of Interpretation,* 44–63.

must not be used in order to validate the interpretations of his text, but to show the discrepancies between the author's intention and the intention of the text."[41] This may perhaps be a little too comfortably provocative, since of course an author might be perfectly aware that the act of clarifying his writerly intentions itself participates in "a complex strategy of interactions which also involves the readers." However that may be, what becomes clear from an extensive investigation into Stevens's commentary on "The Snow Man" is the drastically *restricted* authority of such authorial self-explanations. This is not the same as saying that Stevens's commentary is of no value to us whatsoever and cannot be returned to whenever it happens to support a particular reading, but only that interpretations of "The Snow Man" are not necessarily accountable to this small piece of self-exegesis and need not be measured by the yardstick of the poet's single scant remark.

The Plurality of Critical Selves

Critics who do not primarily cross "The Snow Man" with other texts (as opposed to those who do, discussed in the next section) tend to focus their analysis on one or another conception of the self. This apparently gives them sufficient leeway in appropriating the text, so that they can tailor it to their personal, subjective agendas and bring into play something of their own selves. Tracing four of the more prominent instances of such thematic, non-intertextual appropriations should help provide us with insight into both the disseminating potential of "The Snow Man" and the workings of the critical rhetoric that is typically developed for responding to that potential. Helen Vendler is the first case in point; she comments on the poem as follows:

We are drawn by all of Stevens' syntactic involutions into the vertiginous abyss of things thought too long . . . Stevens' bold stroke of the three "nothing's" closing *The Snow Man* announces, as with a closing of one door and the opening of another, the discovery of the abolition of one old self by a new one, which necessitates at first the contemplation of an absolute void. . . . [W]e see in *The Snow Man*, through its vertigo of receding planes, the very moment in which Stevens first discovered that the self, pursued to invisibility, makes itself metaphysically visible again, if only in the form of a terrifying blank.[42]

41. Umberto Eco, *Interpretation and Overinterpretation*, 67, 73.
42. Vendler, *Words Chosen Out of Desire*, 49.

Vendler is at her best when able to distill such graceful narratives—half paraphrase, half personal meditation—out of Stevens's poetry. Yet we should stop to consider what her narrative, generically speaking, signals: it throws into relief not only the constant critical need to shuttle back and forth between text and critically fabricated context, but also how this context is a function of the critic's personal agenda. Why else would Vendler insist so strongly on the inevitability of running into the self again, even if that self becomes only "metaphysically visible" (whatever that may mean)? To let "the nothing that is" which rounds off the poem stand for the (displaced, reconfigured) self is a personal readerly decision, groundable at most in intuition, but not prompted with any demonstrable urgency by the text. The fact that Vendler champions such a reading is indissociable from her own ideological preference for the "universal" psychological-existential topics of individualism, identity-building, and humanism, and, *ex negativo*, from her dislike of philosophical theorizing and sociopolitical contextualizing. Thus, her critical insight—to make the most rudimentary use of Paul de Man's well-known opposition—is clearly limited and produced by a blindness to other possibilities.

Vendler's image of an abyss of thoughts grown stale is close to the metaphor that figures in Geoffrey H. Hartman's interpretation of the poem. Hartman believes it to be no less than "a virtue" of this poem that its long-winded syntax depicts a "defense against overthink, against our relentless mental pollution of nature." But the way Hartman frames the poem is entirely different:

> The hygiene, the cleansing power of this wintery mind is clear, whether or not we understand the poem. Stevens's poetry is in fact so difficult to understand because our mind is not wintery enough. It tends to be too spiritual, or too fictional, or simply eager for thought. . . . [I]f we pollute our environment by "meanings," by pathetic fictions, we see merely ourselves in nature when our real desire is to see nature. Stevens asks us, therefore, to reverse ourselves and become what we see instead of seeing what we are. . . . Unless we stop occupying nature with our ideas and anxieties we shall be in the dilemma recently expressed by Theodor Adorno. "I cannot look at nature," said Adorno, "I cannot look at the shadow of trees without the shadow of Buchenwald interposing." . . . What man has made of man and what man has made of nature are intimately joined, yet through the politics of poetry we may still open a chink in this claustrophobic mind and see "Nothing that is not there and the nothing that is."[43]

43. Hartman, "Poet's Politics," 256–57.

Hartman's reading appears in an article entitled "The Poet's Politics," which is about the last title one would expect from Helen Vendler—or, for that matter, from the very Geoffrey Hartman who was later for some time to be associated with the razzle-dazzle of deconstruction "on the wild side."[44] The critic's opening gambit in this article is to state his purpose in unmistakable terms: "I start with the assumption that ours is a political age and even, as Napoleon said, that politics is destiny. What good, then, is poetry in this age?"[45] Like Vendler, Hartman is interested in constructions of the self and reads the poem as a reshuffling of the cards in this respect. But instead of swerving to a metaphysical region, he worries over the political world and the dire need to escape its oppressive traumas. His emphasis is on the indispensable sanity of forgetting and on the strength of the urge to delete from consciousness, however temporarily, the unspeakable character of the human race.

A diminished emphasis on the political is to be found again with a third critic to have interpreted "The Snow Man" primarily as a text on the self. Richard Poirier considers the poem in a patient and subtle meditation on "Writing Off the Self" (the title of the concluding chapter of *The Renewal of Literature*). He takes issue with Bloom's indomitable need to both assert his own will and find a similar resilience of willpower in Stevens. While "self-fracturing and self-dissolution" in Bloom's view invariably lead to "enormous crises and potential catastrophes," Poirier is inclined to see them rather as "benign," "liberating," and "exhilarating." As a result, he detects in "The Snow Man" "a slackening out of the self, an expiration into passivity. We are allowed to think of misery in the wind but we are also invited *not* to think of it; it is possible for a human to be like a snow man and also not to be like one."[46]

Poirier's teasing out of a double bind in Stevens's text—the attempt simultaneously to state a feeling of misery and not to think about it—is not done for the classic deconstructive purpose of pointing up an epistemological aporia, but rather with an eye to giving a specific affective resonance to the poem. Yet the attribution of this resonance once again shows itself to be motivated at least as much by the construction of a personal critical voice as by the reconstruction of an authorial poetic one. Poetic commentary cedes

44. Christopher Norris, *Deconstruction: Theory and Practice*, 92–99.

45. Hartman, "Poet's Politics," 247. The essay appears in Hartman's *Beyond Formalism: Literary Essays 1958–1970*, and is the only one not noted as having earlier appeared in print, so it was probably written shortly before the collection was published. That would make the political age of which Hartman is speaking the turbulent years 1968 and 1969.

46. Poirier, *Renewal of Literature*, 212–13, 219.

to explicit self-presentation and confessionalism when Poirier proclaims the deep affinity he shares with all those who endeavor to set the self adrift by letting things go. Detecting the same inclination in Stevens, he adds: "I confess to being pleased by this receptivity and, when faced with uncertainties as to my own existence, feeling temperamentally in favor of relaxation rather than self-assertion, of drift rather than aggressive deployments."[47] It is this temperamental inclination, arguably, that has set Poirier off from his more lionized celebrity colleagues (not just Bloom but also, in her own way, Vendler) and that is responsible for his position as a relative outsider easily ignored in the academic warfare between critical egos and schools. But beyond illustrating the relatively trivial fact of a critic's sociological positioning in the academic market, Poirier's defense of his temperamental inclination also highlights the ease with which any interpretation of a poem like "The Snow Man" shades into readerly self-analysis. The poem possesses such an archetypical, generalizable quality that its meaning cannot be restricted to a specific textual event, but demands to be negotiated and dynamically produced *between* text and reader.

Since the interpretation of poetry—more than that of scientific, political, or even philosophical writings—generally depends on a rapprochement of spirits, Poirier's reading is not necessarily discredited by its blatant subjectivity. As a matter of fact, it happens to square well with the most extensive and ambitious discussion "The Snow Man" has been awarded, that by William W. Bevis, who has written a hefty book about his original puzzlement over this one small poem and the readings it has received. In *Mind of Winter: Wallace Stevens, Meditation, and Literature*, Bevis makes a compelling case for seeing Stevens's recurrent ascetic streak, so ostensibly on display in "The Snow Man," as essentially "meditative," in the rather specific sense of meditation as practiced in Eastern philosophies like Zen Buddhism. To Bevis, what "The Snow Man" represents is "a state of consciousness," an "experience" that exists in an inevitably uneasy tension with the act of representation and traditional notions of the self, since such a state of consciousness is itself "aconceptual" and involves a loss of the self qua self. "Stevens often tired of the triumph of self," writes Bevis, but "[u]nlike Eliot, [he] evolved a benign, secular, and noninstitutional alternative to the 'prison of the self.'" Making use of two forms of expertise, the "advanced phenomenology" of the meditative state of consciousness recorded by especially Buddhist testimonies and the scientific results of neurophysiological

47. Ibid., 211.

and experimental states-of-consciousness research, Bevis fleshes out the following arguments:

> A *meditative state of consciousness* is a naturally occurring physiological phenomenon, possible for any person in any culture and probably experienced by everyone to some degree. There are several characteristics common to its various stages: (1) transience, (2) ineffability, (3) sensations of time and space changed or transcended, (4) sensations of self-loss—that is, absence of thought or feeling according to later reports, and minimal cortical activity as measured by machines during meditation. Such a state of consciousness differs in report and measurable characteristics from other states such as waking, dreaming, day-dreaming, and hypnotic trance, and such calm self-loss differs also from the other mystical categories of the occult, vision, and ecstasy (excited self-loss).[48]

Some of these claims, to be sure, are further modified in the course of Bevis's elaborate exploration. Of most immediate critical importance, however, is the fact that Bevis's intriguing investigation leads to a scientific delineation of that notoriously elusive and intuitive catchall fetish of Anglo-romanticism and American intellectual life in general, the "self." Thus, we learn that "[t]he self as we usually think of it is not so much the more automatic activity of the peripheral nervous system or the spine or brainstem, but the highly individualized association patterns of the cortex, created and shaped by one's personal history and one's personal needs."[49] It is this originally "uncommitted," interpreting part of the cortex that, according to Bevis, can be shut down upon occasion, leading to a meditative state of consciousness for which "The Snow Man" could be taken to stand as one of the aptest literary evocations in the whole of American and even Western poetry.

Bevis's patient elucidation, which cannot be done justice by a single-page synopsis, is so persuasively argued that it may well be deemed to bring us closest to the poet's inspiration and the poem's intentions, yet it, too, crucially depends on a particular coloring—in this case, a refusal to color—of the tone of "The Snow Man." When juxtaposed with Vendler's, Hartman's, and Poirier's appropriative ventures, Bevis's interpretation is revealed as yet another attempt, be it ever so inspired and exhilarating, at negotiating a

48. Bevis, *Mind of Winter*, 4–5, 10, 6, 12.
49. Ibid., 125.

poem whose signifying intention is ultimately too dispersed and variously reconfigurable to be reduced to a single scenario.

IV. INTERTEXTUAL APPROPRIATIONS

Eleanor Cook warns us about the final line of "The Snow Man" that "[w]e should beware of changing 'a' or even 'the nothing' to 'nothingness,' a word which comes with portentous metaphysical associations. (Consider the effects of *le néant* or *das Nichtige*.)"[50] From a historical point of view, however, Cook is fighting a losing battle, and not surprisingly so. The effort to keep readers from flying off on philosophical tangents, however much inspired by an understandable fear of stifling the poem by swaddling it in philosophemes, lacks a solid textual basis. The final grammatical ambiguity of "the nothing that is," by its double interpretability as an ordinary ellipsis and a widening ontological statement, almost automatically sets readers off on a philosophical chase. Such textual ambiguity may not be deemed an aesthetic *réussite* by everyone, and some readers (mainly those who dislike their poetry contaminated by philosophy) might deplore Stevens's final flourish as a trick or even a mannerism that turns sour upon further inspection and produces infelicitous critical aftereffects. But for every such reader there will also be one who is fascinated by the text precisely as it ambiguously stands.

To draw upon other writers and texts in trying to understand, put to intellectual use, or simply prolong the aesthetic play of "The Snow Man" is a legitimate critical move. In the foregoing overview of what were called, reductively, "formal" and "thematic" appropriations, links have already been established, almost inadvertently, to writers like Emerson and Derrida. It is in some Ecoesque (or should we say Ecological?) sense the poem's intention to be crossed with other texts (both by other writers and by Stevens himself), even if the concrete process of intertextualization proves to be, in the final analysis, no more than an associative readerly function. After all, "The Snow Man" so patently stages the old-time epistemological debates of subject versus object and presence versus absence, and hinges so clearly on tantalizing paradoxes and logical aporiae, that it easily achieves an almost archetypical or paradigmatic effect.

50. Cook, *Poetry, Word-Play, and Word-War*, 49.

To aim at exhaustiveness in listing the intertextual links that critics have established with "The Snow Man" would be impracticable, tedious, and ultimately pointless.[51] The existence of what has by now become a very rich intertextual fabric, a fine-meshed net collectively woven by critics, provides a poignant example of the critical need to somehow limit options in reading Stevens. In the following pages on non-Stevensian intertexts, I will limit myself, therefore, to the possibilities opened up by three philosophical to semiphilosophical writers: Schopenhauer, Nietzsche, and Emerson. The justification for choosing this ultimately arbitrary trio is in turn triple: it lies, first, in a remarkable textual closeness that raises questions of influence and affinity; secondly, in the usefulness (with an eye to the second half of this study) of the topics foregrounded by the intertexts; and thirdly (in some cases), in the personal appropriative pleasure of swerving from the beaten track established by earlier critics. In a second section, the most momentous possibilities for intertextualizing "The Snow Man" from within Stevens's own tentacular oeuvre will be demonstrated as well.

Non-Stevensian Intertexts

Schopenhauer and the Question of the Subject

In a little-noted article of 1972, Richard P. Adams analyzed the possible influence of Schopenhauer on Stevens's poetry. His self-declared purpose in doing so was to engage in traditional source study, based on the seemingly moderate assumptions "first that Stevens read at least some parts of *The*

---

51. The most important crossings with non-Stevensian texts that remain unmentioned in the following discussion are those with Valéry, Poulet, Heidegger, and Merleau-Ponty in Macksey, "Climates of Wallace Stevens," 195–200; Derrida in Paul A. Bové, *Destructive Poetics: Heidegger and Modern American Poetry*, 192–93; Keats's "To Autumn" and "In Drear-Nighted December" in Vendler, "Stevens and Keats," 187–88, and *Words Chosen Out of Desire*, 47–48; Nietzsche (various quotations) in Geoffrey H. Hartman, *Saving the Text: Literature/Derrida/Philosophy*, xxiv, and Leggett, *Early Stevens*, 187–95; Shakespeare's sonnet 73 in Cook, *Poetry, Word-Play, and Word-War*, 50; Shelley's "Ode to the West Wind" in Schwarz, *Narrative and Representation*, 66; Ruskin, Whitman, and once again Shelley and Nietzsche in Bloom, *Poems of Our Climate*, 53–63; Friedrich Schlegel in Anthony Whiting, *The Never-Resting Mind: Wallace Stevens' Romantic Irony*, 64–65; Wittgenstein in Maeder, *Experimental Language*, 106; Shakespeare's *King Lear* and Jane Austen's *Emma* in Sharpe, *Wallace Stevens*, 12–13; Kandinsky, Larkin, Frost, Heidegger, and Dickinson in Lensing, *Seasons*, 136–43; and Buddhist texts, reports on scientific experiments, William James, Virginia Woolf, and much more in Bevis, *Mind of Winter*.

World as Will and Idea, probably in the translation of Haldane and Kemp, and probably before 1914, and second that this is one of the philosophical works from which he borrowed ideas for his poetry."[52] Whether either of these assumptions is justified remains hard to decide in the absence of any explicit, written evidence; we know of only one surviving book by Schopenhauer in Stevens's library, *The Wisdom of Life: Being the First Part of Arthur Schopenhauer's Aphorismen zur Lebensweisheit*—a typical buy which moreover postdates the writing of "The Snow Man."[53] Still, one cannot help but be struck by the remarkable aptness and affinity of the quotation from Schopenhauer dug up by Adams. In what is surely one of the German philosopher's most heavily romantic, grandiose, and accumulative sentences, Schopenhauer describes an essential tenet of his philosophy as follows:

> If, raised by the power of the mind, a man relinquishes the common way of looking at things, gives up tracing, under the guidance of the forms of the principle of sufficient reason, their relations to each other, the final goal of which is always a relation to his own will; if he thus ceases to consider the where, the when, the why, and the whither of things, and looks simply and solely at the *what;* if, further, he does not allow abstract thought, the concepts of the reason, to take possession of his consciousness, but, instead of all this, gives the whole power of his mind to perception, sinks himself entirely in this, and lets his whole consciousness be filled with the quiet contemplation of the natural object actually present, whether a landscape, a tree, a mountain, a building, or whatever it may be; inasmuch as he *loses* himself in this object (to use a pregnant German idiom), *i.e.*, forgets even his individuality, his will, and only continues to exist as the pure subject, the clear mirror of the object, so that it is as if the object alone were there, without any one to perceive it, and he can no longer separate the perceiver from the perception, but both have become one, because the whole consciousness is filled and occupied with one single sensuous picture; if thus the object has to such an extent passed out of all relation to something outside it, and the subject out of all relation to the will, then that which is so known is no longer the particular thing as such; but it is the *Idea,* the eternal form, the immediate objectivity of the will at this grade; and, therefore, he who is sunk in this perception is no longer individual, for in such perception the individual has lost himself; but he is *pure,* will-less, painless, timeless *subject of knowledge.*[54]

52. Richard P. Adams, "Wallace Stevens and Schopenhauer's *The World as Will and Idea*," 135.
53. Moynihan, "Checklist," 97.
54. Quoted in Adams, "Stevens and Schopenhauer," 137–38.

Although far from evincing Schopenhauer's expansiveness, the second half of "The Snow Man" can easily be taken to describe the same experience —the experience, that is, of canceling the will and the intellect by concentrating on the visual scene at hand, until all sense of individuality is lost and inside and outside are lifted up (sublated, as later Hegelians would say) into one quasi-mystical whole. Of course, while Schopenhauer imagines and describes this experience as leading to a form of plenitude—to the absolute knowledge of an eternal Idea—Stevens ostensibly does the opposite by finishing on an absence: "the nothing that is." But whether this actually amounts to a diametrical opposition is far from certain. If we attribute any authority at all to Stevens's own comment that "The Snow Man" seeks to *understand* (and enjoy) reality, the element of being filled by a certain desirable knowledge is one that both texts could be taken to have in common. From such a perspective, the main difference would merely lie in the fact that Stevens keeps his conclusion more open and paradoxical, appears more willing to deconstruct his own desire. Not even the fact that he claims to be after "reality," whereas Schopenhauer winds up with an "Idea," necessarily constitutes a contrast, since "The Snow Man" can be read as an early variation on what Stevens was to call, famously and problematically, the "first idea" (a phrase that will be explained in the section on Stevensian intertexts).

Once we are prepared to grant Schopenhauer's text a fair share of intertextual relevance (and the decision to do so is an entirely readerly one based on one's proper interests), we may detect an element in it that deserves to be followed through: the philosopher's endeavor to become "the pure subject, the clear mirror of the object," or again, at the end, a *"pure, will-less, painless, timeless subject of knowledge."* In both formulations the word "subject" takes pride of place. Schopenhauer's use of it transparently displays the etymological background of the word. This inscribes his discourse in a complex philosophical tradition traced out by Rudolf Boehm. *Subject*, says Boehm, derives from the Latin *subiectum* (whatever lies underneath, the fundamental, *das Grundlegende*), and was originally used as one possible translation for Aristotle's concept of *hypokeimenon*. Until the Middle Ages (most notably in the theological philosophy of Thomas Aquinas), *subiectum* remained the name for something indeterminate requiring determination from outside, from other things to which, as the English verb still has it, it is *subjected*.[55]

55. Rudolf Boehm, *Das Grundlegende und das Wesentliche—Zu Aristoteles' Abhandlung "Ueber das Sein und das Seiende"* (Metaphysik Z); Rudolf Boehm, *Kritik der Grundlagen des Zeitalters,*

Boehm tries to show that at the beginning of the modern era, in Descartes's writings—which, since Hegel and Heidegger, are supposed to have inaugurated a philosophy and an age of *subjectivity*—the subject still retained its medieval sense. The idea of man as a nonentity submitting to outside determination continued to inform—indeed to pervert, in Boehm's opinion—not only philosophy but also modern science, which began to develop its ideal of objectivity at precisely this point in history, and soon began to split off from philosophy. The much-flaunted "modern" subject at the center of the world of philosophy thus surreptitiously turns out to be grounded on submission, surrender, and disempowerment.[56]

If we condense Boehm's comprehensive argument and apply it to the texts at hand, we find that Schopenhauer precisely embodies the modern ideal criticized by Boehm: the romantic philosopher stakes his hopes on an existence that surrenders all sublunary freedom and concomitant personal responsibility to the chimerical "knowledge" of an absolute, eternal "Idea." This philosophical background adds a special tension to Stevens's text. "The Snow Man" may be read from an antagonistic angle (which may or may not be the same as reading against the grain of the text), in which case the text may be construed as *seeing through* the Cartesian-Schopenhauerian ideal of subjectivity: what remains, the poem indicates, when you allow your will and individuality to be radically canceled until you become nothing yourself is not the vision of an absolute reality or idea, but simply nothing. You acquire the pure, will-less, painless, timeless character of what is indescribable, inhuman, unproductive: nothing. This is a legitimate reading, but it does cast the poem in one particular template only—that of Western humanist philosophers' long-standing rejection of values like impassiveness, as Bevis argues.[57] It also suppresses the ambiguity that resides in Stevens's final affirmation that he is nevertheless still able to behold something that

---

177–97. The old meaning of *subject* can also still be heard in the English noun that is used to refer to people owing obedience to a higher power, as in "the Queen's subjects."

56. From this point of view, the fact that Schopenhauer in the above fragment paraphrases his wish to become "pure subject" as a longing to become "the clear mirror of the object" is no coincidence, since the most famous image of the subject as a mirror is to be found in John Locke, who, in Boehm's thesis, was one of the first philosophers to stretch Descartes's ideas to the point of life-threatening absurdity (Boehm, *Kritik*, 209–29).

57. To Bevis, the mistake commonly made by Western readers of the poem is that of confusing a state of consciousness (supposedly portrayed here) with an idea (or, in its expanded form, an ideology), in this case of nothing or nothingness (*Mind of Winter*, 12). He points to a strong tradition in the West that assumes that "negations are depressing" (ibid., 28) and that mistakes a "disappearance of intellect" for "a distancing of the intellect" (32). Bevis, by contrast, argues at length that a state of passive meditation does not require any "noetic . . .

truly *is*—even if that something happens to be a nothing and may conse-quently be tainted with irony. What "The Snow Man" manages to do, in other words, is to stage the conflict of a whole hotly debated philosophical tradition in the tantalizing, incantatory shape of a lyric.

Nietzsche, as is commonly known, took Schopenhauer to task for the mis-anthropic and escapist streak in his notion of the subject. Denouncing his predecessor in *The Genealogy of Morals*, he wrote:

> Let us, from now on, be on our guard against the hallowed philosophers' myth of a "pure, will-less, painless, timeless knower"; let us beware of the tentacles of such contradictory notions as "pure reason," "absolute knowledge," "ab-solute intelligence." All these concepts presuppose an eye such as no living being can imagine, an eye required to have no direction, to abrogate its active and interpretative powers—precisely those powers that alone make of seeing, seeing *something*.[58]

Unsurprisingly, Nietzsche's invective, too, can be used as a template, anal-ogously with Boehm's. In such a scenario, "The Snow Man" shows the ef-fect of an absolute subjection to the outer world: ultimately, you cannot see anything *concrete*. To the extent that the snow man claims to "behold," to experience the senses *purely*, he can do so only by canceling things and experiencing things *abstractly*.[59] Halfway through the poem, Stevens already begins to take away human involvement—in the form of emotional invest-ment ("not to think / Of any misery")—in order to let his snow man listen ever more abstractly, extending "the sound of a few [particular] leaves" to "the sound of the [whole] land / Full of the same wind / That is blowing in" what ultimately becomes a "*bare* place," thus gradually canceling all the precise perceptions of particular visual phenomena that took up the poem's

---

enlightenment" (see esp. 88). To the extent that a state of passive meditation depends on its own sort of subjection, then, the notion of subjection is viewed as positive (or neutral) by Bevis, not as the negative (epistemological and existential) subjection deplored by Boehm.

58. Friedrich Nietzsche, *The Birth of Tragedy* and *The Genealogy of Morals*, 255.

59. Such abstraction in turn begs to be compared with Heidegger's critique in "The Origin of the Work of Art" of the belief that "the thingness of the thing" (22) is what the senses convey, "the *aistheton*" (25): "We never really first perceive a throng of sensations, e.g., tones and noises, in the appearance of things . . . ; rather we hear the storm whistling in the chim-ney, we hear the three-motored plane, we hear the Mercedes in immediate distinction from the Volkswagen. Much closer to us than all sensations are the things themselves. We hear the door shut in the house and never hear acoustical sensations or even mere sounds. *In order to hear a bare sound we have to listen away from things, divert our ear from them, i.e., listen abstractly*" (26; emphasis added).

first half, until the snow man's beholding is no longer a beholding-something but only a beholding-nothing. Beyond this point of abstraction, the poem literally cannot speak; all the rest is silence.

Nietzsche and the Question of the Will

Nietzsche's above-quoted diatribe against Schopenhauer (and, in one fell stroke, against Kant and Hegel) appears in the third and largest essay of *The Genealogy of Morals* under the title "What Do Ascetic Ideals Mean?" This essay famously lambastes the Christian denial of life, which in Nietzsche's opinion finds its clearest expression in the nihilistic ideal of asceticism. Nietzsche's central argument in the essay rests on a thesis that is prominently stated at the end of both the first and the final paragraphs. The thesis, cast in one of the philosopher's most incisive and haunting aphorisms, has become so well known that it has associatively popped up in more than one critical narrative on "The Snow Man." It centers on the relationship between asceticism and the human will: "The fact that the ascetic ideal can mean so many things to man is indicative of a basic trait of the human will, its fear of the void. Our will requires an aim; it would sooner have the void for its purpose than be void of purpose."[60]

Bloom mentions the aphorism only in passing, unsure of its relevance here. And Leggett believes it to be in no way "illuminating . . . despite the similar phrasing." But could it not be used to open up a new perspective on the poem after all? Admittedly, Stevens gives no sign of wishing to emphasize the workings of the will at the end of his poem; he only seems to "surrender to the reality principle."[61] To this extent, the critical usefulness of juxtaposing Nietzsche's proposition indeed seems minimal. But it is precisely Nietzsche's intention to make us question the ascetic act of surrendering and passivity, to force us to ask how much that act, too, is ultimately informed by the human will. What the Nietzschean juxtaposition does is to let us read Stevens's text in light of the momentous category of the will. This may help us see better how the "listener" in the poem, having already turned into "nothing himself," still claims he is able to "behold," and that although what he beholds should not be thought of in terms of anything he would want or wish to see ("Nothing that is not there"), it does seem to embody an ascetic

60. Nietzsche, *Genealogy of Morals*, 231.
61. Leggett, *Early Stevens*, 187–88; Bloom, *Poems of Our Climate*, 61.

ideal. What this snow man finally does behold is not simply "nothing" but "the nothing that is"—a formulation which may be taken to betray a wish that nothing be experienced as something, too. Stevens's snow man proves unable (or unwilling?) to completely cancel his own will: the nothing he winds up with must somehow still be taken to exist or empower.

A discussion of the will also enters into Bevis's exposition of the poem, although it is approached there from an entirely different angle. Bevis talks of the snow man's "willed will-lessness" and develops this notion in contrast with that of the romantic (i.e., uniquely individual) "self" and that of the "animal will." If the self, in neurological terms, is composed of the experience collected in the uncommitted cortex of the brain, and if the animal will may be understood as the "sensory and motor operations made within the committed cortex in pursuit of a goal," such a self and an animal will are themselves still governed at a lower level (probably that of the midbrain or brainstem) by a human "free will." And since current scientific inquiries suggest the possibility of a distinction between self, animal will, and free will along these lines, the paradox of willed will-lessness "may very well refer to the brainstem willing the cortex will-less." Thus, freedom is retained and indeed wielded at one level, often to the incomprehension of Western thinkers. "On the issue of will, perhaps, Western conceptions of meditation as quietist, passive, nihilist, depart farthest from meditative testimony. Meditators believe they are strong, persevering, disciplined, courageous, decisive: this could be true, while the result is passivity in isolated functions."[62] The attainment of a state of will-lessness requires an enormous will effort (one must have a mind of winter for it), though the effort is not registered in the language of conflict, tension, and strife, since those are exactly the states to be dispensed with or overcome. The question of the will, in other words, could very well be all the more relevant to "The Snow Man" for being almost inaudibly voiced and illegibly inscribed.

The phenomenon of inscription, in fact, offers yet another angle for raising questions of the will about this poem. To readers less interested in the representational and referential accuracy of the poem, there is always the possibility of letting the text fold back on itself as text. Thus, Hartman in his deconstructive phase claimed that what remains in Stevens's snow man, in the last analysis, is "the *will to write*." "Language itself," Hartman added, "nothing else, or the Nothing that is language, is the motivating residue."[63]

---

62. Bevis, *Mind of Winter*, 81, 141, 143.
63. Hartman, *Saving the Text*, xxiv.

To turn texts into metatexts and to call language a nothing are, of course, characteristic of deconstructionist readings, yet the idea of a "motivating residue" does also happen to square well with Stevens's own later gloss that "The Snow Man" achieves some *enjoyment* of reality. Did the act of *writing* the poem, we might wonder with some justification, perhaps contribute toward fostering the illusion of enjoyment? In other words, did Stevens's aesthetic-creative satisfaction, his exhilaration at delivering a well-crafted text that poetically snaps into place, translate afterwards into an unambiguously affirmative interpretation of the text? "The Snow Man" would then do more than figure the will to will-lessness: it would also come to embody the will to write—and write resistingly, teasingly—about the will to will-lessness.

Emerson and the Question of the Sublime

If conjectures about conscious allusion in Stevens's poem had to be made, the ancestral figure of Ralph Waldo Emerson would probably loom largest.[64] From its opening onwards, the first chapter of *Nature* can be brought to bear on the poem: "To go into solitude, a man needs to retire as much from his chamber as from society." As with Emerson, so with Stevens, one could argue: seeking to be alone, he leaves behind the protective cocoon of his house as well as other people, and walks off into nature. The reward for acting thus, according to Emerson, is "the perpetual presence of the sublime." And the terms in which Emerson goes on to elucidate this presence sound like a potential first gloss on Stevens's poem: "The lover of nature is he whose inward and outward senses are still truly adjusted to each other."[65] More important, though, than any of these preparatory and merely implicit similarities is the passage that follows—a passage which, in Bloom's opinion, may be called "without hyperbole, the central passage in American literature, since it is the crucial epiphany of our literature's Central Man":[66]

> In good health, the air is a cordial of incredible virtue. Crossing a bare common, in snow puddles, at twilight, under a clouded sky, without having in

---

64. Critics who have used Emerson to discuss "The Snow Man" include Bloom, *Poems of Our Climate*, 60ff.; Cook, *Poetry, Word-Play, and Word-War*, 48ff.; Vendler, *Words Chosen Out of Desire*, 49; Milton J. Bates, *Mythology of Self*, 132; and Bevis, *Mind of Winter*, 43ff.
65. Ralph Waldo Emerson, *Nature*, 9–10.
66. Bloom, *Poems of Our Climate*, 60–61.

my thoughts any occurrence of special good fortune, I have enjoyed a perfect exhilaration. I am glad to the brink of fear. In the woods too, a man casts off his years, as the snake his slough, and at what period soever of life, is always a child. In the woods, is perpetual youth. Within these plantations of God, a decorum and sanctity reign, a perennial festival is dressed, and the guest sees not how he should tire of them in a thousand years. In the woods, we return to reason and faith. There I feel that nothing can befall me in life,— no disgrace, no calamity, (leaving me my eyes,) which nature cannot repair. Standing on the bare ground,—my head bathed by the blithe air, and uplifted into infinite space,—all mean egotism vanishes. I become a transparent eyeball; I am nothing; I see all; the currents of the Universal Being circulate through me; I am part or particle of God.[67]

At least four parallels between Emerson's rapturous effusion and Stevens's poem are manifest: Emerson writes about walking across a "bare common," while Stevens stands in a "bare place"; both writers are—at some point at least—surrounded by snow; both turn into "nothing"; and despite doing so, the one still "see[s]" and the other still "beholds."[68] These parallels support the ironical possibility of some form of conscious influence (although the hypothesis of influence remains ultimately unverifiable). The opening of *Nature*, as Frank Lentricchia notes, is symptomatic of

the archetypal and revolutionary American desire for radical origination in a new land . . . In order to kill himself off as an expression of history and simultaneously re-birth himself as the first man living utterly in the present, a man must "go into solitude," not only from society but also from his "chamber"— the place where "I read and write," where though no one is bodily present, "I" am "not solitary," because "I" have the unwanted company of all those represented selves who populate my books. The "I" must therefore be emptied of everything, including its literary company.[69]

The irony of Emerson's possible influence on Stevens resides in the fact that the older writer's story of solitude and rebirth into the present and the new, to the extent that it is not only original but originary, creates an unresolvable plight for Stevens: the plight of being in the "unwanted company" of a literary forefather at the exact point of trying to get away from the echo chamber of literature.

67. Emerson, *Nature*, 10.
68. See Bloom, *Poems of Our Climate*, 61.
69. Lentricchia, *Modernist Quartet*, 201.

Once the possibility of influence has been established, the question crit-
ics naturally feel like asking is: How does "The Snow Man" rewrite or recast
Emerson? We know that Stevens was familiar with the Emersonian epiphany
of the transparent eyeball early on: not only did he receive Emerson's *Works*
as a gift from his mother during his student days at Harvard, subsequently
marking and annotating in particular the essay on "Nature,"[70] he also (ar-
guably) made a grim, caustic allusion to Emerson's epiphany in the third of
his "Phases," a cycle of poems written during and about the First World War:

> This was the salty taste of glory,
> That it was not
> Like Agamemnon's story.
> Only, an eyeball in the mud,
> And Hopkins,
> Flat and pale and gory!
>   (OP 10)

To be able to answer the question of how Stevens revises his ancestor,
one needs to scrutinize the passage from *Nature* first. Emerson's book opens
with an unalluring—or at best, rather vague and generalized—scene, and ex-
presses the serendipity of experiencing the sublime there. This experience,
though dependent on the writer's surroundings, involves a transcendence of
these surroundings that expands as far and wide as the whole cosmos. (The
sublime has often been described in terms of "a transcendence of limits" or
"a fiction for transcendence.")[71] The overall gesture is sweepingly panthe-
istic and the tone, so essential to the influence Emerson was to exert upon
American culture, literally evangelical. Also important is that, a few lines
after the reprinted passage, Emerson specifies that "the power to produce this
delight, does not reside in nature, but in man, or in a harmony of both."[72]
The experience of the sublime, in other words, requires either the applica-
tion of what John Ruskin famously called the "pathetic fallacy," or else a
perfect fusion between human inside and natural outside.

Much as was the case with Schopenhauer, Stevens's restaging of Emerson's
trance turns out to be ambivalent. On one level, it might seem as though
the later poet wished to counter or deflate all the Emersonian ingredients.

---

70. Milton J. Bates, "Stevens' Books at the Huntington," 48, 51.
71. Harold Bloom, *The Western Canon: The Books and School of the Ages*, 524; Mary Arens-
berg, introduction to *The American Sublime*, 2.
72. Emerson, *Nature*, 11.

He sets his own contrasting story in a scenery to which he gives the devoted and crystalline brilliance of a painter,[73] and when he proceeds to reduce this landscape to an equally bare place, he apparently refuses to find the sublime there. A frozen-over "mind of winter" does not bespeak much affinity with Transcendentalism and does not seem to reach out to a divinely empowered universe.[74] Stevens's tone does not wax rapturous or patently celebratory. One reason for this is the poet's stubborn resistance to the all-too-human temptation (reductively associated, because of Ruskin, with romanticism) to commit the "pathetic fallacy"—to project, that is, his own feelings (of "misery," in this case) onto the scene. Stevens's vision, if such it can be called, comes across as either much bleaker or more neutral and indeterminate. Whereas in Emerson the act of looking is invested by a sense of filling and fulfillment, the momentum in Stevens seems to be toward emptying and being emptied.[75]

But despite its elegance, this diametrical opposition breaks down upon careful inspection. As both Vendler and Cook have observed, Stevens (or at least his "listener" in the snow) in his own way, too, tries to change into a transparent eye (and "I": the pun is a favorite with both writers). Indeed, he merges inside and outside so strongly that one nothing is mirrored by another. In doing so, he can be felt to continue the deconstruction that, as Bloom suggests, is already at work in Emerson's text.[76] For the epiphany of the transparent eyeball also rests on the instability and fluidity of paradox, on a gladness that is hard to tell from fear, on a nothing that becomes all. "Nothing" and "all" notoriously have a way of flipping around; pantheism and nihilism are two sides of the same coin. And so the superficial opposition between the writers collapses at a deeper level: we find a repressed shudder at the void in Emerson's apparent elation, just as we hear the possibility of a muted exhilaration in Stevens's apparent iciness. It proves easy enough to historicize these readings: as a high romantic, we might note, Emerson had

73. Vendler, *Words Chosen Out of Desire*, 49.

74. Eleanor Cook, alluding to Stevens's own formulation of the meaning of "The Snow Man," sums up the contrast as follows: "If Emerson had a 'mind of winter' like Stevens' snow man, he would accept or enjoy his bare scene, and there would be nothing special in the place of his experience, or in himself for experiencing it there" (*Poetry, Word-Play, and Word-War*, 48).

75. In Cook's reading, a final opposition is to be found between Emerson's "bare common" and Stevens's "bare place," with the latter "moving against the community and the commonalty of the topoi or commonplaces, and back to a 'bare place,' no longer common" (ibid.).

76. Vendler, *Words Chosen Out of Desire*, 49; Cook, *Poetry, Word-Play, and Word-War*, 50; Bloom, *Poems of Our Climate*, 61.

to repress an awareness that his sublime was founded on an abyss, whereas Stevens, as a latter-day, skeptical high modernist, was forced to repress or downplay his deep longing for the sublime. Bevis's argument that we should distinguish between two states of consciousness here—the one, depicted by Emerson, typical of ecstasy (excited self-loss, in which the intellect but not the emotions go blank), the other, evoked by Stevens, typical of meditation (calm self-loss, in which both the intellect and the emotions go blank)[77]— is a useful elaboration, but it does not preclude the possibility of a more confused, less rigorous conceptualization on Stevens's part. When Stevens explicitly addressed the possibility of an American Sublime in the epony-mous poem of 1935, he not only established a direct link between the words "behold" and "sublime," but also went on to write what sounded like a para-phrase of "The Snow Man"—namely, that

> the sublime comes down
> To the spirit itself,
>
> The spirit and space,
> The empty spirit
> In vacant space.
>   (CP 131)

If the category of the sublime is supposed to depend on *excited* self-loss, then this is not what Stevens appears to be giving us here. In other words, Stevens may not always have distinguished so tidily between *excited* and *calm* self-loss, treating both rather as manifestations of the larger phenomenon of the sublime.

Given Stevens's own much-discussed postromantic involvement with the sublime, "The Snow Man" may be felt to thicken by the end into a text that intertwines frosty passivity with barely contained ecstasy, exhilaration with anxiety, the pounding of the blood with the prospect of death—for we have been told at least since Edmund Burke, its master student, that the sensation of the sublime is always ultimately informed by death.[78] Apart from raising

---

77. Bevis, *Mind of Winter*, 43–51.

78. See esp. *The American Sublime* edited by Mary Arensberg, where Stevens is the only poet to be the topic of two individual essays. In her introduction to this volume, Arensberg discusses the possibility, suggested by Thomas Weiskel, that "in an age when we have lost the obsession with natural infinitude," the sublime is a "moribund aesthetic" (Weiskel quoted in Arensberg, introduction, 2) and proceeds to call Stevens's sublime "so belated" that for him

existential questions on the status of the subject or the self and on the role of the will in asceticism, "The Snow Man" now also appears to possess the uncanny ability to spur thoughts both on the sublime in a postromantic world and on the ultimate frontier of death—and it has the ability to do so while being drained of all traces attesting to the inner perturbations and turmoil ordinarily attendant upon such thoughts. No matter which of these questions or themes any one reader may happen to favor, however, the fact remains that they can all be pursued, and be most profitably pursued by inserting the poem in a dialogue with other reflective and thought-provoking texts that share similar concerns. And it is this fact (if that is what it may be called) that, more than any intrinsic aesthetic qualities perhaps, manages to explain the continuing critical popularity of the poem.

Stevensian Intertexts

The First Idea and Decreation

Stevens introduced the term "first idea" as late as 1942 in the opening cantos of "Notes toward a Supreme Fiction," but the notion had unmistakably been with him in one form or another for many years. Both the genesis of the term and its exact denotation as it moves from context to context are hard to determine, though. Bloom suggests that the "only relevant philosophical notion would seem to be C. S. Peirce's Idea of Firstness." Peirce defined his term as follows: "The idea of the present instant, which, whether it exists or not, is naturally thought as a point of time in which no thought can take place or any detail be separated, is an idea of Firstness."[79] Stevens's "first idea" was likewise strongly involved with a sense of full presence—in

---

it is "already a fiction" (16). For another extended analysis of the sublime in Stevens, see Paul Endo, "Stevens and the Two Sublimes." The connection between the sublime and death in Burke's work is most clear in the following passage: "Whatever is fitted in any sort to excite the ideas of pain, and danger, that is to say, whatever is in any sort terrible, or is conversant about terrible objects, or operates in a manner analogous to terror, is a source of the *sublime*; that is, it is productive of the strongest emotion which the mind is capable of feeling. . . . But as pain is stronger in its operation than pleasure, so death is in general a much more affecting idea than pain; because there are very few pains, however exquisite, which are not preferred to death; nay, what generally makes pain itself, if I may say so, more painful, is, that it is considered as an emissary of this king of terrors" (Edmund Burke, *A Philosophical Enquiry into the Origin of Our Ideas of the Sublime and Beautiful*, 39–40).

79. Bloom, *Poems of Our Climate*, 49; Peirce quoted in Poirier, *Poetry and Pragmatism*, 71.

particular the presence of the senses per se, unencumbered by thought and language. In calling this sense of presence, paradoxically, an "idea," he was ostensibly playing on etymology, for the pre-Platonic meaning of the word in Greek primarily refers to the realm of the visible: before Plato, *idea* simply meant "look, semblance," deriving from the verb *idein* (to see), which in turn is related to *eidos* (that which is seen). Thus, Stevens's use of the word is enantiosemic: it unites contrary meanings, for the word inevitably also retains its present post-Platonic meaning of abstract concept—which becomes clear from the following definition he gave to his friend Henry Church: "If you take the varnish and dirt of generations off a picture, you see it in its first idea. If you think about the world without its varnish and dirt, you are a thinker of the first idea" (*L* 426–27). Seeing and thinking are collapsed here to form an indivisible Gordian knot, and their relationship is further complicated by metaphors of painting and restoration, with all the historical-philosophical questions *these* entail. This phenomenological knot is one with which the sophisticated later Stevens would repeatedly, and often playfully, juggle, fascinated as he continued to be by "the flux // Between the thing as idea and / The idea as thing" (*CP* 295). Suffice it at this point to recall Stevens's recurrent attempts, early and late, to experience a purely sensuous reality, to experience the surrounding world as immediately and, so to speak, objectively as a baby or an animal, without the interference of verbalized thoughts and emotions.[80] In "Prelude to Objects," for instance, the poet muses upon the supposition that

> if, without sentiment,
> He is what he hears and sees and if,
> Without pathos, he feels what he hears
> And sees, being nothing otherwise,

---

80. The blotting out of emotions in this nostalgia for the first idea—specifically with respect to "The Snow Man"—may be grounded intertextually in the poet's journal. Joan Richardson refers to the following 1908 entry in order to buttress her thesis that "The Snow Man" pictures an attempt on Stevens's part to extract himself from his social bourgeois identity: "Paul Bourget in 'Une Idylle Tragique,' p. 65—Je me dis: Il n'y [a] qu'une chose de vraie ici-bas, s'assouvir le coeur, sentir et aller jusqu'au bout de tous ses sentiments, désirer et aller jusqu'au bout de tous ses désirs; vivre enfin sa vie à soi, sa vie sincère, en dehors de tous les mensonges et de toutes les conventions, avant de sombrer dans l'inévitable néant" (*SP* 178; see Richardson, *Early Years*, 256–57). To this passionate outburst, Stevens's only comment was the dry "('farouche nihilisme')"—thereby suggesting a deep distrust of Bourget's romantic, revolutionary adoration of the emotions. "The Snow Man" may be construed, at one of its many signifying levels, as a reply to Bourget as well.

Having nothing otherwise, he has not
To go to the Louvre to behold himself.
(CP 194)

The passage echoes "The Snow Man" in several ways: by its incantatory repetitions; by its refusal to let sensation be muddied by "sentiment" (the pathetic fallacy that would hear misery in the sound of the wind); by its insistence on becoming "nothing"; and finally by the verbal echo of "behold." "Let's see the very thing and nothing else," Stevens proposed in "Credences of Summer" (CP 373), and his many thrusts in this direction all provide usable material for juxtaposing with "The Snow Man."

Nearly ten years after composing "Notes toward a Supreme Fiction" and bringing the term "first idea" into the debate, Stevens hit upon another welcome—because sufficiently slippery—term that has since provided critics with a vocabulary for framing those poems under the spell of an untainted sort of immediacy. In a 1951 lecture delivered at the Museum of Modern Art in New York, he observed that "Simone Weil in *La Pesanteur et La Grâce* has a chapter on what she calls decreation. She says that decreation is making pass from the created to the uncreated, but that destruction is making pass from the created to nothingness. Modern reality is a reality of decreation, in which our revelations are not the revelations of belief, but the precious portents of our powers" (NA 174–75). The relevance to Stevens's own work is obvious and so the notion of decreation, too, has been called upon to explain and appropriate "The Snow Man." Weil's opposition between destroying and decreating offers one more theoretical foil, amplified by Stevens's embroidery that what remains after decreation is not "the revelations of belief" but a sense of empowerment.[81] How much the snow man is nourished by a comparable power—the power, perhaps, of *mere being*, in spite of extreme

---

81. For "decreation" and "The Snow Man," see Thomas J. Hines, *The Later Poetry of Wallace Stevens: Phenomenological Parallels with Husserl and Heidegger*, 40; Roy Harvey Pearce, "Toward Decreation: Stevens and the 'Theory of Poetry,'" 290; James S. Leonard and Christine E. Wharton, *The Fluent Mundo: Wallace Stevens and the Structure of Reality*, 64; Whiting, *Never-Resting Mind*, 64–65. Already in 1942, in a letter to Hi Simons, Stevens had centered an explanation of the poetic task of unseeing the world on the question of power: "When a poet makes his imagination the imagination of other people, he does so by making them see the world through his eyes. Most modern activity is the undoing of that very job. The world has been painted; most modern activity is getting rid of the paint to get at the world itself. Powerful integrations of the imagination are difficult to get away from. I am surprised that you have any difficulty with this, when the chances are that every day you see all sorts of things through the eyes of other people in terms of their imaginations. This power is one of the poet's chief powers" (L 402).

cold and the blowing out of thought and emotion, the power of just standing in the snow as a bare but vital minimum—is impossible to tell. But a reader's empathy easily operates along such lines, projecting an irreducible vitality onto "The Snow Man" that makes of the poem an expression of invigorating and life-affirming rather than of depressing and life-threatening powers.

Antithetical and Dialectical Readings

Not only concepts that are *analogous* with those expressed in "The Snow Man" invite juxtaposition; Stevens's oeuvre is shot through with so many conspicuous *oppositions* that critics are rarely at a loss to set up one or another poetic binarism as well. Eleanor Cook, for example, links "The Snow Man" to the poem that immediately precedes it in *Harmonium* (and in *The Collected Poems*), the strangely ritualistic and eerie "Domination of Black" (*CP* 8–9): "The two poems make a fine study in contrast: black versus white, night versus day, fire versus ice, 'I' versus 'one,' past tense versus present. What they have in common are leaves and wind and boughs, the sensations of seeing and hearing, places that are full of sounds, and referential words that gradually take on literary significance like the history of the words themselves."[82]

More commonly, however, than "Domination of Black," the poem that originally followed "The Snow Man" at the time of first publication in Harriet Monroe's *Poetry*, "Tea at the Palaz of Hoon" (*CP* 65), is used as a counterpart. As Robin Gail Schulze argues, "Stevens made a habit of publishing poems in carefully organized sets, particularly in pairs in which one poem questions, undercuts, and cycles into the other." "The Snow Man" originally appeared in a set of twelve poems under the title "Sur Ma Guzzla Gracile"—a "buffo title," as Schulze calls it, meaning "From Out of My Slender Gullet" and "mark[ing] the cycle as an exercise in ventriloquism." According to Schulze, "The Snow Man" should not be read independently of its counterpart:

> Each pair of poems in Stevens's set constitutes an imaginative cycle. Linking oppositional lyrics, Stevens implies that no one mental state can satisfy for long. Hoon, for all his fiery fancy, will tire of his palace, cast off his protective images, and become the snow poet. The snow man in turn will yield to

82. Cook, *Poetry, Word-Play, and Word-War*, 47.

the warming sun of the imagination until he shines like Hoon. Stevens's set portrays the act of imaginative creation as an endless cartwheeling motion—the mind makes, the creations become old, stale, abstract, and the mind tears them apart only to start the cycle again.[83]

The fact that Stevens tore the snow man and Hoon away from each other by the time of book publication somewhat downplays the importance he is supposed to have attached to their contrastive unity, but the opposition between the two poems has nevertheless proved to be particularly productive. Not only did Milton J. Bates put it to work on at least two occasions, it is also used throughout James Longenbach's *Wallace Stevens: The Plain Sense of Things*, where it leads to a reading in which " 'The Snow Man' is the alternative vision to the aristocratic Hoon, and together these companion poems of 1921 have often seemed to condense the aesthetic dialectic of Stevens's entire career: discovering and imposing, the poet as finder and the poet as maker, the world within and the world without."[84]

In this description, Longenbach uses the word "dialectic" rather loosely, merely indicating by it the existence of two poles between which Stevens's poetry may be said to oscillate. But the word may also be used more rigorously, in the Hegelian triadic sense that passes from thesis over antithesis to synthesis. Harold Bloom is strongly committed to this form of reasoning—witness the triad of ethos, logos, and pathos that undergirds his study of Stevens—and it does not come as a surprise to see him inscribe "The Snow Man" in a truly dialectical scenario:

> The reader who masters the interrelationships of these three brief texts, *The Man Whose Pharynx Was Bad*, *The Snow Man*, and *Tea at the Palaz of Hoon*, has reached the center of Stevens' poetic and human anxieties and of his resources for meeting those anxieties. I will read the three poems as though they formed one larger, dialectical lyric when run together, akin to Coleridge's *Dejection: An Ode* and Wordsworth's *Intimations* ode. The *Pharynx* poem states the crisis of poetic vision; *The Snow Man* meets the crisis by a reduction to the First Idea; exuberantly, the great hymn of Hoon, so invariably misread as irony, reimagines the First Idea and restitutes, momentarily yet transumptively, the contraction of meaning provoked by the crisis.[85]

83. Robin Gail Schulze, "Teaching Wallace Stevens and Marianne Moore: The Search for an Open Mind," 181; Schulze, *Web of Friendship*, 25–26.
84. Milton J. Bates, *Mythology of Self*, 153, and introduction to *Sur Plusieurs Beaux Sujects: Wallace Stevens' Commonplace Book*, 10; James Longenbach, *Wallace Stevens: The Plain Sense of Things*, 35.
85. Bloom, *Poems of Our Climate*, 50.

Whether we are willing to subscribe to Bloom's psychological teleology is beside the point here. Richard Poirier, for one, has extensively quarreled with it, and Daniel R. Schwarz rearranges the order of the three poems into "a three-act lyric monodrama" in which Hoon comes on stage in the second act and the snow man only in the third and final act. What Bloom's critical appropriation patently signals, though, is the strong potential for setting up triadic constructions—alongside antithetical ones—in the reading of Stevens in general, and of "The Snow Man" in particular.[86] Judith Butler addresses this aspect of a modernistically inflected post-Hegelianism in Stevens most explicitly. "In twentieth-century reflections on history and metaphysics," she observes,

> Hegel's romantic postulation of a dialectical unity of opposites has come to seem irreconcilable with the assertion of human finitude, the ineluctability of temporal experience, the hermeneutical fusion of cultural horizons, and the refutation of language as a closed system of signs. And yet, true to its own logic of inversion, the dialectic reemerges within the confines of twentieth-century thought, deprived of the possibility of synthesis, of systematic closure, and of the claim to ontological truth. As a persistent wish, the structure of a metaphysical longing, the dialectic survives as that precise metaphysical possibility that can no longer be realized.

Stevens's work, according to Butler, offers one of the most striking poetic illustrations of this lingering wish for dialectical thinking, at the same time as it offers some of the most playful twentieth-century mockeries and deflations of the dialectical drive for unification. For Stevens, "the dialectic no longer denotes the ontological unity of opposites or the logical principle of dialectical reversal" but "becomes instead a performative moment in a language, an occasion in which the loss of metaphysical moorings clears the way for a poetic affirmation of what is."[87] Such performative moments, we might add, are precisely what allow critics to engage in their own provisional types of

86. Poirier, *Renewal of Literature*, 211–20; Schwarz, *Narrative and Representation*, 58; see also Suberchicot's *Treize façons*, which divides each of its thirteen chapters neatly into triads and argues that Stevens's widespread use of antithesis is to be understood as a positive rhetorical strategy intended to preclude the arrival at simple affirmative meanings (275). Recent examples of enlisting "The Snow Man" as part of a critical triad that cuts a path into Stevens's poetry come from Douglas Mao, who falls back on Bloom's trio of poems (*Solid Objects*, 219), and Tony Sharpe, who believes that "Earthy Anecdote," "Anecdote of the Jar," and "The Snow Man" "offer useful triangulation points from which to map Stevens's poetic terrain" (*Wallace Stevens*, x).

87. Judith Butler, "The Nothing That Is: Wallace Stevens' Hegelian Affinities," 269.

dialectical performance, casting Stevens as a poet whose work moves in and out of certain recurrent theses, antitheses, and syntheses.

Palimpsests

In Thomas F. Walsh's *Concordance to the Poetry of Wallace Stevens*, the rare and poetically self-conscious word *behold* is listed no less than thirty times, *snow* (in one form or another) more than twice as often, and *nothing* (together with *nothingness*) over 160 times. (It is indeed "As if nothingness contained a métier," in the remarkable line from "The Rock" [*CP* 526]).[88] And this is to pay no attention to other staple ingredients of "The Snow Man" such as *mind, sun, sound, wind,* and *leaves:* in all these cases, counts run up to a few hundreds. Stevens was a poet who, for all his stylistic extravaganza and outré preciosity, returned to the same nuclear words over and over again—propelled by a kind of repetition compulsion—and who insatiably strove to explore the multiple reconfigurability of these words. In this respect, he stands as the culmination and perfect embodiment of literary modernism in Poirier's definition: "A modernist writer keeps going . . . because in reading what he has just written he finds provocations only for alternatives."[89] Few other writers have composed an oeuvre that so incessantly and in such multiple ways folds back on itself, is so strongly interconnected, with nearly every poem containing one or another echo, allusion, motif, or mirror figure—be it formally, acoustically, or thematically—pointing to other texts from the same corpus.

The possibilities for reading later poems as palimpsests of "The Snow Man" are, as a result, legion.[90] To investigate a number of them will allow us a sharper insight into both the way Stevens may have retrospectively

---

88. The early J. Hillis Miller, under the influence of Heideggerian phenomenology, went so far as to claim that "[i]n the later poetry nothingness is source and end of everything, and underlies everything as its present reality" (*Poets of Reality,* 277).

89. Poirier, *Renewal of Literature,* 110.

90. Poems (or parts of poems) that have been viewed as rewrites of "The Snow Man" but that will not be discussed in the following pages range from such relatively neglected lyrics as "Snow and Stars" (*CP* 133), "Man Carrying Thing" (350–51), "In a Bad Time" (426–27), "Vacancy in the Park" (511), "Long and Sluggish Lines" (522), "A Quiet Normal Life" (523), "As You Leave the Room" (*OP* 117–18), and "On the Way to the Bus" (*OP* 136) to major constituents of the Stevens canon, like "The Comedian as the Letter C" (*CP* 27–46), "The Poems of Our Climate" (193–94), "The Latest Freed Man" (204–5), "Esthétique du Mal" (313–26), "The Auroras of Autumn" (411–21), "The Plain Sense of Things" (502–3), "Not Ideas about the Thing but the Thing Itself" (534), and "The Course of a Particular"

interpreted his own earlier text and the way he may have come to *feel* about it at particular points in time. Interestingly, two of the poems apparently intended in some sense as rewrites of "The Snow Man" were composed in 1940, shortly after the war in Europe had broken out. In the first, "Man and Bottle," Stevens is still trying to salvage some aspects of the earlier text:

> The mind is the great poem of winter, the man,
> Who, to find what will suffice,
> Destroys romantic tenements
> Of rose and ice
>
> In the land of war. More than the man, it is
> A man with the fury of a race of men,
> A light at the centre of many lights,
> A man at the centre of men.
>
> It has to content the reason concerning war,
> It has to persuade that war is part of itself,
> A manner of thinking, a mode
> Of destroying, as the mind destroys,
>
> An aversion, as the world is averted
> From an old delusion, an old affair with the sun,
> An impossible aberration with the moon,
> A grossness of peace.
>
> It is not the snow that is the quill, the page.
> The poem lashes more fiercely than the wind,
> As the mind, to find what will suffice, destroys
> Romantic tenements of rose and ice.
>
> (CP 238–39)

"Man and Bottle" approaches the predecessor it identifies in the first line with a twist. The "mind of winter" earlier associated with turning into a snow man now becomes itself "the great poem." And it does so not by simply decomposing itself into nothing, even if the proposed movement is again

(OP 123–24). The last poem, especially, has been frequently read in conjunction with "The Snow Man": see Litz, *Introspective Voyager*, 291–94, and " 'Compass and Curriculum,' " 237; Bové, *Destructive Poetics*, 212–15; Vendler, *On Extended Wings*, 67; Bevis, *Mind of Winter*, 52ff.; Lensing, *Seasons*, 144–47; and the lengthy reading of the poem as a "palinode" of "The Snow Man" in Macksey, "Climates of Wallace Stevens," 194–218. Some of the poems listed here will be discussed in Part Two.

one of reduction "to find what will suffice." The mind must above all remain that of a "man"—more particularly of a man who shows himself sufficiently aware of the condition of living in a "land of war." The reductive and de-structive task the mind sets itself in the later poem is an essentially human, not a seemingly dehumanizing, one that has to be undertaken archetypically in the name and place of all humanity. The task belongs to a "man at the centre of men." Stevens longs to retain the mental "mode / Of destroying" he evinced in the guise of a snow man—and which he would later come to de-fine, more felicitously, as a mode of decreating or uncreating—but he strives to provide a better justification and rationale for it in terms of the more ur-gent and oppressive reality of his historical situation. The old mental mode should now seek to internalize war—should do so, moreover, without giving up the poet's humanity, without amounting to a surrender to nothingness. It is no longer the snowscape *outside* that is allowed to drive "the quill" and fill "the page"; nor is it enough to just float on "the wind" and lose one's sense of selfhood in the blowing of the wind all over the bare land. "The poem [must lash] more fiercely" than that, and the mind must remain fully conscious of, and responsible for, its act of destroying. By the time Stevens has reached the end of "Man and Bottle," he no longer seems to level his attack against the poetry of his overtly "romantic" predecessors alone (in particular, as George Bornstein argues, against Coleridge's "Kubla Khan"), but also, secondarily and more ambiguously, against the socially withdrawn, largely aestheticist invention of his own earlier crystal "tenements" of snow.[91]

· · ·

91. Bornstein, *Transformations of Romanticism*, 6. Apart from harking back to and rewriting "The Snow Man," "Man and Bottle" also offers a fine illustration of how variously Stevens weaves his textual web, how endlessly he provokes intertextual disseminations. One need only juxtapose the poem's opening lines and those of its better-known companion piece written at the same time, "Of Modern Poetry" ("The poem of the mind in the act of finding / What will suffice" [CP 239]), to realize that "Man and Bottle" is simultaneously enlisted in a definitional and apologetic task aimed at positioning and justifying high modernist art in the embattled circumstances of a deep political crisis. That the "mode / Of destroying" upon which the poem hinges in turn recalls Picasso's aphorism that a painting forms a "hoard of destructions"—a phrase Stevens had earlier borrowed for "The Man with the Blue Guitar" (CP 173)—only serves to extend the intertextual network, as does the claim that the mind "has to persuade that war is part of itself," which anticipates the apologetic supplementary canto to "Notes toward a Supreme Fiction" about the poet's war running parallel to the one waged by soldiers (CP 407–8). Almost vertiginously, finally, the search for "A light at the centre of many lights, / A man at the centre of men" recurs in several later poems, not the least of which is "A Primitive Like an Orb" (CP 440–43). Clearly, Stevens allows his readers to go on combining texts almost *ad infinitum*.

The second palimpsest from 1940 is considerably more outspoken in the way it takes issue with "The Snow Man." It also develops a different perspective from the one that inspires "Man and Bottle." In the fourth canto of "Extracts from Addresses to the Academy of Fine Ideas," Stevens no longer follows the dubious and dangerous course of interiorizing an all-too-real and lethal war, of recuperating it as a model for modernist artistic strategies and relocating it in the mind's destructive discontinuities. (Perhaps because he sensed that he was "flirting with the aestheticisation of history which is Benjamin's definition of fascism," Stevens soon felt uncomfortable with "Man and Bottle.")[92] This time he takes a different slant by rereading "The Snow Man" with an eye to the ethical question of losing the self. Recounting another one of his walks, at the end of the winter of 1940, when a three-month snow had just melted, the poet stops to recollect how

> The wind blew in the empty place.
> The winter wind blew in an empty place—
> There was that difference between the and an,
> The difference between himself and no man,
> No man that heard a wind in an empty place.
> It was time to be himself again, to see
> If the place, in spite of its witheredness, was still
> Within the difference. He felt curious
> Whether the water was black and lashed about
> Or whether the ice still covered the lake. There was still
> Snow under the trees and on the northern rocks,
> The dead rocks not the green rocks, the live rocks. If,
> When he looked, the water ran up the air or grew white
> Against the edge of the ice, the abstraction would
> Be broken and winter would be broken and done,
> And being would be being himself again,
> Being, becoming seeing and feeling and self,
> Black water breaking into reality.
>
> (CP 255)

The snow man, Stevens now believes, was actually "no man," and the wind "blowing in the same bare place" was not so much blowing in *the* but

92. Jenkins, *Rage for Order*, 45; see also Longenbach, *Plain Sense*, 216.

in *an* empty place, in a locus no longer circumscribable, a no-place. "It is time to be myself again, to restore the difference between Me and Not Me, between inside and outside," he continues, "time to look again and notice the specific details of the place that surrounds me, to give up my liking for abstraction." Whether this rebirth of the self (metaphorically figured by the final image of "water breaking") results from the nightmare of history and a corresponding conviction that the writer in a time of global crisis cannot afford to escape into self-dissolution or whether it is merely prompted by a momentary mood cannot be inferred from the text. What this extract from "Extracts" does indicate, however, is Stevens's unwillingness to freeze his attitude programmatically into that of a socially nonexistent snow man; it signals his awareness, in other words, of some of the limits of the reductive strategy that is part of the earlier poem.

While the lines in "Extracts" that respond to "The Snow Man" typically suppress much of their affective amplitude—they bespeak an urgency only in the insistence of their repetitions and suggest an eventual willingness to confront the world's darker side ("Black water")—"No Possum, No Sop, No Taters" contains several stanzas that reintroduce the pathetic fallacy with a vengeance. The poem was written in the peculiarly Siberian New England winter of 1943, when the war seemed like it would last forever and oil on the home front was becoming so scarce a commodity that even a citizen as well-off as Stevens was afraid he would be unable to heat his house any longer.[93] Reality was closing in on the poet, then, and walks could not so easily dispel the mind's grinding anymore:

> He is not here, the old sun,
> As absent as if we were asleep.
>
> The field is frozen. The leaves are dry.
> Bad is final in this light.
>
> In this bleak air the broken stalks
> Have arms without hands. They have trunks
>
> Without legs or, for that, without heads.
> They have heads in which a captive cry

93. Filreis, *Actual World*, 46.

Is merely the moving of a tongue.
Snow sparkles like eyesight falling to earth,

Like seeing fallen brightly away.
The leaves hop, scraping on the ground.

It is deep January. The sky is hard.
The stalks are firmly rooted in ice.

It is in this solitude, a syllable,
Out of these gawky flitterings,

Intones its single emptiness,
The savagest hollow of winter-sound.

It is here, in this bad, that we reach
The last purity of the knowledge of good.

The crow looks rusty as he rises up.
Bright is the malice in his eye . . .

One joins him there for company,
But at a distance, in another tree.

(CP 293–94)

How different this January scene from the one in "The Snow Man": it contains snow and leaves and "single emptiness," but no possibility of wiping the slate of the mind until it is blank by concentrating on the natural ambience and forgetting all feelings of misery. The lines are clipped and jerky instead of meandering and long-winded. They ask to be delivered in an exhausted, disappointed voice that lacks the breath—the inspiration—to reach any expansiveness of statement: Stevens's favorite stanzaic form of the tercet is conspicuously absent. The horrors of war, we feel, make themselves poignantly felt everywhere around; they cry to be heard on all sides, infecting a landscape suddenly grown eerie and gruesome. The poet's attitude toward winter scenes has changed from a largely *aesthetical* to a mostly *ethical* one, from an exercise in surrendering to the unspeaking senses to an expression of the morally unspeakable. The "solitude" of the inhospitable landscape no longer allows the poet to forget his fellow humans, nor to experience, Emerson-wise, the sublime. It merely forces him to hanker after, and testify to, some "last purity of the knowledge of good"—a purity that must be affirmed as a vital residue, as a self-saving moral base that steadies us in the bleakest times of crisis.[94] "The outcome of 'No Possum, No Sop, No Taters,' " says Alison Rieke, "in terms of discovery and potential closure, is more complex than 'The Snow Man.' "[95] That may be a daring claim to make, yet the poem's ending is unmistakably enigmatic and more than usually successful at resisting the intelligence. We can only wonder: Do the concluding stanzas perhaps picture a tentative, ethically wary, diffident attempt at resocializing? Do they display a readiness to risk life again by searching out the "company" of all those whom we know to be ultimately full of "Bright . . . malice"? The poem, significantly, was written shortly before "Esthétique du Mal," at a time when Stevens was particularly involved with the relationship between ethics and aesthetics and his place as a social being among people. It was a time when a poem like "The Snow Man" could not have been written.

In all three presumed palimpsests of "The Snow Man" composed during the war, the pressure of history can be felt and the earlier poem is adapted accordingly. By the fifties, however, such urgency had subsided and the septuagenarian Stevens felt free to concentrate on his own mental life. In several poems of this period, he once more appears to have recalled and remolded "The Snow Man." One of them is "A Clear Day and No Memories," published in 1955, the year of Stevens's death. It is a limpid and economical poem typical of the very late work:

> No soldiers in the scenery,
> No thoughts of people now dead,
> As they were fifty years ago:
> Young and living in a live air,
> Young and walking in the sunshine,
> Bending in blue dresses to touch something—
> Today the mind is not part of the weather.
>
> Today the air is clear of everything.
> It has no knowledge except of nothingness

94. Peter A. Brazeau explains that the poem's "folksy title is meant to heighten the sense of *mal* by contrasting this winter scene to the down-home version of paradise, the South, which had meant so much to Stevens over the years. As he wrote to Philip May [who lived in Jacksonville, Florida], 'How happy you all seem to be down there; how you go on living in a land of milk and honey, or, to be more exact, possum, sop and taters' " (*Parts of a World*, 109). "No Possum, No Sop, No Taters" has understandably been interpreted as a rewriting of "Farewell to Florida" (CP 117–18) as well (Filreis, *Actual World*, 48).

95. Rieke, "Wallace Stevens in the Classroom," 137.

> And it flows over us without meanings,
> As if none of us had ever been here before
> And are not now: in this shallow spectacle,
> This invisible activity, this sense.
>
> (OP 138–39)

"A Clear Day and No Memories" opens with the faintest possible recollection of the poem previously discussed, "No Possum, No Sop, No Taters," which imagined people mutilated (arguably by war) and spread out all over the natural scenery. But the recollection is there to be negated, even if the effort of negation simultaneously betrays the lingering psychic force of what must be suppressed. The first stanza offers a choice example of what is undoubtedly one of Stevens's main rhetorical characteristics—a feature that we will see several times more in the second half of this study. Critics have used various labels for it: P. Michael Campbell and John Dolan have chosen to call it "praeteritic antithesis," which, in their definition, "differs from a typical antithesis in that 'the rejected thing, the thing denied' (to borrow a phrase from Stevens) ends up becoming the focus of attention, with the ostensibly endorsed term fading into the background." In deconstructionist quarters, this rhetorical figure has been popularized and endlessly deployed under the name of "double bind," and Daniel R. Schwarz has unearthed another ancient rhetorical name to pin it down, that of "occupatio" ("speaking of what he says he will not speak of").[96] To erase the past Stevens has to face it first; he cannot help but become conscious of what it is the weather allows him—or should allow him—to forget. Memories have a way of surreptitiously resurfacing and lingering on: they demand to be dwelt on in some detail and with some sense of nostalgia before they can be loosed to the wind. If they are libidinally cathected, moreover, as they seem to be here, they also have to be repeated, in accordance with the deep structure and the most fundamental workings of desire itself: the anaphora of lines 4 and 5 illustrates this in the simplest possible manner. It is this cathecting aspect, in fact, that most clearly sets off the repressive effort in this poem from that in "The Snow Man": whereas the snow man's "mind of winter," for all we knew, managed only to dispense with its *own* "misery," Stevens's older mind shows itself prepared to embrace *other* people as well—those once loved in the bloom of his youth. "A Clear Day and No Memories" is

---

96. P. Michael Campbell and John Dolan, "Teaching Stevens's Poetry through Rhetorical Structure," 119–20; Schwarz, *Narrative and Representation*, 225 (see also 59).

in some respect a farewell poem, but a farewell poem in which a remarkable serenity of tone is achieved—if serenity is what we may infer from the fact that "the poem evinces no density of resistance, no symptomatology . . . The profundity of the labor of the negative and of the task of repression is the one thing absent."[97]

It is a strikingly *knowing* poem also, as we move on to the stepped-up negations of the second stanza. The poet (or, more accurately, "the air" he looks at in a meditative identification that avoids any pathetic fallacy) attains a "*knowledge* . . . of nothingness" (a seemingly ironic claim that goes beyond the mere *beholding* of nothing by the snow man and recalls Schopenhauer). He subsequently expresses an awareness of both the necessary fictionality of dissolving the self (necessarily fictional, that is, within the realm of writing) and the need for a will to believe (or a willing suspension of disbelief) if one nevertheless wants to achieve this dissolution: "*As if* none of us had ever been here before / And are not now." The poem ends with what can be construed as this poet's late, toned-down, even dispassionate version of the sublime. "The world is a force, not a presence," Stevens had proclaimed in one of his more arresting aphorisms (*OP* 198), and what we are ultimately left with at the end of "A Clear Day" is a "sense" of just such a force, of an "invisible activity" in a world unable to transcend its status of "shallow spectacle." For the Stevens approaching death, it would seem, a vitality that suffused this imperfect world could be enough, for the moment.

V. READING NOTHING THAT IS NOT THERE AND THE NOTHING THAT IS

"How I wish great poems could be written about nothing," A. R. Ammons once wistfully sighed.[98] In a way, of course, they can: one of them is called "The Snow Man," and it abundantly shows that to *write* about nothing is not therefore to *mean* nothing—quite to the contrary. And to *read* about nothing is not to *understand* nothing either. Indeed, Stevens's little poem at one of its many signifying levels offers a metacommentary on its own workings. For we are invited to mirror the snow man's act or condition: we are invited

---

97. Steven Shaviro, " 'That Which Is Always Beginning': Stevens's Poetry of Affirmation," 221.

98. Quoted in Anthony Libby, *Mythologies of Nothing: Mystical Death in American Poetry 1940–70*, 1.

to read (behold) nothing that is not there and the nothing that is, as if the text had reversed the classic graffito "Do not read this"[99] by another double bind: "Go ahead and read, there's nothing to be seen anyhow." This is the paradoxical act or condition of all reading, to the extent that language, too, as Geoffrey H. Hartman suggests, can be considered a nothing of sorts. "The Snow Man" thus heightens our awareness of its textual-linguistic status as a something-nothing that is at once determinate and indeterminate, material and disembodied, present and absent—like the vicarious visions and sensations it sets off in the reader's imagination: at one or more removes from reality, yet in its own imaginary and potent way quite real. The poem enhances our awareness, in other words, of the act of reading by proposing that we address the question of how much we are reading—are forced to read— between the lines.[100] The issue is almost as vexed and contested in literary criticism as in the making of music: How much are we reading between the notes or staves when playing music? How far does our performative franchise extend? How much may this franchise fluctuate from day to day, mood to mood, moment to moment? No pianist wants to play the same piece identically every day: bringing music to life is a matter of exploring and testing its many signifying and aesthetic possibilities and of searching out those realizations that, for the time being, make most sense and are most satisfying. The score and its historical context obviously limit the performer's options in myriad ways: only through the artistic mastery of delimitation does any attempt at realization acquire its purpose and meaning. But those limits are in no sense meant to close off the musician's freedom; they are rather meant to *enable* it.

99. Peggy Kamuf, "Reading between the Blinds," xiv.

100. Instead of emphasizing the paradoxical nature of language in Hartmanian fashion, Stanley Fish characteristically prefers to frame the poem in terms of the operations of a reader's mind in the act of producing an interpretation of the poem: "Only . . . when [the snow man] is nothing himself, will his self not be interposed between him and the nothing— the thing that is not an object of human thought—that is. But the reader who understands that this is what it means to have a mind of winter purchases that understanding at the price of being able to have one, since the act of understanding, of apprehending from a distance, is precisely what must be given up. What we finally discover is that what is required is a mind not active in the way it must be for the discovery to be made. The demand that the reader reanalyze does not parallel a program for the achieving of a pure perception; rather it is inseparable from the realization that such a perception is forever unavailable" (*Is There a Text in This Class?* 257). Fish's "hypothetical reading," as he calls it (ibid.), is not, however, meant to demonstrate a need for reading "between" the lines, for in his theory such a reading practice would be altogether impossible.

No doubt, one could raise serious objections to the way I have allowed "The Snow Man" to get snowed under—or, to stay within the same tropological field, to melt away into increasingly gray and opaque slush. In particular, one could argue that bringing into the game non-Stevensian, philosophically biased intertexts is to fly off on ever so many tangents and that "The Snow Man" is better read as an atmospheric poem evoking a moment of strong, purifying cold that reduces the hiking poet's mind to a blank slate, wipes away the musty thoughts produced by *Sitzfleisch*, and invigorates him by the brilliant immediacy of its imprint on the retina. This would be close to Bevis's Buddhist state-of-consciousness reading, and its musical equivalent would be something like the third part of John Cage's *String Quartet in Four Parts*, "Nearly Stationary," or even, more extremely, the same composer's notorious *4'33"*, four minutes and thirty-three seconds of silence on the piano. One could object that it is misguided to read the poem's final lines in an almost doggedly literal manner, as though they contained a nugget of deeper understanding and were not merely meant to be indeterminately suggestive and logically inconclusive without further ado. We know that the poem was composed at a time when Stevens's principal purpose was to write a "pure" poetry that attached more value to the play of sounds and images than to the formulation of ideas. Do not all my laborious attempts at multiple contextualization threaten to rob the text of its freshness? Do they not tax the poem's elasticity to the point where it may snap? Do they not mistake the finishing flourish of a pretty, witty paradox for a metaphysical conundrum? These are all valid objections. But they are only valid insofar as they help to raise the question of the poem's communicative and aesthetic force and the existence of limits to that force. Any fine poem possesses the power to transcend both its historical conditions of production and the authorial intentions that originally informed it, and any poem must reckon with what Milton J. Bates calls "revisions of the implied reader-writer contract" that historically alter perceptions and appropriations. If "The Snow Man"—in particular its ending, which partakes of an "energetic, extended series of researches into the methods of closure"—offers a site where one may watch, in a nutshell, the conflicts of a whole philosophical tradition and a whole poetic oeuvre, it is only the very force of the paradoxes Stevens creates that can keep such interpretations going. These paradoxes, as Barbara M. Fisher observes, are at once "logical," "ontological," and "rhetorical," and their unquantifiable force is, for better or worse, as much a function of the *intentio lectoris* as of the *intentio operis:* it depends not only on the aesthetic effectiveness of the poem's textual economy and polysemy but just as much on the reader's temperament, needs, and interests.[101]

Despite my attempts at organization, it has not really proved possible to follow a beautifully calculated, rigorously developing course in setting up the preceding case study, nor is that study now leading up to a nicely rounded conclusion about the precise limits of a poem's signifying potential. "Close reading," says J. Hillis Miller, "reaches its limit in the constantly renewed experience of its failure to take you where you think you want to go and ought to go." The limits of reading "The Snow Man," it turns out, are not so easily established. But perhaps the difficulty comes with the territory. As Mario J. Valdés maintains, "the idea of fixed identity for a literary text" may well be "contrary to the spirit of humanistic inquiry." A literary text has no fixed identity because its identity is, in Owen Miller's words, "a relational rather than a constitutive notion."[102]

The relational quality of a text's identity has come to the fore with a vengeance in the case of my intertextual readings. Such readings, as I was able to experience in a vividly empirical manner while writing, are potentially inexhaustible. An unstopping flock of associations and possibilities for establishing sensible links came flying in my window (many of them duly dying in the wastebasket). One of them was Heidegger's 1929 inaugural address as a professor at the University of Freiburg, entitled "What Is Metaphysics?"—a lecture that famously posits "the basic question of metaphysics": "Why are there beings at all, and why not rather nothing?" Had "The Snow Man" been written a decade later, critics would no doubt have tried to argue for a direct influence of Heidegger in much the same way Richard P. Adams did with Schopenhauer. The following Hegelian quotation, dug up by Judith Butler, seemed no less promising at one point: "If we take a closer look at what a limit implies, we see it involving a contradiction in itself, and thus evincing its dialectical nature. But, again, the limit, as the negation of something, is not an abstract nothing, but a nothing which is what we call an 'other.'" Other links were suggested to me in conversation by philosophers who pointed to Parmenides' thesis that the same can be known only by the same and to Maurice Merleau-Ponty's analogical idea

101. Milton J. Bates, "'The Emperor' and Its Clothes," 24; Reddy, "'As He Starts the Human Tale,'" 4; Fisher, *Intensest Rendezvous*, 39.
102. J. Hillis Miller, preface, ix; Mario J. Valdés, "Conclusion: Concepts of Fixed and Variable Identity," 301–2; Owen Miller, preface to *Identity of the Literary Text*, xix.

that you have to be a thing yourself to understand the thingness of a thing. Richard Wilbur's memory of an epistolary exchange with Stevens, finally, proved equally teasing: "I had been reading Gaston Bachelard, the Sorbonne philosopher and aesthetician. Bachelard says somewhere that the human imagination simply cannot cope with polar conditions, and so I shot off a postcard to Stevens. He wrote back some splendid sentence about Bachelard is wrong, most art is created out of a condition of winter."[103]

The fact that such new tracks are theoretically always available does not of course mean that in matters of literary interpretation "anything goes." It only means that my own interpretation of the poem is caught up in its proper historicity: my "understanding" of the text has evolved in the process of bringing all the above materials together and working some of them out, and it has evolved in such a way as to let any attempt at stabilizing this understanding appear to be an act of foreclosure. At the same time, however, *some* stabilization—be it ever so provisional—is always necessary, and we should recall Umberto Eco's caveat: "To say that a text potentially has no end does not mean that *every* act of interpretation can have a happy ending."[104] For all its tonal undecidability, as we have seen, even "The Snow Man" disallows certain readings, at least by the standards of a community of modestly competent readers: one cannot claim about the poem, say, that it expresses a state of hysteria without fundamentally damaging the text's semantic, syntactic, and logical coherence, just as it would be ridiculous to purport that the text was really an encrypted laundry list. We have no need for an absolute, transcendental Authority vested in the objective essences of a Text or of Language to dismiss such interpretations as absurd, sterile, or paranoid.

But those are the easiest interpretive limits to set here. More to the point may be a complaint once made by Robert Frost against what he called "this spreading of every word into all its denotations and connotations . . . as if it had been written on blotting paper."[105] Frost was not the sort of poet to appreciate too many associative fantasies on the reader's part; he was rather someone who sought to carefully control and mete out his own textual ambiguities. With Stevens, things were arguably different. Not that this poet was any less disciplined or less bent on accuracy than Frost, but with him

103. Martin Heidegger, "What Is Metaphysics?" 112; Hegel quoted in Butler, "The Nothing That Is," 281; Wilbur quoted in Brazeau, *Parts of a World,* 170.

104. Eco, *Limits of Interpretation,* 6.

105. Quoted in Helen Vendler, "Dark and Deep," 5.

such discipline and accuracy were preferably wedded to the greatest possible denotative and connotative variety. It was part of Stevens's project of resisting the mind almost successfully that his texts should be able to branch out as much as possible within the limits of an aesthetically effective economy.

For limits there are, it bears repeating, and they are not set only by the text but also by the reader. If the signifying process is theoretically open and, therefore, nonfinalistic, it is practically always in need of finalization. Because the erudition and associative possibilities of individual readers are of necessity limited, the interpretive process appears itself limned by the phenomenon of repetitiveness. Cross-fertilizing "The Snow Man" with more and more intertexts, I have necessarily also illustrated how my analysis gradually fell prey to the law of diminishing returns. In the end, every interpreter is forced to circle around a few recurrent observations about the poem—that it can be made to affirm as well as undercut certain propositions, that it does not allow itself to be interpreted in either/or terms but, largely because of its flat tone and suppressed polyphony, seems to offer always a case of both/and. This sort of undecidability is a favorite conclusion of deconstructionists, who tend to be particularly sensitive to differences *within* rather than differences *between,* and who have a penchant for "infinitely deferring the possibility of adding up the sum of a text's parts or meanings and reaching a totalized, integrated whole."[106] Still, the theoretical impossibility of "reaching a totalized, integrated whole" should not blind us to the threat of "infinite deferrals"—a luxury we can never really afford in life, or only at the price of irresponsibility. The necessarily limiting practice of any concrete interpretation should not be stalled by the limitlessness of its theoretical options. A constant insistence on a *regressus in infinitum* in the field of signification betrays, in Eco's words, a fundamental "epistemological fanaticism."[107]

So, even if we must beware of lapsing into a fanatical epistemological relativism, the experience, fostered by the emblematic reading of a single Stevens poem, that contexts are nonsaturable and that the process of contextualization is an open-ended process has its undeniable heuristic importance. It is an importance that extends beyond the analysis of poetry to involve any humanly urgent reality that one may set out to comprehend. The best literary evocation of the potential drama of this heuristic *condition humaine*—one that displays its existential, ethical, and political

106. Barbara Johnson, *The Critical Difference: Essays in the Contemporary Rhetoric of Reading,* 4.
107. Eco, *Limits of Interpretation,* 24.

implications with greater urgency than any poem could—is probably to be found in Don DeLillo's *Libra*. The novel presents us with the plight of a character, Nicholas Branch, who, as a retired senior analyst of the CIA, is hired to write the secret history of the assassination of John F. Kennedy. "He is in the fifteenth year of his labor," writes DeLillo, "and sometimes wonders if he is becoming bodiless. He knows he is getting old." Branch has studied the twenty-six-volume addendum to the notorious Warren Report, as well as the 125,000-page FBI file and loads of insignificant details, from Jack Ruby's mother's dental chart down to a microphotograph of three strands of Lee Harvey Oswald's pubic hair. "He sits in the data-spew of hundreds of lives. There's no end in sight," notes DeLillo. "Branch must study everything. He is in too deep to be selective." Everything is connectable to everything else and any overlooked detail may contain the key to the crime. "He takes refuge in his notes. The notes are becoming an end in themselves. Branch has decided it is premature to make a serious effort to turn these notes into coherent history. Maybe it will always be premature. Because the data keeps coming. Because new lives enter the record all the time. The past is changing as he writes."[108] It is impossible for Branch to dam the branching facts that may be linked to the assassination, to set limits to the ever-expanding and ever-changing context that must explain the event. Every conclusion seems premature; every interpretation involves a risk, an exclusion of contradictory data, a commitment that plays with and endangers the lives of others. Instead of erasing moral dilemmas, undecidability only sharpens them.

Professional readers of "The Snow Man," to be sure, do not share the existential, ethical, and political urgency of Branch's plight, but their situation is not intrinsically or fundamentally different. Tracking down and linking up all the possible intertexts that can be used to elucidate the poem, they too may start wondering if they are becoming bodiless and know that they are growing old. Time takes its toll in the form of fatigue and a neurobiologically explicable desire for new horizons, a natural longing for a change of environment. It is no coincidence that bringing into the game a number of non-Stevensian as well as Stevensian intertexts took us gradually away from the poem and made us follow a series of topics and options hinted at, but not worked out, by the poem itself. In this light, we would do well to recall Owen Miller's analysis of intertextuality, for, drawing on concepts from gestalt psychology, Miller attests to "the phenomenon of reversibility: figure

108. Don DeLillo, *Libra*, 14–15, 59, 301.

becomes ground and ground figure. Intertextuality viewed in this light takes on a new sheen. For if we speak literally of a focused text, we must envisage a reversal between figure and ground, between text and intertext as we reverse focus. The reversibility of figure/ground relationships in perception, we are told, is caused by *perceptual fatigue* on the part of the perceiver" (emphasis added).[109]

What ultimately remains, when one tries to theorize an intertextualizing reading practice, is little else than a few metaphors of focus and perspective, tropes of zooming in and out. The eye is a restless muscle; like the mind, it can never be satisfied. Reading "The Snow Man" from various angles and developing intertextual crossings has clarified how naturally we are inclined to jump backwards and forwards between the figure of a text and the ground of its possible contexts. These jumps depend to a considerable extent on what happens to hold our attention and what seems to warrant further investigation. "What the text means to its readers now matters more than what the author meant when he wrote it," Valdés argues. This primacy of personal readerly interests is only the corollary of a natural, biological self-interest. It should not be taken, however, to entail a lack of readerly humility and respect vis-à-vis the text. The very possibility of interpretive excess is simply built-in, not epiphenomenal. "Ultimately the identity of the text depends on how the text relates to our human interests and purposes."[110]

In the final analysis, the limits of reading "The Snow Man" are determined by how the poem manages to relate to our human interests and purposes. We have seen how the text can help us ponder questions of considerable existential importance—questions on the status of the self as it subjects itself to reality, on the role of the will in asceticism, and on the place of the sublime in a postromantic world, but also more poetic questions on the autonomy of the individual lyric and the value of explicit authorial intentions (specifically in the case of Stevens), and still other, heuristic questions on some of the favorite maneuvers of critical appropriation. Collectively, these possibilities for discussion, together with the formal riches and tonal insecurities of the text, help to explain why "The Snow Man" has managed to rouse so much critical interest and why the poem should actively invite so much interpretation and reinterpretation. *Interpretation*, etymologically speaking, means translation: it denotes an attempt to translate a text into a language that is no longer the text's but our own (or that of other texts)—an

109. Owen Miller, "Intertextual Identity," 35.
110. Valdés, "Conclusion," 300, 306.

attempt undertaken with an eye to determining what is, or may be, at stake in the text. The major risk with a poet like Stevens will always be that this act of interpretation becomes a critical end in itself. Stevens's belief, as he wrote to Stevens T. Mason, that "a poem consists of all the constructions that can be placed upon it" and that its measure is "the variety of meanings that can be found in it" is, after all, a one-sided belief that should not be understood outside its sociological context—that of the professionalization of literature and the rise of certain elitist forms of art-making that we have come to group under the heading of (high) modernism. The final measure of Stevens's poetic success, as of any writer's, is not a simple matter of variety of meaning, but rather of whether his writings can delight, enlighten, and empower us and whether they have the potential to change our lives. This is a matter for every reader to decide, not for critics to decree.

Chapter 6

Triangulating Pleasure, Doubt, and Irritation

To THE EXTENT THAT Stevens's poetry (a) resists the closure of intelligence almost successfully, (b) manages to incorporate or accommodate simultaneously a variety of tones and voices, and (c) is characterized by a high degree of intertextualizability (if such a cumbersome sesquipedalian word is allowed), it puts the reader in a situation that some of today's more influential theoreticians have emphasized as eminently literary. Thus, Derrida insists that literature is that institution "which allows one to *say everything, in every way*. The space of literature is not only that of an instituted *fiction* but also a *fictive institution* which in principle allows one to say everything."[1] Being no more than a "fictive institution," literature cannot be distinguished categorially from more common, daily usages of speech and writing; it cannot (and should not) be enshrined or encased in an autonomous niche. Nevertheless, even if it proves theoretically possible to "re-read everything as literature, some textual events lend themselves to this better than others, their potentialities are richer and denser. Whence the economic point of view. This wealth itself does not give rise to an absolute evaluation—absolutely stabilized, objective, and natural. Whence the difficulty of theorizing this economy."[2] Derrida's elliptic formulation sounds almost like a synopsis of the previous chapters of this book. For if anything has become clear, it is that Stevens's texts involve a remarkable richness and

---

1. Jacques Derrida, "'This Strange Institution Called Literature': An Interview with Jacques Derrida," 36. The phrase used by Derrida is "tout dire," which, as interviewer and translator Derek Attridge explains, means "both to 'say everything,' with a sense of exhausting a totality, and to 'say anything,' i.e., to speak without constraints on what one may say" (ibid.).
2. Ibid., 46.

density of potentialities, but also that the economy of this rich and dense production of signification, the actual workings of this dissemination, are hard to theorize—which is to say, hard to delimit, outline, and systematize in any rigorous sense.

It is not only Derrida who has been so tentative about the possibility of characterizing and analyzing objects in the field of literary studies. Umberto Eco's no less ingenious and erudite attempts at constructing a theory of semiotics have likewise faltered in the face of art, both literary and nonliterary. Throwing up his hands in despair, Eco seeks refuge in paradox: "The contextual interaction brings to life more and more meanings and, as soon as they come to light, they seem fraught with yet other possible semantic choices. It is indeed difficult to avoid the conclusion that a work of art *communicates too much* and therefore *does not communicate at all*, simply existing as a magic spell that is radically impermeable to all semiotic approach." A poem like "The Snow Man" almost epitomizes high art from this perspective, since it, too, finally seems to live more off an untheorizable "magic spell" than off the communicative transparency or lucidity of its denotations. Theoretical rigor is hard to achieve in the face of this phenomenon, witness also Derrida's blatantly unrigorous definition of the category of the poetic as "that which you desire to learn . . . by heart" and Helen Vendler's analogous insistence, expressed from the opposite side of the critical spectrum, that "the best way into a poem is to learn it by heart."[3] We are back to the imagery of magnetism and our opening question of what it is in Stevens that has attracted so many critics and sparked so many readings. Many provisional and partial answers have been provided as we went along, but at the most synthetic, general level, the conclusion nevertheless seems to be that what appears most literary about Stevens is also what is least theorizable about him. It has to do with a quality of open-endedness, a multiplicity of ideas he manages to stimulate and of sensations and voices he serves to express, an aesthetic aura with which he surrounds his thinking and feeling (including, not to forget, the aura of music, which has such a dark and deep impact on the thinking and feeling body), and an underlying force (a "personality," perhaps?) that drives all these. Clearly, none of these features are the sort that lend themselves well to objective and rigorous analysis.

· · ·

3. Umberto Eco, A *Theory of Semiotics*, 270; Jacques Derrida, "Che cos'è la poesia?" 227; Vendler, "Teaching the Anthology Pieces," 6.

A poetry of this type can be expected to cast a particularly strong spell on more "inventive" critics with a penchant for "free play." They are the critics who are most immediately responsive to Stevens's own freewheeling and playful mind. What the finest of these critics have done over the years is to extend a writerly praxis beyond Stevens's own mind by developing a living dialogue between what the writer arguably tried to say and what a critic can take the texts to say. Most symptomatic in this respect are Stevens's several deconstructionist readers, especially J. Hillis Miller and Joseph N. Riddel during the seventies and eighties.[4] These readers pushed the appropriation of Stevens to its controversial limits by exploring and exploiting the self-consciousness of his texts *as* texts. The word *appropriation* may best display the tension that informed the resulting controversies, for it is itself uneasily suspended between the category of the "proper" and that of the "appropriate" and thus combines vexed questions of what, on the one hand, is intrinsic and essential to a text, and which readerly strategies for attributing meaning, on the other hand, are acceptable and permissible. "The crucial test of significance," observes Eleanor Cook, sensing what deep down often troubles us about Stevens criticism (as well as about the poetry itself), "is partly a matter of limits, for, *pace* the joys of deconstructionist polysemy, not every echo can or should be brought into play."[5]

With a writer who is, at the most basically textual level, as pluralistic and democratic as Stevens, the limits of critical appropriation are not in any strong sense authorially determined or dictated. More frequently they are a function of psychological, existential, and practical restrictions on the reader's part. They are shaped, that is, by such textually extraneous conditions as the reader's mood, his or her overall temperament, taste, intelligence, attention span, physical health, purposes of reading, environmental circumstances, available time, and the general economy of weighing input

4. See esp. Joseph N. Riddel, "Interpreting Stevens: An Essay on Poetry and Thinking," "Decentering the Image: The 'Project' of 'American' Poetics?," "Metaphoric Staging: Stevens' Beginning Again of the 'End of the Book,'" and "The Climate of Our Poems"; and J. Hillis Miller, "Stevens' Rock and Criticism as Cure," "Theoretical and Atheoretical in Stevens," "Impossible Metaphor: Stevens's 'The Red Fern' as Example," *The Linguistic Moment: From Wordsworth to Stevens*, "When Is a Primitive Like an Orb?," and "Prosopopoeia in Hardy and Stevens." For a well-judged critique of Riddel's and Miller's sometime tendency to idealize the concept of the text to the point where no extralinguistic dimension is any longer recognized, and a concomitant attempt at reestablishing the central place in Stevens's writing of an irreducible materiality that constantly limits linguistic free play, see Alex Argyros, "The Residual Difference: Wallace Stevens and American Deconstruction."

5. Cook, *Poetry, Word-Play, and Word-War*, 88.

against output that comes with any investment of mental energy. From this perspective, the existence of a number of playfully ad-libbing appropriations of Stevens cannot be separated altogether from the institutional opportunities and demands of a heavily professionalized and competitive American critical industry: for it is these institutional conditions that offer the time and the logistics needed for such readerly performances, as well as the symbolic and literal capital that act as incentives in the quest for critical distinction. Likewise, the relative tolerance or intolerance with which such playful readings have been met often depends as much on psychological, existential, practical, and institutional restrictions as on the intentions of Stevens's texts or on any strong ideological divergence in theories of reading.

Beyond these sociological factors, however, we should not overlook what constitutes the major motive for engaging in play: that it affords pleasure. It is not for nothing that Cook speaks of "the *joys* of deconstructionist polysemy": according to Derrida, there can be "no deconstruction without pleasure and no pleasure without deconstruction."[6] In this respect, Stevens again appears to be a precursor or modernist father figure to some of the more influential postmodern critical theories that came in his wake, for the third and final imperative around which "Notes toward a Supreme Fiction" is organized precisely states that "It Must Give Pleasure." Current debates on the nature and place of pleasure in the critical appropriation of literature can be referred back in part to Stevens's own poetry, and to that poetry's reception—a reception that extends from early hesitant remarks like Randall Jarrell's that "one is uneasy about objecting to the play—to the professional playfulness, even—of a large mind and a free spirit" to Cook's use of the concept of "*serio ludere*" in analyzing "The Man with the Blue Guitar."[7] For present purposes, it should be enough to remind ourselves of the diversity of types of pleasure that need to be recognized in Stevens's case. The possibilities for deriving pleasure from reading his poetry are many: they have

6. Derrida, "'Strange Institution,'" 57. As Derrida muses: "Deconstruction perhaps has the effect, if not the mission, of liberating forbidden *jouissance*. That's what has to be taken on board. It is perhaps this *jouissance* which most irritates the all-out adversaries of 'deconstruction.' Who, moreover, blame those they call the 'deconstructionists' for depriving them of their habitual delectation in the reading of the great works or the rich treasures of tradition, and simultaneously for being too playful, for taking too much pleasure, for saying what they like for their own pleasure, etc. An interesting and symptomatic contradiction. These masters of 'kettle logic' understand in some obscure way that the 'deconstructionists,' to use that ridiculous vocabulary, are not those who most deprive themselves of pleasure. Which is sometimes hard to put up with" (ibid., 56).

7. Randall Jarrell, review of *The Collected Poems of Wallace Stevens*, 64; Cook, *Poetry, Word-Play, and Word-War*, 136.

to do not only with the teasingly suggestive and far-reaching tentacularity of the ideas he provokes or with the aesthetic effects of a *joie d'écrire* that subordinates a play with content to one with matter and form, but also with the easily overlooked or naturally underdiscussed facet of humor in his work (arguably the richest and most sophisticated humor in all Anglo-modernist poetry). Stevens is the most prominent high modernist poet, in fact, to have composed an oeuvre that is so consistently born of the mutually reinforcing tension between the pleasure principle and the reality principle.

"Pleasure," as Derrida reminds us, "can accumulate, intensify through a certain experience of pain, ascesis, difficulty, an experience of the impasse or of impossibility." Indeed, among the many forms of pleasure afforded by Stevens's poetry, some are obviously quite serious in nature and require their own sort of mental labor. One of the most paradoxical pleasures is that of being actively, almost constantly made to doubt, not only about the meanings of this poet's texts and the appropriateness of one's response to them, but also about the vast and tentacular topics addressed by them. In 1965, Riddel described *Harmonium*—hardly the most philosophical or meditative of Stevens's volumes—as "a poetry of spontaneous celebrations of pleasure and delight, but spontaneous celebrations of doubt and uncertainty and searching as well. The two are fused." More than thirty years later, Alain Suberchicot could still argue for the greatness of Stevens's poetry by pointing above all to its constant staging of instabilities and uncertainties that undermine the ossifications of thought.[8] Stevens's work acts as a particularly vivid reminder of the fact that the readerly confrontation with doubt often plays as important a function in the fascination with, and the valuation of, art as the so much more immediately gratifying attainment of pleasure. We need only single out the following passage by Barbara Herrnstein Smith, one of those all-too-rare critics who have extensively pondered the axiological aspects of reading, to realize how much the experience of doubt must be taken to inform the category of the "intrinsically rewarding" (her topic of analysis):

> First, in speaking of certain objects and activities [like reading] as "intrinsically rewarding" or done "for their own sake," what we usually mean is that

8. Jacques Derrida, " 'There Is No *One* Narcissism' (Autobiophotographies)," 198; Joseph N. Riddel, *The Clairvoyant Eye: The Poetry and Poetics of Wallace Stevens,* 42; Suberchicot, *Treize façons,* 10, 209.

the rewards involved (a) are not predictable or quantifiable; (b) are likely to be heterogeneous and ongoing rather than specific and terminal; and, in the case of an object (for example, a painting or a child), (c) are produced more or less uniquely by that object as distinct from any other of its kind. . . . Second, although we may be individually motivated to engage in various ludic, aesthetic, or artistic activities only for the sake of the ongoing pleasure they provide (or other, less readily nameable or specifiable, ongoing satisfactions), our doing so may nevertheless yield a long-term profit in enhanced cognitive development, behavioral flexibility, or other kinds of advantage for survival, and our general tendency to *find* pleasure in such activities may, accordingly, be the product or by-product of our evolutionary development.[9]

Despite Stevens's intermittent love of the categorical and the point-blank, the laconically assertive and the aphoristic, his basically evasive and provisionally experimental poetry primordially functions as the work of a mental disturber. What his near-successful resistance to the intelligence necessarily fosters in the first place is doubt. His staging of resistance, as so many critics have noted, stands in a Keatsian tradition; it is meant to test the reader's "Negative Capability," as Keats momentously defined it: "when man is capable of being in uncertainties, Mysteries, doubts, without any irritable reaching after fact & reason." Daniel R. Schwarz is right to argue that "Stevens requires an exegetical reader, one committed to unravelling the mysteries of the text, to finding mysteries within and collating them with mysteries of other poems. . . . Poised between insight and puzzlement, between exultation and despair, between the creative moment and paralysis, his poems create a reader whose stance has similar ambiguities and oscillation."[10]

Among critics, R. P. Blackmur was the first committed Keatsian to respond to Stevens's poetry, for in 1931 he wrote of "The Ordinary Women" (*CP* 10–12): "I am at a loss, and quite happy there, to know anything literally about this poem."[11] Blackmur posted his essay to Stevens and received wholehearted support for his embryonic New Critical defense of an ethically responsible sort of ambiguity. The subsequent interaction between poet and critic has been restaged by James Longenbach, who carefully delineates and amply substantiates Stevens's wariness of dogmatism throughout the

9. Barbara Herrnstein Smith, *Contingencies of Value: Alternative Perspectives for Critical Theory*, 34.
10. John Keats, *Letters of John Keats 1814–1821*, 1:193; Schwarz, *Narrative and Representation*, 17.
11. Blackmur, "Examples of Wallace Stevens," 225.

thirties and his conviction that poetry is best at questioning and complicat-
ing reality.[12] Longenbach demonstrates in particular Stevens's strong affinity
with Kenneth Burke, who in the shrill ideological cross fire of the thirties
wrote:

> Since the body is dogmatic, a generator of belief, society might well be bene-
> fited by the corrective of a disintegrating art, which converts each simplicity
> into a complexity, which ruins the possibility of ready hierarchies, which con-
> cerns itself with the problematical, the experimental, and thus by implication
> works corrosively upon those expansionistic certainties preparing the way for
> our social cataclysms. An art may be of value purely through preventing a
> society from becoming too assertively, too hopelessly, itself.[13]

The deconstructionists' belief that "the motif of homogeneity, the theologi-
cal motif *par excellence*, is decidedly the one to be destroyed," in fact repeats,
thirty-odd years later and at the end of a similarly oppressive ideological era,
the belief that prompted Stevens for a good deal of his writing life to write
as he did—to write, that is, in search of heterogeneity, complexity, ambigu-
ity, ambivalence, pluralism, indeterminacy, paradox, aporia, provisionality,
and evasion. What Stevens set out to do much of the time was to actively
explore ways of precluding an easy yes-or-no response. In his world, conclu-
sive answers tend to stick in the throat, like the Joycean Siamese word pair
"Nes. Yo."[14]

There is an all too easily neglected sanity to this—the sort of sanity that
once prompted Graham Greene in a French interview to formulate the idea
that "doubt is fertile. It is the most important of human qualities." A simi-
lar belief informs Thomas C. Grey's refreshing analysis of Stevens's poetics
from the point of view of a pragmatist law professor, in which Grey affirms
that "Wallace Stevens can speak to the lawyer or legal theorist as a kind of
therapist for the habitual and institutional rigidities of binary thought."[15]
Whether therapeutic or not, Stevens's poetry serves to remind us, in classi-
cally pragmatist fashion, that we are more divided creatures than we often
pretend to be or care to notice and that the human invention of language,

---

12. Longenbach, *Plain Sense*, 148–75, esp. 150–51; see also Newcomb, *Literary Canons*,
86–97.
13. Quoted in Longenbach, *Plain Sense*, 98.
14. Jacques Derrida, *Positions*, 63–64; James Joyce, *Ulysses*, 430.
15. Graham Greene, "Graham Greene à l'écoute du monde," 14 (my translation); Grey,
The Wallace Stevens Case, 6–7.

as some evolutionary philosophers have argued, has made us more assertive, affirmative, and positing than the inner conflicts of our body and mind frequently warrant.[16] One of the principal (and typically modernist) effects of the doubts cast by Stevens is that they estrange us—"defamiliarize" us—from the reductive generalizations that we so easily allow to become self-fulfilling prophecies in our views of the world. In so doing, they have the potential to sharpen our sensitivity to subtlety, contamination, and complexity. Yet they need not do so automatically: for every state of doubt that is fruitful, productive, and empowering, there is one that comes untimely, throws us into despair, and stalls us. Because doubt sets the reader up against himself, the outcome is unpredictable and the coin may fall either way. This is true of all the ploys Stevens uses for raising doubt. With respect to his love of ambiguity, for instance, Longenbach usefully historicizes the phenomenon by distinguishing between different eras and political contexts: "[I]t is chastening to remember how [the New Critics' interest in ambiguity] was sometimes enlisted in a program of self-conscious conservatism; in his final years following the Second World War, Stevens himself would find the house of ambiguity a rather more comfortable than tenuous place in which to dwell. More recently, the deconstructive critics' interest in a text's radical ambiguity has been condemned for similar reasons."[17]

Longenbach judiciously talks of "the strength of Stevens's position (its skeptical and antidogmatic flexibility) and its weakness (its inability to distinguish dogmatism from a productive political commitment)."[18] Historically speaking, Stevens's efforts in the early to middle work were all toward a radical individualism at a time of overbearing collective and monolithic ideologies whose disciplinary effects he took to be oppressive. Among other things, he wanted his work to testify to the several conflicting selves that lodge within any single individual and that often remain suppressed and unrecognized. But this also means, inevitably, that the sociopolitical importance of his literary efforts has changed and continues to change in accordance with larger societal evolutions. Today, in a more individualistic and pluralistic world that has to a certain extent commodified and assimilated avant-garde experiments and accustomed itself to various strands of postmodern thinking, Stevens's poetry no longer finds itself caught so perilously in a cross fire over its intellectual and aesthetic value. It has come to offer

16. See Dennett, *Kinds of Minds*, 127–28.
17. Longenbach, *Plain Sense*, 162.
18. Ibid., 165.

exercises in the negotiation of doubt above all in a more narrowly pedagog-
ical environment, among the members of an academic community. Within
that environment, however, Stevens apparently does remain a figure with
the ability to keep unsettling and disorienting students, even to the point
of being viewed as one of the most intimidating of canonical writers.

Any attempt at setting up resistance to the reader, at unsettling and dis-
orienting him and throwing him into doubt, will automatically call forth its
own forms of counterresistance. And so the analysis of critical responses to
this poet cannot be called complete with the detection of a simple tension
between the potential pleasures of doubt and the occasional doubtfulness of
pleasure. As so often with this poet, we need to triangulate the debate by
acknowledging a third term—that of irritation. For there is no denying that
Stevens criticism, despite the principle that critics write books about poets
to whom they feel attracted, is also repeatedly marked by moments of impa-
tience. The guises such impatience and irritation can take are many (they
are frequently subcutaneous and displaced), but not so the major reasons for
irritation, which always pertain to either the issue of intelligibility or to that
of topical value. In the first case, Stevens of course shares his fate with most
other high modernists, and has done so from the start. The earliest reviews of
Harmonium, as John Timberman Newcomb demonstrates, simply swarmed
with complaints about obscurity. Seventy years and a critical industry later,
there is still no getting around the issue of obscurity, even if the boundaries
have been pushed back a long way by much concerted critical effort. As
one honest and sober-headed critic testifies: "If sometimes his poems resist
the intelligence completely, then we can either blame him or blame our-
selves, but we must not pretend that this obscurity does not exist, or that
the knotty lines and seductive puzzles are not part of the charm and power
and exasperation of Stevens's work."[19]

Exasperation there must be upon occasion, and it does not merely result
from characteristics like density, ellipsis, and discontinuity, which Stevens
shares with many another high modernist poet, but also from difficulties
that can be called more properly his own: complications pertaining to the
opacity, extravaganza, and many layers of his diction, to the short-circuiting
counterintuitiveness of his ideas, to the many ambiguities of his syntax, and
to the rarefied abstractions of, especially, the middle to late work. "One reads

---

19. Newcomb, *Literary Canons*, 52, 63; Elton Glaser, "Stevens at the Seminar Table," 72.

poetry with one's nerves," as we saw (*OP* 189), and this is one Stevensian aphorism that has at times boomeranged. Stevens, particularly the poet of the late forties whose work was collected in *The Auroras of Autumn*, can still strike us as treading a narrow line between experimentation and self-parody, until little remains, in Randall Jarrell's image, than the "passagework" of a virtuoso, a latter-day Lisztian pyrotechnics. At such times, Stevens's mastery of technique turns into a technology—a snowballing technique that becomes its own purpose and requires an investment of readerly energies sometimes out of proportion with the insights and satisfactions it brings. In this respect, it remains a telling fact that literary historians bent on painting a panoramic overview of poetic developments seldom feel comfortable venturing beyond the early writer.[20] Only those critics who are sufficiently well-versed in Stevens—most of them with at least one monograph on the poet to their name—seem to dare tackle the middle to late poetry. And even in their case, there is no simple riding of the waves, no easy surrendering to the text with an incrementally achieved pleasure: considerable toil continues to be required to attain a communicable grasp of this work. Every once in a while, therefore, a certain animosity may be seen to erupt and disrupt even the most expert and admiring of critical narratives.

The second major reason why Stevens's poetry has at times drawn caustic reactions is its (alleged) topical poverty. Again, the phenomenon has a pedigree reaching back to the earliest reception of his works. Even Marianne Moore, who stands on record as one of the first people to have championed Stevens's poetry, started out by having her doubts about the contents of *Harmonium*. Other more or less contemporary reactions expressed bemusement at what was seen as an "elaborate prestidigitation, plucking shining phrases out of a vacuum."[21] The crassest instance of a content-oriented critique, however, came more recently in the form of Marjorie Perloff's 1985 essay "Revolving in Crystal: The Supreme Fiction and the Impasse of Modernist Lyric." In this controversial essay, Perloff crudely and rather demagogically juxtaposes, on the one hand, Stevens's bibliophilia, his worries over raising and funding a poetry chair at Princeton, and "Notes toward a Supreme Fiction," and, on the other, the attack on Pearl Harbor, the fighting on the European front, and other wartime events that occurred more or less

20. Randall Jarrell, "Reflections on Wallace Stevens," 133. For literary historians, see M. L. Rosenthal, *The Modern Poets: A Critical Introduction*, 121–31, and David Perkins, *A History of Modern Poetry: Modernism and After*, 276–99.

21. For Moore, see Schulze, *Web of Friendship*, 19–23; Louis Untermeyer quoted in Newcomb, *Literary Canons*, 54.

simultaneously—thereby implying that sixty-year-old poets and insurance lawyers on the home front with no immediate war experience neverthe-less had the moral obligation to respond constantly, directly, and graphi-cally to the war. Perloff's innuendoes served an unspoken personal agenda, continuing as they did her "quixotic attempt to promote the Pound Era as a politically progressive version of modernism."[22] But insofar as they were also responsive to some of the more intrinsic qualities of Stevens's work, they could be viewed in addition as the (somewhat self-congratulatory and sensationalist) displacements of an understandable irritation that intermit-tently characterizes the reading and study of Stevens. For the gist of Perloff's argument is shared by less vituperative, more apologetic colleagues. Harold Bloom's near-rhetorical question quoted at the outset of my second chap-ter, about Stevens as "the Grand Defender of our sanctified evasions, our privileged status as the secular clergy of a society we cannot serve, let alone save" is only one of many possible examples. Stevens has often been taken to task over the narrowness or slightness of his poems' contents. The oft-quoted repartee from Robert Frost when finding himself accused by Stevens of writing poetry "about things" has become legendary. "The trouble with you is you write about bric-a-brac," Frost shot back.[23] Less snappily and more academically, there is Fredric Jameson's assessment in his single, short con-tribution to Stevens criticism:

> Any evaluation of Stevens' work must start from an initial axiological para-dox, which is surely more intense with Stevens than with any other major modernist figure. It must somehow be able to accommodate the seeming ir-reconcilable impressions of an astonishing linguistic richness on the one hand and an impoverishment or hollowness of content on the other, each of these in constant tension with one another and on various readings each seeming to draw the other into its force field and transfigure it.[24]

At the level of subject matter, more than one reader has testified to feel-ing shortchanged by Stevens. Certainly it is hard to overlook a number of glaring absences in his case, the most conspicuous of which is probably a developed interest in other people—even if we take into consideration that lyric poetry is conventionally the most solitary and inward-oriented of all

---

22. Newcomb, *Literary Canons*, 10.
23. Quoted in Brazeau, *Parts of a World*, 160 (the anecdote may be apocryphal, since our only source for it is Stevens himself).
24. Fredric Jameson, "Wallace Stevens," 11.

literary genres. "Life is an affair of people not of places," noted Stevens, adding: "But for me life is an affair of places and that is the trouble" (*OP* 185). This piece of self-analysis has been grist to the mill of at least one critic, who has taken the trouble to write a book-length study for the main purpose of lambasting Stevens's blindness to, and denial of, the interpersonal in life. Mark Halliday's *Stevens and the Interpersonal* is built on the premise that "there are omissions and distortions in [Stevens's] account of human life more drastic and pervasive than the omissions that can be cited in the work of other great poets."[25]

Real people of flesh and blood indeed rarely enter the picture in Stevens's poetic and mental world, but we should not fail to attend to the second term of the dichotomy in his self-analysis. For instead of setting up an opposition between other people and his own self or ego, Stevens in the quotation bypasses all such romantic reflexes to affirm the importance of places to him. Hence those other aspects of the poetry whose rarity is so commonly deplored by readers (*pace* Helen Vendler): emotional directness, passion, even existential urgency. These "absences"—which are, in fact, only relative invisibilities or lower frequencies—cannot but strike readers even if we gradually realize that "places" in Stevens may function as ever so many "displacements" ("The subjects of one's poems are the symbols of one's self or of one of one's selves" [*OP* 191]) and even if we are able to dig up several counterstatements proclaiming that "[l]ife is not people and scene but thought and feeling" (*OP* 196). There is, as I have argued, a reticence and coldness to Stevens that, although explicable with reference to temperamental as well as cultural and ideological factors, must meet with at least a modicum of irritation and incomprehension in an age that has accustomed itself to all manner of confessionalisms, lavishly poured-out self-expressions, and heavily mediatized displays of in-your-face sensationalism. In such a day and age, not everybody will be sympathetic to an observation of the following sort: "Emotion is thought to lie at the center of aesthetic experience. That, however, is not how the matter appears to me. If I am right, the essence of art is insight of a special kind into reality" (*OP* 1957, 238).

In fact, one final observation still has to be made, in retrospect and *ex negativo*, about "The Snow Man": that the possibilities for biographical and historical contextualization—despite attempts like that by George S. Lensing—prove to be sparse.[26] As a lyric that expresses a state of mind and

25. Mark Halliday, *Stevens and the Interpersonal*, 3.
26. Lensing, *Seasons*, 143.

describes a landscape, "The Snow Man" may offer an extreme case in this respect, yet the fact remains that Stevens, overall, does not readily lend himself to extensive appropriation in the field of the extratextual. "Stevens has been *the* poet of the 'inside' of 'literature,'" says Frank Lentricchia. "This is a place where it's very hard to open the poem up to the flow of his larger social existence."[27] And although this claim has been contested with at least some measure of success in recent years (most recently by Lensing in his *Wallace Stevens and the Seasons*), it has by now also become an *idée reçue* and as such is almost ideally corroborated by Paul Lauter's singling out Stevens as the prime embodiment of an autonomistic, ivory-tower attitude toward literature that Lauter, as the leading champion of a preeminently moral and political criticism, strongly opposes:

> What I am calling aesthetic or formalist criticism began in our time by view-ing literature as in some sense a special kind of discourse, composed by spe-cially talented individuals called poets (and, more recently, theorists), and offering unique forms of knowledge or experience, interpreted by specially-sensitized individuals called critics, whose job it was, among other things, to distinguish poetic discourse from that of science or journalism or rhetoric (propaganda). . . . The universe of aesthetic discourse, at least as it largely has come to be defined by academic critics *and by poets like Wallace Stevens as well,* is thus distinct, removed, even self-enclosed—a singular place where initiates speak mainly to one another in special languages and discuss texts in hermeneutical modes whose authenticity seems measured by their density.[28] [emphasis added]

It might even be claimed that Lentricchia's career as a Stevens critic it-self (and not always intentionally) illustrates the vicissitudes of reading this poet from a socioeconomic, historical, and/or political perspective. In order to draw up an ideological and economic context for Stevens, as he came to prefer doing after his original work in the sixties, Lentricchia practically had to ignore the poetry itself (except for an occasional poem treated synec-dochically) and redirect his attention to the journals, letters, and juvenilia.[29]

---

27. Frank Lentricchia, interview by Imre Salusinszky, 202.

28. Paul Lauter, "The Two Criticisms—or, Structure, Lingo, and Power in the Discourse of Academic Humanists," 135–36.

29. See esp. Lentricchia, *Ariel and the Police,* 136–95, and *Modernist Quartet,* 124–79. Lentricchia points to the fact that "Stevens' most distinguished critics, Harold Bloom and Helen Vendler, have led the way by proceeding as if they had never read the poet's letters and journals, or as if, having read them, they had come to the conclusion that the worldly life

Scanning the terrain of Stevens criticism in the late eighties, Steven Gould Axelrod and Helen Deese had good reason to wonder: "Whether the poet's standing can survive a paradigm shift, whether the current turn to New Historicism, Marxism, psychoanalysis, feminism, and new biography will adversely affect his prestige: these questions currently remain open to speculation."[30] More than ten years later, they are still open to speculation, but less so. The "paradigm shift"—which by now must also be taken to incorporate such trends as cultural and multicultural studies, postcolonialism, ethnic studies, LGBTQ studies, cybertheory, and globalization studies—has over the last few years taken its toll in the form of a relatively diminished overall attention to Stevens among cultural theorists, if perhaps not yet in the form of a diminished prestige among the thinned-out students of modernist poetry.[31] The latest academic evolutions have led Harold Bloom to a dystopian prediction which one need not underwrite in order to consider the appearance of the final name to be telling: "What are now called 'Departments of English,'" Bloom assures us, "will be renamed departments of 'Cultural Studies' where *Batman* comics, Mormon theme parks, television, movies, and rock will replace Chaucer, Shakespeare, Milton, Wordsworth, and Wallace Stevens."[32]

. . .

---

portrayed therein pertained to somebody else" (*Ariel and the Police*, 159; see also interview, 184). As of the mid-eighties, admittedly, several studies have redirected critical attention toward biographical and historical materials, but the biographies by Brazeau and Richardson and the studies by Milton J. Bates, Longenbach, Newcomb, Schulze, Lensing, and Angus Cleghorn collectively come close to exhausting what is of immediate importance in this sense. The two impressively researched archival studies by Filreis are fine examples of the establishment of historical contexts taking over until the interpretation of Stevens's poetry proper is of only marginal importance. And the recent biographical portrait by Sharpe, although commendable as a British outsider's synopsis of existing data, makes no claim to contribute novel findings based on original fieldwork.

30. Axelrod and Deese, "Critical Reception," 10–11.

31. Among currently prestigious trends, only postcolonialism and globalization studies would seem to offer extensive possibilities for rereading Stevens, given the poet's worldwide web of correspondents and go-betweens (from Cuba to Ceylon) and his heavily affective, idealistic, and ideological appropriation of the material and mental pieces of exoticism provided by those contacts. In his study on *Orientalism, Modernism, and the American Poem*, Robert Kern unfortunately forgoes the opportunities both of drawing amply on Stevens and of providing a sufficiently ideological-historical slant on his subject. By contrast, Lee Margaret Jenkins's recent analysis of Stevens's relationship with his Irish correspondent, Thomas MacGreevy (*Rage for Order*, 94–105), and Stephen Matterson's "'The Whole Habit of the Mind': Stevens, Americanness, and the Use of Elsewhere" provide a number of starting-points for a wider postcolonial reading of Stevens's work.

32. Bloom, *Western Canon*, 519.

The limits of reading Stevens have become clearer, then, in the last two decades. But limits are meant to be productive. We can learn from them the best way to be effective. The final question that must be raised, therefore, is: What is the most rewarding method for reading Stevens at the beginning of a new century if we want to contribute to the huge body of extant criticism? Clearly, the method must be one that continues to triangulate the pleasure, doubt, and irritation that Stevens's work characteristically induces. And it is arguably only the analytic work of close reading that, for better or worse, can keep providing us with a felt sense of the textual characteristics that produce such pleasure, doubt, and irritation. More than anything else, it is at the microlevel of the poetic text that Stevens continues to be fascinating, in the specific conflicts he enacts, the evasions and pirouettes he performs, the self-blindings he needs for producing his insights, the multiple forms of aesthetic play he engages in. The method of close reading required for de-tailing this fascination has come under much justified attack in the course of the last three decades, but the pendulum has perhaps swung too much to the other extreme, especially in today's academic market, where, as Stefan Collini notes, a critical dilemma results from the fact that "the traditionally canonical works of literature have by now been very thoroughly studied. An essential condition of launching a successful and high-profile professional career is the promotion of some striking novelty; mere intelligent endorse-ment of the more persuasive of the available interpretations of major works is not enough."[33]

Yet it *should* be enough, of course, or should be enough, at least, as the starting point for new readings, which are valid only if they build on the many persuasive interpretations already on record. That such an incremen-tal close-reading procedure can continue to be productive derives from the fact that in Stevens's case, as I have argued, *close* reading can never be *closed* reading. "It Must Change," Stevens said of the supreme fiction he envisaged, and the formula was precise: it did not say "It Must *Record* Change" or "It Must Be *about* Change." The text *itself* must change before our eyes, con-stantly, like a protean creature or like a landscape viewed through a walker's mobile eyes. Stevens's poetic thought experiments

> are not like statuary, posed
> For a vista in the Louvre. They are things chalked
> On the sidewalk so that the pensive man may see.
>   (CP 216)

33. Stefan Collini, "Interpretation terminable and interminable," 20.

This fleeting, provisional quality affects not only the interpretation of specific texts but also the extendability of such interpretations. The transition from an individual poem to the poetry overall is peculiarly treacherous in the case of Stevens. To read individual poems as ever so many synecdoches of a larger theory, attitude, or belief is often enticing in the case of an oeuvre that resonates with echoes and derives much of its power from an irrepressible aphoristic zest. Yet, synecdoche, that "most seductive of metaphors" in Paul de Man's words, is a trope that often integrates too easily, and particularly so with Stevens.[34]

This is not to say that a synthetic component must not always accompany the analytic close reading of Stevens. Texts should be framed in terms of recurrent themes, topoi, and motifs that extend beyond the individual poem. But any combination of synthetic and analytic reading in Stevens's case must walk a thin line: attempts at generalization are continuously frustrated and in need of being curbed, while too particularly detailed readings threaten to move myopically against the sweeping gestures and implications of Stevens's writing. It is no coincidence that the old paradoxical relation between the peculiar and the general in literature should have been thematized and worried by Stevens, most specifically in "Notes toward a Supreme Fiction":

> Is the poem both peculiar and general?
> There's a meditation there, in which there seems
>
> To be an evasion, a thing not apprehended or
> Not apprehended well. Does the poet
> Evade us, as in a senseless element?
>
> Evade, this hot, dependent orator,
> The spokesman at our bluntest barriers,
> Exponent by a form of speech, the speaker
>
> Of a speech only a little of the tongue?
> It is the gibberish of the vulgate that he seeks.
> He tries by a peculiar speech to speak
>
> The peculiar potency of the general,
> To compound the imagination's Latin with
> The lingua franca et jocundissima.
>
> (CP 396–97)

---

34. Paul de Man, "Semiology and Rhetoric," 11.

It is a task worth emulating in criticism: "by a peculiar speech to speak //
The peculiar potency of the general"—to gloss the fundamental abstrac-
tions of language by tracing their most concrete workings. And the inter-
stices in which this task has to be performed have already been indicated by
Stevens himself, for his own dictum is significantly split by an enjambment
that breaks up the would-be dialectical unity of the tercets and spills over
into the next stanza, thus opening up the field of inquiry.

Part Two

The Limits of Perception,
Thought, and Language

That the unknown as the source of knowledge, as the object of
thought, is part of the dynamics of the known does not permit
of denial. It is the unknown that excites the ardor of schol-
ars, who, in the known alone, would shrivel up with boredom.
We accept the unknown even when we are most skeptical.
We may resent the consideration of it by any except the most
lucid minds; but when so considered, it has seductions more
powerful and more profound than those of the known.

~Wallace Stevens, "The Irrational Element in Poetry"

Chapter 7

Infuriating Philosophers

WALLACE STEVENS'S REPUTATION, for all the different ways in which his work has been framed, continues to rest largely on the critical possibilities he offers for pondering epistemological, language-philosophical, and literary-theoretical questions. It is no coincidence that his rise on the academic firmament from the sixties onwards ran parallel with that of the interdisciplinary work that went by the awkward and somewhat dubious collective name of "theory." As John Timberman Newcomb notes, "it would hardly be an exaggeration to assert that intellectually and institutionally no single author was more important to the rise of American critical theory than Stevens." Reading Stevens from a theoretical and philosophical angle nevertheless presents unmistakable dangers, and these dangers are both categorial and specific. Frank Kermode's previously quoted warning that it is a "mistake" (literally, a *wrong take* on the subject) to read Stevens seriously as a philosopher rather than as a poet with an impressive "peripheral awareness of the important issues in philosophy" remains as valid as ever. Kermode is right to insist that "[c]ritics who systematize Stevens, work out what, under all his vatic obscurities, his tranced and sometimes impassioned mimesis of thinking, he was really getting at, have occasionally come quite close to making him a bore."[1] It is easy enough, moreover, to find support for this critical verdict from the poet himself. Some passages in the letters echo Kermode's blunt dismissal almost verbatim. This is the case, for instance, when we find Stevens wrapping up a paraphrase of "Sunday Morning" in a

1. For the term "theory," see esp. Jonathan Culler, *On Deconstruction: Theory and Criticism after Structuralism*, 8, and *Framing the Sign: Criticism and Its Institutions*, 15. Newcomb, *Literary Canons*, 207; Kermode, interview, 115; Kermode, preface, xvii.

letter of 1928 to L. W. Payne Jr. by saying: "Now these ideas are not bad in a poem. But they are a frightful bore when converted as above" (*L* 250).

Repeatedly, Stevens defined his own work in opposition to that of philosophers. "The poet must not adapt his experience to that of the philosopher," he proclaimed in the *Adagia* (*OP* 196), or, even more provocatively: "Perhaps it is of more value to infuriate philosophers than to go along with them" (*OP* 192). We should realize, however, that both poetic credos were flung in the face of a particular *type* of philosopher: the type who is committed to constructing comprehensive and coherent worldviews, the type who operates under what the pragmatic, skeptical, and elusive Stevens regarded as *Systemszwang*. One of the most telling anecdotes in this respect involves the critic Bernard Heringman, who in 1951 sent Stevens the final chapter of C. Roland Wagner's dissertation—a chapter in which reference was made to Stevens's poetry. Heringman received the following reply:

> Last Sunday I spent several hours and was able to give it careful attention, but it really requires more than that. For me it is a way of synthesizing things that I am never likely to synthesize for myself. It is always somebody else that does this sort of thing. As both you and Mr. Wagner must realize, I have no wish to arrive at a conclusion. Sometimes I believe most in the imagination for a long time and then, without reasoning about it, turn to reality and believe in that and that alone. But both of these things project themselves endlessly and I want them to do just that. (*L* 710)

Stevens's poetry, it is important to remind ourselves, belongs far less to a philosophical tradition based on logic and rationality than to an Emersonian tradition epitomized by such well-known aphorisms as "A foolish consistency is the hobgoblin of little minds" and vitalistic lines like Walt Whitman's "Do I contradict myself? / Very well then I contradict myself, / (I am large, I contain multitudes.)"[2]

In another letter to Heringman, Stevens went so far as to deny any serious influence from philosophers on his work, protesting in the following terms: "I have never studied systematic philosophy and should be bored to death at the mere thought of doing so. . . . I could never possibly have any serious contact with philosophy because I have not the memory" (*L* 636). The most immediately important word in this dismissal is clearly "systematic," though one should not overlook how the hyperbole of "bored to death" (again that

---

2. Ralph Waldo Emerson, "Self-Reliance," 265; Walt Whitman, *Song of Myself*, 246.

image) is straightaway modified by the admission of an underlying inability: "because I have not the memory." The factual tone in which Stevens declares his memory to be inept, moreover, may be taken as something of a smoke screen: we know that this was a man who had a capacious memory, and we also know that his memory was not merely anecdotally or quixotically structured but proved capable of serving him in fields of systematic knowledge-gathering and knowledge-use—he was, after all, an outstanding and highly disciplined lawyer.[3] His downplaying of philosophy, in other words, may be construed, on one level, as a testimony to his anxiety of influence and his deep-rooted desire for originality. Stevens had always been influenced by philosophers. By the end of the same letter to Heringman, for example, he refers to his former Harvard mentor, George Santayana, as "the decrepit old philosopher now living in a convent in Rome," hastening to add that of course "Santayana is not a philosopher in any austere sense" (L 637). And in Peter A. Brazeau's oral biography, *Parts of a World*, Richard Wilbur recalls that after Stevens's last public reading at Harvard, in 1952, the older poet reminisced at great length about his Harvard days and "that it was all about his teachers in philosophy."[4] It is in the works of these same philosophers also—above all, Santayana, William James, and Josiah Royce—that Frank Lentricchia in *Modernist Quartet* elaborately situates the germs of Stevens's art and ideas. In short, it was not philosophy as such against which Stevens was quick to bristle, but a specific, rigorously and logically organized manner of thinking with which the word could be associated—that of "analytic philosophy," the dominant trend in American universities at midcentury, when the reputation of the humanistic, antiessentialist, and antisystematic pragmatism that was congenial to Stevens happened to be at an all-time low.[5]

American pragmatism is in fact the philosophical tradition within which Stevens's ideas are most easily inscribed, if for no other reason than the intrinsic vagueness and polysemy of the term. "The pages of just one pragmatist work," notes Russell B. Goodman with reference to James's 1907 book *Pragmatism*, "contain at least six accounts of what pragmatism is or contains:

---

3. See esp. Grey, *The Wallace Stevens Case*, 10–21, for an authoritative assessment. We might note here Stevens's insistence to one correspondent: "I don't have a separate mind for legal work and another for writing poetry. I do each with my whole mind" (L 414).

4. Quoted in Brazeau, *Parts of a World*, 169.

5. See Russell B. Goodman, introduction to *Pragmatism: A Contemporary Reader*, 1, corroborated by Stevens's confession in a letter of November 1944: "I think that most modern philosophers are purely academic" (L 476).

a theory of truth, a theory of meaning, a philosophical temperament, an epistemology/metaphysics stressing human interest and action, a method for dissolving philosophical disputes, and a skeptical anti-essentialism." In the same book, James wrote: "The philosophy which is so important in each of us is not a technical matter; it is our more or less dumb sense of what life honestly and deeply means. It is only partly got from books; it is our individual way of just seeing and feeling the total push and pressure of the cosmos. . . . The history of philosophy is to a great extent that of a certain clash of human temperaments." Stevens, the tentative but eager and self-reliant thinker, would have willingly consented with words like these. Indeed, the inspiration for his early antisystematic and pluralistic poetic manifesto, "Thirteen Ways of Looking at a Blackbird" (1917), may well have derived in part from a classic paper published by Arthur Lovejoy in *The Journal of Philosophy* one year after James's *Pragmatism* was published, for that paper carried as a title "The Thirteen Pragmatisms."[6] Thirteen, it may be worth recalling, has always been the favorite number for representing uncontainability and irreducible plurality.

We must turn to the 1951 lecture "A Collect of Philosophy" (*OP* 267–80) to find Stevens pondering what were to him the essential divergences between poetry and philosophy, and to observe which intellectual and rhetorical moves he typically deployed to that end. Thanks to Brazeau, we know that the third and final part of this lecture gave him much trouble.[7] Having established, in the first two parts, a degree of similarity and convergence between the disciplines, he proposes to embark on a rundown of fundamental differences. His painstaking attempt is interesting not so much for its results (in terms of clarity and usefulness of its categorial distinctions, that is) as for the illustration it provides of how Stevens's antisystematical, improvisatory mind went to work on the question. The attempt shows, in particular, how his "Emersonian disregard for the syntax of thinking" breaks with the discursive rigor of well-structured argumentations.[8] "The habit of forming concepts unites [poetry and philosophy]," he suggests as a first working hypothesis, quite in tune with one of the more venerable Aristotelian traditions. "The use to which they put their ideas separates them." The difference is developed as follows:

6. Goodman, introduction, 3; James quoted in ibid., 10; for Lovejoy, see ibid.
7. Peter A. Brazeau, "'A Collect of Philosophy': The Difficulty of Finding What Would Suffice"; Wallace Stevens, "Three Manuscript Endings for 'A Collect of Philosophy.'"
8. Sharpe, *Wallace Stevens*, 179.

The philosopher searches for an integration for its own sake, as, for example, Plato's idea that knowledge is recollection or that the soul is a harmony; the poet searches for an integration that shall be not so much sufficient in itself as sufficient for some quality that it possesses, such as its insight, its evocative power or its appearance in the eye of the imagination. The philosopher intends his integration to be fateful; the poet intends his to be effective.

This is immediately slippery. The integrations of philosophy would be autotelic, while those of poetry would live off an external quality—like "insight"? This sounds like turning the tables on philosophy's principal claim for self-legitimation, and so Stevens quickly backtracks:

And yet these integrations, although different from each other, have something in common, such as, say, a characteristic of the depth or distance at which they have been found, a facture of the level or position of the mind or, if you like, of a level or position of the feelings, because in the excitement of bringing things about it is not always easy to say whether one is thinking or feeling or doing both at the same time. (*OP* 276–77)

The second half of this sentence takes issue, quite in passing and maybe unintentionally, with Eliot's then-influential "dissociation of sensibility": to Stevens, it does not prove easy at all, either in poetry or in philosophy, to disentangle and sort out thinking and feeling. By dwelling upon this aspect of the creative process shared by both disciplines, however, he is significantly shifting the debate from a cognitive and methodological to a largely psychological one. What is more, he almost immediately manages to modify and qualify his original opposition to the point of collapse. Maybe, Stevens tries again, the main difference lies in the fact that "the probing of the philosopher is deliberate" and "the probing of the poet is fortuitous." At once he chooses to swerve from the idea of depth and distance just broached:

In any case, it is misleading to speak of the depth or distance at which their integrations are found, or of the level or position of the mind or feelings, if the fact is that they probe in different spheres and if, in their different spheres, they move about by means of different motions. It may be said that the philosopher probes the sphere or spheres of perception and that he moves about therein like someone intent on making sure of every foot on the way. If the poet moves about in the same sphere or spheres, and occasionally he may, he is lightfooted. He is intent on what he sees and hears and the sense of the certainty of the presences about him is as nothing to the presences themselves. (*OP* 277)

How odd again: the philosopher's sphere appears to be that of "perception" (a word itself a little too ambiguous to bring much clarity to the discussion) rather than that of ideas and abstractions, and the philosopher walks in this sphere only as a rational Cartesian obsessed with "certainty," never apparently as a phenomenologist whose primary interest is in "what he sees and hears" and in the fickle "presences about him." The latter sort of interest is a poet's habit—at least when that same poet enters the sphere of perception, which happens only "occasionally." The drift of Stevens's argument becomes no clearer when next the "philosopher's native sphere"—perception, we have just been told—turns out to be "only a metaphysical one." And when that hypothesis, in turn, is swallowed, we begin to feel caught in the revolving door of what a more impatient reader will be inclined to call prevarication or tergiversation.

The same impatient reader will presumably experience considerable relief to find that Stevens, too, feels it is high time for wrapping up a few things, for finally raising "the question of the final cause of philosophy and the final cause of poetry" (OP 278). But the relief is short-lived, since Stevens appears unable to stop putting ideas under erasure. "The answers to this question are as countless as the definitions of philosophy and poetry," he continues. "To define philosophy and to define poetry are parts of the repertory of the mind. They are classic exercises. This could not be true if the definitions were adequate." Lines like these, at the heart of what Stevens's fugitive and wayward lecture tries to enact, have been understandably inviting to both pragmatist and poststructuralist critics, for they seem to express a basic belief in provisionality as well as in a binary thinking that can be neither upheld nor simply dispensed with. Wishing to extract himself from an intellectual stalemate, Stevens flaunts a radical relativism and fundamental theoretical undecidability, implicitly calling for the endless deferral of intellectual play. Yet this, too, proves to be but one stage in an ongoing exercise. Stevens does not leave off at relativity and undecidability. A less skeptical voice in him takes over, and-yetting one more time:

> And yet for all the different kinds of philosophy it is possible to generalize and to say that the philosopher's world is intended to be a world, which yet remains to be discovered and which, at bottom, the philosophers probably hope will always remain to be discovered and that the poet's world is intended to be a world, which yet remains to be celebrated and which, at bottom, the poets probably hope will always remain to be celebrated. (OP 278)

The elaborate rhetorical flourish of parallelism clearly signals an insistent wish to reach a climax: Stevens *would* arrive at an insight into what separates both intellectual enterprises. Or rather, more recalcitrantly, he would and he would not. He would have his own poetic celebrations, as much as the philosopher's discoveries, be temporary and transient, the finite and provisional products of time, but he would not have the underlying drive that propels all searches for celebration and discovery be diminished thereby and lose its infinitely vital, wholly insatiable character. Desire, as so often, is what ultimately inspires his thinking and writing: both the heuristic and celebratory activities of philosophers and poets are informed by a fundamental sort of human passion whose existence, no matter how aimless and sterile it can at times prove to be, was in the eyes of this poet almost always the one remaining mainstay in life. To be alive, for Stevens, was to desire, and to keep one's desire burning was to stay alive. This was his deep-rooted conviction, and it could never have been the conviction of a melioristic utilitarian or of a sociopolitically committed activist—despite all affirmations of a world to be discovered and celebrated—but only of a man whose frustrations and alienations ran so deep as to require a basic vitalizing prop otherwise void of purpose or content.

"A Collect of Philosophy" does not end with this projection of endless desire, and makes a few more surprising sidesteps in its labyrinthine progress, but the point should be taken: even for such a relatively homogeneous unit as a single lecture, Stevens's thought is well-nigh impossible to synthesize or recast in the shape of a narrative that manages to trace the development of a systematic theory. His restive and evasive theoretical quests can only be halted by the illusory dogma of the moment. That dogma of the moment, at the same time, remained what one part of him looked for and even craved, for there is a sort of transcendental power and sincerity to the moment— to the experience of the present in all its possible urgency and with all its possible needs—that cannot be so simply reduced or denied. There is always the serendipitous possibility of happening upon a delimitation of reality that would suffice, for the moment. Without this possibility, we are all condemned to lapse into indifference—a danger that constantly haunted Stevens.

Clearly, it is impossible to pin this poet's work down to a handful of ideas, opinions, and beliefs. We cannot contain his intellectual world in any systematic form and present it as some sort of developed philosophy.

Nevertheless, what remains possible, and becomes all the more useful for being possible, is to set up a conceptual *framework* within which to analyze and understand Stevens's poetic experiments. With a poet noted for his remarkable "awareness of the important issues in philosophy," no matter how "peripheral" this awareness may have been, it should be possible to circumscribe a number of these "important issues."

In his own muted and rhetorically deflected way, Stevens was an obsessive man. And his most famous obsessions were with a handful of issues: the workings of desire (in the physical as well as the idealistic senses of the word); the role and theory of poetry in a world fundamentally uprooted by the death of God and the social and political drama of Stevens's own age (including two world wars, a major economic depression, and a cold war); the need for originality (where his obsession could become so compulsive as to border on an originality neurosis); and the aesthetic and performative potential for play in poetry. But no obsession was arguably as striking, as idiomatic and poetically defining, as that with the epistemological nexus of perception, thought, and language—a nexus often parading in the post-Coleridgean guise of a reality-imagination debate. No reader can engage this poetry without a smattering of epistemology, and every literary critic has to take the risk of amateuristic dabbling in this field. More than three decades after the Stevens industry started to boom (and its bias was heavily philosophical to begin with), critical studies still open by claiming that "[t]he essence of a Stevens poem is the continuing dialogue—the ever-changing process—between the mind and the world, and the continuing quest within the mind for the appropriate language—what might be called the semiological quest—to render that dialogue."[9] More particularly, Stevens appears to have been fascinated, time and again, by the *irreducibility* of the three categories of perception, thought, and language, and by the question of their *interaction* and *(in)separability*. This fascination is itself so intimately linked with the Kantian question of conditions that it would not be too philosophically extraneous to call Stevens a poet obsessed with conditionality.

One illuminating theory of the conditions governing the relations between perception, thought, and language is offered by the French phenomenological philosopher Maurice Merleau-Ponty. It is a theory that is all the more apposite for coming from a phenomenologist, since we have already seen that one of the early philosophical labels to be stuck on Stevens's poetic

9. Schwarz, *Narrative and Representation*, 1.

ideas, however approximative, was precisely that of "phenomenological."[10] Merleau-Ponty expounds the matter as follows:

> The relation . . . of thought to language or of thought to perception is this two-way relationship that phenomenology has called *Fundierung*: the founding term, or originator— . . . language, perception—is primary in the sense that the originated is presented as a determinate or explicit form of the originator, which prevents the latter from reabsorbing the former, and yet the originator is not primary in the empiricist sense and the originated is not simply derived from it, since it is through the originated that the originator is made manifest.[11]

The issue described here has affinities with Derrida's theory of iterability as discussed in Chapter 4. Once again the debate hinges on the difference between "necessary conditions" and "sufficient reasons" and on the complication that results from the fact that the two should be kept apart. Language and perception, argues Merleau-Ponty (and for present purposes we suspend the question of the justifiability of this argument), are both necessary conditions for thought, but they are not sufficient reasons for it: they do not in themselves produce or warrant any concrete thoughts. They precede thought in such a way that thought can never fully encompass perception or language, since thought is determined by these, or developed on the basis of these. But the dependence is mutual and not unidirectional: perception and language themselves derive their foundational status only from thought and are themselves manifested only through thought.

It is not difficult to see how a philosopher originally schooled in phenomenology like Derrida was able to extend this irresolvable ambivalence and interaction into a theory of difference, or even, suspending the notion irresolvably in time and in between activity and passivity, of "differance." From the very first, Derrida emphasized the antitheological and antihomogenizing nature of his philosophical enterprise.[12] Any attempt at inscribing a

---

10. The most prominent instances of this link with phenomenology are J. Hillis Miller, *Poets of Reality*; Hines, *Later Poetry of Wallace Stevens*; Jeanne Ruppert, "Nature, Feeling, and Disclosure in the Poetry of Wallace Stevens"; Bevis, *Mind of Winter*, 110–11; Leonard and Wharton, *Fluent Mundo*, 83–102; and Paul Kenneth Naylor, "'The Idea of It': Wallace Stevens and Edmund Husserl." As recently as 1997, critics were still describing Stevens as a poet who moved from the romantic to the phenomenological (Voros, *Notations of the Wild*, 11).
11. Maurice Merleau-Ponty, *Phenomenology of Perception*, 394.
12. Derrida, *Positions*, 63–64.

constitutive difference *within* (the experience of) reality is ultimately anti-originary in that it disallows a single point of origin where necessary condition and sufficient reason are conflated—a conflation that is precisely typical of monotheistic worldviews. (That the word *originary* itself has been popularized in academic jargon almost single-handedly by Derrida only serves to underscore the importance of Kantian questions of conditionality in his work.) Both Merleau-Ponty and Derrida, we could say, have taught us the dangers of privileging any of the entangled, interacting, and even mutually productive categories of perception, thought, and language. The fact that Stevens, in his own poetic way, often highlighted these dangers, entanglements, and interactions helps to explain why critics have moved with remarkable ease from Stevens the phenomenologist to Stevens the deconstructionist.

The middle ground from which Stevens pushed out to the frontiers of the perception-thought-language nexus shares a lot with Kantian, Nietzschean, phenomenological, and pragmatist topoi and perspectives—in particular, the topos of perspectivity itself. Reality to Stevens tended to mean reality *as perceived*. "Things seen are things as seen," he proclaimed in his *Adagia* (*OP* 188), and in "The Pure Good of Theory" he insisted: "It is never the thing but the version of the thing" (*CP* 332). In this perspectivist attitude much of his philosophical modernity resides, although it is a modernity that has been nearly defeated by its own success, since we have come to assimilate the idea of perspectivism (and of its descendant, social constructivism) so widely in the humanities as to render it inconspicuous and seemingly "natural." "It is possible," Stevens wrote at the outset of one of his most theoretically sophisticated poems, "Description without Place," "that to seem—it is to be" (*CP* 339). And by entertaining this hypothesis he was merely unrolling another stretch of a long intertextual thread that reaches back at least to his own boisterous injunction in "The Emperor of Ice-Cream": "Let be be finale of seem" (*CP* 64). To seem is to be *to a perceiver*, and Stevens, early and late, was fascinated by the freedom (both opportunity and danger) that the human mind is left with in the act of perceiving, as well as by the strictures that operate upon (both limiting and enabling) this freedom. A. Walton Litz describes him as a poetic Ernst Gombrich, who saw the artist "as a creator of *schema* for apprehending the physical."[13] It is part of Stevens's modernist moment that he should have opened "An Ordinary Evening in New Haven" by calling houses "difficult objects" (*CP* 465), that he should

13. Litz, "'Compass and Curriculum,'" 239.

have talked in that same poem of the "difficulty of the visible" (CP 474), and composed what reads like a variation on the famous concluding question to Yeats's "Among School Children" ("How can we know the dancer from the dance?"):

> Suppose these houses are composed of ourselves,
> . . . .
> So much ourselves, we cannot tell apart
> The idea and the bearer-being of the idea.[14]
>
> (CP 466)

Starting out from his perspectivist middle ground, Stevens was nevertheless given to exploring the various limit situations of the perception-thought-language nexus—limit situations that are, not coincidentally, crucial to the act of writing. And since that nexus is triadic, those limit situations are themselves of three kinds. Each one of the three interacting terms offers the possibility for autonomization or hypostatization, to the point where they may try to swallow the other two whole. Stevens liked to experiment with such situations—instances where limits come close to being lifted up or falling away, thus paradoxically announcing themselves:

> One of the limits of reality
> Presents itself in Oley when the hay,
> Baked through long days, is piled in mows. It is
> A land too ripe for enigmas, too serene.
>
> (CP 374)

The first manifestation of a limit situation, illustrated by these lines from "Credences of Summer," has to do with what we have earlier touched upon in the context of "The Snow Man." It occurs whenever Stevens falls back on the irreducibility of the real and seeks to express a sense of full presence and satisfaction in immediate reality or, as his color symbolism would have it, in "green's green apogee" (CP 373). At such times, he tends to be

---

14. Allusions to Yeats's "Among School Children" can arguably also be heard in lines like "He is the heroic / Actor and act but not divided" from "Examination of the Hero in a Time of War" (CP 279) and in the scene with the "negresses" brought in "to dance, / Among the children" in "The Auroras of Autumn" (CP 415). Surprisingly, not even Harold Bloom has recognized the intertextual possibilities of this link, though we know Yeats to have been one of the few writers from whom Stevens explicitly borrowed lines (in "Page from a Tale" [CP 421–23]; see Lensing, *Poet's Growth*, 224, and Jenkins, *Rage for Order*, 123–24).

impressed by, or attracted to, the possibility of an unmediated perception of the world. He then seeks to cancel the conflict between perception and thought (which in this case includes language) by deactivating one side, that of thought (and language). But inevitably this also means that he moves, in Jerry Fodor's terms, "very close to the edge of what we know how to talk about at all sensibly," since "perception is a hybrid of what the senses are given and what the mind infers. . . . Granting something unconceptualised that is simply *given* to the mind in experience has generally been supposed to be the epistemological price one has to pay for an ontology that takes the world to be not itself mind-dependent."[15] Analogously with how the category of the "real" functions in Lacanian psychoanalysis—as something that falls outside the symbolic order and whose existence can only be affirmed, not further discussed—Stevens's rock-bottom reality tends to show itself in its irreducible alterity as that residual other of thought and language which cannot ultimately be incorporated in terms of knowing or describing. In "On Poetic Truth," a text by H. D. Lewis which Stevens considered so fascinating that he transcribed it for his own use (thereby misleading Samuel French Morse into including it in the first edition of *Opus Posthumous*), this otherness of reality is precisely central to the argument. What we want from art, argues Lewis, is to be brought into contact with "reality as it impinges on us from the outside, the sense that we can touch and feel a solid reality which does not wholly dissolve itself into the conceptions of our own minds. . . . And the wonder and mystery of art . . . is the revelation of something 'wholly other' by which the inexpressible loneliness of thinking is broken and enriched" (*OP* 1957, 236–37).

The attachment to "the wonder and mystery of art" that consists in breaking the shell of the self and striking out to something "wholly other" (like nature, or in George S. Lensing's most recent book, the four seasons) was undoubtedly great in Stevens. But it was not a naive attachment. For all his longing to invoke the real, material world in its untainted alterity, Stevens simultaneously showed himself to be exceptionally sensitive to the fact that we ultimately cannot have unmediated access to that something other which exists in excess of all intentionality and interpretation. And so the earnestness and eagerness of his representations of an immediately, transparently perceived reality treacherously fluctuate from poem to poem. The fact that the (re)presentation of the *fondant* (perception) can happen only

15. Jerry Fodor, "Encounters with Trees," 10–11.

by way of the *fondé* (thought, here again including language) produced an irresolvable irony that left Stevens in a predicament he sometimes tried to efface and suppress, but more often allowed to be inscribed in his rhetorically self-conscious texts. To what extent these textual forms of self-consciousness were intentional is frequently hard to tell and often depends on the way we are willing to color the tone of the poems. But on the whole, Stevens was only too aware that if language and thought could be deactivated experientially, they could not therefore be deactivated performatively: they are the indispensable tools for the communication of this deactivation; they are the means for the simple attestation of unmediated perception. The furthest a poet can go is to use suspension points (and Stevens, as I have argued elsewhere, was one of the two prominent high modernist poets in English, the other being Hart Crane, to have made repeated and astonishingly rich use of that typographical device).[16] Falling back on the stop-stand-and-listen sign of suspension points and the concomitant rhetorical ploy of aposiopesis was the most extreme maneuver he had at his disposal for conjuring up moments when the senses tried to take over entirely from the perceiving subject, as in the following instances:

> Look, Master,
> See the river, the railroad, the cathedral . . .
>
> (CP 227)

> Here, being visible is being white,
> Is being of the solid of white, the accomplishment
> Of an extremist in an exercise . . .
>
> (CP 412)

> The leaves cry . . . One holds off and merely hears the cry.
> (OP 123)

William W. Bevis's case for seeing Stevens as somebody who meticulously tried to represent a meditative state of consciousness works as an important reminder of the insufficiency of epistemological readings on those occasions when Stevens's poems seem to be deactivating thought and language. The poet recollecting his meditative tranquilities in writing was a variously divided person, alternately contented and calm, restive and skeptical, or more

---

16. Bart Eeckhout, "When Language Stops . . . Suspension Points in the Poetry of Hart Crane and Wallace Stevens."

playful and ironical. Yet Bevis's de-epistemologizing argument should not be pushed to such an extreme as to blind ourselves to the many ways in which Stevens's self-conscious rhetoric—perhaps at a different level from that of the attempt to report meditative experience—is replete with self-undercutting scenes.

In sharp contrast with the deactivation of thought (which may be interpreted as the deactivation of all cortical activity), we find in Stevens's work several forms of extreme idealism in which the thinking mind appears to encompass or envelop the entire world. Writing in his usual paternal tone to José Rodríguez Feo in 1945, Stevens insisted that "there is no passion like the passion of thinking which grows stronger as one grows older, even though one never thinks anything of any particular interest to anyone else. Spend an hour or two a day even if in the beginning you are staggered by the confusion and aimlessness of your thoughts" (L 513). It was precisely the strength of this passion for thinking that called forth countermoments of complete surrender to perception, for Stevens knew only too well how dangerous the aimless and fruitless confusions of a spinning mind could be. "The mind is the most terrible force in the world," he wrote in his *Adagia*, "principally in this that it is the only force that can defend us against itself" (OP 199). One of the most arresting manifestations of Stevens's inclination to autonomize, or even ontologize, thought (or the inventions of the mind; we are not, here, in a cognitive-scientific realm where we may always rigorously distinguish between categories) was his long-standing interest in fiction and the possible fictionality of the world.

The word *fiction*—a "terribly equivocal word," according to Derrida[17]—appears for the first time in Stevens's poetry in the opening line of *Harmonium*'s "A High-Toned Old Christian Woman," with its resounding prolepsis: "Poetry is the supreme fiction, madame" (CP 59). The Christian addressee of that poem reminds us of the soil from which Stevens's further theorizations sprang: a concern with the death of the gods, associated with Nietzsche's famous proclamation. Significantly, it was Nietzsche who provided Frank Kermode with the first epigraph to his chapter on "Fictions" in *The Sense of an Ending*, where the philosopher is quoted as saying: "What can be thought must certainly be a fiction." The epigraph immediately following Nietzsche's was borrowed, just as significantly, from Stevens, to whom

17. Derrida, "'Strange Institution,'" 49.

Kermode's whole book was a disguised "love-letter." This second epigraph concerns "the nicer knowledge of / Belief, that what it believes in is not true." The link between Stevens and Nietzsche has often been made, and B. J. Leggett has gone to great lengths in comparing the two writers' respective views of fiction. But Nietzsche stands in a longer Kantian tradition, which he radicalized and polemicized and which in Stevens's own day was continued by phenomenology. Paul Kenneth Naylor, for example, quotes Husserl as saying that "the element which makes up the life of phenomenology as of all eidetic science is 'fiction.'" In this perspectivist and subjectivist tradition, it became possible to construct fiction as a "transcendental" illusion—a necessary illusion, that is, not a delusion, or, as Rudolf Boehm explains the concept, an appearance that does not disappear when seen through.[18]

Stevens can be situated in that tradition, if perhaps only on the margins of it, in that eccentric, nonphilosophical realm where less systematically conceptualized, more improvisatory and intrinsically poetic concerns contaminate the notion of fiction. The following lines from *Adagia*, for example, which are among the most-quoted of his many obiter dicta, must be read as a post-Coleridgean defense of the imagination mixed in with a wider philosophical claim about the necessarily fictional structure of reality: "The final belief is to believe in a fiction, which you know to be a fiction, there being nothing else. The exquisite truth is to know that it is a fiction and that you believe in it willingly" (*OP* 189). Having made this claim, Stevens was able to write his best-known long poem, "Notes toward a Supreme Fiction," providing for it the following instructively confusing explanation:

> One evening, a week or so ago, a student at Trinity College came to the office and walked home with me. We talked about this book ["Notes"]. I said that I thought that we had reached a point at which we could no longer really

18. Epigraphs: Frank Kermode, *The Sense of an Ending: Studies in the Theory of Fiction*, 34; "love-letter": Kermode, interview, 113; Leggett, *Early Stevens*, 213–52; Naylor, " 'Idea of It,' " 47; Rudolf Boehm, *Aan het einde van een tijdperk: Filosofisch-economische aantekeningen*, 20. Freud, in *The Future of an Illusion*, likewise drew a distinction between illusions, on one hand, and factual errors and delusions about reality, on the other (30–31). Stevens, unsurprisingly, took a strong interest in the notion of illusion as well. He picked up Freud's question of whether there could possibly be a science of illusions in his own essay "Imagination as Value" (*NA* 139) and wrote in a 1942 letter to Hi Simons: "The use of the word illusion suggests the simplest way to define the difference between escapism in a pejorative sense and in a nonpejorative sense: that is to say: it is the difference between elusion and illusion, or benign illusion. Of course, I believe in benign illusion" (*L* 402).

believe in anything unless we recognized that it was a fiction. The student said that that was an impossibility, that there was no such thing as believing in something that one knew was not true. It is obvious, however, that we are doing that all the time. There are things with respect to which we willingly suspend disbelief; if there is instinctive in us a will to believe, or if there is a will to believe, whether or not it is instinctive, it seems to me that we can suspend disbelief with reference to a fiction as easily as we can suspend it with reference to anything else. There are fictions that are extensions of reality. There are plenty of people who believe in Heaven as definitely as your New England ancestors and my Dutch ancestors believed in it. But Heaven is an extension of reality. (*L* 430)

In this excerpt from a letter to Henry Church (which finds Stevens proceeding to dismiss Nietzsche in ambiguous terms well analyzed by Leggett),[19] Stevens typically vacillates between broader and narrower conceptions of fiction. This leads him to contradict his provocative opening proposition that we can really believe in something only if we recognize it to be a fiction—a proposition we might gloss as: only if we recognize it to be a construction and structuration by the mind, an experience of the world that is always, necessarily, mentally and subjectively shaped, not simply imprinted from the outside on a blank slate. Stevens immediately undercuts the universalizing sweep of this idea by moving on to the particularity of "things with respect to which we willingly suspend disbelief" and by winding up with the classic opposition between reality and narrowly defined fictions, of which there are some that can be seen as "extensions of reality."

To realize the full range of Stevens's poetic exploitations of the concept of fiction, we should in fact turn to etymology. Stevens was an addict of the Lewis and Short *Latin Dictionary*,[20] and so would have known that *fiction* derives from *fingo* (infinitive *fingere*) and that this verb in general means "to form, shape, fashion, frame, make," as well as "to form mentally or in speech, to represent in thought, to imagine, conceive, think, suppose" and "to contrive, devise, invent, feign," and is additionally able to take more specific meanings like "to make into something or in a certain manner" or "to form by instruction, to instruct, teach, train." All of these meanings went into his use of the word as it moved from context to context. He conceived of *fiction* as an umbrella term for the entertaining of hypotheses that explored the inescapability, primacy, even self-sufficiency of the mind (or consciousness,

19. Leggett, *Early Stevens*, 47ff.
20. Cook, *Poetry, Word-Play, and Word-War*, 40.

or thought) in our human experience of the world—the only experience available to us.

Stevens's concern with fictionality runs deep in his work, and one of the most pervasive lexical indices signaling its constancy is that of the conjunctive cluster "as if."[21] In the concordance to his work, the cluster figures no less than 113 times. It is, we might quip, as if Stevens possessed a special feeling of *as if*—a feeling that accorded well with William James's remark from his epoch-making chapter on "The Stream of Thought": "We ought to say a feeling of *and*, a feeling of *if*, a feeling of *but*, and a feeling of *by*, quite as readily as we say a feeling of *blue* or a feeling of *cold*. Yet we do not: so inveterate has our habit become of recognizing the existence of the substantive parts alone, that language almost refuses to lend itself to any other use."[22] As a poet, Stevens was ceaselessly out to undercut the priority that our linguistically molded minds tend to attribute to the substantive (the material, the solidified, the static, or, in one of his preferred shapes, the statuesque) by foregrounding the role of grammatical connectives and shifters (the immaterial, the fluid, the dynamic, the relational, the provisional, the hypothetical, the transitory).

Yet the phrase "as if" does more in Stevens than function as a token of the skeptically qualifying and dynamic mind: it tends to open up the world to observability as well. As Wolfgang Iser argues: "Self-disclosure of fictionality puts the world represented in brackets, thereby indicating the presence of a purpose which turns out to be observability of the world represented." Stevens's insistent as-ifness is part of his modernity, situating us at the heart of a dynamic and open-ended heuristic process that conditions and shapes our human self-consciousness. We cannot even begin to understand the world unless we fall back on as-if reasonings and approach nature by way of what Daniel C. Dennett calls "approximating confabulation." For Stevens,

---

21. The recurrent "as ifs" in Stevens, increasing in frequency over time, are at the heart of Jacqueline Vaught Brogan's study *Stevens and Simile: A Theory of Language*. The conjunction has inevitably spurred critics into establishing intertextual extensions, the most eye-catching of which is with Hans Vaihinger's *Die Philosophie des "Als Ob"* (The philosophy of "as if"), a turn-of-the-century classic dug up by, among others, Frank Kermode (see esp. *Sense of an Ending*, 39–41, and preface, xvii; also Frank Doggett, "This Invented World: Stevens' 'Notes toward a Supreme Fiction,'" 20, and *Stevens' Poetry of Thought*, 105–6, 185). Vaihinger himself feeds into a longer tradition that runs from Kant through Nietzsche, though he appears to have written independently of the latter. Freud, in *The Future of an Illusion*, dismissed Vaihinger as patent nonsense (28–29), and both Joan Richardson (*Wallace Stevens: The Later Years, 1923–1955*, 58–62) and James Longenbach (*Plain Sense*, 287–88) have analyzed Stevens's familiarity with, and response to, the Vaihinger-fiction-Freud connection.

22. William James, *The Principles of Psychology*, 159.

as Lee Edelman wittily points out, " 'is' is only made available to us as 'as.' "[23]
Or in the language of "An Ordinary Evening in New Haven": the world is
only available to us "in the intricate evasions of as" (CP 486).

Although today's scientific cognitive and neurolinguistic evidence sug-
gests that thought and language are clearly divided from each other and
thinking is far less a matter of words and sentences than writers and aca-
demics in text-oriented disciplines are inclined to believe,[24] in Stevens's
case the extremes of idealizing and hypostatizing thought, on one hand,
and language, on the other, are often difficult to disentangle. What is clear,
though, and what has been noted over and over again, is that Stevens's texts
are more than usually self-referential and that the question of the limits of
language was often at some level involved in his writing. With the possible
exception of Gertrude Stein, he is the most "textual" and (meta)linguistic
of high modernist poets in English (and for that reason, he stands as a father
figure to many postmodernist poets and critical theorists).

Language, as the sometime popularity of deconstruction has shown, has an
extraordinary potential for being idealized and hypostatized. Its "invention,"
after all, is the great watershed in the evolution of the human species. As
Steven Pinker notes: "People can be forgiven for overrating language. Words
make noise, or sit on a page, for all to hear and see. Thoughts are trapped
inside the head of the thinker."[25] During the past century, when modernist
artists started focusing their attention on the formal aspects of art-making
and, no less important, Saussurian linguistic theory began to foreground the
arbitrariness of the sign, the inclination to let language fall back on itself
became stronger than ever. Stevens did not know the structuralist jargon
we use to talk of the radical alienability of signifiers from signifieds and of
signifieds from referents, but that did not prevent him from having his own
sense of these things: a similar insight, for instance, underlies the polysemous
title of one of his most crucial language-philosophical poems, "Description
without Place." His work offers multiple illustrations of the heavily ideal-
istic notion that things not described do not exist (or that describing the
world actually creates it), as well as of the Hegelian idea that no concrete

23. Iser, "Feigning in Fiction," 220; Dennett, *Kinds of Minds*, 127; Edelman, *Homograph-
esis*, 141.
24. Steven Pinker, *The Language Instinct: The New Science of Language and Mind*, 55–82.
25. Ibid., 67.

empirical experience or phenomenon can be communicated, since language is essentially general and abstract. The related notion that we are captives of language (the strongest possible form of limitation) can also be found upon occasion. Such language-philosophical ideas frequently underlie his alternatively exasperating and exhilarating moments of blatant, laconic circularity in formulation and imagery.

What is more, the philosophical limits of language were not the only ones with which Stevens was preoccupied. Margaret Dickie calls him a poet who was more than usually given "to arrest attention at the letter itself, both as a character of the alphabet and as a material token." The limits of the materiality of language, too, were repeatedly tested by him. This could take the moderate form of a search for exotic and foreign scraps of diction or of an at times outré sesquipedalophilia—two stylistic habits that signaled a high verbal and linguistic self-consciousness and were meant to be in large part self-sufficient. But occasionally, Stevens went further and struck out for the most distant frontiers of verbal sense—to those regions where sense passes into nonsense and only acoustical materiality seems to remain. Alison Rieke, in *The Senses of Nonsense*, studies this aspect most extensively, following the poet into the Joycean realm of "ithy oonts," "tunk-a-tunk-tunk," "ti-rill-a-roo," and "hoobla-hoobla-hoobla-how," where he was "purposefully manipulating language at its limits to confound his readers." For strategical reasons, Eleanor Cook avoids the word "nonsense" in her own *Poetry, Word-Play, and Word-War in Wallace Stevens*, but she does an even more convincing job of showing the many ways in which this poet sprang the bounds and straitjacket of hackneyed denotation. "More even than Joyce," she provocatively claims, "[Stevens] can make us hear the words we have inherited in a new way." His "sophistication in etymological word-play and word-war is extraordinary. So is his multilingual punning."[26] We would be much amiss, in other words, to restrict Stevens's exploration of the limits of language to a metapoetic realm of philosophical ideas only: it is just as diversely and richly worked into his handling of words at the most immediately poetic level.

These are, in a nutshell, the limits of perception, thought, and language that constitute the core dynamic out of which Stevens's poems are generated

26. Dickie, *Lyric Contingencies*, 11; Alison Rieke, *The Senses of Nonsense*, 96; Cook, *Poetry, Word-Play, and Word-War*, xii, 7.

and to which they continually return. A critical framework of the kind just elaborated contributes to our understanding and appreciation of the work even if, and precisely because, such a systematized overview was constantly resisted by Stevens himself. Indeed, we should not forget this element of tactical resistance. It was above all by resisting the limitations of limits at the same time that he established them—by problematizing identities, if you like, in the very process of defining them—that Stevens betrayed his obsession with our human finitude. When pressured, for instance, to elucidate the notion of "supreme fiction," he typically preferred to be evasive by coming up with his own version of Joyce's notorious (though probably apocryphal) claim that *Ulysses* is so filled with "enigmas and puzzles that it will keep the professors busy for centuries arguing over what I meant."[27] Stevens merely substituted a different brand of scholar for the Joycean professor: "The next thing for me to do will be to try to be a little more precise about this enigma. I hold off from even attempting that because, as soon as I start to rationalize, I lose the poetry of the idea. . . . As I see the subject, it could occupy a school of rabbis for the next few generations" (L 435). And almost twelve years later, pressed by another critic, Stevens was still adamant: "That a man's work should remain indefinite is often intentional. For instance, in projecting a supreme fiction, I cannot imagine anything more fatal than to state it definitely and incautiously. . . . I don't mean to try to exercise the slightest restraint on what you say. Say what you will. But we are dealing with poetry, not with philosophy. The last thing in the world that I should want to do would be to formulate a system" (L 863–64).

Poetry, Stevens was convinced, is not meant to offer an awkwardly elaborate and circumstantial, somewhat frivolously attired, repetition of philosophical tenets and reasonings. It is not a literally misplaced illustration of philosophical ideas. Although it can contain such ideas—and even does so lavishly in his case—it assimilates them to its own imaginative purposes and sets them to work on a poetic level. As early as his Harvard years, Stevens protested (in the margin of his copy of James Russell Lowell's letters) against the idea that poetry should "in some way convey a truth of philosophy" when he observed: "I like my philosophy smothered in beauty and not the opposite."[28] The critical longing for a minimal systematicity in coming to terms with Stevens's explorations of the limit situations of perception,

27. Quoted in Don Gifford, Ulysses *Annotated,* v.
28. Quoted and reproduced in Milton J. Bates, "Stevens' Books at the Huntington," 49, 50.

thought, and language can never escape a tension with Stevens's own poetic project, rightly inscribed in the native tradition of Emersonian pragmatism by critics like Richard Poirier. That tradition "depends on certain key, repeated terms," says Poirier. "But to a wholly unusual degree it never allows any of these terms to arrive at a precise or static definition. Their use is conducive less to clarification than to vagueness." As readers who want to get a purchase on these repeated terms in Stevens's poetry, we are forced to negotiate between pleasure, doubt, and irritation as we shuttle back and forth between positions, cross boundaries, slide from perspective to perspective, watch the dance of the signifiers, and enjoy the aesthetic play of the text. A certain cognitive dissonance, after all, is one of the major motivations for appropriating cultural artifacts, and the act of shifting and shuttling is simply inherent in dealing with the question of limits: the condition of liminality, as Angus Fletcher emphasizes, is precisely a condition of betweenness.[29]

The following chapters are organized so as to deepen our understanding of that condition of betweenness in Stevens's poetry. From a methodological point of view, they are even subject to that condition themselves, for they try both to credit the specific performativity of Stevens's irreducibly concrete extemporizations and to take into account the powerful human need for binding specific readings together under larger, synthetic rubrics. My strongest emphasis, admittedly, will be on the detailed reading of a handful of shorter lyrics that are particularly well-suited for showing the knottedness and contaminations of the perception-thought-language nexus that we so hastily cut up for the sake of analysis. To study individual poems is, I would argue, crucial for appreciating the different, complex ways in which Stevens's poetic efforts at limitation not only succeed in clarifying boundaries but also require our constant attention to the necessity of traversing these boundaries. This bifurcation means that the conceptual dividing lines among the ensuing chapters are necessarily porous. My particular clustering of poems cannot escape the largely associative, unrigorous principle expressed in the poet's motto "Thought tends to collect in pools" (OP 196). Yet if the metaphor used by Stevens is a treacherously organic one, it nonetheless offers an image of delineation. Each of the following four chapters is thus intended to test what is limited by limitation in his poetry and then folded over again: in the effort to separate the painterly gaze from various domains of immediacy (Chapter 8); in the effort to sort out our "sense" of reality from

---

29. Poirier, *Poetry and Pragmatism*, 129; Fletcher, foreword, xvii.

what the senses convey as well as from the translations of these impressions by our sense-making brain (Chapter 9); in the effort to disentangle mimesis from music and description from elucidation and artifice (Chapter 10); and in the effort, finally, to trace the "other" that is implicitly circumscribed by the identifications of metaphor (Chapter 11).

Chapter 8

Between Matter and Mind

"NOTHING IS ITSELF TAKEN ALONE. Things are because of interrelations or interactions," Stevens famously mused in his *Adagia* (*OP* 189). The idea for this epigram may have originated with Emerson, in particular with the poem "Each and All," where Stevens's literary father pondered how "All are needed by each one; / Nothing is fair or good alone."[1] But the intellectual ramifications of the epigram extend far beyond this single intertextual connection. One of the possible ways of understanding the statement is by reformulating it as follows: no thing is "the thing itself." Things are differential and relational; they can come to exist only through interrelations and interactions with their environments, including, above all, the interested minds that perceive them. This wider idea, arguably, is the point of departure for what has come to be constructed as Stevens's near-compulsive involvement with "the thing itself." The intellectual antecedents of that involvement are so easily traced that they have been summoned onto the stage time and again in Stevens criticism. As a philosopheme, "the thing itself" is shopworn; it has been around since Kant's *Ding an sich,* and in fact for some time longer: since Berkeley's "things in themselves" and since the birth of modern science, which based its ideal of objectivity precisely on forsaking all human intentionality and surrendering to the thing itself.

Almost too conspicuously, the so-called thing itself makes a couple of literal appearances in Stevens's work. It is even referred to pontifically in its German format when Crispin, the verbal prankster, sheds his old self in the first stage of his poetic voyage from an Old to a New World and marvels, "Here was the veritable ding an sich, at last" (*CP* 29). Thirty years

1. Ralph Waldo Emerson, "Each and All," 258.

157

later, in "The Course of a Particular," Stevens is still writing of "the thing / Itself" (OP 124), and the most eye-catching appearance of the phrase in his oeuvre occurs in the concluding title in The Collected Poems, "Not Ideas about the Thing but the Thing Itself" (CP 534). Countless are the examples, moreover, of variant phrases, as when the speaker of "Credences of Summer" enjoins us (and prompts himself): "Let's see the very thing and nothing else. / Let's see it with the hottest fire of sight" (CP 373).

William W. Bevis remarks that such appearances—and the obsessive theme they signal—"[have] naturally been traced by Western intellectuals (and Stevens) to sources in Kant." Kenneth Burke was one of the first cases in point. "Is it not a bit ironical," he asked Allen Tate in a letter of November 1944, "to see a supposedly fairly relatively new poet like Stevens trying to explain his supposedly fairly relatively new esthetic by discovering the Kantian line-up somewhat more than 150 years late? I think you'll have to let more philosophy into your criticism, if only to avoid its coming in thus unnoticed, and naively."[2] The warning sounded by Burke was valid insofar as Stevens's poetry, as I have indicated, is rightly famous for providing a treacherous admixture of specificity and generality (or particularity and universality), which renders it peculiarly susceptible to philosophical contextualizations and cross-fertilizations. It was even valid insofar as philosophical concepts already have a tendency to sneak in by the back door during literary discussions, whether invited or not. Yet its validity was at the same time importantly limited. There is obviously a lot more to Stevens's ideas, beliefs, and attitudes about the thing itself than epistemology. Criticism with a particularly theoretical agenda runs the risk of forgetting how happy this poet was to exploit the many poetic ambiguities made available to him by the philosophical overtones of both term and concept.

From a nonphilosophical angle, it may be argued, the thing itself functions as an important, even a necessary, poetic illusion for Stevens—as it did for so many other high modernists. This claim is made convincingly by Douglas Mao in a recent book on the modernist obsession with objects. Although Mao's book is mostly concerned with the ideological analysis of literary responses to a material culture, it begins with the observation that the "feeling of regard for the physical object as object—as not-self, as not-subject, as most helpless and will-less of entities, but also as fragment of Being, as solidity, as otherness in its most resilient opacity—seems a peculiarly

2. Bevis, Mind of Winter, 8; Burke quoted in Filreis, Actual World, 97.

twentieth-century malady or revelation." In Stevens's case, what the object qua object was meant to accommodate appears to have been above all a painterly desire to see the world as immediately and originally as possible, to see it with eyes cleansed of all the darkening and dulling films of habituated sight. The poetic-cum-painterly quest for the thing itself, in such instances, works aesthetically to *intensify* rather than epistemologically to dismantle and strip down reality. In other words, the thing itself on such occasions is not so much that phantom excluded by Kant as inevitably beyond our ken as it corresponds to Kant's (and, we might add, Nietzsche's, William James's, and Husserl's) perspectival thing-as-perceived. The issue, then, turns out to have less to do with tracing the limits of epistemology than with pursuing tangential experiences: various possible states of consciousness, various possible qualities of perception, and various possible modes of projecting desire. Dwelling on objects is thus often a matter of safeguarding the individuality of such experiences. As Mao insists, a typically "modernist vision of the predicament of the object" resides precisely in the contemporary conviction that "the particular, the concrete, and the auratic were threatened as never before by habits of generalization and abstraction serving a newly triumphant science. The reading of the discrete thing as representative or symptom of anything other than itself, that is, could become unsettling to the degree that it seemed to partake of the subordination of individuals (humans *and* objects) to system, a process that for the modernists as for their Romantic predecessors represented the essential direction of modernity at its most destructive."[3]

In this chapter, I would like to attend to three emblematic ways in which Stevens sets out to "paint" the thing itself, even though I realize that in this particular poet's case the "habits of generalization and abstraction" decried by so many of his Anglo-American high modernist contemporaries were never easily countered or assuaged. In fact, the verb *paint* itself immediately proves to be characteristically problematic, since all three instances I intend to look at somehow display the metaphorical character of this activity of "painting" in poetry. Each poem in its own way involves the setting up of the poet's *resistance* to the act—or to particular ideologies—of painting. Stevens, we should recall, was a poet of resistance. Much as he resisted philosophical appropriations at the same time that he invited them, he also resisted alignments with painting even as he shared a number of painterly concerns. Two

---

3. Mao, *Solid Objects*, 4, 6–7.

poems of 1938, "Study of Two Pears" and "The Latest Freed Man," and one of 1940, "Landscape with Boat," illustrate this resistant interest in painterly takes on the thing itself. Belonging as they do to the most perspectival of Stevens's volumes, *Parts of a World,* they also develop three different perspectives on the subject. In the first poem, we see Stevens putting on the guise of a painter only to destabilize the painterly attempt at representing the thing itself. In the second poem, he sounds an echo to painterly visions only *after* his attempt at identifying with the thing itself has elapsed. And in the third, he sets off from one of his favorite pictorial genres, the landscape, to develop a polemical and somewhat dogmatic antidogmatic dispute with one particular type of painter's parallel quest to get at the thing itself. That "type" of painter, I will argue, may be fleshed out most convincingly by drawing on the writings of Piet Mondrian.

"Study of Two Pears" sounds like the title of a painting (a still life, specifically). By its very title, in other words, the poem sets up an analogy between the poet's and the painter's task. "As you know," Stevens explained to José Rodríguez Feo, "I pay just as much attention to painters as I do to writers because, except technically, their problems are the same" (*L* 593). We should notice the wording here, not just the characteristic idea: "problems" is the term Stevens uses, rather than "task" or "project" or "endeavor." It is useful to bear this in mind when we read through his seemingly straightforward "Study of Two Pears":

I

Opusculum paedagogum.
The pears are not viols,
Nudes or bottles.
They resemble nothing else.

II

They are yellow forms
Composed of curves
Bulging toward the base.
They are touched red.

III

They are not flat surfaces
Having curved outlines.
They are round
Tapering toward the top.

IV

In the way they are modelled
There are bits of blue.
A hard dry leaf hangs
From the stem.

V

The yellow glistens.
It glistens with various yellows,
Citrons, oranges and greens
Flowering over the skin.

VI

The shadows of the pears
Are blobs on the green cloth.
The pears are not seen
As the observer wills.

(CP 196–97)

Is this a poem that merely "discourse[s] with pleasant dogmatism on the familiar themes of the irreducible world of sense," as A. Walton Litz proposes?[4] On a first reading, it certainly appears to be so. It even tries to outdo painting in registering, or responding to, the irreducibility of our world of sense. The poem opens by declining the imaginatively and associatively twisted painterly representations that allow pears to look like "viols, / Nudes or bottles"—three of the classic ingredients of cubist painting—and goes so far as to denounce any two-dimensional representation whatsoever: "They are not flat surfaces / Having curved outlines."[5] "The new painting has to be sculpture," in Helen Vendler's paradoxical paraphrase. What is more, even sculpture—and one might think of Claes Oldenburg in this case, an artist who is known to have drawn inspiration from Stevens—would be inadequate for the requested literalness, since it, too, constitutes a representational detour that in the end would fail to catch the sensuous individuality of the actual material pears in front of the speaker.[6] In the quest for the

4. Litz, *Introspective Voyager*, 261.

5. For a reading in which Stevens responds to cubism in particular, see Bonnie Costello, "Effects of an Analogy: Wallace Stevens and Painting," 78. The poem's opening quatrain is singled out by P. Michael Campbell and John Dolan as one of the more conspicuous instances of Stevens's use of "praeteritic antithesis": the act of denial precisely foregrounds the topic denied, in this case the resemblance between pears and other objects as brought to light by painters ("Teaching Stevens's Poetry," 124–25).

6. Vendler, *On Extended Wings*, 144. For Oldenburg, see Glen G. MacLeod, "The Influence of Wallace Stevens on Contemporary Artists," 158–60. As Charles Altieri notes, though the

pears' identity, no traces of difference seem to be allowed. Stevens is playing with the farthest boundaries of representation, those limit situations where the act of representation itself becomes an act of betrayal and must strive—desperately and/or ironically—to cancel itself. The poetic result, however, is not so much annihilating as intensifying: much of what Stevens achieves is to stimulate us so that we "piece together a pear as if the object were freshly before us, seen for the first time."[7] There are other, diametrically opposed ways of achieving similar results: in the poem "Someone Puts a Pineapple Together," it happens by the invention of a series of twelve wildly fantastic and delightfully astonishing metaphors (NA 86). Here it happens by insisting on concrete and detailed literalness. The starting point of "Study of Two Pears" is that the objects "resemble nothing else": a pear is a pear is a pear, and not a metaphor. The poem's conclusion consists of an emphasis on the fact that the materiality of the pears imposes important limits on what the retina registers. There is, in Joyce's words, an "[i]neluctable modality of the visible": we cannot see the pears whichever way we want. "The mind is smaller than the eye," Stevens noted in "A Fish-Scale Sunrise" (CP 161). Between starting point and conclusion, we get a number of specific descriptions, so freshly detailed that Eleanor Cook is no doubt right to single out this poem as one that shows how "Stevens' sensuous particulars do not pall. He keeps them simple, often short, and sometimes achieves a remarkable sense of presence. . . . This is a side of Stevens that we tend to underestimate."[8]

Yet there is more than meets the eye here. Even if we may reasonably feel that the speaker of "Study of Two Pears" is content with a more naively enjoying reader than is usually the case in Stevens's poems, we are still in the company of a poet who loves to "make the visible a little hard // To see" (CP 311) and who is given to pondering certain theoretical "problems." The extended reading that Charles Altieri gives of the poem is symptomatic in this respect. Although Altieri sets out by talking of a fresh piecing together in front of our eyes, he winds up commenting in terms that are much more philosophical. "Physical shadows," he writes, "become metaphorical shadows, which then become metapoetic shadows serving as an emblem for the

---

pears in the text may be interpreted as painted rather than real ones, such a reading would impoverish the poem ("Why Stevens Must Be Abstract, or What a Poet Can Learn from Painting," 117–18). In that case, the remark "They are not flat surfaces" could no longer be descriptive and the poem's whole urge for vivid immediacy would be blunted.

7. Altieri, "Why Stevens Must Be Abstract," 98.
8. Joyce, Ulysses, 31; Cook, Poetry, Word-Play, and Word-War, 154.

very overdetermined absence language is in the process of creating."[9] If the pears are not *seen* as the observer wills, they nevertheless seem to possess the uncanny ability to decompose in a critic's hands. Stevens is a poet who was always inclined to demonstrate at some level that "if it were not for the fact that substance is problematic and absent, there would not be art."[10] Altieri's remark on the poem's "overdetermined absence" is not simply attributable to his own theorizing and philosophical bias: he would not have been brought to such theoretical speculations had the poem been written by William Carlos Williams.

Indeed, the counterexample of Williams, as several critics have suggested, is more than a useful shorthand expedient.[11] Probably the best question to ask of "Study of Two Pears" is: What keeps this from being a Williams poem? (Or conversely: What makes it so Stevensian?) We quickly notice a few unmistakable differences—to begin with, the very first line: "Opusculum paedagogum." The introduction of a small pedagogical manual, in slightly pedantic and self-mocking Latin to boot, is irreconcilable with the poetic program of someone like Williams, who was known for his hypercorrectively American attempts at fighting Latin and Greek with his bare hands and who would have been horrified to see his pictorial poems lose their would-be "objective," "imagistic," referentially unproblematic specificity by being abstracted into pedagogical paradigms. In Stevens's case, however, the phrase betrays a characteristic theoretical bias—the wish to pass from the particular to the general—along with an inclination to play a few cavalierly executed epistemological finger exercises. The poem's formal presentation in six numbered sections, with its faint pretense of organized steps in the logical development of an argument, adds to this theoretical impression. In this context, Williams's reaction to Stevens's later "Description without Place" is worth recalling. Williams interpreted the Spanish "hidalgo" in that poem as a critical allusion to himself and to his own poetic enterprise, and he responded by writing "A Place (Any Place) to Transcend All Places."[12] This poem tries to get a lick in at Stevens on several levels, one of them allusion.

---

9. Altieri, "Why Stevens Must Be Abstract," 99.

10. Paul de Man, *Blindness and Insight: Essays in the Rhetoric of Contemporary Criticism*, 244.

11. See Altieri, "Why Stevens Must Be Abstract," 98, and Jacqueline Vaught Brogan, "Wallace Stevens: Poems Against His Climate," 80.

12. See *The Collected Later Poems of William Carlos Williams*, 113–15. For analyses of this poetic tit-for-tat between Stevens and Williams, see Alec Marsh, "Stevens and Williams: The Economics of Metaphor"; Albert Gelpi, "Stevens and Williams: The Epistemology of Modernism," 19–21; Paul Mariani, *William Carlos Williams: A New World Naked*, 517; and Filreis, *Actual World*, 180–83. As to the nearly lifelong relationship between the two poets,

Thus, we come across the phrase "Pears / philosophically hard." Williams's pears, the poem suggests, are not exactly like Stevens's, since Williams's philosophy is restricted to their materiality and nothing else. Despite all the descriptive delicacy and concentration Stevens achieves in "Study of Two Pears," *his* pears are not entirely kept from serving extraneous philosophical purposes, for they are caught between the pedagogical ambition voiced in the first line and the epistemological verity of the final lines. Stevens's poem, it turns out, is not simply a "Study" in a painterly sense, but also in a more scholarly, intellectual sense.

There is a second, more subtle way in which the poem diverges from Williams: in the alliterative impulse of its second and third quatrains. "Composed of curves / Bulging toward the base. / . . . Tapering toward the top." Stevens, it appears, cannot be all eye; he must have his music, too. Though the music does much here to underscore the ostensible delight he takes in depicting the pears, it also has a momentum of its own that works independently of the visualizing experiment and signals how for this poet the stark objectivity of a "Polaroid poetry" can never really suffice.[13] Neither can an entirely lean, unambiguously exact diction, since we also get, in the fourth quatrain, the dissonant word *modelled*. "In the way they are modelled" suggests some hidden agent—a Pygmalion or a divine creator, perhaps. Even if we are at a loss to explain the appropriateness of this suggestion of agency, we cannot avoid the feeling that the pears are strangely doubled: they are not truly original, the text suggests, but (always already?) imitations modeled upon something else. They seem irrecoverable from an originary difference. The result of this lexical dissonance is that our attention is diverted from a

---

we had better distrust the tendency of Williams's biographer, Mariani, to take an entirely benign view: "Always in public and in their exchanges there was the utmost cordiality and deference between these two giants while each jockeyed for position and watched the other" (*William Carlos Williams*, 499). Jacqueline Vaught Brogan catches more of the ambivalence with which the two men regarded each other when she observes that "Stevens' and Williams' friendship was alternately bullying, playful, respectful, and somewhat 'uneasy'" ("Poems Against His Climate," 76). That last word is also foregrounded by Martha Helen Strom in her essay "The Uneasy Friendship of William Carlos Williams and Wallace Stevens." For more extended comparative analyses of Stevens and Williams, see esp. Kurt Heinzelman, "Williams and Stevens: The Vanishing-Point of Resemblance"; David Walker, *The Transparent Lyric: Reading and Meaning in the Poetry of Stevens and Williams*; Mao, *Solid Objects*, 229–36; and the various contributors to the special issue on Williams and Stevens published by the *William Carlos Williams Review* and edited by Glen G. MacLeod.

13. The phrase "Polaroid poetry" was used by John Frederick Nims to characterize Gary Snyder's *Selected Poems*, and, in Richard Wilbur's explanation, refers to the sort of poetry that "follows William Carlos Williams' weaker poems" (Wilbur, "The Art of Poetry," 89).

rigorously or naively transfixing look at the pears to the workings of language and to theories of representation. The same result issues from the "unobtrusive metaphors" that are subsequently brought into play.[14] "Flowering" and "blobs" give us slight nudges and once more open up the poem to theoretical ruminations. The first of these words inspires Altieri to muse:

> As the pear becomes most fully itself before the eye, it must become something else: the fruit must act as a flower does if the mind is to appreciate fully its appearance as a fruit. Then, as flowering seems to capture the particular act of emergence, we recognize that the term applies to a good deal more than the pear. The flowering is also a process of the mind's own blossoming within a world formerly perceived only from a distance. The painting brush, the writer's recasting, and the observer's attention all here flower, suggesting that when mind too becomes fully itself it must at the same time become other, must take on an identity that no perception qua perception can register. Perception at its most intense requires our entering the order of metaphor, requires the intensification of art. This indeed is why we need a painting to learn how to see a pear.[15]

Altieri gets a lot of mileage out of a single word here, but the fact is that Stevens's tropology proves sufficiently impure to support critical narratives of this sort—an impurity that a Williams poem would try much harder to avoid. Bonnie Costello argues that Stevens's relation to painting overall was "far more figurative and conceptual" than Williams's literal analogies, which aimed at "an equivalency of effect in words."[16] The difference between the approaches shows even in this near-literalist poem.

The difference becomes even more evident in the final couplet, for Williams would not be likely to end a radically descriptive poem with a general observation, and would certainly avoid the sort of syntactical ambiguity teasingly inserted by Stevens. Altieri unpacks that ambiguity most clearly: " 'As the observer wills' can refer either to a temporal state (observing cannot take place at the same time as willing) or to a modal state (observing cannot be brought into accord with the dictates of will). In either case, the as marks the deep problem."[17] Stevens, as suggested, possessed a Jamesian sense of the intricate evasions of the obscurest as, and the poem's final statement does

14. Vendler, On Extended Wings, 146.
15. Altieri, "Why Stevens Must Be Abstract," 98.
16. Costello, "Effects of an Analogy," 66; see also MacLeod, Wallace Stevens and Modern Art, xxiii.
17. Altieri, "Why Stevens Must Be Abstract," 99.

not simply pin the pears down as we would expect it to do, but rather allows the text to fork. Spontaneously, we interpret: the pears are not seen the way we would like to see them, for their materiality imposes severe limits on our perception. But we must also hear a more pedagogical, philosophical, and doctrinaire voice saying: the pears cannot be seen as long as we want anything from them—that is, until we are prepared to subject ourselves to their objectivity and turn into blank slates or mirrors (or are willing to pacify the cortex, as Bevis would say). This second voice undercuts the poet's previous insertions of alliteration, dissonant diction, and metaphor. As a result, the text neither reaches the closure of simple aphorism nor manages to leave us with fully present, tangible pears.

Does this mean that Jacqueline Vaught Brogan is right to see "Study of Two Pears" as "rather obviously pitted against 'objective' poetry"?[18] Probably not, for that would mean tilting the balance too easily in a counterintuitive direction: after all, we *have* "naively" enjoyed painting and sculpting along with the poet. It is only when we linger over the text that we find the act of reading somebody in the act of writing about the act of looking at two pears to pose its own sort of enigma—or, as Stevens wanted it, its own sort of "problem." The problem is that of a disparity between the thing itself in its most literal identity and the necessary doubling of representation, which can bring the thing to life only in a relational and analogical manner. A poet like Stevens, working in the medium of language and hence at one further remove from the visual than a painter, tended to be particularly sensitive to this disparity and often sought to inscribe it even at the point of greatest immediacy. "A pear is a pear is a pear—or is it?" the poem seems to be asking, and Stevens's characteristic answer sounds: "It is and it is not." The pear has sufficient materiality to impose its own sensuous restrictions and not to comply with our silly fancies, but if it is to be *seen* at all, it must adapt to the fact that seeing is a relational category that can never, in the final analysis, be contained by the object of perception. "Things seen are things as seen" (*OP* 188).

"The Latest Freed Man," unlike "Study of Two Pears," is neither a precision exercise nor an "opusculum paedagogum." In fact, it does not even appear much involved with the painterly attempt to seize the thing itself, and comes to its subject from an entirely different angle. What it does manage to

18. Brogan, "Poems Against His Climate," 80.

suggest, however, is the strength of the basic motivations behind Stevens's recurrent interest in—and even desire for—the uncontaminated thing itself. Things seen in this poem are still things *as* seen, but the question becomes one of how the act of seeing should meet unspoken desires even as the sensuous "how" displaces the epistemological "what." Staging what we may surmise to be his own experience in the third person, Stevens recalls how he got up one morning at six o'clock—his usual hour on working days—and felt once again empowered by the rising sun:

> Tired of the old descriptions of the world,
> The latest freed man rose at six and sat
> On the edge of his bed. He said,
>   "I suppose there is
> A doctrine to this landscape. Yet, having just
> Escaped from the truth, the morning is color and mist,
> Which is enough: the moment's rain and sea,
> The moment's sun (the strong man vaguely seen),
> Overtaking the doctrine of this landscape. Of him
> And of his works, I am sure. He bathes in the mist
> Like a man without a doctrine. The light he gives—
> It is how he gives his light. It is how he shines,
> Rising upon the doctors in their beds
> And on their beds. . . ."
>
>   (CP 204–5)

Waking up as the incorrigible modernist that he is, Stevens immediately dismisses the "doctrine to this landscape," its "old descriptions."[19] He has "just / Escaped from the truth"—a statement that is much denser than we might infer from the almost perfunctory way in which it is delivered. (It is, grammatically speaking, a dangling participle.) "The Latest Freed Man," it should be remembered, is the third in a trio of poems not only composed around the same time, but also published together (with nine other poems, including "Study of Two Pears") in the *Southern Review* under the title "Canonica."[20] Its two predecessors in *The Collected Poems* are "The Man on

---

19. A useful gloss on how "descriptions" may be viewed as a "doctrine" can be found in "Of Modern Poetry," composed shortly after "The Latest Freed Man." There the opening lines suggest a modernist's typical simplification of history into a premodern world that is stable, simple, and legible, and a modern one that is fickle, complex, and illegible: "The poem of the mind in the act of finding / What will suffice. It has not always had / To find: the scene was set; it repeated what / Was in the script" (CP 239).

20. Milton J. Bates, *Mythology of Self*, 227.

the Dump" and "On the Road Home," the first of which famously builds
toward the striking final line, "Where was it one first heard of the truth?
The the" (CP 203). This rejection of *the* truth becomes still more apparent
in the second poem, with its explicit claims that "There is no such thing as
the truth" and "There are many truths, / But they are not parts of a truth"
(CP 203). In one sense, then, "having just / Escaped from the truth" refers
to Stevens's apparently new insight expressed in the two immediately pre-
ceding poems. (The seeds of this insight may of course reach back several
decades, more particularly to William James at Harvard, and the effects
of it would continue to show, as we will see in a moment, in "Landscape
with Boat.")

Color, mist, rain, sea, and sun must replace "the doctrine of this land-
scape." They are what the senses record and nothing more. The sun holds
pride of place in this group—as it commonly does in this most heliocen-
tric of poets, for whom "All things in the sun are sun" (CP 104)—and
quickly acquires a certain synecdochic stature. Its image serves complex
purposes, though. For no sooner has Stevens mentioned the sun in "The
Latest Freed Man" than he calls it a "strong man," which is evidently a
highly self-conscious fictionalization and anthropomorphization pulling us
away from what is imprinted on the retina. With a glaring prosopopoeia,
he ascribes human attributes to it, thus parading the one trope that in Paul
de Man's view may be even more essential to lyric poetry than metaphor.[21]
In addition, the sun-man is turned into an almost Cartesian foundation of
certainty: "Of him / And of his works, I am sure." The certainty is charac-
teristically represented by a circular formulation, a shrug of the shoulders:
"The light he gives—" (and we linger expectantly over the dash, only to
be wrong-footed, since no real enjambment follows, only an anacoluthon)
"It is how he gives his light." Sun and light are what they are, phenomena
antedating ideas, not to be reached by asking definitional questions of *what*
they are, but only by settling for the perceptual experience of *how* they are.
"The light he gives—" is a sentence that cannot be completed by a definition
but only by a change of topic and perspective: "It is *how* he gives his light
[that matters]. It is *how* he shines [that is of importance to somebody who
refuses to address anything except the thing itself]" (emphasis added). In
"The Figure of the Youth as Virile Poet," Stevens would return to this irre-
ducibility of light when claiming about the imagination that "[l]ike light,

21. Paul de Man, "Hypogram and Inscription," 44–51; see also J. Hillis Miller, "Prosopo-
poeia."

it adds nothing, except itself" (*NA* 61). Sunlight to Stevens embodied one of the principal limits of reality: as vital to human perception, experience, and consciousness (and to their derivative, the imagination that projects prosopopoeias) as it is to the life of plants.

Having shifted to an experience of the irreducibility of the sun and its light, Stevens indeed chooses to forgo any elaboration of his sun-man prosopopoeia, returning instead to how the sun simply shines on the human and the inanimate alike, the perceiving and the unperceiving—"the doctors in their beds / And on their beds. . . ."[22] The speechifying halts, trailing off in suspension points that suggest both the speaker's dismissal of doctrinaire discussions and his surrendering to pure sensation.

> And so the freed man said.
> It was how the sun came shining into his room:
> To be without a description of to be,
> For a moment on rising, at the edge of the bed, to be,
> To have the ant of the self changed to an ox
> With its organic boomings, to be changed
> From a doctor into an ox, before standing up,
> To know that the change and that the ox-like struggle
> Come from the strength that is the strength of the sun,
> Whether it comes directly or from the sun.
> It was how he was free. It was how his freedom came.
> It was being without description, being an ox.
>
> (*CP* 205)

With an idiomatically Stevensian syntactical trick, the "It is" of the previous soliloquy ("It is how he gives his light. It is how he shines") is picked up, but in such a way as to become more and more referentially unfocused. The triple anaphora "It was" (which becomes quadruple if we count both hemistichs in the penultimate line, and which will become septuple by the time we are through with the poem) does not really attach itself to any specific antecedent or implied subject. Rather, it comes to express something as

---

22. "Doctors" recalls in one and the same gesture those thinkers/writers who would find a "doctrine" to the landscape—including, possibly, such theological doctors as Thomas Aquinas (Cook, *Poetry, Word-Play, and Word-War*, 156; Maeder, *Experimental Language*, 38–39)—and colleagues like "old Dr. Williams" (*L* 286), whose poetic project of bringing to light and elucidating objects Stevens at this point is inclined to share (Brogan, "Poems Against His Climate," 81).

all-embracing as the voice of Being. Not coincidentally, "to be" and "being" predominate as verb forms, appearing no less than six times in a sequence of infinitival clauses that are suspended in the air like "a free-floating series of verbal impulses."[23] The grammatical subject, that prime guarantee of self and identity, recedes as Stevens momentarily tries "To be without a description of to be." We are very much in the realm of what a few years later he would call the first idea, and Stevens picks his words with the utmost care. As in the later "Description without Place," he seems to play on etymology: to describe is always also to de-scribe, to pass by the detour of scription, and thus to falsify the experience of mere being. The desire for the apperception of the thing itself is a desire for a state of being (meditative perhaps, in Bevis's special sense) that occurs without the slightest verbal interference. In Stevens there is, as Richard Poirier notes, "an unsatisfiable aspiration, the dream of an impossible possibility: to see something without having to name it, without having to think about it, to see it without having to re-create it, to see it as would a transparent eyeball, with no sense of its dependence on the human will. This, it might be recalled, is Emerson's dream of 'genius': to know a world without knowing it as a text."[24]

To figure this "dream of an impossible possibility," Stevens needs to fall back, as he repeatedly did, on the rhetorical ploy of an animal's perception of the world. He inflates himself and gets under the skin of an ox, there to enjoy the unthinking ease of bovine being. The "strength" he thus experiences derives "from the sun," whether directly or indirectly (no metaphysics and disputations on cause and effect for animals; no Cartesian principles of certainty about the strong man and his works).[25] The feeling is meant to be liberating: "It was how he was free." But free from what? From a nagging need for *the* truth, we may presume, and, more generally, from the endless inroads into reality of a mind that can never be satisfied, from a self that feels constrained by its insatiable desire. The primary impulse for searching out such freedom shows itself to be above all negative and antithetical: what the latest freed man wants is more a matter of negative freedom *from* than of positive freedom *for* or *with an eye to*. For all we know, he does not want his freedom for any social or ethical purpose but only as a personal psychological

23. Vendler, On Extended Wings, 115; see also Maeder, Experimental Language, 40.
24. Poirier, Renewal of Literature, 210.
25. Given his focus on Bergson, Tom Quirk has no trouble providing a Bergsonian reading of the poem as pointing to an elementary, all-suffusing élan vital (Bergson and American Culture: The Worlds of Willa Cather and Wallace Stevens, 241–42).

antidote to the general misery of living. His freedom, at this point, is not that of the existentialist philosopher: like the "freedom" of animals, it is amoral, not burdened with responsibility.

It is typical of Stevens's texts, nevertheless, that they are themselves rarely naive, innocent, or blank, even at the point of recording a deep wish for naïveté, innocence, or blankness, and even when they are getting across with considerable incantatory force the pleasurable sensation of imagining oneself—if only "For a moment on rising, at the edge" of social and ethically responsible life—to be an ox. There is no way, for example, in which the text can wrest itself entirely free from its image: the ox. For where does that image come from? Partly from broadly cultural stereotypes, as expressed in certain idioms like "strong as an ox" and "dumb as an ox." But the image could also have been inspired by a more strictly *literary* heritage, if it was borrowed from Zarathustra's advice to the truth-seeker: "As the ox ought he to do; and his happiness should smell of the earth, and not of contempt for the earth." Nietzsche is not the only intertextual candidate here, for Stevens's animal also looks like one of the Oxen of the Sun, and that legendary breed of animal has its own literary history, all the way down from the *Odyssey* to *Ulysses*.[26] The image, in short, remains culturally entangled and open to textual dissemination. The first idea is unable to do without one or another image. "It was being without description, being an ox": the syntactical parallelism suggests near-synonymity, but the tag dramatically subverts Stevens's self-declared ambition. What must be de-scribed nevertheless gets re-scripted in the image. A similar rhetorical sensitivity informs the poem's final lines:

> It was the importance of the trees outdoors,
> The freshness of the oak-leaves, not so much
> That they were oak-leaves, as the way they looked.
> It was everything being more real, himself
> At the centre of reality, seeing it.

26. For the ox idioms and Nietzsche quote, see Leggett, *Early Stevens*, 245. Stuart Gilbert, in his search for analogies between *Ulysses* and the story of the *Odyssey* as interpreted by Victor Bérard, points out that the "Oxen of the Sun are symbols of fertility" (*James Joyce's Ulysses: A Study*, 297). Stevens-the-ox, too, is arguably fertilized by "the strength of the sun." His ox may even be seen, as Beverly Maeder reminds us, as "an avatar of the sun that comes up 'bull fire' in 'Add This to Rhetoric' (CP 198), the catalyst that allows the man to become ox-like" (*Experimental Language*, 39).

> It was everything bulging and blazing and big in itself,
> The blue of the rug, the portrait of Vidal,
> *Qui fait fi des joliesses banales*, the chairs.
>
> (CP 205)

This is not just a passage in two different languages, but in at least two different voices as well. One voice that may be heard—and we should not hesitate to call it the dominant one—is that of the lover of the first idea and the thing itself, the man who wants to become all seeing, who wants his eye to pierce material reality at its most intense, who simplifies his diction and would ultimately dispense with language altogether: "not so much / That they were oak-leaves, as the way they looked" (which is to say, again, not so much the *what* as the *how*). We should understand and value the moving quality of this voice coming from an almost sixty-year-old, essentially solitary man who wished that his life could be occasionally reduced to standing, looking, marveling, and feeling rejuvenated—like drawing a breath of Alpine air. But there is also a countervoice that registers the ceaseless tension between sensibility and language. This voice knows it must mention the "oak-leaves" *as* "oak-leaves" in order not to wind up stammering about the amorphous or to disable the reader from vicariously re-presenting the scene. (This is not the same thing as saying that the word *oak-leaves* is necessary in order to experience the sensible specificity of oak-leaves, as overly enthusiastic and idealistic Wittgensteinians tend to conclude.) Time and again, Stevens anticipates the Heideggerian and Derridean ploy of writing words *under erasure*—of writing them, that is, then crossing them out, but without making them fully illegible, so that the word is at once there and not there.[27] This does not mean that Stevens's second voice simply speaks the deconstructive language of a compulsively sobered-up linguistic existentialism (though it can always be made to do so). Other, less philosophical notions are at least as much implicated in it, such as the awareness of how the gap between senses and language, between feeling and thought, precisely opens up a space for the poet to play with rhetoric and imagination. For it is hard to turn a deaf ear, in the final three lines, to the boisterously paraded alliteration of "bulging," "blazing," "big," and "blue," as well as to the witty

---

27. Although it is Derrida who most conspicuously publicized the device of writing words under erasure (especially in *Of Grammatology*), he derived the practice from Heidegger, who applied the same technique to the word *Sein* in *Zur Seinsfrage* (Gayatri Chakravorty Spivak, translator's preface, xiv–xviii). Coincidentally or not, the context in which we are talking about Stevens's poem is also one that involves descriptions of "being."

inner rhyme on "Vidal" and "*banales*" and the conspicuously inserted, fastidious French. It is even tempting to read in the description of Stevens's room with the "chairs" a faint allusion to Van Gogh.[28] At the same time that the poet withdraws from the natural outdoor scenery to his own room— a movement that suggests a return to the self that had been momentarily suspended—he hints at Van Gogh's paintings, the products not of photographic mimesis but of a strong imagination and an idiosyncratic artistic vision.[29] It is no longer the poet-as-ox, then, that appears to be speaking at the end of the poem, but once again the modernist artist tired of the old schemata of perception and experience, looking for new ones to replace them. (Coincidentally or not, the "blue" of the rug is associated with the poetic imagination in Stevens's usual color symbolism, and the objects that finally come into view—the rug, the painting, and the chairs—are all manmade.) The experience of the first idea or of the thing itself, whether the immediately physical sensation of an ox's body or the perception of objects registered in a state of oxhood, has already slipped through his fingers. It has served its function of rekindling the poetic imagination. "May there be an ennui of the first idea?" Stevens wonders in "Notes toward a Supreme Fiction," providing himself the rhetorical answer: "What else, prodigious scholar, should there be?" (*CP* 381).

The first idea, or the thing itself, we may infer from "The Latest Freed Man," is no more than the name for an infinitely renewable, necessarily short-lived strategy. This is finally also what the poem's title tells us. Stevens knows the illusion of being an ox and of perceiving the thing itself is an illusion in need of continual renewal. For this is only the story of the *latest*

28. Anatole Vidal, it may be recalled, was the owner of a Parisian bookstore who acted as Stevens's cultural connection with Europe during the thirties, sending him anything he requested, "from bonbons to books to an occasional painting" (Brazeau, *Parts of a World*, 27). Stevens had a painting of Vidal by Jean Labasque in his bedroom. Glen MacLeod suspects that by choosing to "emphasize the elements of everyday domestic life" at the end of "The Latest Freed Man," Stevens "was consciously indulging [the] Dutch aspect of his sensibility" represented by seventeenth-century indoor paintings (*Wallace Stevens and Modern Art*, 87), but the association with another Dutchman, Van Gogh, adds a dimension that is better attuned to the modernist exercise undertaken in the poem.

29. This powerful artistic vision is also what Labasque's painting of Vidal supposedly embodied. In an unpublished letter of June 4, 1938, recently uncovered by Beverly Maeder, "Vidal praises Labasque's art, saying that 'l'art de Jean Labasque est par dessus tout moderne et toujours à la recherche de l'idée forte, dominante, de l'individualité,—que cet art ne peut être qualifié de joli, d'aimable, de gracieux' ('Jean Labasque's art is above all modern, and constantly driven by the search for a powerful governing idea of individuality. It cannot be called pretty, pleasant or graceful')" (*Experimental Language*, 216, Maeder's translation).

freed man. There have been other such stories before, and still more are to follow. Many more indeed followed as Stevens kept trying to close the gap between matter and mind, in the full awareness that the human mind plays a paradoxically double role in this: at once material and immaterial, at once materializing and immaterializing. For the human mind, even as it tries to seize upon the thing itself, is, in the rambunctious paronomasia of "Repetitions of a Young Captain," a "make-matter, matter-nothing mind" (CP 307).

In 1940, two years after the appearance of "Study of Two Pears" and "The Latest Freed Man," Stevens wrote a much different poem, this time fore-grounding the artistic quest for the thing itself in more orthodox fashion with the overt purpose of denouncing such a quest. "Landscape with Boat" is more philosophically oriented and more clearly programmatic than either of its two predecessors. It has also been somewhat neglected in the canon of Stevens criticism—a neglect that may have been prompted by its dis-putatious and dogmatic ring, by a certain declarative tone that leaves little room for ambivalence, and by the fact that its flat and unredeeming language enacts only too well what it sets out to represent. According to Lucy Beck-ett, " 'Landscape with Boat' is not a distinguished poem. It is as if Stevens, having arrived with sudden clarity at an idea of immense importance to himself, had simply allowed himself to write it down as fast and as lucidly as possible."[30] Yet, in more than one sense, the text does offer an interesting case study, and if caught in an appropriate intertextual web amply resonates with artistic relevance.

The offset line that introduces the poem reads like a dramatis personae (but in the singular): "An anti-master-man, floribund ascetic" (CP 241). This man is the subject of the poem, and he predictably reminds B. J. Leggett of the object of scorn in Nietzsche's diatribes against ascetic truth-seekers and concomitant eulogies of the master-man groping for power.[31] However, even if that is where Stevens got (part of) his inspiration, the poem profits more from a less compulsory intertext—one that cannot perhaps pretend to any direct allusiveness on Stevens's part, but that nevertheless enhances the aesthetic significance of the text. We should follow the lead of Bonnie

30. Lucy Beckett, *Wallace Stevens*, 125.
31. Leggett, *Early Stevens*, 221; see also David Bromwich, "Stevens and the Idea of the Hero."

Costello, who believes the "anti-master-man," in general terms, to be a modernist counterfigure to the old masters in painting.[32] It is indeed to the language and theory of painting that the poem immediately turns to characterize its protagonist:

> He brushed away the thunder, then the clouds,
> Then the colossal illusion of heaven. Yet still
> The sky was blue. He wanted imperceptible air.
> He wanted to see. He wanted the eye to see
> And not be touched by blue. He wanted to know,
> A naked man who regarded himself in the glass
> Of air, who looked for the world beneath the blue,
> Without blue, without any turquoise tint or phase,
> Any azure under-side or after-color. Nabob
> Of bones, he rejected, he denied, to arrive
> At the neutral centre, the ominous element,
> The single-colored, colorless, primitive.
>
> (CP 241–42)

There is no compelling reason to believe that the character described in these lines needs to be identified as a specific artist (a painter or, more metonymically, a painter-poet).[33] Still, the artistic perspective evoked here is evidently that of a form of radically abstract art, and if there is one exemplary figure whose theories may be fruitfully crossed with the text, it is that of the Dutchman Piet Mondrian. At the time of composing "Landscape with Boat," Stevens was moving in the direction of an outspoken interest in Mondrian's art (especially the works of the twenties and after): only two years later, as Glen G. MacLeod demonstrates, the reading of an essay by the emigré painter would become one of the inspirational sources for "Notes toward a Supreme Fiction." Stevens had seen Mondrian's work on several occasions during the thirties, both at the Museum of Modern Art in New York and at the Wadsworth Atheneum in his hometown, Hartford. The

---

32. Costello, "Effects of an Analogy," 78.
33. Anna Balakian interprets the lines as a response to the Mallarméan struggle with the word and idea of *ciel* (both "sky" and "heaven")—which takes up a central place in symbolist and postsymbolist poetry—without, however, suggesting that the character in Stevens's poem is intended as an allusion to the French poet (*The Fiction of the Poet: From Mallarmé to the Post-Symbolist Mode*, 146–48).

Wadsworth, at the time "the most modern museum in the United States," had been championing artists from the De Stijl movement for years, had purchased a Mondrian painting for its permanent collection in 1936, and was showing three more of his paintings as part of an exhibition mounted in the year "Landscape with Boat" was written. What is more, throughout the thirties Stevens is known to have grappled with the claims made on him by surrealist and abstract painting, respectively, and thanks to MacLeod we also know that during that same era he kept himself from siding with abstract art, associating it with its most radical and dogmatic branch of geometric abstraction.[34]

"Landscape with Boat" is inexplicably absent from MacLeod's study of Stevens's interaction with the painterly climate of his day, yet it fits in well with the critical narrative presented there. Or so it does if we are willing to dissociate the Mondrian-like figure taken issue with in the poem from the Mondrian whom Stevens would come to value much more positively by the time of his work on "Notes" (and also later, when he continued to hail the painter's "integrity" [L 628]). To most of the ideas attributed to the "floribund ascetic" we can even find verbal and pictorial counterparts in Mondrian. "He wanted the eye to see / And not be touched by blue," observes the speaker, while Mondrian wrote: "We do not have to see beyond the natural, but we have to see, as it were, *through* it: we have to see deeper—see *abstractly*, and above all *universally*."[35] Mondrian, too, in his most radical work, "looked for the world beneath the blue, / Without blue, without any turquoise tint or phase, / Any azure under-side or after-color." He would not allow any "turquoise tint" or "azure . . . after-color," any variegated shades of color that impress and obsess the eye of romantic, realist, and impressionist painters alike. Instead, he reduced his palette to "The single-colored, colorless, primitive"—that is, to the three primary, unshaded or "single" colors (red, blue, and yellow), and to the three so-called "colorless" noncolors (white, black, and gray).[36]

---

34. For Mondrian's influence on "Notes," see MacLeod, *Wallace Stevens and Modern Art*, xxiv–xxv, 114–21; for the Wadsworth, see ibid., 27–28, 109, 221; for Stevens's attitude toward abstract art in the thirties, see ibid., 92–96 and chapters 3 and 4 overall.

35. Piet Mondriaan, "Natuurlijke en abstracte realiteit," 99. Here as elsewhere, translations from the Dutch are my own; English-language versions of Mondrian's writings are available from Harry Holtzman and Martin S. James, in *The New Art—The New Life: The Collected Writings of Piet Mondrian*.

36. "The natural color of material things has to disappear, as far as this is possible, preferably by a layer of pure color or 'non-color' (black, white, and gray)" (Piet Mondriaan, "Neo-Plasticisme: De Woning—De Straat—De Stad," 17).

In Mondrian's case, moreover, these primary colors and noncolors were not used to any superficially sensuous effect, for the Dutchman was after "the appearance of the aesthetic idea, in itself."[37] His basic attitude toward the senses (and, inseparably, toward our human physical condition) was negative: he, too, "rejected, he denied, to arrive / At the neutral centre, the ominous element." "Ominous" wickedly puns on the root word *omen*, as if the ascetic and abstracting artist had exclaimed: "We want to see a sign!" The wickedness first appears when the speaker christens his protagonist "Nabob / Of bones." A nabob, as the dictionary tells us, is a rich indigenous chieftain, but, especially at this point in the poem, the word is a conspicuously disruptive, stylistically self-conscious lexical item that no ascetic would ever dream of using. So it comes as no surprise to see the enjambment lead to a skeletal bareness: this painter, who is ostensibly so eager to pierce all superficies with his X-raying eyes, is rich only in the hard and dry country of the bones, in the Sahara of skeletons and death. The poem starts to adopt a critical stance here, so that we hark back to the oxymoron of "floribund ascetic" posited at the outset and become aware of the scathing irony in it. Suddenly, we are made aware that the adjective "floribund" contains an echo of "moribund"—or, in James S. Leonard and Christine E. Wharton's somewhat more florid formulation: "The anti-master-man's floribundness, perverting the rose-potentiality of the class floribunda, renders it a rosaceous equivalent of the moribund."[38]

In the following lines, the poem strikes an increasingly antagonistic posture as the figure of Mondrian continues to offer an interesting point of comparison:

> It was not as if the truth lay where he thought,
> Like a phantom, in an uncreated night.
> It was easier to think it lay there. If
> It was nowhere else, it was there and because
> It was nowhere else, its place had to be supposed,
> Itself had to be supposed, a thing supposed
> In a place supposed, a thing that he reached
> In a place that he reached, by rejecting what he saw
> And denying what he heard. He would arrive.

37. Piet Mondriaan, "De nieuwe beelding in de schilderkunst. IV. Beeldingsmiddel en compositie. (Vervolg.)," 42.
38. Leonard and Wharton, *Fluent Mundo*, 111.

He had only not to live, to walk in the dark,
To be projected by one void into
Another.

It was his nature to suppose,
To receive what others had supposed, without
Accepting. He received what he denied.
But as truth to be accepted, he supposed
A truth beyond all truths.

(CP 242)

Does the ascetic persona, rationalizing his procedure, have any real idea of what he is after? The speaker mocks the anti-master-man's tergiversations in lines that bear the outline of step-by-step rational progress but lead only to a cul-de-sac. The accumulative repetitions—"its place had to be supposed, / Itself had to be supposed, a thing supposed / In a place supposed, a thing that he reached / In a place that he reached"—create a singsong effect that ridicules the anti-master-man's attempt as amounting to no more than self-hypnosis. The choice of words, especially the quadruple "supposed," is also highly significant. To look for a thing sup-posed (or hypo-thesized) suggests a quest for a sub-stance (or, in the Greek of Aristotle, a *hypo-keimenon*), which is precisely what the theosophically and neoplatonically influenced Mondrian, situating his own artistic search in a philosophical history of long standing, sought to establish in figuring the "deepest general": "This *deepest general* has been indicated by Aristotle as *substance*, as *that which something is*, as *the thing on its own*, as that which exists on its own independently of the accidents of size, form—characteristics that merely form the *exterior* by which the substance reveals itself." This irreducible "thing on its own" un-derlying all variable outward appearances or "accidents," this *hypokeimenon*, is an entirely spiritual "phantom," as the poem calls it, that can be reached only "by rejecting what he saw / And denying what he heard." The ironical reassurance that follows is caustic: "He would arrive. / He had only not to live, to walk in the dark, / To be projected by one void into / Another." Again we may juxtapose textual material from Mondrian, for whom "not to live" was in some sense imperative as well: "As long as the individual pre-dominates in the consciousness of the age, art remains *tied to (ordinary) life* and is, primarily, the expression of that life."[39] An alternative art that strives

39. Piet Mondriaan, "De nieuwe beelding in de schilderkunst. VII. Van het natuurlijke tot het abstracte, d.i. van het onbepaalde tot het bepaalde. (I)," 88; Mondriaan, "Nieuwe beelding in de schilderkunst. IV," 51.

to transcend all embodied individuality, however, can only "be projected by one void into / Another."

Stevens's ascetic quester for the fundamental—a fundamentalist of sorts, who cannot live with contingency and provisionality but "would arrive"— turns a deaf ear to the social world as well. His principled unconcern with lived experience makes him "receive what others had supposed, without / Accepting." He is prepared to embrace only "A [transcendent, absolute, divine] truth beyond all [human, relative] truths."[40]

> He never supposed
> That he might be truth, himself, or part of it,
> That the things that he rejected might be part
> And the irregular turquoise, part, the perceptible blue
> Grown denser, part, the eye so touched, so played
> Upon by clouds, the ear so magnified
> By thunder, parts, and all these things together,
> Parts, and more things, parts. He never supposed divine
> Things might not look divine, nor that if nothing
> Was divine then all things were, the world itself,
> And that if nothing was the truth, then all
> Things were the truth, the world itself was the truth.
>
> (CP 242)

This is the rhetorically most accomplished moment in the poem, and Helen Vendler understandably cites it as a classic instance of Stevens's style.[41] "Landscape with Boat," for all its uncharacteristically blunt assertiveness, here shows itself to be a programmatically central text to the volume of which it is part: *Parts of a World*. Piecemeal, the poem restores the various phenomenal "parts" that compose our *être-au-monde*—to use Merleau-Ponty's felicitously polysemous phrase.[42] It does so with a barely concealed passion for the things of this world, snowballing and roller-coastering for

---

40. In a letter of 1914 to H. P. Bremmer, Mondrian explained his artistic project by saying: "I wish to approximate the truth as closely as possible and for that reason to abstract everything until I arrive at the foundation (always still an exterior foundation) of things. For me it is a truth that by saying nothing determinate one is precisely saying the most determinate, the truth (that of the great comprehensiveness)" (quoted in Saskia Bak, "Visies op Mondriaan," 70).

41. Vendler, *On Extended Wings*, 16.

42. The phrase appears in the title of part 3 of Merleau-Ponty's *Phenomenology of Perception*.

what feels like forever and building up to a jubilant, voluptuous climax. Nevertheless, any return to an embodied human state and any reestablishment of a relationship to the world based on passion will always also involve the possibility of conflict, and a small fissure in the climactic outburst dramatizes this possibility. When Stevens reaches the point of invoking "all these things together, / Parts, and more things, parts," the enjambment raises the question of the relationship between sprawling parts and overarching whole. The squirming facts exceed the squamous mind, if we may say so. Throughout *Parts of a World*, Eleanor Cook tells us, "Stevens is wary of themes that commonly give a sense of unity or wholeness, whether war and nation, whether old ideas of light and space, whether home or heaven or the quest for either. . . . He is equally wary of rhetorical patterns that commonly give a sense of unity or wholeness: synecdoche, metaphor, symbol, closure."[43] We have already had occasion to observe Stevens's scant and disruptive use of metaphor, as well as his refusal of closure, in "Study of Two Pears" and his inability to find full satisfaction in old ideas of light in "The Latest Freed Man."

We should, however, remind ourselves that shoring up the parts of his world did not always prove as easy to Stevens as it might appear from "Landscape with Boat." If the "parts" in that poem work strongly against all totalizing, holistic gestures, if, as James Longenbach maintains, they are even "divided against themselves, repeated so often that they diffuse the very sense of a whole to which a part belongs," several other lines and poems may be produced that surrender much more willingly to a totalizing and integrating nostalgia. This oscillation between diversity and unity has been linked by Longenbach and other critics to the poet's political stance during most of his writing life: "Stevens's politics often appear divided on precisely this fulcrum: wanting to preserve the integrity of every part of the world, he nevertheless fears the anarchic energy those parts set free."[44] In the "parts" climax of "Landscape with Boat," the fear of anarchy is so successfully suppressed that Stevens turns reckless. He enthusiastically adopts a sweeping Whitmanian posture—not really his most congenial stance, though he was given to trying it out now and then—and allows himself to embrace

43. Cook, *Poetry, Word-Play, and Word-War*, 153. Stevens's obsession with parts has an interesting prehistory that can be retraced by following the course of his pet phrase "odds and ends" from its earliest appearance onwards (see esp. *SP* 87, 104, 157, 175, 177, 244, 245). The most aphoristic example of Stevens's unremitting partiality in *Parts of a World* states that "In the sum of the parts, there are only the parts" (*CP* 204).

44. Longenbach, *Plain Sense of Things*, 217.

a pantheistic world view ("if nothing / Was divine then all things were"). More than that, he subsequently moves on to formulate a principle that comes dangerously close to courting an absolute relativism: "if nothing was the truth, then all / Things were the truth, the world itself was the truth." From a philosophical point of view (to be distinguished from the emotive and persuasive intentions of the text, which are far less question-begging), the speaker's reasoning continues to operate by the yardstick of what it denounces: the absolute. To move from a denunciation of absolute truth into an equally absolute relativism is, of course, to stick to the primacy of the absolute.

The poem, fortunately, does not end with the rash generalization of all things being divine and true, but returns to the seductive, sensuous appeal exercised by that divine and true world which philosophical fundamentalists and artistic ascetics forsake in their respective quests for the truth:

> Had he been better able to suppose:
> He might sit on a sofa on a balcony
> Above the Mediterranean, emerald
> Becoming emeralds. He might watch the palms
> Flap green ears in the heat. He might observe
> A yellow wine and follow a steamer's track
> And say, "The thing I hum appears to be
> The rhythm of this celestial pantomime."
>
> (CP 243)

To move from "emerald" to "emeralds" means more than to move away from primary colors: it is to step from homogeneity to heterogeneity, from monolithic identity to pluralistic difference, from the unified to the diversified. To "watch the palms / Flap green ears in the heat" is to stage the world's potential for imaginative and poetic investment, figured here by a dense admixture of metaphor and metonymy: the palm leaves do not merely resemble, say, a rabbit's drooping ears, but the metaphor of "Flap[ping] ears" is also metonymically inspired by the sound of the leaves rustled by the wind. The hedonist's eye and ear (and even, because of the "yellow wine," taste and smell) are gratified by the Mediterranean "Landscape with Boat," so much so that the ambiance makes the speaker "hum" out of sheer delight. Such humming is Stevens's downplayed metaphor for writing poetry—downplayed because it is inspired by the "celestial pantomime" of the environment, and the one thing pantomimes by definition lack is the spoken word. The world and reality constitute a mute spectacle that needs poets to give it voice and music.[45] With typical etymological subtlety, Stevens gives his final word an unexpected resonance by inscribing a fundamentally mimetic trait in all of reality (panto-mime). Not only does language seek to mirror the world, he seems to suggest, but the world itself also mirrors language. This is no cause for epistemological despair but only for a relaxed celebration of our "celestial" condition.

Stevens's final scene of a Mediterranean landscape with boat functions as an attractive, sensuous antidote to the world-renouncing austerity evinced by the floribund ascetic. But it, too, has its limits. If we think of the scene against its biographical background, for instance, we cannot help but notice the status of this Mediterranean seascape as a somewhat bourgeois paradisal fantasy, appropriately disinfected and aestheticized, the imaginary toy of a settled insurance lawyer who, at sixty, knew he would never actually see Europe, but who relished visiting it, as an armchair traveler, in his mind. This background acquires a special poignancy from the poem's date of composition: 1940. Europe was a battlefield in that year, not a holiday destination. In Stevens's American mind, political isolationism proved sufficiently entrenched to allow him to overwrite historical reality and picture himself humming and sipping wine among the palm trees at the French Côte d'Azur or the Italian Riviera. His own poetic rejection of the ascetic's radical rejection of life in a material world was thus also a rejection of a major part of that life and that material world. Though his aestheticized world of delightful objects and impressions could figure "the noble repose that comes of being out of reach of human persuasion," it could not extricate itself from "the human power to destroy"; like so many other high modernist depictions of an object world, it could only represent "a realm beyond the reach of ideology but not secure against the material consequences of ideological conflicts."[46] This is the fate not only of modernist utopias organized around the innocence of objects, but, more widely, of all advocacies and apologies of hedonism: such prelapsarian utopias and idealizations have their own severe restrictions, their own self-blinding partialities. A reply to the Mondrians of art (and philosophy) can make beguiling use of parts of the world to celebrate life—but only of certain parts and no others. The sociopolitical world

45. Marie Borroff usefully reminds us of the music in the final lines, those "repetitive phonic patterns that make us conscious, as we read, of the sounds of words, including the *m*- and *p*-systems to which *Mediterranean, emerald[s], palms, hum, appears, rhythm,* and *pantomime* belong" ("Making Sense of the Sleight-of-Hand Man," 98).

46. Mao, *Solid Objects,* 9.

of conflict and potential violence needs to be hummed away into oblivion. The imperfect, as we all know, is not *just* a paradise.

And there is yet another act of forgetting that enabled Stevens to write "Landscape with Boat." Even if a modicum of self-irony may be held to inform the description of the ascetic, Stevens still manages rather easily in this poem to come down on one side of the debate, ignoring for the moment his own strong inclination toward abstraction and his own regular distrust of the sufficiency of sensuous particulars. MacLeod convincingly demonstrates how much more divided and ambivalent Stevens could be, as early as the late thirties, about abstract art, and how he would soon come to latch on to justifications for abstraction, which he found, among other places, in Mondrian's writings.[47] "Landscape with Boat" thus possesses all the momentary strength of its humanistic and phenomenological appeal, but not the strength of representativeness with respect to Stevens's poetry overall. This is not Stevens at his most polyphonic, dramatizing the difficult polylogue inside his head, but a more monologic poet, setting up a rhetorical divide between self and opponent for the sake of disputation and programmatic affirmation. "Landscape with Boat" is an affirmation of the sensuous particulars of this world, and may be enjoyed as such by the reader; but it is also, surreptitiously, an exorcism. To make the visible a little harder to see and enjoy, we need to return to more subtly ambiguous texts like "Study of Two Pears" and "The Latest Freed Man"—poems that have always been taken to belong to this writer's greatest lyric achievements.

47. MacLeod, *Wallace Stevens and Modern Art*, 95.

Chapter 9

Between the Senses of Sense

IF WE NEED TO RECKON WITH the human mind to be able to develop a sensible relationship with the thing itself, we also need to reckon with human sensibility and with the role of the external senses. The word *sense* is one of the most crucial, though least-noted, nodal words around which Stevens's thought and work collects in pools. It is a characteristically polysemous word that carries ample epistemological ramifications, so much so that definitions and illustrations in the *Oxford English Dictionary* run to several pages. Stevens tapped into a remarkable number of those meanings and followed through on many of the potential ramifications. Simply culling from the *O.E.D.* those sections that are of direct relevance to his work, we quickly require all of the following (slightly stylized) entries:

I. Faculty of perception or sensation.
    1. Each of the special faculties, connected with a bodily organ, by which man and other animals perceive external objects and changes in the condition of their bodies. Usu. reckoned as five—sight, hearing, smell, taste, touch. Also called *outward or external sense*.
    pl. The faculties of physical perception or sensation as opposed to the higher faculties of intellect, spirit, etc.
    2. An instinctive or acquired faculty of perception or accurate estimation. E.g. a sense of locality, of distance.
    5. Capability of feeling, as a quality of the body and its parts; liability to feel pain, irritation, etc.
    7. Applied to faculties of the mind or soul compared or contrasted with the bodily senses; usually with some defining word, as *inner, interior, internal, inward sense*.
    11. Natural understanding, intelligence, esp. as bearing on action or behaviour.

II. Actual perception or feeling.

13. A more or less vague perception or impression *of* (an outward object, as present or imagined).

14. A more or less indefinite consciousness or impression *of* (a fact, state of things, etc.) as present or impending.

16. Emotional consciousness of something.

18. An opinion, view, or judgment held or formed.

III. Meaning, signification.

19. The meaning or signification of a word or phrase.

20.b. The meaning or interpretation of a dream, or of anything cryptic or symbolical.

20.c. The gist, upshot, or general purport of words spoken or written.

23. The meaning of a speaker or writer; the substance, purport, or intention of what he says.

27. Discourse that has a satisfactory and intelligible meaning. Phr. *To make sense of,* to find a meaning in.

28. What is wise or reasonable.

In the most general terms, these definitions run the gamut of possibilities between two semantic poles. At one extreme, we find bodily perceptions and sensations in their utmost immediacy and presence; at the other, a thinking consciousness interpreting the world that is composed, by and large, of those perceptions and sensations. In between these extremes, however, a considerable twilight zone stretches out—a zone for which "feeling" presents a faintly synonymous but barely helpful alternative. It is especially because of this twilight zone that lexicographers (those cryptometaphysicians) are forced to fall back on such unrigorous and approximative markers as "more or less vague" and "more or less indefinite."

The word *sense,* it turns out, operates at the very intersection between human perception, feeling, and consciousness, on one hand, and the world, on the other. It has semantically assimilated various types of interaction and interplay between humans and their environment. That is why it has so easily acquired some of the more plural, conflicted, and elusive qualities of human life itself insofar as we try to understand, appreciate, and express our experiences. How great in particular is the potential for ideological contestability may be gauged from a derived concept that was the locus of a whole poetic-metaphysical debate in Stevens's day: the concept of "sensibility." Raymond Williams, in his invaluable little study of "keywords" in the English language, traces the word *sensibility* back to the eighteenth century, where it came to suggest "taste," "cultivation," and "discrimination."

Throughout the nineteenth century, he illustrates, it retained the overall meaning of "aesthetic feeling," until in the early years of the twentieth century T. S. Eliot made it serve his own ideological agenda by coining the phrase (for the purpose of deploring) "the dissociation of sensibility" supposedly typical of the modern era. To Eliot, says Williams, the phrase referred to "a supposed disjunction between 'thought' and 'feeling.' *Sensibility* became the apparently unifying word, and on the whole was transferred from kinds of response to a use equivalent to the formation of a particular mind: a whole activity, a whole way of perceiving and responding, not to be reduced to either 'thought' or 'feeling.' "[1]

Stevens, as is known, did not share Eliot's postlapsarian scenario. The need to ideologically reunify modern man failed to electrify him sufficiently for him to be willing to march to Eliot's reactionary drum. What he did come to favor doing in his own work, though, was to explore and exploit a word like *sense* for the purpose of teasing out the limits of his and other people's art-making. The following meditations from "Effects of Analogy" (1948), dealing with the issue of resemblance and its relation to poetry, are but one case in point:

> Another mode of analogy is to be found in the personality of the poet. . . . This mode proposes for study the poet's sense of the world as the source of poetry. The corporeal world exists as the common denominator of the incorporeal worlds of its inhabitants. If there are people who live only in the corporeal world, enjoying the wind and the weather and supplying standards of normality, there are other people who are not so sure of the wind and the weather and who supply standards of abnormality. It is the poet's sense of the world that is the poet's world. The corporeal world, the familiar world of the commonplace, in short, our world, is one sense of the analogy that develops between our world and the world of the poet. The poet's sense of the world is the other sense. It is the analogy between these two senses that concerns us. . . . A man's sense of the world is born with him and persists, and penetrates the ameliorations of education and experience of life. His species is as fixed as his genus. For each man, then, certain subjects are congenital. Now, the poet manifests his personality, first of all, by his choice of subject. Temperament is a more explicit word than personality and would no doubt be the exact word to use, since it emphasizes the manner of thinking and feeling. . . . What is the poet's subject? It is his sense of the world. For him, it is inevitable and inexhaustible. (*NA* 118, 120, 121)

1. Raymond Williams, *Keywords: A Vocabulary of Culture and Society*, 235–38; "dissociation of sensibility": T. S. Eliot, "The Metaphysical Poets," 64.

The argument sounds at least partly apologetic, and understandably so: as an idiosyncratic avant-garde poet, Stevens belonged to a rare "species" himself. Moreover, with the passing of the years he became more and more obsessed with the question of genetic predisposition—what he called "the unalterable necessity / Of being this unalterable animal" (CP 324)—to the point of spending large sums of money on tracing his genealogical family tree. But what is of more importance to the argument pursued in the above excerpts is that it conspicuously hinges on a fuzzy kind of logic. By the time Stevens gets around to setting up an analogy between various "senses" of the world, he begins to sound circular and we are not really led beyond the mysterious "sense of the world" with which "normal" people and artists alike appear to be impregnated. This sense involves both "thinking and feeling"—no emphasis on a culturally widespread dissociation here—but, partly because of this amalgamation, does not appear to open itself up to further definition and theorization. If someone's innate sense of the world is "inevitable and inexhaustible," it also proves to be to a large extent inexplicable. When the painter Raoul Dufy died in 1953, Stevens pointed to some of the ingredients and backgrounds that went into the artist's lithographs, only to wind up saying that "all the ideas, documentation, study and observation . . . are subdued, finally, by Dufy's sense" (OP 282). And in answer to a 1938 questionnaire from *Twentieth Century Verse* asking whether a representative American poetry existed distinct from English poetry, Stevens characteristically hedged his bets and politically wrote back that "there exists a clear sense of what is American. Conceding that we are racially a bit tentative, does not the sense of what we are answer your question?" (OP 308).

The pat statement and rhetorical question in the elliptical reply to *Twentieth Century Verse* were not only sufficiently vague to be able to accommodate a wide range of ideological appropriations at a time of stringent ideological altercations. They also betrayed the limitations of a word like *sense* in a political context. There the word could at most act as an evasive, circumspect locution that resisted coming down firmly on either side of the divide in a nationalistically and even jingoistically loaded debate between the political right and the political left. Indeed, immediately following Stevens's affirmation of the existence of "a clear sense of what is American," we find his answer to the second half of the question ("do you think the American Renaissance of 1912 and the following years had permanent value?"): "The less said about permanent values now-a-days, the better" (OP 308). The ideological difficulties attached to Stevens's formulation of a tentative sense of Americanness spotlight the fact that his habit of using the word *sense* was bound to be more effective in the restricted, nonpolitical, and nonracialized contexts in which he usually turned to it—contexts in which he rather sought to express an aesthetic personality, a certain philosophical thoughtfulness, and/or a lyrical susceptibility. It was in those three contexts, above all, that Stevens was able to put the word to satisfactory use by playing on its several enumerated meanings.

Exploring the poetics of modern punning, Eleanor Cook wonders: "What words come with so venerable a history of paronomasia that no self-respecting modern poet can use them without making choices? That is, poets may use these words if they wish, but they must decide what to do about the standard paronomasia—whether to distance it, or merely to acknowledge it, or to carry on with it."[2] Cook's examples are words like *turn, leaves, room, immaculate* and *maculate*, and *infans*—all of them, she goes on to demonstrate, staples of the Stevens canon. If *sense* belongs in this category, we should of course start by observing that Stevens does not always actively pursue the paronomasia. Sometimes the meaning of the word can be determined quite precisely and unequivocally on the basis of context. We have no trouble, for instance, understanding what the poet refers to in the fourteenth of his "Variations on a Summer Day":

> Words add to the senses. The words for the dazzle
> Of mica, the dithering of grass,
> The Arachne integument of dead trees,
> Are the eye grown larger, more intense.
>
> (CP 234)

The "senses" here are the five external faculties of perception and sensation, represented synecdochically by the eye. If there is anything that is poetically foregrounded in these four lines, it is not the semantic potential of the word *sense* but the self-conscious vocabulary that follows in its wake, as well as the dense and forbidding classical allusion to a girl, Arachne, whose mythical story tells of weaving, artistry, and spiderwebs. Similarly, when in "Arcades of Philadelphia the Past," Stevens ponders the fact that "A man must be very poor / With a single sense," we interpret this in light of the preceding

---

2. Eleanor Cook, "The Poetics of Modern Punning: Wallace Stevens, Elizabeth Bishop, and Others," 175.

stanza: "To see, / To hear, to touch, to taste, to smell, that's now, / That's this" (*CP* 225). The illustrations that follow make clear that the reference in this case is again primarily to the external senses.

More frequently, however, Stevens's use of *sense* is denotatively insecure, spreading out into its more elusive, contaminated, and enigmatic meanings (or senses). The excerpt from "Effects of Analogy" provides only one of many instances, and it is easy enough to find near-literal echoes of its contents and language in adages like "A poem should be part of one's sense of life" (*OP* 191) and "Reality is the object seen in its greatest common sense" (*OP* 202). Especially in the later poetry, we may notice how the word crops up in ways that simultaneously evoke irrational qualities of being, mix external perception with internal perception, and point to an unaccountable temperamental inclination. "Ill of a constant question in his thought," for example, Stevens grows "Unhappy about the sense of happiness," and stops to ask the riddling questions:

> Was it that—a sense and beyond intelligence?
> Could the future rest on a sense and be beyond
> Intelligence? On what does the present rest?
> (*CP* 331)

Not on language, Stevens seems to be implying, for language can provide us only with an approximating "sense" of what is at stake here and no full-blown "intelligence." Analogously, there is no way we could ever pinpoint the precise referent of a line like "There is a sense in sounds beyond their meaning" (*CP* 352). Does *sense* here stand for some ulterior purpose? Or is it merely a sort of acoustical first idea, sound *as* sound, with all human meanings (thought and feeling) sifted out? Part of our being-in-the-world, Stevens seems to be saying, consists of a "feeling" or "feelings" that remain forever beyond understanding and language. There is always a sense to Stevens's use of the word *sense*, but sometimes language can do no more than grope for it, casting a wide-meshed net, surrounding it periphrastically, acknowledging an irreducible alterity and irrationality. The five external senses and even our overall sense of the world may come from outside language, but within language they reside not *in* but *between* the senses of the word *sense*.

Two consecutive poems from *The Auroras of Autumn*, "The Ultimate Poem Is Abstract" and "Bouquet of Roses in Sunlight," turn around, upon,

or toward the word *sense*. The first and more forceful of the poems offers an-
other version of Stevens's longing to escape from the treadmill of the mind,
expressed this time with a wry and caustic desperation:

> This day writhes with what? The lecturer
> On This Beautiful World Of Ours composes himself
> And hems the planet rose and haws it ripe,
>
> And red, and right. The particular question—here
> The particular answer to the particular question
> Is not in point—the question is in point.
>
> If the day writhes, it is not with revelations.
> One goes on asking questions. That, then, is one
> Of the categories. So said, this placid space
>
> Is changed. It is not so blue as we thought. To be blue,
> There must be no questions. It is an intellect
> Of windings round and dodges to and fro,
>
> Writhings in wrong obliques and distances,
> Not an intellect in which we are fleet: present
> Everywhere in space at once, cloud-pole
>
> Of communication. It would be enough
> If we were ever, just once, at the middle, fixed
> In This Beautiful World Of Ours and not as now,
>
> Helplessly at the edge, enough to be
> Complete, because at the middle, if only in sense,
> And in that enormous sense, merely enjoy.
>
> (CP 429–30)

Hardly a better word could have been chosen for voicing the vague dis-
comfort-without-origin that plagues the poet and provokes the poem than
the verb *writhe:* its faint suggestion of strangling and suffocation (as if the
speaker were trying to wrest himself free from a straitjacket), its obstruct-
ing materiality (evident from the uncomfortable way the word sits in the
mouth), and its contorted near-homonymity with *write* all add to its ex-
pressive effect. Being in a foul, unsparing mood, Stevens quickly turns to
mockery, leveled both at other poets—Helen Vendler suspects "The lecturer
/ On This Beautiful World Of Ours" to be Keats or some blood brother—and

at himself.[3] The self-mockery may be heard above all in the bathetic disso-
nance and the hollow virtuosic rotundity of "hems the planet rose and haws
it ripe, // And red, and right." Prettifying the day into cheaply alliterative
poetry will not do at this point, for such a slick trick amounts to no more
than an evasive expedient, a "particular [aestheticized] answer" that cannot
satisfy the larger "particular question." Once again, Stevens's restless mind,
craving to know and understand yet feeling impotent and defeated, "goes on
asking questions," until the world is robbed even of the certainty of its blue
skies. "The Ultimate Poem Is Abstract" predates "Effects of Analogy" by
only a year, and so is roughly contemporaneous with the previously quoted
claim that "[i]f there are people who live only in the corporeal world, enjoy-
ing the wind and the weather and supplying standards of normality, there
are other people who are not so sure of the wind and the weather and who
supply standards of abnormality."

Abnormality, this poem reminds us, is not always easy to live with. It can-
not always be handsomely contained by claiming an artistic ability to offer
"standards" for it. Sometimes it merely confirms one in feeling "helplessly
at the edge." Even the act of writing a poem about this helplessness can
be unmasked as a futile "dodg[ing] to and fro" in a world where the intel-
lect manages only to "writh[e] in wrong obliques and distances" instead of
reaching the dynamic centrality of a swift yet omnipresent "cloud-pole // Of
communication." The poem, in one interpretation, "develops by exhausting
itself and its composer, who wants only to bring himself to the point where
he has nothing to say, where something will be said for him."[4] The two final
stanzas are infused with a psychic tension whose exact cause remains unde-
cidable (at least to the reader) but whose urgency is all the more evident. "It
would be enough," Stevens sighs, if one could ever feel "at the middle" of
reality, "if only in sense, / And in that enormous sense, merely enjoy." The
ambivalence of the ending, its divided sentiment, is patent. For in one of his
favorite rhetorical maneuvers, Stevens works hard to overwrite the optative
character of his fantasy by paratactically heaping up reformulations and ex-
emplifications of a state of well-being until we finish reading the poem with
a sense of affirmation and enjoyment. "The poem itself is a fine example of
Stevens's sleight-of-hand with verbs," notes William W. Bevis, pointing to
"the prestidigitation that Vendler first revealed: 'enjoy' *cannot* be parallel
to either the infinitive 'to be,' or the adjective 'complete.' To be parallel,

3. Vendler, "Stevens and Keats," 190.
4. Roy Harvey Pearce, *The Continuity of American Poetry*, 408.

the form would have to be 'to enjoy,' or 'enjoying.' Instead, the declarative 'enjoy' gives the lie to 'and': there has been a hiatus, and in that hidden moment the wished-for state of mind has suddenly been accomplished."[5]

Whether we can really talk of any accomplishment, however, is not so certain. The ending, as Margaret Dickie argues, "opens out rather than closes the subject."[6] The momentary illusionism of the final rhetorical trick may not be strong enough to cancel the strength of the cafard that only two lines before disrupts the crescendo Stevens is trying to build up. The "enormous sense" of enjoyment remains written in the form of an irrealis, and we are made to feel that if "The Ultimate Poem Is Abstract," this cannot be that ultimate poem. We are instead made to marvel at what it might mean to reach a place "at the middle, fixed" where we are "present / Everywhere in space at once," a place where we have ultimately succeeded in abstracting ourselves entirely from a turmoil of writhing questions. How far indeed should we take the qualification "ultimate" to extend? Would not the attainment of an ultimate abstraction require us to surrender the very illusion of an "enormous sense" in which we can "merely enjoy"? Can any poem that goes beyond the merest vocalization of a hemming and hawing meet the requirement of ultimate abstraction? And how can we ever hope to *share* a sense of both the enormity and the mereness of an ultimate, abstract joy? Language itself is too helplessly at the edge to pull this off. At most, it can only hint at what this enormous enjoyment might be; it can only provide us with a vague *sense* of it, point *toward* it, and in the act of hinting, in the act of writing a poem about this hinting, not only *provide* a sense of it but *make* sense of it for us, now, here, who have not yet succumbed to the ultimate abstraction that is death.

The twin text that follows "The Ultimate Poem Is Abstract" picks up the word *sense* again. Recalling in the process poems like "Study of Two Pears," "The Poems of Our Climate" (*CP* 193–94), "Add This to Rhetoric" (*CP* 198–99), and "Woman Looking at a Vase of Flowers" (*CP* 246–47), it turns to look at a bouquet of roses in sunlight:

> Say that it is a crude effect, black reds,
> Pink yellows, orange whites, too much as they are
> To be anything else in the sunlight of the room,

---

5. Bevis, *Mind of Winter*, 103.
6. Dickie, *Lyric Contingencies*, 159.

Too much as they are to be changed by metaphor,
Too actual, things that in being real
Make any imaginings of them lesser things.

And yet this effect is a consequence of the way
We feel and, therefore, is not real, except
In our sense of it, our sense of the fertilest red,

Of yellow as first color and of white,
In which the sense lies still, as a man lies,
Enormous, in a completing of his truth.

Our sense of these things changes and they change,
Not as in metaphor, but in our sense
Of them. So sense exceeds all metaphor.

It exceeds the heavy changes of the light.
It is like a flow of meanings with no speech
And of as many meanings as of men.

We are two that use these roses as we are,
In seeing them. This is what makes them seem
So far beyond the rhetorician's touch.

                                   (CP 430–31)

"Bouquet of Roses in Sunlight" is a considerably less tormented poem
than its predecessor, more classically epistemological and perceptual in its
concerns. Stevens returns to the ineluctable modality of the visible that
he so frequently explores as an antidote to his fantasticating habits. The
roses are "too much as they are" not to be diminished by any of his artificial
"imaginings." Yet their immediate materiality as objects cannot be severed
from the perceiving subject's receptivity: their colors are "a consequence
of the way / We feel." In the condensed play on *sense* that follows, we are
made to hear all of the word's major significations in an uncertainly shifting
interaction: external visual perception shades into an almost ineffable fun-
damental feeling (echoing the previous poem in being called "Enormous"
and "a completing," and further complicated by the pun on lying) and then
into personal meaning ("a flow of meanings with no speech / And of as
many meanings as of men"). A still later poem, "Things of August," pro-
poses that "the beholder . . . is the possessed of sense not the possessor" (*CP*
492). If "sense exceeds all metaphor," this is because, unlike the inventions

of metaphor, sense cannot be "reached at will";[7] it is a happening, a state of mind or mood that occurs *to* the beholder, that befalls him inexplicably, that determines his state of being. But it is also responsible for a dynamic, vitalizing rapport with the world of objects that surrounds us. "Our 'sense' of the world," Beverly Maeder writes, "is in a dialectical relationship with it, and as our experience heightens it, it brings about a change in the world that is greater than the change produced by metaphor."[8]

As a poet intermittently given to casting a cold eye on the instruments and pretensions of his own art, Stevens winds up siding once again with a nonverbal "sense" of the world, "beyond the rhetorician's touch." Or so it would "seem," for seeing can never really transcend seeming, as a poet can never really step outside the illusionism of language and metaphoricity to communicate his "sense" of the world around him. The implicit opposition set up between the rhetorician and (for want of a better alternative) the realist is itself a momentary rhetorical ploy reminiscent of the opposition between an "evading metaphor" and "the figure" in "Add This to Rhetoric" (CP 199). The only way to let the bouquet of roses be registered by the senses alone is to fall silent, as the poem does at the point of reaching out to a reality "beyond the rhetorician's touch." As long as we keep verbalizing, we are condemned to embrace the contamination of words in their botched and bungling attempts at making sense. Sensation, feeling, and meaning all weave into our sense-making words, for they are part of a single experiential nexus that we can disentangle and name only at the expense of dissolving or disfiguring it. The bouquet of roses may *seem* to exist "far beyond the rhetorician's touch," but only because the rhetorician in Stevens is doing his level best to lay low, to play the linguistic opossum.[9]

·   ·   ·

7. Riddel, *Clairvoyant Eye*, 233.
8. Maeder, *Experimental Language*, 57.
9. This implies that the intrinsic textuality of the text, as so often with this poet, may easily be played off against the poet's ostensible desire (be it ever so momentary) to transcend the disfigurations of language and metaphoricity. Maeder offers one eloquent example of such a reading when she comments that "what the poem affirms and what it does are opposed. A paraphrase of the poem's statements affirms that there is a subjective plane of sharable or shared experience in which metaphor is illegitimate because the kind of change it produces would be purely external. Metaphor is opposed to meaning that is human, whereas the objects of sense perception are not because they give life to feeling and feeling to life. Metaphor would be the touch that separates us from our 'meanings,' from applications to each individual's life. But what the poem's metaphorical work does is to apprehend indirectly yet respect the integrity of the things perceived. The shifting words for colors, the slippage and

The same three facets of sensation, feeling, and meaning return, finally, in one of Stevens's late and most widely appreciated poems, "The Plain Sense of Things" (1952). As so often in the case of the late work, one needs to be familiar with the preceding poetic output and its recurrent topoi to appreciate fully the power of this poem's simplicity, the stamina of its backward glance, and the weight of its personal involvement. "The Plain Sense of Things" belongs to the poems that Bevis calls "an old man's art, with everything to say and nothing to prove, poems saturated with patient intensity."[10] When submitting the poem to Margaret Marshall as one of a group of seven short lyrics, Stevens austerely commented: "Now that these poems have been completed they seem to have nothing to do with anything in particular, except poetry, and you will have to determine for yourself whether they are appropriate for use in The Nation" (L 764). However, if this comment ostensibly works to downplay "The Plain Sense," it may be counterbalanced by pointing to the amplitude that at least two of Stevens's most prominent critics have given to the poem. Thus, Frank Kermode saw fit to borrow both title and subject matter for an extended analysis of what he claimed to be a central theme, no less, in modern philosophy, and James Longenbach did not hesitate to subtitle his major contribution to Stevens scholarship simply *The Plain Sense of Things*. Not coincidentally, perhaps, a similar dialectic between gestures of deflation and inflation characterizes critical responses to the poem's tone, which vary from Roy Harvey Pearce's "mood of calmness and certitude (transcendent as opposed to transcending)" and Lensing's insistence upon "blankness" to Vendler's emphasis on the poet's "immense effort" and "heroic" attempt.[11]

Stevens was seventy-three as he observed how, after an exceptionally dismal summer, one more fall was passing into yet another New England winter:

> After the leaves have fallen, we return
> To a plain sense of things. It is as if

---

transformation of the word 'sense(s),' the metaphor of 'the rhetorician's touch,' and the other similes and metaphors all point to the very intervention of metaphorical language as what allows us to 'use' (in the last stanza)—and be consciously active in using—the objects we observe" (*Experimental Language*, 60).

10. Bevis, *Mind of Winter*, 112.

11. Frank Kermode, *An Appetite for Poetry*, 172–88; Longenbach, *Plain Sense of Things*; Pearce, "Toward Decreation," 302; Lensing, *Seasons*, 52; Vendler, *On Extended Wings*, 112, 114.

We had come to an end of the imagination,
Inanimate in an inert savoir.

It is difficult even to choose the adjective
For this blank cold, this sadness without cause.
The great structure has become a minor house.
No turban walks across the lessened floors.

The greenhouse never so badly needed paint.
The chimney is fifty years old and slants to one side.
A fantastic effort has failed, a repetition
In a repetitiousness of men and flies.

Yet the absence of the imagination had
Itself to be imagined. The great pond,
The plain sense of it, without reflections, leaves,
Mud, water like dirty glass, expressing silence

Of a sort, silence of a rat come out to see,
The great pond and its waste of the lilies, all this
Had to be imagined as an inevitable knowledge,
Required, as a necessity requires.

                                        (CP 502–3)

"The Plain Sense of Things," says Longenbach, "begins where the consol-
ing fiction of 'The Rock' ends. The leaves disguising the barrenness of our
world have fallen." We may hear a faint echo of Stevens's favorite Shake-
spearean sonnet, number 73, on the time of year when only a few leaves, or
none at all, still hang upon the boughs. The poet does not merely "return /
To a plain sense of things," but also to a poetic topos—that of the autumnal
experience of transience, the nostalgia of old age, and the elegiac and conso-
latory functions of poetry. With its "suppression of the imagination," "return
to ignorance," "sense of discomfiture," and "tropes of reduction," the poem is
to Lensing "a summary of [all of Stevens's] poems of autumn."[12] The opening
mood is one of finality and impotence, only to be rescued from the bleakest
despair of the literal (the inescapable, the immobile) by the insertion of an
"as if" and the use of the indefinite article: "*as if* / We had come to *an* end of
the imagination." Still, the sense of impotence appears to be great; it speaks
sardonically from the remarkably self-conscious fourth line: "Inanimate in

12. Longenbach, *Plain Sense of Things*, 303; Lensing, *Seasons*, 62.

an inert savoir." The rhetoric in this line seems to be hollowed of all life; it is in the same league with the hemming and hawing, the "rhetorician's touch," decried in "The Ultimate Poem Is Abstract" and "Bouquet of Roses in Sunlight." It is the jugglery of an old hand that knows the ropes. The principal effect of the French nominalized verb is not to enchant or amuse, but rather to twist the mouth, to strike us as vapidly sophisticated. Suspended by itself, the word *savoir* lacks the "conjunction with 'faire' or 'vivre' and is left in a kind of limbo on the page."[13] It is introduced, moreover, by a stammering series of no less deadening words. Ronald Schleifer's suggestion of "a kind of negative materiality," for all the stretching it involves, seems apt: "'inanimate' is reduced to its material sound, *in-an-imate*, the ghostly repetition ('return') of its sound that is there all along, 'in an inert': where meaning (or 'spirit,' or the imagination) was, there shall non-sense (or the blank cold of 'matter' and the 'letter') come to be."[14] By the end of the first stanza, Stevens's "return / To a plain sense of things" becomes in fact almost a return to *nonsense*—the nonsense of a poetry that falls apart, a language that falters.

The feeling, expressed in "The Man with the Blue Guitar," of a "heraldic center of the world" containing "The amorist Adjective aflame" (CP 172) has forsaken the poet as well. The very choice of an "adjective / For this . . . cold" has become "difficult," and if Stevens, describe as he must, nevertheless comes up with "blank," the word can only communicate the inventive poverty of his mind by forgoing any positively concrete description. There is no point even in questioning the origin of this mood, "this sadness," for it is sprung upon the poet "without cause," like a mere sense of things. Disaffection toward all the poetry that has gone before cannot itself be the direct cause, then, yet it does appear to be one of the more subtly registered effects. The "great structure" that "has become a minor house," suggests, by its very wording, the attempted construction of an architecturally connected oeuvre. And the absence of a "turban" synecdochically recalls that fantastic and fictive fabric out of which Stevens's poetry at its most exotic used to be woven—like the "Arabian" who had earlier visited the poet's room "With his damned hoobla-hoobla-hoobla-how" (CP 383).

The third stanza, despite the simple, matter-of-fact depiction in its first two lines, arguably throws another backward glance at Stevens's poetic achievement. At first "The greenhouse" that "never so badly needed paint"

13. Jenkins, *Rage for Order*, 113.
14. Ronald Schleifer, *Rhetoric and Death: The Language of Modernism and Postmodern Discourse Theory*, 224.

looks only like the literal thing, an understandably disconcerting sight to the old poet, filling him with a sense of depleted energies at the prospect of the never-ending need for material reconstruction.[15] But it may also be read as "a place of artificial growth," as a trope for the poetic imagination.[16] Looking at house, greenhouse, and chimney from the windblown, relativizing perspective of the outdoors, Stevens is visited by doubts about the artificiality and circularity of much of his lifetime's work. "A fantastic effort has failed, a repetition / In a repetitiousness of men and flies." The "men" in his poetry, to be sure, had never been *actual* men (or women), but a collection of invented, allegorical men (and women), both in the form of extravagantly made-up creatures and of displaced self-portraits. As early as April 27, 1906, Stevens had recorded in his journal: "There is a perfect rout of characters in every man—and every man is like an actor's trunk, full of strange creatures, new & old" (SP 166). Almost fifty years later, the act of fleshing out these gaudily appareled creatures strikes Stevens as having led only to a "repetitiousness" and, in a self-deprecating juxtaposition, the creatures are flicked off in one and the same gesture as irritably buzzing "flies."

At this point, the nadir of the poem has been reached and something of a traditional volta is required if the poem is not to fall prey to an unremitting gloom. Not surprisingly, what opens up a gap for Stevens is his habit of questioning the structure of experience and perception. Turning against his own despondency, he finds a redeeming force in a structural necessity, a necessary condition: "the absence of the imagination had / Itself to be imagined." The inconspicuous shift from present to past tense helps to record a sense of overcoming, of surrendering the literalness that until this moment seems to have kept the poet in its grip. All the poem's descriptions,

---

15. At seventy-three, we should remember, Stevens was still holding a full-time job as a vice president at the Hartford Accident and Indemnity Company, refusing to retire out of an overscrupulous sense of financial responsibility for the futures of his wife, his daughter, and his grandson. On October 24, 1952, which must have been no more than a couple of days before he composed the poem, he wrote to Thomas MacGreevy grudgingly and plaintively: "At my age it would be nice to be able to read more and think more and be myself more and to make up my mind about God, say, before it is too late, or at least before he makes up his mind about me. And I should like to walk more and be in the air more and get around more. But it is all incompatible with paying taxes and trying to save a little money. More particularly, at this very time of year when we are in the midst of autumn and well aware that the cold is coming on, I keep thinking that I would like to go South. Who doesn't? Then a day or so ago I received a note from Sweden with a little picture showing the ground covered with snow before the leaves had fallen (a sign, if not a proof, of a long winter), and a man walking across country with his dog, and I'd like that too" (L 763).

16. Michael Beehler, *T. S. Eliot, Wallace Stevens, and the Discourses of Difference*, 161.

we are made to feel, have at least one irreducible quality in common: that the act of figuring an absence or shortcoming makes for its own imaginative productivity. Presenting the "plain sense of things" still requires something minimally positive (something minimally posited) like the stubborn materiality of a "great pond," even if that pond must be "without reflections, leaves, / Mud, water like dirty glass," without the possibilities for inventive naming and describing, without the mirror surface into which a decrepit Narcissus might hope to stare. A "plain sense," in fact, must be so barely something as to facilitate the escape from an inner "sadness without cause" into a state of "silence." Not absence, but silence, and this silence, spilling over the stanza's rim in a telling enjambment, proves to be "Of a [particular] sort," more specifically: the "silence of a rat come out to see." It is, in other words, again the silence of an animal state of perception and sensation, but now in an even more diminished form. This time Stevens is willing to forgo the grander or more benignly funny connotations that cling to such images as the strong ox (in "The Latest Freed Man"), the lion and bear (in "Poetry Is a Destructive Force," CP 192–93), the self-inflating rabbit (in "A Rabbit as King of the Ghosts," CP 209–10), and the donkey Pompilio in his correspondence with José Rodríguez Feo.[17] The "rat's low vantage point on the world," as James Longenbach judiciously comments, serves the purpose of canceling an unwanted view: "viewed from the higher perspective that human beings usually occupy, the surface of the water would be clouded by mirror images."[18] Stevens evidently does not want the boomerang interiority of self-"reflections" at this point. He is trying to derive strength and enjoyment rather from a stoically dispassionate, almost ataractic attachment to the material world around him—the sort of snow-man perspective that allowed him to write in the fall of 1952, in a letter to Sister M. Bernetta Quinn: "This morning I walked around in the park here for almost an hour before coming to the office and felt as blank as one of the ponds which in the

17. Stevens's conscious association with a rat may involve a sly reply to the pontifex of poetry in the early fifties, T. S. Eliot (see also Leonard and Wharton, Fluent Mundo, 27). After all, rats stand for revulsion, horror, and death in The Waste Land: "I think we are in rats' alley / Where the dead men lost their bones. / . . . / A rat crept softly through the vegetation / Dragging its slimy belly on the bank / While I was fishing in the dull canal / . . . / And bones cast in a little low dry garret, / Rattled by the rat's foot only, year to year" (T. S. Eliot, Collected Poems 1909–1962, 57, 60). From this point of view, it may not be a lexical coincidence that Stevens-as-rat sees a "waste of the lilies." At least to him, we might interpret the possible allusion, there are still lilies, and the waste can be accepted without lapsing into Eliot's barely withheld neurasthenia.

18. Longenbach, Plain Sense of Things, 303.

weather at this time of year are motionless. But perhaps it was the blankness that made me enjoy it so much" (*L* 762).

Despite this image of concentration, a great variety of perspectives is nevertheless needed to throw light on the poem's quintessentially Stevensian conclusion: "all this / Had to be imagined as an inevitable knowledge, / Required, as a necessity requires." Diction, for one thing, is of unexpected importance here, especially if we follow up Eleanor Cook's casual suggestion that there may be an "unobtrusive" "play with 'in'" in the poem.[19] Indeed, the first, middle, and final stanzas appear to be clinched by formulations that hinge on *in*: "*In*animate *in* an *in*ert savoir. // . . . a repetition / *In* a repetitiousness of men and flies. // . . . an *in*evitable knowledge, / Required, as a necessity requires." The prepositions and prefixes trace out much of the poem's progress: from being locked in lifeless inertia, through the hopelessness of intellectual and emotional circularity, to a positive affirmation of fate and the material world. "It is as if / We had come to an end of the imagination," but we have not: there is no end of the imagination as long as there is no end *to* the imagination, and there is no end to it as long as there is a material world perceived by human consciousness.

Stevens's reaffirmation of the imagination is couched in abstractions that collectively recall the ambiguities of the word *sense* in his title. His pictured attempt at reaching the plain sense of things is at once perceptual ("The great pond . . . without reflections"), affective (signaled by the repetition of "Had to be"), and cognitive ("imagined as an inevitable knowledge"). As so often, this mixture turns upon the double use of *as* in the final two lines. It is the urge to understand our condition and communicate it to others that requires us to view the signifiers and the signifieds we live by as "an inevitable knowledge" (which is also, in one sense, inevitable *for* knowledge) and "a necessity." What is more, the poem also suggests that referents are no different in this respect from signifiers and signifieds. For referents, too, are arbitrary and contingent *as images* for conveying the poet's state of mind: other realities than a great pond and a rat could have served the purpose. The referents that kindle the imagination may even be viewed as arbitrary and contingent from the deeper Nietzschean perspective of a radical fictionalism that conceives of every plain visual perception as already metaphorical.[20] This is the fundamental philosophical skepsis, at the cognitive or perceptual level, that deconstructionists have found inscribed in the

---

19. Cook, *Poetry, Word-Play, and Word-War*, 297.
20. For more on this, see Chapter 11.

poem's ending.[21] Yet this skepsis constitutes but one level of Stevens's poetic enterprise. The evocation of an underlying desire is at least as important to him. And how this desire should be understood, particularly in relation to the contingency and necessity of seeing, is not so clear. The poet's "act of re-covering the ordinary world," offers Longenbach, "is not in itself inevitable or necessary—nothing can force us to be like a rat when we have the power to be an old philosopher: we must make the act necessary through the power of perceiving."[22]

The emphasis in Longenbach's reading comes to lie on an effort of the will, but the relation between will and necessity in this poem is problematic, as Steven Shaviro's elaborate Deleuzean-Nietzschean interpretation beau-tifully illustrates. To Shaviro, the world on which the poem ends precedes or exceeds the cognitive and the epistemological world; it is "inescapably linguistic, but it cannot be reduced to the effects of language as an instru-ment of knowledge or assertion. It inescapably implicates subjectivity, but it cannot be reduced to effects generated by a subject or in the course of a subject's grappling with external objects." Nevertheless, this extralinguistic and extrasubjective world, this resistant residual otherness, is affirmed by the text, and this affirmation

> exceeds both voluntarism, which would concentrate, like Bloom's [typical] reading, on figures of will and necessity, and intellectualism, which would stress [in accordance with the "skeptical idealism" of deconstruction] the poem's unavoidable blindness to its own significations. The "inevitable knowl-edge" is a knowledge only of the bafflement of knowledge . . . Yet this impasse is also an imagined necessity, necessity . . . as required by and through imag-ination . . . , and hence a positive projection of the will to power as well. Conversely, the will seems to predominate here only to the extent that it turns against itself to identify with the necessity that constrains and even-tually destroys it. But this destruction is the accomplishment, and not the defeat, of the process of willing . . . [23]

Shaviro allows us to hear in this poem what Bevis has traced in so many other texts and what my intertextual reading of "The Snow Man" via Nietz-sche has further illustrated: a Stevens who wills not to will, even if Shaviro

21. See, for example, Beehler, *Discourses of Difference*, 161.
22. Longenbach, *Plain Sense of Things*, 303. Longenbach alludes to George Santayana, the implicit dedicatee of "To an Old Philosopher in Rome," which was written soon after Santayana's death, as was "The Plain Sense of Things."
23. Shaviro, " 'That Which Is Always Beginning,' " 230.

links this up to the willing of necessity expressed by Nietzsche's *amor fati* rather than to Bevis's meditative states of consciousness pursued in Buddhist philosophies.

"Knowledge and will," argues Shaviro, "are both positively implicated as local possibilities within a larger economy of repetition without identity, so that the limitation of each is exceeded without being transcended or dialectically subsumed."[24] The "repetition" that, earlier in the poem, had seemed a "fantastic . . . fail[ure]," has not so much been dispelled by the end as reaffirmed and valorized. The structure of reality, according to this poem, is one of fundamental repetition—the repetition of a plain sense of things that exceeds the thinkable, the perceptible, the sensible, and the effable—but not the repetition of identity: the thinkable, perceptible, sensible, and effable are not in turn to be transcended or subsumed. The plain sense of things is something we can only encircle, never penetrate, for it is that ceaselessly self-questioning excess at the heart of life that baffles all understanding. In "The Irrational Element in Poetry," Stevens wrote: "That the unknown as the source of knowledge, as the object of thought, is part of the dynamics of the known does not permit of denial. It is the unknown that excites the ardor of scholars, who, in the known alone, would shrivel up with boredom. We accept the unknown even when we are most skeptical. We may resent the consideration of it by any except the most lucid minds; but when so considered, it has seductions more powerful and more profound than those of the known" (OP 231–32). To provide a *sense* of the unknown that excited his scholarly ardor was one of Stevens's major ambitions, and "The Plain Sense of Things" shows this ardor to have been, at times, a truly vital matter, a question of redeeming his existence through asking the question of existence itself at a level that could open it up to the writing of poetry. It is a question of making sense of the plain sense of things while knowing that this plain sense ultimately posits an enigma made all the more powerful and profoundly rewarding for being so enigmatic.

To court the enigmatic generally implies, as Alison Rieke has shown, that a writer be willing to test those situations where sense reaches its limit and passes into nonsense. Only the human animal is a sense-making animal, which means that our five external senses of perception and even our inner temperamental sense of things are not simply given per se, but always, as soon as we try to express them, inflected both by our desire to understand

24. Ibid., 231.

things (even if this desire comes in the form of trying to suspend the desire momentarily) and by the necessity of using contingent images and words. " 'Sense,' " in Rieke's summing up, "begins with physiology, with the body as it takes in data through the five senses. These sensations translate into mental phenomena, perceptions as understanding. Our spoken and written languages then transmit to us the meaning or sense supposedly in our heads."[25] That this process, however, is not nearly as neat and linear as Rieke's summary would have it is often demonstrated by Stevens's poetry and its constant explorations of "New senses in the engenderings of sense" (CP 527).

25. Rieke, *Senses of Nonsense*, 5.

Chapter 10

Between Mimesis and Music

ACCORDING TO J. HILLIS MILLER, "Stevens' poetry is not merely poetry about poetry. It is a poetry that is the battleground among conflicting theories of poetry." These theories, as well as the conflicts between them, are "as old as our Western tradition," and are not simply "alternatives among which one may choose. Their contradictory inherence in one another generates the meditative search for 'what will suffice' in Stevens' poetry."[1] The theories are not strictly poetic either, though they may be most outspokenly embodied by poetry. They have to do with the representational nature of language as it interacts with our outer and inner worlds. Miller identifies three basic theories. Two of these have in common that they take the act of joining or linking representation and that which is being represented (the representamen, in technical jargon) to be somehow possible and valid. This sets them off from the third theory, according to which language helplessly and frustratingly—or, at times, grandly and jubilantly—folds back on itself. We are familiar with the first two theories above all from M. H. Abrams's classic study of romantic perspectives on poetry, *The Mirror and the Lamp*, whose title pits the two most common metaphors for these conflicting theories against each other.

The first theory, according to Miller, is governed by "the idea that poetry is imitation, *mimesis*, analogy, copy. Truth is measured by the equivalence between the structure of words and the structure of nonlinguistic reality."[2] This is the "mirror" of Abrams's book, where the corresponding view of language

---

1. J. Hillis Miller, *The Linguistic Moment: From Wordsworth to Stevens*, 5.
2. Ibid., 5–6. Miller omits mention of the immediate sources of his inspiration, which undoubtedly include Derrida's meditations on truth and mimesis as either *alētheia* or *homoiōsis* in "The Double Session."

is proposed to be "characteristic of much of the thinking from Plato to the eighteenth century." Abrams shows that it was above all John Locke who came to be associated with this view, because the metaphor of the mirror takes pride of place in his *Essay Concerning Human Understanding*—along with alternative images like the "white paper," the "empty cabinet," and the "dark room"—as a figure of the operations of the mind.[3] The fact that Miller, in his paraphrase of the mimetic theory of language, feels able to recycle Stevens without so much as marking the allusion ("Things as they are on the blue guitar must reflect things as they are in nature," he writes) works as an important reminder: for all Stevens's metalinguistic and modernist preoccupation with the formalist and structuralist potential of language, the most "natural" view of language as mimetic is by no means absent from his work. After all, the mimetic view of language is one of those transcendental illusions without which we cannot even begin to approach the world or reason about it. Without the illusion of (the possibility of) mimesis, of a correspondence between world and representation, the whole literary drive for representational accuracy and precision would be unthinkable. That such mirroring is nevertheless at some level illusory—that, in Wolfgang Iser's words, language is "an analogue which merely contains the conditions that will allow a reference to be conceived, but cannot be identical to that reference"—Stevens was sharply aware of.[4] He knew the art of poetry to be basically no different from that of painting, the field in which his younger contemporary Ernst Gombrich was busy demonstrating the existence of codes and schemes underlying all forms of would-be mimetic realism.

A mirror cannot function as a mirror without the intentionality of an onlooker, and so, Miller continues, at least since Aristotle "the notion that poetry is imitation was inextricably involved with the notion that poetry is also unveiling, uncovering, revelation, *alētheia*." In Abrams, this second idea is summed up by the image of the lamp, which, in the wake of what Abrams likes to see as Kant's "Copernican revolution in epistemology," is "the prevailing romantic conception of the poetic mind." Miller does not speak of lamps, but of the importance of *alētheia* all the way from Aristotle to Heidegger's *The Origin of the Work of Art*. In doing so, he points to the pivotal role played by the entangled and impure concept of *logos*, which to the Greeks could mean "mind," "intelligence," "message," "idea," "word,"

---

3. M. H. Abrams, *The Mirror and the Lamp: Romantic Theory and the Critical Tradition*, [viii]; for Locke's metaphors, see ibid., 57, and Boehm, *Kritik*, 210–11.
    4. Miller, *Linguistic Moment*, 6; Iser, "Feigning in Fiction," 213.

"ground," "measure," "order," "ratio," "proportion," or "being." It is this impurity, analogous in its operations to that of the word *sense*, that is largely
responsible for producing those notoriously aporetic moments when Being
is caught in language at the same time as it recedes. "Poetry," writes Miller,

> is a revelation in the visible and reasonable of that which as the base of rea
> son cannot be faced or said directly. . . . Being vanishes, dispersed into its
> representation. This annihilation cannot be shown directly, though it is the
> source of all poetry, for the moment of the origin of language cannot be shown
> in language. . . . This annihilation, in the root sense of a transformation into
> nothing at the moment of greatest illumination, is a crucial instant in Stevens'
> experience of the power of the poetic word.[5]

Behind such lines, we can easily hear the conclusion to "The Snow Man,"
and we should not be surprised to observe that Miller at this point in his
narrative restages, in the sketchiest of outlines, his earlier Heideggerian-
phenomenological analyses of Stevens's concern with a basic nothingness.

The third theory of poetry (or, more widely, of language in general) involves "the notion that poetry is creation, not discovery. In this theory there
is nothing outside the text. All meaning comes into existence with language
and in the interplay of language." This is, of course, the Miller of the seventies and early eighties speaking, the critic whose thinking had been stamped
by his then-colleagues at Yale, Jacques Derrida and Paul de Man.[6] But the
formulation is not off the mark. We have already had the opportunity to
see such a theory at work in Stevens's poetry. And we need only turn to
the final section of "Description without Place" to hit upon proclamations
like "It is a world of words to the end of it" (CP 345). The polysemous title
of that poem, moreover, itself invites a radically skeptical interpretation in
which language is construed as autotelic or circular, a tool that is supposedly descriptive but is unable in actual fact to affect what lies beyond its
own perimeter and become one with an outside place or reality. There is

---

5. Miller, *Linguistic Moment*, 6; Abrams, *Mirror and the Lamp*, 58, [viii]; Miller, *Linguistic Moment*, 7.

6. Miller, *Linguistic Moment*, 10. Miller has been accused of taking Derrida's statement "il n'y a pas de hors-texte" too literally; see Argyros, "Residual Difference." Derrida himself has repeatedly protested against misrepresentations of his claim: "I never cease to be surprised by critics who see my work as a declaration that there is nothing beyond language, that we are imprisoned in language; it is, in fact, saying the exact opposite. The critique of logocentrism is above all else the search for the 'other' and the 'other of language'" (quoted in Derek Attridge, "Derrida and the Questioning of Literature," 20).

no question that Stevens can be aligned—as has often been the case—with "deconstructive" notions of an aporia underlying the very concept of description. "Writing," says Lee Edelman, "though it marks or describes those differences upon which the specification of identity depends, works simultaneously, as Logan puts it, to 'de-scribe,' efface, or undo identity by framing difference as the misrecognition of a 'différance' whose negativity, whose purely relational articulation, calls into question the possibility of any positive presence or discrete identity."[7]

An interpretation along these lines is made possible by the unmoored, dangling status of the phrase "Description without Place" as a title disconnected from the body of the text. But this is different from saying that we should give precedence to such an interpretation. Here, as elsewhere, the most interesting thing about Stevens's poem is not that it intuitively confirms a single philosophical theory. It is rather the way the poem is able to contextualize and tap the various significations of its title. No iconoclastic radicalism and linguistic idealism is needed, for instance, to realize that any poetic invention of the imagination can also be called a description to which no place in the real or actual world corresponds. It is simply in the nature of fiction to describe what never took place in the first place. Alternatively, Stevens's poem reminds us that any description of the past or of the future is ultimately textual, too: the corresponding material world no longer is, or is yet to be, and can never overlap entirely with the poet's representation. "Description without Place," it turns out, just as readily accommodates aphorisms that are in agreement with the *second* theory in Miller's triad. "Description is revelation," we hear at one point. "It is not / The thing described, nor false facsimile" (CP 344). In other words, Stevens's idea that "It is a world of words to the end of it" does not necessarily imply a cavalier, counterintuitive denial of nonverbal material reality as the necessary "other" of language.

What cannot be denied, though, is that Stevens's repeated thrusts for the thing itself and the first idea, his regular attempts at reaching a pure vision of the world uncouched in language, gave him a strong, almost Wittgensteinian sense of the role of verbalization in thinking about, understanding, and representing the world. As shown in the preceding chapters, the structuring force and irreducible materiality of Stevens's rhetoric often surfaces and manages to make itself heard at the exact point of his attempts to surrender to the nonverbal. It is characteristic of Miller's third theory—that

7. Edelman, *Homographesis*, 10.

all reality is somehow textual—that world and language tend to "change places constantly," if only because of the simple fact that the textuality of the world cannot logically be denied within text itself. " 'Things below are copies,' " Miller offers as a Platonic example from Yeats, "but that which is copied can come into language only by way of the transfers of metaphor. In that sense, things above are copies of what is below."[8] In Stevens's own language, this sounds like: "things are as I think they are / And say they are on the blue guitar" (CP 180).

Stevens's handling of language has always attracted critical attention, even more than that of other high modernist poets. This is a poet, after all, who made his name as a word-juggling virtuoso—"the playboy of the western *word*" in Conrad Aiken's quip[9]—capable of the most inspired and scintillating razzle-dazzle. Witness the famous opening couplet of "Bantams in Pine-Woods":

> Chieftain Iffucan of Azcan in caftan
> Of tan with henna hackles, halt!
>
> (CP 75)

Or the exuberantly playful and intoxicating first tercet of "Snow and Stars":

> The grackles sing avant the spring
> Most spiss—oh! Yes, most spissantly.
> They sing right puissantly.
>
> (CP 133)

In early poems like "Sea Surface Full of Clouds" (CP 98–102), Stevens carried his language to sumptuous extremes of mellifluousness and sensuality, and his strong liking for onomatopoeic coinages and nonsense is responsible for much of the vitalizing and humorous appeal of his work. But the gaudiness gradually went underground and much of the wordplay got displaced to other, less conspicuous levels like the beguiling polysemy of abstractions and their surprising etymological layers, the ambiguities of syntax, the disruptive possibilities of arcane and out-of-place items of diction, and inconspicuous forms of allusion. As the boisterous bravura and pyrotechnics receded and

8. Miller, *Linguistic Moment*, 11–12.
9. Quoted in Charles Doyle, *Wallace Stevens: The Critical Heritage*, 87.

Stevens became less inclined to reenact "the linguisticity of being" that we find in his Crispin mode,[10] his concern with the *theory* of language and poetry grew in inverse proportion. And predictably, given the self-referential quality of modernist art in general and of Stevens's metawriting in particular (both of them out to problematize "naive" notions of mimetic representation), the mimetic theory came under some heavy fire. The theoretical possibility of mimesis showed its practical limits especially when Stevens was engaged in his search for, or tried to affirm, the thing itself and the first idea. When he was *not* directly engaged in that project, his interest tended to lie more exclusively with Miller's second and third theories. Thus, the classic lamp of romanticism found its counterpart in a wealth of candles, all the way from the early theatrical experiment *Carlos among the Candles* (OP 163–67), through lines like "A candle is enough to light the world" in "The Man with the Blue Guitar" (CP 172), up to the "scholar of one candle" cowed by the inhuman "Arctic effulgence flaring on the frame / Of everything he is" in "The Auroras of Autumn" (CP 417). It is also Stevens the candlelighter who berates himself, deep into "Notes toward a Supreme Fiction," that "to impose is not / To discover," and expresses a continuing hope that "to find, / Not to impose . . . // It is possible, possible, possible. It must / Be possible" (CP 403–4).

The hope of finding and discovering through language shows itself to be an indomitably human one in Stevens. Sometimes, however, what is found or discovered turns out to be only the dissociated and dissociating power of language itself, the autonomy of a world of words. A "green queen" that "seems to be on the saying of her name" (and on the singing of her assonances) (CP 339) is one of many possible examples. She is a relatively innocent creature, existing as she does primarily for the purpose of indulging in and celebrating the imagination. But other instances are more daring (or self-ironizing): "There it was, word for word, / The poem that took the place of a mountain" (CP 512). The material world in middle to late Stevens is often on the verge of ceding to language. And when it does, we get poems like "The Owl in the Sarcophagus," one of his darkest and most artificial texts, where personified peace-after-death is paraded as

> An immaculate personage in nothingness,
> With the whole spirit sparkling in its cloth,

10. Sharpe, *Wallace Stevens*, 100.

Generations of the imagination piled
In the manner of its stitchings, of its thread,
In the weaving round the wonder of its need,

And the first flowers upon it, an alphabet
By which to spell out holy doom and end . . .
(CP 434)

The master imagery of "cloth," "stitchings," "thread," and "weaving" plays on the etymology of one unstated word—*text*—whose Latin root, as post-structuralists never tire of telling us, is a term derived from the world of weaving. And this imagery of textual weaving, in turn, is mixed with "flow-ers" (a classic figure for tropes) and "alphabet" to augment our sense of a poet trying his hand at a textual and verbal creation ex nihilo. "The Owl in the Sarcophagus," for all its incantatory elegiac power, consists almost entirely of a self-generated and self-generating rhetoric. It points up one of the limits of poetic composition itself, the boundary where technique turns into technology.

One of Stevens's most classic meditations on the delimiting quality of rep-resentation, specifically as it affects the production of art, is "The Idea of Or-der at Key West" (CP 128–30). Situated in the liminal space between solid land and fluid sea, moreover, the poem participates in a particularly fertile American tradition of seashore poems, ranging all the way from Emerson's "Seashore" and Whitman's "Out of the Cradle Endlessly Rocking," through Frost's "Neither Out Far Nor In Deep" and Crane's "Voyages," to Bishop's "At the Fishhouses," Ammons's "Corsons Inlet," and Plath's "Point Shirley." The seashore, which was frequented by Stevens especially in his Floridian poems, constitutes one of the most visited topoi in American poetry and has come to sustain an unusual tropological diversity. Frequently suggesting a marine version of the self-defining American confrontation with frontiers and the exploration of new worlds, it no less often figures a crisis of identity— social, political, psychological, metaphysical, artistic, and/or linguistic. In this respect, the choice of location in Stevens may be seen to transcend the poem's anecdotal inspiration. More than simply an exotic tropical island that Stevens happened to like visiting, Key West also marked the circum-ference of his world: it did so by constituting at once the furthest extreme of the physical space he inhabited in his life (with the exception of an oc-casional trip to Cuba and a cruise that took him further into the Caribbean and through the Panama Canal) and the farthest southern border of his own nation. The last in a long tail of keys at the tip of Florida, Key West is to the American South what Provincetown, at the tip of Cape Cod, is to the East Coast: a strikingly marginal extension. (Not coincidentally, both places have since been appropriated by traditionally marginalized groups: gays and lesbians.) To Stevens, as Miller notes, the island "was an outer edge, horizon, or boundary to his travels, a limit from which the more domestic landscapes of Pennsylvania and Connecticut were measured."[11]

Aside from Miller, few of Stevens's most famous critics have taken the time to observe how complex the ideas and textual fabric of Stevens's poem in this extreme locale really are. And none, as far as I can see, have addressed how the poem interlocks the three theories of language that may be summed up by the images of a mirror, a lamp, and a world of words. "It is, as meditation, relatively simple to follow," writes Frank Kermode, finding support in this from Helen Vendler, who takes "The Idea of Order" to belong to Stevens's "easier discursive poems" and assures us that it "sufficiently resembles its Romantic predecessors . . . to make the inexperienced reader feel at ease." Richard Poirier even slights the poem, telling us that Stevens is "at his best not within the relatively neat structures of a poem like 'The Idea of Order at Key West,' masterful though it is, but in [his] more meandering, ruminative opacities."[12] Stevens himself in later years gave in to a temptation for reductive interpretations as well. Asked in 1954 to prepare an introduction to a selection of his poems that he was to read as part of a radio program on New England authors, he summarized this poem as "designed to show how man gives his own order to the world about him." This sounds almost trite in its generality, especially when compared with Harold Bloom's remarks on what he calls "the most powerful poem in what was to be the *Ideas of Order* volume but also surpassing any single poem in either edition of *Harmonium*." Bloom intones the warning that "The Idea of Order at Key West" "has its desperate equivocations and its unresolvable difficulties, more perhaps than even so strong a poem can sustain. In some respects, it is an impossible text to interpret, and its rhetoric may be at variance with its deepest intentionalities."[13] Even if it is a common maneuver for Bloom to

11. J. Hillis Miller, "The Ethics of Topography: Stevens," 261.
12. Frank Kermode, *Wallace Stevens*, 52; Vendler, "Wallace Stevens" in *Columbia History of American Poetry*, 382; Poirier, *Renewal of Literature*, 211. Poirier's outspoken preference for a "meandering" Stevens is not unfunny in light of Vendler's one-time prohibition against using the word if one wishes to qualify as a serious Stevens critic (see the rapping given to Alan Golding in Helen Vendler, "New Books on Wallace Stevens," 550).
13. Stevens quoted in Filreis, *Actual World*, 252; Bloom, *Poems of Our Climate*, 92–93.

pave the way for one of his grandly idiosyncratic analyses by first upping the critical ante, this self-serving aspect is more often than not only one part of the story. Hyperbole may be a stock ingredient of Bloom's trade, but a lack of lucidity and of responsiveness to complexity generally is not.

Indeed, who would be willing to deny there is already an aspect of "equivocation"—"desperate" or not—in the poem's opening stanza, with its accumulation of qualifications, its pendular swing and prismatic variations?

> She sang beyond the genius of the sea.
> The water never formed to mind or voice,
> Like a body wholly body, fluttering
> Its empty sleeves; and yet its mimic motion
> Made constant cry, caused constantly a cry,
> That was not ours although we understood,
> Inhuman, of the veritable ocean.
>
> (CP 128)

A "genius," Frank Lentricchia reminds us, "in the classical tradition signifies the ordering, tutelary, presiding god or spirit of a place." Hence, "if reality [for which the sea may provisionally be taken to stand as a *pars pro toto*] has a genius, then reality has an inherent order." But that order, which "preceded the place and generated it, speaks in it and through it," is not available to the singing woman along the shore.[14] Her song exists "beyond" any possible ordering and generating power of the sea. The poem opens by establishing a yawning gap between the human and the natural—the gap where poetry can begin to be written and music to be composed.

"There will never be an end / To this droning of the surf," Stevens had written earlier of the same Key West locale (CP 23), but the endlessness now prompts a new question: Could the droning ever turn to articulated music? Does not the seeming limitlessness of the sea preempt "the human power of controlling and ordering," as Miller suggests?[15] "The water never formed to mind or voice." The intransitive usage of the verb is meticulous: to say that the sea never formed *itself* would suggest some underlying agency; to talk intransitively of a forming pure and simple is to surrender the sea to arbitrary, uncontrollable, organic metamorphoses unable to acquire (as well as adapt to) human features like "mind or voice." The division between

14. Lentricchia, *Gaiety of Language*, 180; Miller, "Ethics of Topography," 265.
15. Miller, "Ethics of Topography," 266.

(wo)man and nature appears as solid and radical as the equally time-worn Cartesian dualism of body and soul, or body and spirit. "The water" is merely "a body wholly body, fluttering / Its empty sleeves" like a scarecrow or a fairy-tale ghost.[16] Its self is a mere void that can be filled or inflated only by a spirit coming from outside. Already, however, the strength of the dissociation between the natural/physical and the human/spiritual begins to tell on the poet's language. Since the sea is entirely body, its "motion" can only be a second-best "mimic" or simulation of human gestures. Yet human gestures are informed by conscious intentions and meanings. We are quickly made aware of the seductiveness of personification and the much-maligned pathetic fallacy. The water cannot "mimic" without a mimetic disposition. This explains the hesitation in the fifth line and why its first hemistich is subsequently corrected: the sea's motion "Made constant cry, caused constantly a cry." We need to feel the difficulty of the words. The sea cannot utter any cries, cannot "make" a "cry"—intentionally, that is. At most, it can "cause" a sound that we interpret as a cry while knowing full well that this cry "Was not ours although we understood, / Inhuman, of the veritable ocean." This is the paradox of our human relationship with nature: the sensuous effects we record are "not ours" and yet it is only "we" who can claim to "understand" them; but this understanding itself must in some respect *remain* ours, for it can never be an understanding of the deep alterity of the "inhuman," of "the veritable ocean" *an sich*. Stevens repeats the classic epistemological dilemma that fundamentally affects our drive for mimetic representation. If the human habit of mimetic thinking and speaking belongs to those Kantian categories we cannot (and should not try to) dispense with, we nevertheless need to be aware that it does not bring us any closer to the ghost of an objective reality *an sich*, "fluttering / Its empty sleeves."

Because there emerges, toward the end of the poem, at least one second person who appears to accompany the poet on his walk along the sea, "The Idea of Order at Key West" has been contrasted more than once with Wordsworth's "Lines Written a Few Miles above Tintern Abbey." Yet the

16. For the Cartesian dualism, see Lentricchia, *Gaiety of Language*, 180–81; for the scarecrow association, Bloom, *Poems of Our Climate*, 98–99; for the suggestion of a ghost, which has the advantage of initiating a recurrent ghost imagery in the overall poem, again Lentricchia, *Gaiety of Language*, 181, 185–86. According to Thomas J. Hines, "[t]he 'body' of water is 'wholly body' in the sense that it has no limbs ('empty sleeves') and no head, thus no mind or feeling" (*Later Poetry of Wallace Stevens*, 52). Miller at this point marshals Nietzsche and Beckett to talk of how "Stevens figures the sea's inability to express itself as its being like a body without arms, legs, or head, that is, without all the appendages we human beings use to make gestures, speak, and so communicate with others" ("Ethics of Topography," 268).

contrast has never been made sufficiently explicit. For Stevens is entering into an intertextual dialogue with the romantic poetry that had stamped his own art from the very beginning and in terms of which he kept defining his "postromantic" modernist concerns and endeavors. His opening stanza clearly swerves from the stance taken by Wordsworth, who at one point in his poem hails

> a sense sublime
> Of something far more deeply interfused,
> Whose dwelling is the light of setting suns,
> And the round ocean, and the living air,
> And the blue sky, and in the mind of man,
> A motion and a spirit, that impels
> All thinking things, all objects of all thought,
> And rolls through all things. Therefore am I still
> A lover of the meadows and the woods,
> And mountains; and of all that we behold
> From this green earth; of all the mighty world
> Of eye and ear, both what they half-create,
> And what perceive; well pleased to recognize
> In nature and the language of the sense,
> The anchor of my purest thoughts, the nurse,
> The guide, the guardian of my heart, and soul
> Of all my moral being.[17]

Wordsworth records his experience of the sublime in confronting, among other things, the "ocean"—more particularly in its "motion" and its "spirit" (a word Stevens will pick up in his third stanza, though one can already hear it implicitly in his overture). This spirit infuses all of nature, which is accordingly rendered in a climactic series of metaphors passing from "anchor" through three unproblematized personifications—"nurse," "guide," and "guardian"—to the "soul [is this still a metaphor?] / Of all my moral being." My discussion of "The Snow Man" has demonstrated that Stevens, too, could not really live without some lingering sense of the sublime. The very choice of a seascape for his poem is one that easily conjures up the same notion; seascapes also function as an example of the sublime in Kant.[18] Yet

17. William Wordsworth, *Lyrical Ballads, and Other Poems, 1797–1800*, 118–19.
18. Miller, "Ethics of Topography," 266.

the stage set by "The Idea of Order" bespeaks that, as an ironical modernist and a post-Nietzschean skeptic wary of all religiously inclined holistic gestures of harmony, Stevens refused to surrender himself unquestioningly to this impulse.

From the very beginning, then, the poem makes clear that the poet feels neither like basking in the discontinuity between an alien natural environment and artistic attempts at translating this environment into "mind or voice," nor that he can afford to simply wish the difficulty of translation away. And so he circles around his topic, looking at it again from several sides:

> The sea was not a mask. No more was she.
> The song and water were not medleyed sound
> Even if what she sang was what she heard,
> Since what she sang was uttered word by word.
> It may be that in all her phrases stirred
> The grinding water and the gasping wind;
> But it was she and not the sea we heard.
>
> (CP 128–29)

To Melville's romantic metaphysical monomaniac, Captain Ahab, the sea, like all visible objects, was but one of those "pasteboard masks" that should be ripped off or struck through to reveal the divine or demonic principle underlying the universe. But to the willfully sobered-up, secular modernist Stevens, who at the time of writing is known to have had the question of a viable substitute for religion constantly on his mind, the sea cannot be a sounding device for an ulterior spirit. It is no *per-sona*—the ancient Greek word for the mask used by actors to give voice to their fictive "persons."[19] Nor is the woman a per-sona for the spirit of the sea. She is just herself, apart from and discontinuous with the sea and its self, whatever that "self" may be.

"The song and water were not medleyed sound": Stevens's antiromantic drive reappears, for "[t]he blending of contrived, human music with the spontaneous noises of nature [is] a dominant romantic musical image."[20] Although the woman is supposed to believe that she sings what she hears,

19. Herman Melville, *Moby-Dick; or, The Whale*, 178; for the substitute of religion, see Filreis, *Modernism from Right to Left*, 154; for the per-sona, see John Hollander, "The Sound of the Music of Music and Sound," 236.
20. Hollander, "Sound of the Music," 236–37.

her singing cannot be entirely mimetic. It is in the nature of singing to involve a stylized channeling and translation of incoming acoustical data into humanly felt and meaningful melody. This would be true even if the song happened to be one of those wordless vocalises that were popular with so-called impressionistic composers, witness Debussy's *Sirènes* or Ravel's *Vocalise-Étude*. But the woman—because she is Stevens's postromantic muse, we may legitimately presume at this point, and he wants her attempts to be sufficiently germane to his own poetic vocation—uses language, which means that "what she sang was uttered word by word." Her sound does not flow like the endless droning of the surf, but is analyzed and fractured into different spatiotemporal entities. "In the way you speak / You arrange, the thing is posed, / What in nature merely grows," Stevens was to write only a few years later in "Add This to Rhetoric" (CP 198). Those lines appear in *Parts of a World*, where he could also be heard saying: "Words are not forms of a single word. / In the sum of the parts, there are only the parts" (CP 204). "The Idea of Order" shows him moving toward the Saussurian idea that language is differential and does not rise or grow organically. In the romantic distinction between organical and mechanical/artificial—an offshoot of the classic nature-culture divide—language clearly stands on the second side. Stevens underscores this by suddenly building a triple rhyme, "heard-word-stirred"—an insistent and conspicuous effect because the poem is nowhere else found to highlight its musical artificiality with quite the same self-conscious resonance. What is more, the rhyme suddenly throws into relief the treacherously mimetic relation that might be supposed to link the poem's meter, with its blank-verse alterations of accented and unaccented syllables, to the ebb and flow of waves crashing on the seashore. The regular pattern of systole and diastole seemingly shared by natural phenomenon and literary device cannot really preempt the fundamentally artificial and ordered constructedness of the latter.

The decision to let music stand in for poetry in the first half of "The Idea of Order" adds to the poem's argument, for the mimetic qualities of language and representation are more easily shown to be problematic in the realm of the aural (in the musical key of Key West, so to speak) than in the realm of the visual. Except for a few acoustical realities that can be imitated and re-presented in program music (like the sound of birdsong, thunder, cowbells, car horns, or the surf of the sea), music tends to be cut loose from external referents—*pace* Richard Strauss's claim to be able to paint a redheaded woman in sound. In this respect, music stands a little apart from painting, sculpture, architecture, and literature—those artistic disciplines

to which the epistemological skepticism of deconstructionists has, not coin-
cidentally, been directed much more commonly than to the realm of music.
Music rises largely from the inside; it is no simple representation of an outer
reality. Its referents are almost always located in the dark organic rumblings
of the body and its energies, and in the no more clearly delineated world
of emotions. That is to a large extent why the verbal appropriation of mu-
sic is such a hazardous undertaking and often seems such an unfalsifiable,
associative free-for-all, and why the signifying process to performers and lis-
teners alike is so challenging and hotly disputed. This referential ambiguity
may be one of the reasons why Stevens keeps the precise contents of the
song he hears undescribed. He only reminds us that the link between the
acoustical surroundings and the act of art-making is anything but obviously
representational by letting the woman sing a verbal song, which is at one
further remove from representing the sounds of the sea than merely acousti-
cal, instrumental renderings would be. To sing *by* the sea—perhaps *prompted
by* the grandeur and vitality and power and intoxication that the sound of
the sea so easily induces in us—is not to sing the sea itself. Between mimesis
and music, between the wish to reflect and mirror reality as accurately as
possible and the wish to sing one's own sense of reality, a space stretches out
in which art may be—even must be—produced.

In the final three lines of the second stanza, the skepsis toward romantic
beliefs with which the poem opened is further elaborated. In the modern
world, one cannot be so sure anymore of inspiration—of the possibility for
poetry to be, in Coleridge's favorite image, an aeolian harp on which natural
chords are sounded by the "wind." "That wind gasps in descriptive accuracy,"
writes Eleanor Cook, "but also as if in surprise—surprise that its own mas-
tery of inspiration is being questioned." Even if a productive dialectic and
interplay are at work between nature and the art-making woman, Stevens
remains unable to establish the precise connection: he can only be sure that
"it was she and not the sea we heard."[21]

21. Cook, *Poetry, Word-Play, and Word-War*, 132. As Miller points out, Stevens's voice
in the recording he made of this poem "emphasizes the way 'she' is so close a sound to 'sea,'
differing from it by the variation of a single phoneme: 'It was *she* and not the *sea* we heard.'
Both those sounds are onomatopoeias for the hissing sound the wind makes or the sound
the sea makes as a small wave crests and then flows to its limit up the beach. Though it was
'she' and not 'sea' we heard, the sound 'she' as well as the sound 'sea,' it could be argued, are
initially spoken as meaningless hisses by the grinding water and the gasping wind, whether in
nature or in the human throat and mouth. Human speech proper is made by setting against
one another two such minimally different sounds as 'she' and 'sea.' Meaning arises from the
difference between one sound and the other. The poet's words show this in action" ("Ethics
of Topography," 271).

For she was the maker of the song she sang.
The ever-hooded, tragic-gestured sea
Was merely a place by which she walked to sing.
Whose spirit is this? we said, because we knew
It was the spirit that we sought and knew
That we should ask this often as she sang.

(CP 129)

The claim that the sea is "merely a place by which she walked to sing" is another way of evoking how the art of singing grazes reality only tangentially, how singer and poet alike are walking the liminal lines and edges of representation. It is a way, in other words, of undercutting the pathetic fallacies of the preceding line, with its compactly meaningful Miltonian epithets. "Ever-hooded," for instance, can be seen to carry meaning on at least three levels: "Visually, it works like the famous Hokusai wave, hood-shaped at the point of greatest gathering; conceptually, it reminds us that we cannot truly and finally know outside reality; symbolically, it recalls death's traditional garb, which may hide a skeleton or simply vacancy, mere air." At this third and final level, we recognize the earlier ghost "fluttering / Its empty sleeves" now making a ghostly reappearance.[22] The image of an ever-hooded sea flirts again with the anthropomorphization of prosopopoeia, and the treacherousness of that device is made more vivid still by the second epithet, "tragic-gestured." It may be that the sea bears only the merest gestural outlines of a tragic comportment, but the very inclination to attribute a potential for tragedy to what is "merely a place" all too patently displays the human, and especially romantic, habit of projecting spiritual qualities onto a natural scenery. At the same time, the choice of words—"ever-hooded, tragic-gestured"—may be taken to register the drama that underlies and inspires this poem: a drama resulting from the existential solitude, the darkly inexplicable fate, the vulnerability and mortality of humans in their unsponsored, one-way dependency upon a fundamentally indifferent environment.

Unsurprisingly, then, Stevens turns to address the question of what to do with the "spirit" Wordsworth found "roll[ing] through all things." "Whose spirit is this?" he asks, unable to rest contented with merely and passively riding the figurative waves of the song he hears, spellbound by the resistant

---

22. Cook, *Poetry, Word-Play, and Word-War,* 131; for the ghost imagery, see Lentricchia, *Gaiety of Language,* 183.

enigma of how song and sea relate. What could a Song of the Sea in the final analysis amount to?

> If it was only the dark voice of the sea
> That rose, or even colored by many waves;
> If it was only the outer voice of sky
> And cloud, of the sunken coral water-walled,
> However clear, it would have been deep air,
> The heaving speech of air, a summer sound
> Repeated in a summer without end
> And sound alone. But it was more than that,
> More even than her voice, and ours, among
> The meaningless plungings of water and the wind,
> Theatrical distances, bronze shadows heaped
> On high horizons, mountainous atmospheres
> Of sky and sea.
>
> (CP 129)

This is the one part of the poem that is most frequently sidestepped or given short shrift by critics in favor of the ensuing lines, which offer more plainly propounding answers. Yet one should not miss how the passage stretches language to the limits of self-consciousness. Although the first, seven-and-a-half-line, sentence is broadly understandable in its drift, it is dense and uncertainly ironic in its mixing of natural and human perspectives, as well as in its deployment of inconspicuous verbal games on "colored" (with its classic overtone of "troped," which also underlies "Domination of Black," CP 8–9), "coral" (which faintly plays on a "chorale" sung at the "water-walled" bottom of the sea), and "without end" (meaning both endless and aimless). The spirit Stevens looks for in the woman's voice cannot come from sea, sky, or cloud, for then her song would sound like "The heaving speech of air, a summer sound / Repeated in a summer without end," continuing in an undifferentiated repetition, endlessly and aimlessly, like the droning of the surf. It would be senseless sensuous iteration, not a song of fragmented words and human significance.

But it is especially the second sentence in this passage that produces an uncanny effect. That the "plungings of water and the wind" are so alien and inhuman as to be "meaningless" logically follows from earlier remarks, but the "voice" now appears to transcend not only that of sea, sky, and cloud, but also that of the woman herself, and even the poet's and his companion's. The spirit Stevens finds in the singing suddenly proves to be "more than either the preexisting genius loci, on the one hand, or the creative consciousness of the singer, on the other. The spirit is also more than the voice of the listening and looking 'we' for whom the poet speaks."[23] Significantly, the poem Stevens chose to immediately follow "The Idea of Order" in his second collection is "The American Sublime," where "the sublime comes down / To the spirit itself, // The spirit and space" (CP 131). Representing the sublime of this grand oceanscape is arguably what the middle section of "The Idea of Order" also strives to do. Bonnie Costello, for instance, feels the stanza to be "reminiscent of nineteenth-century American sublime painting." And predictably, one of the few critics not to have turned a blind eye to this stanza is Harold Bloom, whose fascination with the sublime is part and parcel of his academic persona. "What rises up is a voice neither natural nor human," he writes, "yet Stevens cannot tell us, or know himself, what such a voice might be." Referring to the final two and a half lines, Bloom talks of the "daemonic intensity of heaping up the imagery of height, the hyperboles of vision."[24]

Syntactically, these lines are ambiguously suspended: they appear to be almost discontinuous with the main clause (which principally deals with the subject of voice and spirit). If they stand in apposition to water and wind, the link is at best tenuous; we rather experience them as a scene suddenly there, like an epiphany. On the level of diction, too, the lines are mesmerizing and opaque, with their "mixture of abstraction and artifice"[25]—the only lines in the poem to radically leap ahead more than a decade in the way they foreshadow the highly textual creations of poems like "Chocorua to Its Neighbor" (CP 296–302) and "The Owl in the Sarcophagus" (CP 431–36).[26] To express the sublime in a language that is simultaneously evanescent, sonorous, and rhetorically self-conscious is much more characteristic

23. Miller, "Ethics of Topography," 275.

24. Bonnie Costello, "Wallace Stevens: The Adequacy of Landscape," 211; Bloom, Poems of Our Climate, 101, 100.

25. Angus Cleghorn, "Questioning the Composition of Romance in 'The Idea of Order at Key West,'" 29.

26. "Theatrical distances, bronze shadows" also anticipates Stevens's supposedly final poem, "Of Mere Being," in the version that appears in the first edition of Opus Posthumous: "The palm at the end of the mind, / Beyond the last thought, rises / In the bronze distance, // A gold-feathered bird / Sings in the palm, without human meaning, / Without human feeling, a foreign song" (OP 1957, 117; "bronze distance" was later corrected to "bronze decor" on the basis of the only extant typescript). "Of Mere Being," too, deals with the subject of song and likewise figures the irrational quality of the sublime occurring on a level outside "human meaning" and "human feeling."

of the later Stevens, in poems that bring him the closest he was ever to come to that most would-be sublime of American high modernists, Hart Crane.[27] There is no way we could refer Stevens's world of words back to any simple actual referent, to determine its denotation with any accuracy. The conjunction of "Theatrical distances," "shadows" that are "heaped," and "mountainous atmospheres" (perhaps anticipating the "mountainous music" of "The Man with the Blue Guitar," CP 179) is too densely scriptural for that. The appearance, in addition, of "high horizons" is telling, for the experience of the sublime in Stevens precisely involves a grappling with "that which lies beyond the horizon of poetic language as a transcendent" and entails a recurrent use of the very trope of the horizon.[28] At the precise center of "The Idea of Order," the textuality of the poem makes itself heard with a vengeance, and the tracing of horizons announces the later poetic technology that would, among other things, stage "an abstraction given head, / A giant on the horizon, . . . / A definition with an illustration, not / Too exactly labelled, . . . / At the centre on the horizon" (CP 443).

The difficult sublimity of this stretch in the poem is so easily overlooked or forgotten because it is followed by a stanza in which Stevens suddenly comes up with lines that have all the classic sound of an answer. And the answer is not that "It is a world of words to the end of it," but that it is a world made more poignant and significant by the artist's words:

> It was her voice that made
> The sky acutest at its vanishing.
> She measured to the hour its solitude.
> She was the single artificer of the world
> In which she sang. And when she sang, the sea,
> Whatever self it had, became the self
> That was her song, for she was the maker. Then we,
> As we beheld her striding there alone,
> Knew that there never was a world for her
> Except the one she sang and, singing, made.
>
> (CP 129–30)

---

27. For the two most rewarding studies of Crane's rhetoric in its relation to the sublime, see Lee Edelman, *Transmemberment of Song: Hart Crane's Anatomies of Rhetoric and Desire*, and Thomas E. Yingling, *Hart Crane and the Homosexual Text: New Thresholds, New Anatomies*, esp. 24–56 and 145–85.

28. Michael Beehler, "Kant and Stevens: The Dynamics of the Sublime and the Dynamics of Poetry," 135.

This passage is often presented as the poem's center of gravity, its actual philosophical credo. To Joseph N. Riddel, for instance, it expressed no less than "the inflexible pivot of [Stevens's] belief," while Harold Bloom, less sweepingly yet no less decisively, calls "the single artificer of the world" "the poem's central metaphor." Helen Vendler takes exception to the "endangering sentimentality" she perceives "in the girl's becoming entirely the maker of the world she sings," and proceeds to talk of the overall poem's "easy hyperbole." And Alex Argyros opposes "The Idea of Order at Key West" to Stevens's later (and to him more subtly inflected) writings by arguing that the poem "postulates a constitutive imagination creating the world it narrates"—a postulate amounting in his eyes to a "kind of Idealism" and "textual solipsism" all too often found in Stevens's American deconstructive critics.[29] Repeatedly also, one of the poet's most controversial alter egos is summoned to bear witness to such solipsism. For the passage may be read as a palimpsest of the final three stanzas of "Tea at the Palaz of Hoon":

> What was the ointment sprinkled on my beard?
> What were the hymns that buzzed beside my ears?
> What was the sea whose tide swept through me there?
>
> Out of my mind the golden ointment rained,
> And my ears made the blowing hymns they heard.
> I was myself the compass of that sea:
>
> I was the world in which I walked, and what I saw
> Or heard or felt came not but from myself;
> And there I found myself more truly and more strange.
>   (CP 65)

The parallels between these passages are unmistakable, yet they cannot in themselves suffice as evidence for shoring up the claim that the stanza from "The Idea of Order" constitutes that poem's central thesis. Since critical uncertainty reigns on the extent to which Stevens was mocking himself in his portrait of Hoon, the earlier poem cannot help us decide what place in the later poem we should attribute to the palimpsest. What is more, even if a tendency toward solipsism is in evidence when the woman turns into "the

---

29. Joseph N. Riddel, "Walt Whitman and Wallace Stevens," 42; Bloom, *Poems of Our Climate*, 101; Vendler, *Words Chosen Out of Desire*, 70–71; Argyros, "Residual Difference," 30.

single artificer of the world / In which she sang," this momentary change need not constitute the poem's apex and climactic insight.

Solipsism may be an altogether deceptive word for what Stevens is voicing here. We should not overlook, first, the enjambment: we are not told that "She was the single artificer of the world" at large, which would indeed sound presumptuously solipsistic and totalizing, but only "of the world / In which she sang." The woman's singing of the world is not immediately conflated with that world: she is somehow still singing *in* a world, to which she responds. And the claims that "her voice . . . made / The sky acutest at its vanishing" and that "She measured to the hour its solitude" both confirm, with a spatial and a temporal image, respectively, that she is not so much canceling or ignoring the outer world as showing an intensifying interest in it. The woman's art-making, the poem claims, injects the greatest possible human significance into an otherwise alien and meaningless environment. It is the artistic act, the moment of artistic production and performance, that concerns Stevens here—a moment for which the classic Hegelian paronomasia of *Aufhebung* for once seems appropriate: this act of *raising* into art is also, of necessity, a form of performatively *erasing* reality as an unformed, inhuman, chaotic given. "[T]he sea, / Whatever self it had, became the self / That was her song." Art appropriates reality by transforming it. And the ability to make art, the text indicates, is a matter of craftsmanship, of the classical *poeta faber* working upon reality, not of the romantic *poeta vates*, whose visions may be more easily dismissed as simple self-deceptions. "The singer is not an aeolian harp, expressing the words of wind or sea, but a 'maker' in the classical sense of the poet as 'maker,'" observes A. Walton Litz.[30] The words "maker," "made" (twice), and "artificer," and even the pun on "measured," point to this unromantic attitude, much as the words "poetry" and "fiction," so omnipresent in Stevens's oeuvre, tend to return us to their etymological root sense of "fabrication."

Stevens further complicates the picture by explicitly taking up the position of an outsider and observer *speculating on* the woman's art-making. For the first time in the poem, we are invited to step back and wonder about the relationship between woman and speaker. Do the views of Stevens the poet-observer, who talks inclusively in the we-form, mirror those of the singing woman? Or might he somehow be dissociating himself from "her" belief

---

30. Litz, *Introspective Voyager*, 193; see also Cook, *Poetry, Word-Play, and Word-War*, 131, for a further elaboration upon this opposition, in this case with Wordsworth's "Tintern Abbey."

(suddenly more totalizing in its formulation) "that there never was a world for her / Except the one she sang and, singing, made"? Is the woman really his reworked romantic muse inspiring him from outside, or is she merely a mirror figure that can help him construct and validate his own identity in classically Lacanian fashion, as Brooke Baeten argues?[31] How can he speak for his companion (or indeed for his audience) and how can they both "know," as they claim to do, what it is that the woman believes or feels? Only by projection, by empathy, or by appropriation, it would appear, for the singing is apparently not addressed to the poet and his companion at all. The two men are only finding themselves, in the woman, "more truly and more strange."

If the poem ended here, we would feel more justified in interpreting the stanza's final statement as a conclusively affirmed insight. But what we find instead is a poet troubled by his own experience and reflections, turning to question his companion:

> Ramon Fernandez, tell me, if you know,
> Why, when the singing ended and we turned
> Toward the town, tell why the glassy lights,
> The lights in the fishing boats at anchor there,
> As the night descended, tilting in the air,
> Mastered the night and portioned out the sea,
> Fixing emblazoned zones and fiery poles,
> Arranging, deepening, enchanting night.
> (*CP* 130)

These lines effect a remarkable shift in both situation and perspective. The woman's essentially human and finite singing has "ended" and the two listeners have "turned / Toward the town": the world the woman made in her art has run its course and the poet's concern now seems to be with the way such temporary art-making reflects on the social world (if we may be so allegorical) outside art. The poem's perspective becomes more emphatically that of the recipients or consumers of art now that the woman disappears from the scene and Stevens explicitly stages an audience in the form of his walking companion.[32] Both shifts work as a corrective to the idealistic

31. Brooke Baeten, "'Whose Spirit Is This?': Musings on the Woman Singer in 'The Idea of Order at Key West,'" 24, 31–32.

32. The introduction of a character named Ramon Fernandez at this point in the poem has become a bone of considerable critical contention in Stevens studies. The name is that of a

overtones of the preceding stanza, which has been so readily taken to voice
Stevens's article of faith. "The inexplicable magic of 'The Idea of Order,'"
notes Longenbach, "exists not in the private world of the solitary singer but
in the fact that other human beings hear the song and feel its power over
their minds."[33] This power is also that of the language of poetry, which is
now rendered in terms of romantic lamp imagery. "As the night descended"
and the amorphousness of primeval chaos uncontained and undelimited by
language envelops us, "The lights in the fishing boats at anchor there, /
. . . Mastered the night." The boats with their lights are not coincidentally
"at anchor": this tells us how language stabilizes us in the sublime, inhu-
man sea of sensations that would otherwise drown us. Nor are they "fishing
boats" for nothing. When language (or art, or any kind of human making)
is primarily seen as revelatory and enlightening, this ties in with a view of
poetry as fishing for serendipitous words. To "light up" and to "fish" belong
to the same semantic field—that of disclosure and discovery.

The nature of revelations produced by the lights and the fishing, how-
ever, may be various. Several critics have noted Stevens's use of the kind of
geographical imagery so common also with John Donne in the era of great
seafaring discoveries (including the "discovery" of "America"). Language is
able to "[portion] out the sea, / Fixing emblazoned zones and fiery poles."
The "zones" bring to mind the imaginary, but scientifically and practically
very efficient, lines of latitude and longitude by which we "portion out" sea
and earth, much as the "poles" recall the Arctic and Antarctic reference
points that enable us to think and talk about the earth as if it had an upside
and a downside, and also (since they are called "fiery") the stars by which
we perform such measuring. "Before the lines of longitude were conceived,"
comments Eleanor Cook, "navigation was far more hazardous. We are now
much more masters of the sea, having thought of that idea of order for all that
welter." A further allusion to highly practical forms of ordering is reflected

French critic hailing from Mexico (1894–1944) with whom Stevens must have been familiar
from the pages of the *Nouvelle revue française*, *Partisan Review*, the *Criterion*, and *Hound
& Horn* (see Longenbach, *Plain Sense of Things*, 161; Filreis, *Modernism from Right to Left*,
154–56; and Miller, "Ethics of Topography," 262–63). But on at least three occasions, when
tapped for clarification, Stevens denied that the historical person was of any importance to
the poem. So far, no critic has been able to demonstrate convincingly that the actual Ramon
Fernandez is of more than tangential relevance to the interpretation of the text. This only
squares with the fact that, unlike Eliot, Pound, and Yeats, Stevens was a poet who rarely
allowed the interpretation of his work to depend on a knowledge of historical figures and
allusions paraded in the text.
    33. Longenbach, *Plain Sense of Things*, 159.

in the word "arranging." Yet against this, we are also told that the revelations of language are able to "deepen" and "enchant" the night that would otherwise swallow us whole. There are, in other words, not only practical and instrumental but also more mysterious and irrational workings to poetry and singing, as to any human ordering of worlds. "The Latin word for lyric poetry, *carmen*," notes Miller, "means not only 'chant' but also 'incantation.' The boats, like the woman's song, exercise a magical power of enchantment over the scene, changing mere space into a fully differentiated site governed by its own genius of the place. Human acts of building and making, such as the making of the fishing boats, are a species of poetry."[34] Ratio and mystery keep each other in a balance in this evocation of a nocturnal navigation, so that the poem may end in apparent eulogy:

> Oh! Blessed rage for order, pale Ramon,
> The maker's rage to order words of the sea,
> Words of the fragrant portals, dimly-starred,
> And of ourselves and of our origins,
> In ghostlier demarcations, keener sounds.
>
> (CP 130)

Clearly, there is more to these lines than the move toward mysticism and visionary experience that Anthony Libby detects in them. We should notice in them rather a tug between forces. A conscious modernist dissonance speaks from the oxymoronic phrase "Blessed rage for order," which reminds us, among other things, of the fact that "[a] 'rage' for order is not an achievement of order." The phrase, as Filreis shows, collapses romantic and classicist language.[35] Similarly, if the metaphor of the "portals," following so closely upon the word "Blessed," at first seems religious in inspiration, we should notice not only that it is qualified by the this-worldly and sensuous adjective "fragrant," which points back to an attractively concrete Floridian locale, but also that it suggests an image of thresholds. Stevens's search for a valid substitute for religion kept him constantly on the verge of such substitutes (propelling him to compose, among other things, "Notes *toward* a Supreme Fiction"). His pluralistic bias kept him from trying to erect a monotheistic or monovocal church of his own. The image of the "fragrant portals," Costello

---

34. Cook, *Poetry, Word-Play, and Word-War,* 133; Miller, "Ethics of Topography," 278.
35. Libby, *Mythologies of Nothing,* 54–55; Lentricchia, *Gaiety of Language*, 185; Filreis, *Modernism from Right to Left,* 154.

suggests, characteristically "cannot be centered or totalized."[36] Thus, the poem does not end in straightforward affirmation and conclusion but in suggestion and a sense of provisionality and transition: we are kept suspended on the brink of the romantic and even the apocalyptic, at the frontier of an ordered world, with a smell of incense wafted on currents of air. We are left with an index only of the irrationally raging strength of Stevens's poetic desire "to order words of the sea." We are not offered any concrete words that actually capture "ourselves and . . . our origins"—just as we were never initiated into what the woman was singing before she left the scene.[37] After all, to believe that language can in any simple way delimit selves and reach back to the origins of representation (whether sea or self or any other part of our world) may be to forget the Heraclitean wisdom, always dear to Stevens, that we are continuously in flux. And it may be to forget the more modern philosophical wisdom that mimesis is problematic and the originary moment of language ultimately irretrievable. Our "demarcations" of the sea through "words" are "ghostlier," that is, more abstract, conceptual, mental, or imaginary, than we might often wish, yet the "sounds" they produce are also so much "keener," so much more productive, concretizing, delineating, aesthetically pleasing, than those produced by inhuman extralinguistic reality (a "sound" of sorts, too, in the aquatic sense). This polarity precisely constitutes the finitude of the poet's double-edged instrument, language, which simultaneously realizes our world by restricting it and obfuscates it by deploying general words that inevitably exceed their contexts and occasions.

The irreducibility of language to its contexts and occasions brings us round, finally, to the "Idea of Order" announced in the title and to the poem's "dimly-starred" historical context. The poem was first published in 1934, and its call for order must have sounded particularly loud and shrill in the political climate of that year.[38] Across the Atlantic, Hitler was already

36. Costello, "Adequacy of Landscape," 211.
37. Several gender-inflected readings of "The Idea of Order" have demonstrated that Stevens's representation/projection of the woman has its problematic aspects, even if we go along with the poet in interpreting her, alternatively, as his postromantic muse, as an idealized feminine version of the poet, or as a figure for the imagination, and even if we recall Adrienne Rich's envious exclamation: "If a woman had written that poem, my God!" (quoted in Maria Irene Ramalho de Sousa Santos, "The Woman in the Poem: Wallace Stevens, Ramon Fernandez, and Adrienne Rich," 155). For more gender readings, see esp. Jacqueline Vaught Brogan, " 'Sister of the Minotaur': Sexism and Stevens"; Mary Arensberg, " 'A Curable Separation': Stevens and the Mythology of Gender"; and Brooke Baeten, " 'Whose Spirit Is This?' "
38. A few months before the poem was published, Stevens became a vice president of the Hartford Accident and Indemnity Company and, exhilarated by the promotion, left for one

in power, and in the United States the devastating effects of the Depression were rampant. The rhetoric of order was everywhere, and the poem should not be extracted from its zeitgeist. Stevens was at pains to get across, even on a philosophical level, that his "rage for order" was anything but totalitarian: "It may be that every man introduces his own order into the life about him and that the idea of order in general is simply what Bishop Berkeley might have called a fortuitous concourse of personal orders. But still there is order. . . . But then, I never thought that it was a fixed philosophic proposition that life was a mass of irrelevancies any more than I now think that it is a fixed philosophic proposition that every man introduces his own order as part of a general order. These are tentative ideas for the purposes of poetry" (L 293). They are, it should be added, not only tentative ideas, but also unusual words to write at a time when most American artists were at each other's throats over questions of loyalty to the proletariat, to Marxism, capitalism, southern agrarianism, fascism, and other political and ideological subjects on which firm stands had to be taken. It was in such a belligerent context that Stevens wrote his own jacket statement for *Ideas of Order,* the volume that parades "The Idea of Order at Key West" as its nearly eponymous *pièce de résistance*. The full text of that statement reads as follows:

> We think of changes occurring today as economic changes, involving political and social changes. Such changes raise questions of political and social order.
>
> While it is inevitable that a poet should be concerned with such questions, this book, although it reflects them, is primarily concerned with ideas of order of a different nature, as, for example, the dependence of the individual, confronting the elimination of established ideas, on the general sense of order; the idea of order created by individual concepts, as of the poet, in "The Idea of Order at Key West"; the idea of order arising from the practice of any art, as of poetry in "Sailing after Lunch."
>
> The book is essentially a book of pure poetry. I believe that, in any society, the poet should be the exponent of the imagination of that society. *Ideas of Order* attempts to illustrate the role of the imagination in life, and particularly in life at present. The more realistic life may be, the more it needs the stimulus of the imagination. (OP 222–23)

---

of his business-cum-pleasure jaunts to Key West. Longenbach takes the poem to have been written on that occasion and so does Filreis, though inconsistently (on pages 154 and 335 of *Modernism from Right to Left,* he confirms February 1934 as the date of composition, while on page 119 he proposes mid-1933 instead).

This apology is not without its occasional elusiveness: among other things, the description of "Sailing after Lunch" (CP 120–21) sounds more apposite to "The Idea of Order at Key West," which ostensibly does not much toy with the concept of the poet. But caution is above all required in dealing with Stevens's provocative flaunting of "pure poetry." The context of the entire statement in which these words appear makes clear that no radical world-renunciation and retreat into wholly autotelic verbal music is meant. In a letter of 1941 to Henry Church, Stevens asked the rhetorical question: "But is it possible to discuss aesthetic expression without at least discussing Croce?" (L 385). This high esteem for Benedetto Croce is of considerable importance in framing Stevens's endeavor in *Ideas of Order*. As Longenbach, taking up an earlier analysis by Litz, points out: "Stevens owed his understanding of pure poetry less to Mallarmé than to Croce, for whom the Mallarméan concept of the term, which 'excludes, or pretends to exclude, from poetry all the meaning of words,' is paradoxically an 'impure' conception of pure poetry: for Croce, the truly pure poem dwelt in a middle ground between the extremes of reference and music, between the life of the world and the life of the text."[39] What Stevens, following Croce, and in unison with people like Kenneth Burke, especially wanted to drive home was the need to keep making elementary distinctions between various activities— most prominently between the political and the poetic—and to meet poetry on its own grounds. He was aware of the limits of poetry, but did not want to transgress those limits if he risked losing the poetry in the process. From this point of view, we can understand how, in a poem like "The Idea of Order at Key West," he set out to achieve a careful mixture of "reference and music." Only by navigating between these two facets did Stevens feel he could achieve the necessary ambiguity that would keep his poetry alive beyond the anecdotal topicality of its historical moment. By merging classical and romantic imagery, the hard and the ethereal, the scientific and the sublime, he hoped to renew the essentially "romantic" quality of poetry that he spoke of only a few months after composing "The Idea of Order" in a letter explaining his "temporary theory of poetry": "When people speak of the romantic, they do so in what the French commonly call a *pejorative* sense. But poetry is essentially romantic, only the romantic of poetry must be something constantly new and, therefore, just the opposite of what is spoken of as the romantic. Without this new romantic, one gets nowhere . . . What

39. Longenbach, *Plain Sense of Things*, 151. Quotations in this excerpt are from Benedetto Croce's *The Defence of Poetry*, in the 1933 translation by E. F. Carritt.

one is always doing is keeping the romantic pure: eliminating from it what people speak of as the romantic" (*L* 277).

"The Idea of Order at Key West," it should be clear by now, is not nearly as straightforward, monological, or monothematic a poem as it has often been made out to be. To be sure, the poem is a little too continuous and short to belong entirely with the freely associative genre of the "walk poem" as established by Roger Gilbert in his *Walks in the World* (despite the fact that the text is occasioned by precisely such a walk), but it does pass through various stages that cannot be reduced easily to a single perspective and that, as Alain Suberchicot notes, do not permit Stevens to reach a stability of tone.[40] The three conflicting theories of poetry and language identified by Miller are all woven into the text, from the mimetic attempt at representing the sea, to a middle stanza that textually tightens into a world of words, to the romantic lights that are assimilated into a classicist-modernist perspective at the end of the poem. For all the attempts at rooting the poem historically, moreover, "The Idea of Order" remains a text whose ambition first and foremost is to make universalizing statements about the performative act of representation in art, and to make these statements sufficiently elusively, sufficiently open to appropriation by its anonymous audience, to require a responding creativity on the reader's part. For the final irony of the text is that we have been given only an *idea* of what it might mean to order the sea at Key West into a lyric and a song; the "ghostlier demarcations, keener sounds" are for every one of us to invent. In this sense, "The Idea of Order" is a poem that dramatizes both the finite productivity of the limits imposed by language and the simultaneous infinitude of possibilities made available by accepting these limits. To order reality, at Key West as anywhere else, is a matter of tapping the mimetic, revelatory, and/or self-sufficient potentials of language; but to keep poetry alive, for Stevens, was always a matter of, at the same time, evading the entrapments and oppressions of excessive order and of lingering in that realm where the merest suggestion of an idea of order provides the greatest pleasure.

40. Suberchicot, *Treize façons*, 95.

Chapter 11

Between Metaphor and X

To achieve perfection of style, Aristotle advised poets, they should aim at clarity by using "only current or proper words," without lapsing into what is merely "mean." Such meanness, he argued, could be avoided by inventing metaphors, since for poets "the greatest thing by far is to have a command of metaphor. This alone cannot be imparted by another; it is the mark of genius, for to make good metaphors implies an eye for resemblances." Aristotle's opinion has stood the test of time, and few poets even twenty-four centuries later would feel like quarreling with it. So too with Stevens, who, as Beverly Maeder notes, marked the passage in his copy of the *Poetics*.[1] We cannot be surprised, then, to find in Stevens's own theoretical writings the claim that "[p]oetry is a satisfying of the desire for resemblance" (*NA* 77) or to read this Mallarméan entry in the notebooks that he kept late in life:

> It is only au pays de la métaphore
> Qu'on est poète.
>
> (*OP* 204)

The country of metaphors is the poet's kingdom. Yet the borders of this imaginary country are not so easily mapped; it is not clear, for instance, what lies *outside* this country. Metaphors (whether good or bad) and the process of metaphoricity are everywhere present in language. As Paul de Man noted, metaphors may well be "much more tenacious than facts." High modernist poetry brings this home with a vengeance, since it pushes to an extreme the type of metaphor that Northrop Frye considered most essential: "In the

---

1. Aristotle, *The Poetics*, 81, 87; Maeder, *Experimental Language*, 13, 211.

anagogic aspect of meaning, the radical form of metaphor, 'A is B,' comes into its own. Here we are dealing with poetry in its totality, in which the formula 'A is B' may be hypothetically applied to anything, for there is no metaphor, not even 'black is white,' which a reader has any right to quarrel with in advance. The literary universe, therefore, is a universe in which everything is potentially identical with everything else."[2]

Stevens's own foray into the theory of metaphor, "Three Academic Pieces," opens similarly by proposing that "in some sense, all things resemble each other" (NA 71). In literature, and especially in high modernist poetry, everything may resemble everything else, and anything goes. Under such conditions, it is not surprising that Frye followed up his analysis by moving into the realm of religion: "When poet and critic pass from the archetypal to the anagogic phase, they enter a phase of which only religion, or something as infinite in its range as religion, can possibly form an external goal. . . . [P]oets are happier as servants of religion than of politics, because the transcendental and apocalyptic perspective of religion comes as a tremendous emancipation of the imaginative mind."[3] We do not have to be persuaded by Frye's emancipatory rhetoric to acknowledge the remarkable ease with which a discussion of metaphor proves able to shade into metaphysics. Frye's analysis in some sense only paved the way for certain poststructuralists, whose dropping of the religious belief that bolstered his scheme made them fall into an equally "infinite" abyss.

Over the past decades we have witnessed a veritable explosion of theories of metaphor and theories in which metaphor takes a pivotal role, culminating in such provocative claims as Lacan's statement that "the most serious reality, and even for man the only serious one . . . is to be found but in metaphor."[4] One of the most influential texts, however, to connect the fields of metaphor and metaphysics, or literary theory and philosophy, and perhaps the most useful text for framing Stevens's own performative take on the subject, is Derrida's essay "White Mythology: Metaphor in the

---

2. De Man, "Semiology and Rhetoric," 5; Northrop Frye, *Anatomy of Criticism: Four Essays*, 124.

3. Frye, *Anatomy of Criticism*, 125.

4. Jacques Lacan, "La Métaphore du Sujet," 892 (my translation). In 1927, John Middleton Murry could open an essay by saying: "Discussions of metaphor—*there are not many of them*—often strike us at first as superficial" ("Metaphor," 1; emphasis added). But by 1971, Warren A. Shibles managed to record about three thousand entries in his *Metaphor: An Annotated Bibliography and History*. And this was only at the beginning of the decade of "theory"; since 1971, the number of studies has made a few more quantum leaps.

Text of Philosophy." In this many-layered text, Derrida tries to demon-
strate the mutual, ultimately aporetic contamination of metaphor and meta-
physics. Philosophy, so his argument runs, has traditionally sought to exile
metaphor, defining it as a contingent feature of language, a merely formal
vehicle for ideas whose essence remains unaffected by it—at best, a rhetor-
ical tool for ornamentation or condensation. But time and again, this has
led to unsolvable quandaries. Philosophy never manages to fully contain
and theorize metaphor, because the latter always remains at the heart of
the very reasoning that attempts to expel it. In one of Derrida's notori-
ous, irreducible puns, this uncontainability is cast as "La métaphysique—
relève de la métaphore" (meaning both "Metaphysics—the *Aufhebung* of
metaphor" and "Metaphysics derives from metaphor").[5] The contamina-
tion, however, works both ways: if philosophy proves unable to construct
a rigorous metaphorology, metaphor in turn cannot be defined or discussed
without working out a metaphysics. The two-sidedness of this argument has
often been glossed over in literary quarters, where critics have been all too
quick to interpret Derrida as saying that writing is always already metaphor-
ical, and hence that philosophy and metaphysics are but a subgenre of liter-
ature, or that we might as well just collapse philosophy and literature into
one type of writing controlled by metaphor.[6] Derrida's principal argument is
rather about the difficult entanglement of metaphor and metaphysics. Dis-
cussing the one entails drawing on the other, in a continuous and impure
mutual production and limitation.

"Poetry," Stevens noted in one of his many *adagia*, "is metaphor" (*OP*
194), and the statement may stand as an index of how his entire oeuvre
is shot through with this figure of speech. The omnipresence of metaphor
involves more in his case, however, than the mere occurrence of a relatively
high number of metaphors. (Comparative analyses might well show that
the number is lower than that of many another modernist poet, as Alain
Suberchicot argues.)[7] It also involves the presence of metaphor and the
metaphorical process as a key concept informing his theory of poetry; for
much of the time, he regarded the one to be the true subject of the other.
We would be hard pressed to find another major poet who uses the abstract

5. Jacques Derrida, "White Mythology: Metaphor in the Text of Philosophy," 258, and
translator's note, ibid.
6. See Norris, *Deconstruction*, 24, 81–82.
7. Suberchicot, *Treize façons*, 184.

and, to many, unpoetic word *metaphor* itself (or its plural) no less than thirty times in his verse.[8] Stevens's critics have been understandably happy to pick this up and have themselves produced titles like "Metaphoric Staging," "Impossible Metaphor," "World and Word *au pays de la métaphore*," and, most symptomatically of all, "Wallace Stevens' Metaphors of Metaphor."[9]

As with other staple ingredients of this poet's thinking and writing (like his handling of the word *sense*), the term *metaphor* fluctuates and oscillates considerably in what it refers to, almost from one moment to the next. Stevens deliberately makes it hard on us to rest securely on any particular definition or appreciation of the concept. "I do not think Stevens' notions can be readily assimilated to any one current theory of metaphor," writes Eleanor Cook judiciously. "Rather, he seems to challenge theories in his own compact, elusive way."[10] Moreover, as we would expect from a poet who alternates between stripping reality of all its linguistic mediations and surrendering himself to the invention of the most exorbitant linguistic technologies, Stevens tended to view the metaphor-making process with considerable ambivalence. He often hailed the potential of metaphor for bringing together reality and the imagination, or self and world, but at other times he just as strongly denounced its alienating divisiveness, apotropaic evasiveness, and suspicious, inherited ontological equivalences.[11] Poetry and metaphor may have been identical to Stevens, but when he was after the primary and immediate reality of first ideas, he wanted "the figure and not / An evading metaphor" (CP 199) or urged himself to "Trace the gold sun about the whitened sky / Without evasion by a single metaphor" (CP 373). The first idea, though itself a metaphor of sorts, derived much of its obsessive power precisely from the tension it produced with the mediated indirectness of metaphor.

Throughout his poetry, we find Stevens pondering questions of metaphor: How dogged is its presence, really? How hard to subdue is it? How can it be said to reveal and how to obfuscate? How does what it makes present depend upon, or call forth, an absence? How effectively can we try to avoid it, and

8. This is to pay no attention to the fact that several of the poems containing the word *metaphor* are, as Beverly Maeder notes, "collected with other poems of 'transport' (another translation of the Greek *metapherein*) in *Transport to Summer* (1947)" (*Experimental Language*, 46).

9. Riddel, "Metaphoric Staging"; J. Hillis Miller, "Impossible Metaphor"; Maeder, *Experimental Language*, 45–74; Charles Altieri, "Wallace Stevens' Metaphors of Metaphor: Poetry as Theory."

10. Cook, *Poetry, Word-Play, and Word-War*, 174.

11. See esp. Maeder, *Experimental Language*, chap. 1.

alternatively, how great is our need for it and how rich the potential it opens up? One of the best ways of tracing Stevens's partial and local "answers" to such questions—and they are, of course, more often ambiguous working hypotheses than foreclosed answers—is to look at the three most important poems that flaunt the topic in their titles: "Metaphors of a Magnifico," "The Motive for Metaphor," and "Thinking of a Relation between the Images of Metaphors."[12] The first poem makes it perfectly clear that early on in his writing life (the poem was written in 1918), Stevens was already given to engaging most of the above questions. "Metaphors of a Magnifico" offers a shrewdly ironical, elliptical dramatization of the workings and limits of metaphor, though at first it does not seem to present itself like that at all:

> Twenty men crossing a bridge,
> Into a village,
> Are twenty men crossing twenty bridges,
> Into twenty villages,
> Or one man
> Crossing a single bridge into a village.
>
> This is old song
> That will not declare itself . . .
>
> Twenty men crossing a bridge,
> Into a village,
> Are
> Twenty men crossing a bridge
> Into a village.
>
> That will not declare itself
> Yet is certain as meaning . . .

---

12. A fourth poem, "Metaphor as Degeneration" (CP 444–45), is too cryptic in its totality to be profitably included in the discussion. The fact that few critics have given serious attention to "Metaphor as Degeneration" (a recent exception being Beverly Maeder) only corroborates the poem's somewhat dubious status. It should be noted, in addition, that a more exhaustive exploration of the topic of metaphor in Stevens could not bypass the undeservedly neglected "Someone Puts a Pineapple Together" (NA 83–87), which should be read in conjunction with the essay immediately preceding it in The Necessary Angel, as well as two poems analyzed at some length by Eleanor Cook, "Oak Leaves Are Hands" (CP 272) and "Man Carrying Thing" (CP 350–51) (Poetry, Word-Play, and Word-War, 179–81, 184–86), one extensively commented upon by Michael Beehler, "Prologues to What Is Possible" (CP 515–17) (Discourses of Difference, 151–56), and various materials included in the first two chapters of Maeder's Experimental Language (11–74).

> The boots of the men clump
> On the boards of the bridge.
> The first white wall of the village
> Rises through fruit-trees.
>
> Of what was it I was thinking?
>
> So the meaning escapes.
>
> The first white wall of the village . . .
> The fruit-trees. . . .
>
> (PEM 35–36)

"All poetry is experimental poetry," wrote Stevens (OP 187), and this particular poem at first sight presents an experiment in definition. The verb on which the opening stanza hinges is *to be*, the copula that arguably constitutes the most momentous grammatical characteristic of Western European languages and that has been linked directly to the preponderance of metaphysics in Western thought.[13] The poem's speaker apparently seeks to define a scene, "converting fact or event into statement."[14] To this purpose, he tries out two hypotheses. First he abandons the gestalt of the scene and considers the twenty men crossing a bridge as separate individuals. Since the men all subjectively experience the reality surrounding them in different ways (no matter how slight the difference), they cross twenty different bridges into twenty different villages. This is the radically perspectival and particularizing view of things. In the second hypothesis, by contrast, the men are

13. "I am afraid we cannot get rid of God," wrote Nietzsche, "as long as we continue to believe in grammar . . ." (*Götzen-Dämmerung oder Wie man mit dem Hammer philosophirt* [Twilight of the idols], 72; my translation). See also Boehm, *Ideologie en ervaring*, 34, for an interpretation of Nietzsche's aphorism as referring to the "S is P" structure of logic, which prompts Boehm to add that "we cannot get rid of immortality as long as we do not get rid of logic" (my translation); and Derrida's analysis of Emile Benveniste in "The Supplement of Copula: Philosophy before Linguistics," where we learn that Aristotle believed the verb *to be* "did not actually signify anything, that it operated simply as a synthesis" (196). Beverly Maeder draws on Aristotle, Benveniste, and Derrida to explore at great length the poet's conspicuous (over)use of *to be* (*Experimental Language*, 77–123). According to Maeder, "we cannot avoid being struck by the fact that the inflections that characterize English indeed privilege the verb disproportionately. English invests the verb with the ability to express mood, aspect, tense, and sometimes number, often with excruciating precision. . . . I can evoke nuances ad infinitum merely by modifying the various auxiliaries and grammatical forms of *to be*. It might give me a sense of mastering knowledge about the world and mastering the world *tout court*" (ibid., 86).
14. Maeder, *Experimental Language*, 49.

deindividualized and taken collectively, viewed from the outside, so that their situation appears essentially the same and the scene can be reduced to the simple triadic structure of man/bridge/village. This is the abstracting and universalizing view of things that comes almost naturally with language insofar as language tends to synthesize the irreducibly multiple and complex into general concepts.

But of what use are such idealistic, intellectualizing hypotheses? According to the couplet that follows, they are just "old song," timeworn variations on a metaphysical or logical theme. They will not "declare" themselves—a subtly ironical word that does more than point up the absence of an explicit self-identification and clarification: it also echoes the grammatically "declarative" mode of the opening stanza's proposition.[15] And so the speaker must give it another shot: "Twenty men crossing a bridge, / Into a village," (the commas illustrate how carefully and emphatically he ponders his ingredients again) "Are" (this time the crucial verb is highlighted by taking up a monometrical line of its own, before the answer is given with a shrug, all at once and without commas) "Twenty men crossing a bridge / Into a village." Another couplet, trickily modulating the first, interrupts: even if once again nothing has been clarified, at least we can be certain now about the meaning of the statement. Typically, Stevens adopts a jocular tone when struggling with serious, far-reaching questions. If absolute certainty of meaning is wanted, he reminds us, there is but one way to get it: by way of tautology, by using the exactly identical, sterile repetition of 1=1. Absolute certainty of meaning is a snake biting its own tail. Unable to reach out to the world, it is a mere blabbering formula that keeps us forever locked in the mind.

The poem's turning point obviously occurs between the fourth and fifth stanzas. Suddenly, the intellectual exercise appears to have lost its appeal: idealistic hypotheses no longer hold sway over the speaker. His senses call him back to the concrete and the physical, so much so even that he imagines himself to be participating in the scene as one of the men and observes along with them how "The first white wall of the village / Rises through fruit-trees."[16] This time, the speaker is all eye and ear—and consequently forgets what he was thinking. Once more, then, nothing has been explained or

15. Marie Borroff, *Language and the Poet: Verbal Artistry in Frost, Stevens, and Moore*, 18.
16. The men are most naturally imagined as soldiers, both because of the facts that their group is all-male, exactly twenty in number, and wearing boots, and because of the poem's date of composition, 1918, only shortly after Stevens had written an explicit war poem, "The Death of a Soldier" (CP 97). See also Borroff, *Language and the Poet*, 18, and Cook, *Poetry, Word-Play, and Word-War*, 177.

defined: the senses in themselves have no "meaning" or identity; they just *are* and produce certain sensuous *effects*. Even the most sober nominalizations of language deployed for the purpose of mimetically representing these effects are in fact already a detour. And so the poem concludes with two highly charged, but remarkably open lines:

> The first white wall of the village . . .
> The fruit-trees. . . .

This could be the painter's triumph over the philosopher, with the speaker forgetting his desire for the metaphysics of definition and taking pleasure in pure sight. Then the poem might be read as an early stab at reaching the thing itself or the first idea, bringing to mind Merleau-Ponty's phenomeno-logical idea that "to see is the permission not to think the thing *because one sees it*."[17] The closing lines, in that case, should be seen as imagistic in intention and to invite a reading in which they are mumbled softly, warmly, with a touch of love. Or else, in a somewhat different reading, with a touch of nostalgia, fading into memory at the very point of being returned to. But the "closing" lines—if so inept an adjective may be used for lines that are held in abeyance by suspension points—may also contain the germ of a narrative: the village approached by the twenty men may function emblematically as a promise, the final destination of a long, exhausting march—home at last.[18]

Most critics have stopped here and taken the poem to express quite simply the happiness of surrendering metaphysics to the painterly eye. This is, with-out doubt, a valid interpretation and it is not contradicted by a knowledge of the rest of Stevens's oeuvre. Nevertheless, it proves possible to extend this reading to something more equivocal and nuanced by putting some extra pressure on the suspension points with which the final lines trail off. Marie Borroff takes a benign view of them, in accordance with the generally un-problematic reading just described: "I take these to imply that the speaker

---

17. Maurice Merleau-Ponty, "Cinq notes sur Claude Simon," 64 (my translation).

18. A much darker, suppressed scenario is offered by Srikanth Reddy: "The text stops just short of the climactic encounter between soldiers and villagers; the Magnifico's dry, specula-tive consciousness cannot accommodate the impending cruelty of the village's fall, and the poem drifts off into an ellipsis before the narrative moment of arrival and conflict" ("'As He Starts the Human Tale,'" 15). Along analogous lines, Beverly Maeder proposes that "the failure of expression" at the end of the poem "poignantly conveys the hopelessness of the war situation, the unspeakableness of what can be observed, thought, and felt" (*Experimental Language*, 50–51). As it ends with only a few noun phrases, there is of course no way of ascertaining the precise tonality of Stevens's text.

has willingly abandoned syntax in his absorption in the imagined details of the scene." She dismisses out of hand an exegesis by Bruce King, who remarks: "Although the poem involves an argumentative structure, it is clear that the obvious dialectic disintegrates, and resolution is not achieved . . . Thus the poem ends on a note of defeat as the images fade into the tell-tale dots of uncompleted intellectual process."[19]

While Borroff considers such "negative emphasis" "unjustified," what King opens up is in fact a valid perspective.[20] Rhetorically, the two lines under discussion are aposiopeses, sentences that break off and remain uncompleted. But why are they so? Is it possible to see what, if anything, has been left out? From one point of view, we simply witness the speaker lapsing into a stammer. The aposiopeses clip the lines so short that not even a verb is reached, leaving the noun phrases literally unactivated, without any dynamic potential. Language falls apart in front of our eyes, and with it the necessary condition for all poetry. We are back to the kinds of questions that often plagued Stevens in his search for the thing itself: Can a poet still speak if he surrenders fully to the senses? Does he not remain caught—invariably, inevitably—in textuality and its attendant metaphysics? Is there no gap between concept and percept, between language and the senses? What we get, from this point of view, is a meditation on the meaning of meaning. As B. J. Leggett observes: "The speaker is willing to sacrifice the abstract meaning for the particulars of experience, but it is easy to show both that he has merely exchanged one form of abstraction for another, and that his formulation as a whole *means* simply by exhibiting the differences between two conceptions of reality."[21] The emphasis may legitimately be shifted from a registration of gratification by the senses to an inquiry into the limits of language and the structure of thinking. The fact that the two lines immediately preceding the elliptic close are surrounded by blank spaces already indicates that the poem is finally crumbling and falling apart (even if these spaces simultaneously serve to evoke something of the dissipation of distraction).[22] What is more, the suspension points refer us back to the endings of the second and fourth

19. Borroff, *Language and the Poet*, 19; Bruce King, "Wallace Stevens' 'Metaphors of a Magnifico,'" 450, 452.

20. Borroff, *Language and the Poet*, 158.

21. Leggett, *Early Stevens*, 206.

22. The extra spaces have not attracted critical notice, though they make a notable difference between the reedited version of the poem in *The Palm at the End of the Mind* and the way it was reprinted in the *Collected Poems* (19), where the two lines are appended to the four preceding ones, thus forming a single stanza of six lines. (The Library of America version, based on the original 1923 edition of *Harmonium*, opts for a compromise by building

stanzas, where on both occasions an intellectual block was suggested. In one sense, then, these earlier moments of impotence prove germane to the poem's conclusion, which also reaches a stalemate. The final lines may thus be read as hinging on a both/and logic, simultaneously staging an affirmation and an inability to affirm.

What is it that could have prompted the stalemate? To answer that question, we need to turn to the poem's title: "Metaphors of a Magnifico." The second noun is the easier one here. The magnifico—which is the name for a Venetian nobleman, not one of Stevens's funny neologisms—is only a thin disguise for the poet himself. We have seen how Stevens loved to strut in the gaudy apparel of extravagant, invented characters, and in this case there is a sly extra hint that he is actually figuring himself in the fact that *magnifico* contains the letter *c*. In her analysis of "Homunculus et La Belle Étoile," Cook points out that the homunculus is "yet another of those c-sound male figures who are personae for Stevens (Peter Quince, Pecksniff, Crispin)," and she could easily have extended the list with such characters as "mon oncle" and the magnifico.[23] Yet we should not make the mistake of conflating Stevens and the magnifico too naively: the spectacular disguise should remind us of the distancing effect involved in using the third person for self-description, and it should especially alert us to the possibility of self-irony. John Timberman Newcomb, for one, suggests that the magnifico belongs to those early Stevensian personae who are all too aware of a poetry "threatening to dissolve into radically self-conscious parody."[24] At least the possibility of self-parody appears to be inscribed in the text, for although Stevens flamboyantly makes his entry onto the scene in the magnificent cloak of an aristocrat, the poem from one perspective proceeds to subvert this self-image

---

a stanza of five lines and splitting off only the line "So the meaning escapes.") One should note, further, how the blank spaces may be related to the whiteness of the village walls. Whiteness traditionally figures a semantic vacancy; it tropes upon an absence, which it seeks to intensify by suggesting a presence. Nearly thirty years later, in "The Auroras of Autumn," Stevens returned to both the device of suspension points and the image of whiteness to evoke a surrendering of language to sense and a dialectic of presence and absence: "Here, being visible is being white, / Is being of the solid of white, the accomplishment / Of an extremist in an exercise . . ." (CP 412).

23. Cook, *Poetry, Word-Play, and Word-War*, 67. C's in Stevens have a history of their own that reaches its apogee in "The Comedian as the Letter C" (CP 27–46). We should not forget also that this is a poet who loved to compose titles in old French spelling, making use of unvoiced c's, as in "Cy Est Pourtraicte, Madame Ste Ursule, et Les Unze Mille Vierges" (CP 21–22) and "Bouquet of Belle Scavoir" (CP 231–32), and who kept a commonplace book, *Sur Plusieurs Beaux Sujects,* that almost invariably elicits a parenthetical *sic* from critics.

24. Newcomb, *Literary Canons,* 64.

and to show a person who is split right down the middle, unable to piece sense and intellect together.

This conscious (or only half-conscious?) self-ironizing needs to be borne in mind when developing the implications of the crucial first noun in the title, those "metaphors" around which the poem supposedly revolves. The question raised by the word is as obvious as it is puzzling: Where *are* those metaphors? Looked at from a traditional rhetorical point of view, only two potential candidates in the entire poem can be found—"old song" and "Rises"—and they hardly qualify, since the former self-referentially indicates the text and as such is hackneyed in the case of lyric poetry, and the latter is simply a dead (or severely moribund) metaphor. Few critics, surprisingly, have paid enough attention to this crux to come up with a (necessarily displaced) interpretation of the title. Cook offers one of the most compelling scenarios: "With a title like *Metaphors of a Magnifico*, we expect a series of metaphors, perhaps magnificent, certainly magnified. But the point about the magnifico's metaphors seems to be that he has none. Or more precisely, that he cannot reach any, for he keeps trying to get his men across a bridge, like some officer in charge of transport. . . . Clump, clump, go the boots of twenty men on to the bridge of metaphor, but never across." In Cook's view, the entire poem "centers . . . on the one-word line that is the bridge of all metaphor, the verb 'to be.' But 'are' only carries A back to A, and no meta-, no 'beyond,' comes."[25] The "metaphors" of the title do not anticipate any actual figures of speech in the poem proper, but only a number of vain attempts at *making* metaphors. The twenty men do not appear to be crossing the bridge by accident, then, but emblematically, since the word *crossing* itself (significantly used in the dynamic and processual form of the present participle) carries ancient tropological connotations. Thus, it may easily be argued that the failures recorded in the poem *a contrario* help to show *the necessity of metaphors* to bring a world truly to life. The problem with the "isolated facts" of the white village wall and the fruit trees at the end of the text is, as Anthony Whiting suggests, that they, too, are ultimately "not *like* anything." "None of the magnifico's verbal tactics," adds Maeder with reference to the speaker's successive attempts at defining, reverting to old song, and simply naming, "can fulfill the role formerly attributed to metaphor, in which the oblique reference and inclusionary gesture produced by transfer had the potential to multiply the given represented in language."[26]

25. Cook, *Poetry, Word-Play, and Word-War,* 177.
26. Whiting, *Never-Resting Mind,* 68; Maeder, *Experimental Language,* 51.

The paradox of this interpretation is that our willingness to accept it itself depends on an essentially metaphorical willingness to establish connections, for nowhere does the text make explicit that what it is really looking for, even if fruitlessly, is something strictly metaphorical, something along the lines of "Twenty men crossing a bridge, / Into a village, / Are / A flock of geese / Waddling into a farmyard." As a result, Susan B. Weston's different interpretation provides an equally valid and productive perspective: "The title—'Metaphors of a Magnifico'—suggests that his attempt at definition reduces to so many 'metaphors': like the epigrammatic assertions in 'Thirteen Ways of Looking at a Blackbird,' anything short of identity, X is X ('Twenty men . . . are . . . twenty men'), is metaphoric."[27] When sufficiently stretched, all language of the "S is P" type turns out to be metaphorical. Only the circularity of "S is S" (as in the poem's third stanza) can pretend to escape the condition of metaphoricity. In this respect, we are reminded of Nietzsche's influential little essay, "On Truth and Falsity in Their Extramoral Sense," which has become something of a staple among deconstructionists. In this text, Nietzsche argues that world and mind are linked metaphorically: every nervous impulse we receive is translated or transferred into an image, this image in turn into a sound (a word), the word into a concept—and all these trans-fers are, literally, meta-phors.[28] Our whole experience and perception is constituted metaphorically, or as Stevens would say: "The senses paint / By metaphor" (CP 219).

The juxtaposition of Nietzsche's theory and "Metaphors of a Magnifico" allows us to see how much the metaphysical aspect of metaphors is on display in Stevens's writings at a relatively early date. This is not to say that we should be giving priority to a poststructuralist over a more phenomenological interpretation of the text, nor that we should jump to conclusions about Stevens's original intention in 1918. Weighing these various interpretations

27. Weston, Wallace Stevens, 31–32.
28. See Friedrich Nietzsche, "On Truth and Falsity in Their Extramoral Sense"; also Derrida, "Supplement of Copula," 178, and "White Mythology," 217; Paul de Man, "The Epistemology of Metaphor," 22–23; Riddel, "Metaphoric Staging," 318, 356n7; and Spivak, translator's preface, xxii. The question of scientific accuracy in Nietzsche's nineteenth-century scheme is not important here. Contemporary neuroscience refines Nietzsche by talking of transducers and effectors in the nervous system, of electrochemical pulses and the junctures of synapses where neurotransmitter molecules and neuromodulator molecules interact (Dennett, Kinds of Minds, 69, 73–74). It also contests the "Myth of Double Transduction" that involves some final translation into "the mysterious, nonphysical medium of the mind" (ibid., 72). But it still returns to Nietzsche's notion of transfer in talking of "an astronomically high number of points of transduction" (75) and even confirms Nietzsche's sequence of sounds (words) being translated into concepts (151).

against each other is a matter, rather, of showing how the almost success-
fully resisting signifying economy of "Metaphors of a Magnifico" may pro-
duce several legitimate, if divergent, interpretations. The poem does more
than just hail the senses. It also teases us into meditating on the status of
metaphors both in relation to our perception of the world and in relation to
the language with which we try to represent, control, or imaginatively play
with that world.

We next come to "The Motive for Metaphor," written almost twenty-five
years later, in the fall of 1942, and we are told by Helen Vendler not to
expect anything essentially dissimilar, for it is the "most strictly comparable
poem in the later work to 'Metaphors of a Magnifico.'" Yet Vendler does
not tell us how and why this should be so, and her own interpretation, as
we will see in a moment, actually adds to the far-reaching uncontainability
of "The Motive for Metaphor." A close reading of the text makes it easier
to underwrite Patricia A. Parker's claim that "'The Motive for Metaphor'
is both the most complex and the most frustrating of Stevens' meditations
on metaphor," as well as Eleanor Cook's warning that the poem offers "an
inviting puzzle, though its word-play is so intricate that I am not sure we
shall ever untangle it—which means that metaphor's motive, like all deep
motives, stays partly hidden."[29] Bearing in mind that the poem was written
only a few months after "Notes toward a Supreme Fiction," and remember-
ing that the second of the three poetic imperatives there is that the supreme
fiction "must change" (CP 389), let us look at the more straightforward part
of the poem, its opening two-thirds:

> You like it under the trees in autumn,
> Because everything is half dead.
> The wind moves like a cripple among the leaves
> And repeats words without meaning.
>
> In the same way, you were happy in spring,
> With the half colors of quarter-things,
> The slightly brighter sky, the melting clouds,
> The single bird, the obscure moon—
>
> The obscure moon lighting an obscure world
> Of things that would never be quite expressed,

---

29. Helen Vendler, "Apollo's Harsher Songs," 53; Patricia A. Parker, "The Motive for
Metaphor: Stevens and Derrida," 79–80; Cook, *Poetry, Word-Play, and Word-War*, 182.

> Where you yourself were never quite yourself
> And did not want nor have to be,
>
> Desiring the exhilarations of changes:
> The motive for metaphor . . .
>
> (CP 288)

Of the several possible referents for the poem's addressee, the least coun-terintuitive one seems to be (one part of) the poet himself.[30] It is on the basis of such an interpretation, in which Stevens "addresses his new, 'partial' self," that Vendler develops a psychological reading of the poem that once again reminds us of the uncertain tonality and potential for polyphony in Stevens's work. She defiantly asserts that "The Motive for Metaphor" is "a very brutal poem" in which "self-contempt at the beginning" is "evident." "Whatever voice it is that speaks here," she writes, "it speaks dismissively of the poet's love of half colors and quarter-things."[31] This critical move, which presupposes a devastating irony on the poet's part, is a bold one to make, since the voice that speaks appears to be stating the dead opposite of what Vendler believes to be "evident": it claims that the poet actually likes fall and spring, because these are seasons of change and incompletion, producing the imaginative exhilarations he longs for. A passing reference to the poem in a letter to Henry Church supports this straight, nonironic paraphrase. After summarizing the ideas behind "Notes toward a Supreme Fiction" by saying that "the essence of poetry is change and the essence of change is that it gives pleasure," Stevens continues: "There is a magazine being published at Princeton called CHIMERA. They asked me some time ago for a poem and I sent them a thing called THE MOTIVE FOR METAPHOR. This is an illustration of the last remark that the essence of change is that it gives pleasure: that it exhilarates" (L 430). Stevens seems to imply that we should just take the first two lines of the fourth stanza as a synopsis of the poem: the "exhilarations of changes" form "the motive for metaphor." An etymological play on the word *motive*, which relates to *motion* and *movement*, hence to *change*, only enhances the poem's central thesis.[32]

30. A divergent interpretation is offered by Pearce, "Toward Decreation," 295, and Cook, *Poetry, Word-Play, and Word-War*, 183, who both take the text to address the reader. Cook also believes that, at a secondary level, personified metaphor itself is addressed, but such an interpretation may be subsumed without too much trouble under the primary reading of a self-address, if we take the self apostrophized by Stevens to be the metaphor-making poet.

31. Vendler, "Apollo's Harsher Songs," 53, 55, 53, 54.

32. See Parker, "Motive for Metaphor," 77, and Cook, *Poetry, Word-Play, and Word-War*, 182.

Is there any apparent need to distrust Stevens's own comment at this point? The opening stanza contains three odd phrases that could suggest dissatisfaction with a former poetic self: "half dead," "like a cripple," and "words without meaning." Yet a negative interpretation does not impose itself automatically. All three images evoke a reality that is in need of completion by an imaginative act of the perceiver. Stevens likes things to be "half dead," we might argue, because it is then up to him to give them back half of their lives. At the same time the phrase reminds him, a sixty-three-year-old man, how this act of life-giving acquires a special poignancy and urgency in the light of death. The wind "moves like a cripple" because it needs the support of the poet's language. In addition, the simile may be taken to function at the descriptive level in evoking a hampered, irregular shuffle among the leaves. And the wind "repeats words without meaning" because without a metaphorical translation by the poet it is merely, at most, a *flatus vocis* that has no human meaning. Simultaneously, the description may be taken to prepare us for Stevens's later insistence, in his poem about a "gold-feathered bird" singing "without human meaning, / Without human feeling," that "it is not the reason / That makes us happy or unhappy" ("Of Mere Being," OP 141).

If there are no obvious indications that we need to understand Stevens's tone as scathing, we nevertheless cannot dismiss Vendler's interpretation out of hand: the attribution of irony always rests on a critical conjecture that subverts literal, surface meanings. Given the deep interpretive uncertainty and ambivalence that the poem's ending gives rise to (as we will see), the precise affective coloring of the opening stanzas remains up for grabs. At some level, Stevens could indeed be offering a critique of his own too-comfortable and late-romantic stance by constructing a romantic-bourgeois persona that complacently indulges in half-finished realities. Something similar applies to the second stanza. At first we may assume that "the half colors of quarter-things" make the poet happy by supplying him with the most suitable material for inventing metaphors. We might even draw contextual support for this from the fact that Stevens, around the time he wrote the poem, in November of 1942, visited a Corot exhibit in New York and waxed lyrical about it.[33] After all, Corot's misty, monochromatic landscapes *en demi-teintes* are known for their many "half colors of quarter-things" in the distance. Stevens's enthusiasm could thus be expected to extend to "the

33. Richardson, *Later Years*, 212.

melting clouds" in the poem—with the phrase itself an appropriate instance of a metaphor inspired by change (in this case, from winter to spring) and one that carries the additional faint suggestion of a sky that is being wiped clean like a blank slate so that poetry may be written. That the sublunary world subsequently favored is called "obscure" (a word used three times) could be an index of his symbolist heritage as well as of his late-romantic association of the moon with the imagination and his deeply held belief in the poetic need to darken speech.

But here again we are made to wonder: Is there a simple analogy between the first and second stanzas? If the text suggests that "a quality that was positive in spring has become negative in autumn," as Thomas C. Grey proposes, the poet's attitude toward his idealization of incompletions becomes less certain. "We were drawn to metaphor in spring by desire for excitement," notes Grey, "but now in autumn by fear of reality." If this is so, the poem recants the conventional idea of spring as the herald of rebirth and the promise of fruition and may well be taken to express "Stevens's fear that metaphor (and the kind of *symboliste* poetry that is identified with metaphor) represents a morally ambivalent flight into fantasy." Contextual evidence is easily produced in the form of Stevens's attested "distaste for the 'shrinking' aspects of his nature" that were "particularly troubling to him in 1942," when the literal war without inspired a poetic war within.[34]

That we had better beware of the poem's surface expression is made clear by a typically Stevensian disparity between content and form. For one thing, as Grey shrewdly notes, the language of the first three stanzas is remarkably unfigurative: the only exceptions are those of "the melting clouds" and the wind moving "like a cripple" (technically not even a metaphor but a simile).[35] For another, the eulogy of obscurity is made in the most transparent and prosaic of terms. Metaphor, says the poem, exists in an unrelievable tension with its referent (the so-called tenor), with "things that would never be quite expressed." "Both in nature and in metaphor identity is the vanishing-point of resemblance," Stevens would later write in "Three Academic Pieces" (*NA* 72). "The Motive for Metaphor" anticipates this claim, for the idea of an imperfect match is extended in one and the same gesture to all figures of identity, including the poet's own self. The imperfect is our paradise, and absolute certainty, as "Metaphors of a Magnifico" also insists, can be obtained only by way of tautology. The human subject is never quite

34. Grey, *The Wallace Stevens Case*, 54–57.
35. Ibid., 59–60.

itself and should not be, for "[t]he trouble is that once one is strongly defined, no other definition is ever possible, in spite of daily change" (*L* 880). Human identity is a mutable and mutant construction in a nonlogical field governed by metaphors. Anticipating poststructuralist critiques of the subject in a benign and commonsensical format, Stevens seems to insist on the need to question an overassertive ego and to hail the exhilarating sense of liberation produced by the plastic play between self and self-description. Richard Poirier calls this "the salutary activity of troping," which may teach us to be less intimidated by words and prevent us, in Kenneth Burke's words, from becoming "too assertively, too hopelessly" ourselves.[36]

This may all be quite true, but the poem at this point only propounds its idea without enacting it; the images in the opening stanzas, as Maeder observes, do not even denote "changes"—exhilarating or not—but only "approximations."[37] What is more, the text does not end with the straightforward affirmation of a theory of metaphor or of some poetic dogma, but winds up in more complex fashion:

> The motive for metaphor, shrinking from
> The weight of primary noon,
> The A B C of being,
>
> The ruddy temper, the hammer
> Of red and blue, the hard sound—
> Steel against intimation—the sharp flash,
> The vital, arrogant, fatal, dominant X.
>
> (CP 288)

On the face of it, Stevens's preference for "the obscure moon" (or synecdochically, for that twilight region where the literary imagination is free to hatch metaphors) is underscored by his "shrinking from / The weight of primary noon." The latter image suggests the tyranny of some overinsistent reality—embodied by the full sun—which appears too much itself to allow the poet any space of his own to do his poetic work. According to Harold Bloom, Stevens had a Shelleyan predilection for "that moment in the day when light has come but the sun has not yet risen above the horizon." An interpretation along these lines, however, must again reckon with the tonal

---

36. Poirier, *Poetry and Pragmatism*, 129; Burke quoted by Poirier, ibid.
37. Maeder, *Experimental Language*, 69.

insecurities of the text, for against it Vendler proposes that Stevens is secretly *attracted* to the sun at its zenith, which in her opinion stands for "a new sort of self-knowledge, a change into the changelessness of a final, permanent self." The fact that Vendler shows herself to be obviously pleased with Stevens's castigation of his former self, calling it "a relief, after earlier evasions, to hear him being so harsh,"[38] perhaps betrays the rationale behind her assertive analysis of the poem: her interpretation reads like the expression of one of those moments when irritation over Stevens's sometimes exhausting habits—the drive for "obscurity" explicitly hailed by the poem, the endless "evasions" mentioned by Vendler, the oblique confrontation with a world at war, the constant tonal ambiguities—is critically displaced and channeled into an interpretation in which the poet gives *himself* a rapping.

Whether we prefer Bloom's late-romantic or Vendler's adamantly realist interpretation is less important, however, than the fact that both critics, like many of their colleagues, read the appositions on which the poem ends as an unbroken chain of variational images on a single theme, "The weight of primary noon." Vendler even insists on this, protesting that "the old Platonism, the desire for harmony, is smuggled in" by Stevens in using apposition, "a figure which of itself implies that things can be aligned in meaningful parallels, that metaphorical equivalences are a portion of significance." In Vendler's opinion, we witness Stevens betraying a "nostalgia for synthesis and system: brutality has extended to his self-perception, and to his imagery, without yet having reached his syntax."[39] But this is to blind oneself to the problematic character of the poem's syntax. As Parker, who has offered one of the two most extensive and complicating readings of the poem to date (the other is Grey's), notes: "What makes it finally impossible to extract from 'The Motive' any . . . definitive statement is the unsettling undecidability of its syntax, or movement towards conclusion, though criticism with a particular end in view repeatedly makes such an impossible decision, often without signalling that there is any decision to be made."[40]

38. Bloom, *Poems of Our Climate*, 221; Vendler, "Apollo's Harsher Songs," 55.

39. Vendler, "Apollo's Harsher Songs," 55–56. Here again one might venture an explanation for this reading, not by affirming Stevens's "nostalgia for synthesis," but by pointing to the critic's own nostalgia. The reason that Vendler interprets the poem's syntax as unequivocally as she does is that she wants "The Motive for Metaphor" to corroborate a teleological narrative according to which Stevens passes from an embryonic stage in *Harmonium* through a more complex but not yet fully realized middle period (evidenced by "The Motive for Metaphor"), to the final culmination of his late work, where extremes of complexity and awareness are reached.

40. Parker, "Motive for Metaphor," 84.

The phrases following "The weight of primary noon" need not be con-
strued as in apposition to that line—and consequently in opposition to "The
motive for metaphor"—but may also be read the other way around, as ap-
positions to "The motive for metaphor"—and thus in opposition to "The
weight of primary noon." Admittedly, says Parker, this second grammatical
construction

> may seem less likely, partly because it would appear to involve too sharp a
> shift in mood—from the opening "You like it under the trees in autumn, /
> Because everything is half dead" and its complements in the first three stanzas
> to "ruddy temper" and something described as "vital" in the final lines. Yet
> "exhilarations" already effects this shift, and the reading is not precluded by
> the appositives themselves, whose very lack of definitive dependency leaves
> suspended the question of their referent.

While Parker has no wish to call into question Stevens's attempts at setting
up a number of polarities and oppositions in this poem, she points out how
the text at the same time undoes these, disallowing any monological, univo-
cal statement on the poem's subject: "Stevens' poem, in its ambivalences as
much as in its potentially contradictory syntactical possibilities, may provide
a complex reading not of the single, dominant 'motive' for metaphor but
rather of its unresolvedly plural 'motives,' and motifs, the variations within
its poetic history but also within the *va-et-vient* of his own unconcluded
meditations."[41]

The text's final dissemination of significations, it turns out, is dizzying.
Nearly everything may be read in multiple ways. In one reading (which can
be called the prima facie or intuitive one), "The A B C of being" stands for
an ordered, accumulative system that mistakenly believes itself able to en-
compass the totality of being; it represents the "plain, unpoetic, and literal
language in which the world's real business is conducted, by real men."[42]
But in a secondary, disruptive reading, the same phrase appears to be itself a
metaphor of sorts, and an index to boot of the poet's motive for a language in
which to describe being. A similar ambivalence informs all the appositives
in the final stanza: if from one perspective they stand for some reality or
presence that looks so oppressive to the poet that he wants to sidestep and
circumvent it by way of metaphor, they do so while pulsing with rhythmic

41. Ibid., 85–86.
42. Grey, *The Wallace Stevens Case*, 55.

and imaginative vigor and being themselves nothing but metaphors. "The fi-
nal irony," George S. Lensing observes, is "that being ('primary noon'), from
which metaphor is said to shrink, is itself and in its appositives presented
as a succession of metaphors, a truth that Stevens's breathless crowding of
phrases in apposition almost camouflages." Equivocation reigns supreme also
in the case of what Parker calls the "poem's pervasive Hephaistos figure." On
the one hand, the brutal, deafening hammer blows in the final stanza evoke
Hephaistos in the act of forging weapons and preparing for war. The master
metaphor that these lines pursue, as Grey notes, is that of "a workplace, a
forge, where fire imparts a ruddy temper to metal, which the smith shapes
decisively with his steel hammer, amid hard sounds and sparks, before it cools
and fixes into final form"[43]—the pointed form of an X, in this case, the shape
that is held up to the reader at the end of the poem with an almost cubist
sense of angularity and juxtaposition. Again, we need to recall that this is
a 1942 poem, and the "red and blue" may not just refer to uncontaminated
reality and pure imagination in Stevens's favorite color symbolism but also
hint at the patriotism of an America at war, just as the "hammer" conjures
up its symbolic twin, the sickle.[44] Yet the same Hephaistos, on the other
hand, turns out to have made an earlier, potentially positive appearance in
the poem, in the guise of the "cripple" shuffling through the first stanza,
revealing himself to be also a "culture-bringer."[45]

It is above all the poem's final line, though, that produces a vertiginous ef-
fect. A comedian as the letter X seems at work here and he does not bring us
the promised antithesis to a world of obscurity, movement, and metaphoric-
ity, but rather its forbidding, "oracular" enactment.[46] If we follow through
Parker's radically plural reading of the poem's ending, "X" should be regarded
as both telos and threat. This implies that almost any reading is open, and
critical ingenuity is taxed. In the most frequently pursued interpretation, "X"
simply symbolizes pre- or extralinguistic, phenomenal or material reality—
the sort of reality that "Metaphors of a Magnifico" appeared to be after,
and that proved to be ultimately unavailable without the deployment of

43. Lensing, "Stevens's Prosody," 115; Parker, "Motive for Metaphor," 85; Grey, *The Wal-
lace Stevens Case*, 55.
44. See Parker, "Motive for Metaphor," 82, and Grey, *The Wallace Stevens Case*, 57–58.
Grey expands this reading to involve the coercive and masculinist aspects of Stevens's legal
and business activities, and goes on to distill as many as five different meanings from the
phrase "steel against intimation" (67, 137).
45. Parker, "Motive for Metaphor," 86.
46. Grey, *The Wallace Stevens Case*, 60.

metaphors. The most apposite gloss in this case comes from "Someone Puts a Pineapple Together," which is built up around "the irreducible X / At the bottom of imagined artifice" (*NA* 83). Phenomenal/material reality, or so the "X" in "The Motive for Metaphor" seems to say, ordinarily strikes us as irreducible (it is "vital" and "dominant"), even to the point of becoming dictatorial ("arrogant" and "fatal"), and the only way to escape from its too-literal, too-oppressive insistence is by the exhilarating imaginative leaps of metaphor. Stevens does not choose his symbol fortuitously: ever since Descartes, who invented the symbols (not the letters) X, Y, and Z as counterparts to A, B, and C, the X-sign has represented a variable, unknown quantity—something that exceeds containment and definition. Nietzsche used the same sign in "On Truth and Falsity in Their Extramoral Sense" to refer to the amorphousness of a reality *an sich*: "The disregarding of the individual and real furnishes us with the idea, as it likewise also gives us the form; whereas nature knows of no forms and ideas, and therefore knows no species but only an *x*, to us inaccessible and indefinable." In Helen Regueiro's formulation, the X on which Stevens's poem ends "is the enigma of reality not contained in metaphor." But the poem's syntactical ambiguity forces us to put this even more paradoxically: X is the unavoidable metaphor for the nonmetaphorical base and condition of all metaphoricity. (In accordance with J. Hillis Miller's observation that X is "a sign for signs generally," one could rewrite this as: X is the unavoidable signifier for the nonsignifying base and condition of all signification.) The paradox is clear and it is vintage Stevens, for we know that "a Stevens poem that starts by equating metaphor with the obscure-transitory-unreal and the literal with the clear-stable-real will not continue by simply charting out these binary oppositions in all their classic symmetry."[47]

Such a poem, moreover, will not simply conclude on a clever paradox either, but will seek to resist our intelligence in more ways than one. Unsurprisingly, then, there prove to be other ways of glossing Stevens's final X, and one of them follows the path of personalization. Although we may not intuitively read the X as referring to a person, we should not ignore how humanized are the adjectives that precede it. This strong humanization may be read as a striking instance of the irrepressibility of prosopopoeia even in the face of the most objective reality,[48] but it may also be taken to support,

47. Nietzsche, "On Truth and Falsity," 91–92; Helen Regueiro, "The Rejection of Metaphor," 53; J. Hillis Miller, *Ariadne's Thread: Story Lines*, 24; Grey, *The Wallace Stevens Case*, 61.
48. J. Hillis Miller, "Prosopopoeia," 258.

secondarily, an interpretation in which the X functions as a poetic antagonist. In "Extracts from Addresses to the Academy of Fine Ideas" (1940), Stevens had already set up such an antagonist in the guise of "X, the per-noble master" (CP 254). And he returned to the same strategy shortly after composing "The Motive for Metaphor," in a poem also included in *Transport to Summer*, "The Creations of Sound." There, the infamous X is character-ized as "an obstruction, a man / Too exactly himself" (CP 310), the natural antagonist of a poet who proclaimed he "did not want nor have to be" quite himself. "The Creations of Sound" famously continues:

> Tell X that speech is not dirty silence
> Clarified. It is silence made still dirtier.
> It is more than an imitation for the ear.
>
> He lacks this venerable complication.
> His poems are not of the second part of life.
> They do not make the visible a little hard
>
> To see . . .
>
> (CP 311)

The drift of this passage is all toward the obscure, the difficult, and the sec-ond order of metaphor-making, and away from the kind of ultimate purity and transparence (of language, of self, and of the sociopolitical world) for which many an Anglo-modernist writer (including, at times, Stevens him-self) felt such a profound ideological need. The vitality, arrogance, fatality, and dominance figured at the end of "The Motive for Metaphor" appear to be, then, those of a certain style of writing and a certain type of self (Eliot's? Williams's? various names have been suggested) that generally met with more success than did Stevens's own complicating poetic project and self-conception.

And there is still a third track that may be profitably pursued in read-ing the tantalizing X toward which "The Motive for Metaphor" builds up. This track involves a short detour via Derrida. It requires us to recall how the French philosopher's Heideggerian habit of putting terms under erasure (precisely by overwriting them with an X) has led some of his critics to accuse him of practicing a form of negative theology. In "How to Avoid Speaking: Denials," Derrida sums up the issue as follows:

> Suppose, by a provisional hypothesis, that negative theology consists of con-sidering that every predicative language is inadequate to the essence, in truth

to the hyperessentiality (the being beyond Being) of God; consequently, only a negative ("apophatic") attribution can claim to approach God, and to prepare us for a silent intuition of God. By a more or less tenable analogy, one would thus recognize some traits, the family resemblance of negative theology, in every discourse that seems to return in a regular and insistent manner to this rhetoric of negative determination, endlessly multiplying the defenses and the apophatic warnings: this, which is called X (for example, text, writing, the trace, differance, the hymen, the supplement, the pharmakon, the parergon, etc.) "is" neither this nor that, neither sensible nor intelligible, neither positive nor negative, neither inside nor outside, neither superior nor inferior, neither active nor passive, neither present nor absent, not even neutral, not even subject to a dialectic with a third moment, without any possible sublation ("Aufhebung"). Despite appearances, then, this X is neither a concept nor even a name; it does *lend itself* to a series of names, but calls for another syntax, and exceeds even the order and the structure of predicative discourse. It "is" not and does not say what "is." It is written completely otherwise.[49]

This disquisition may at first seem alien to Stevens and his poem. Derrida is obviously using the symbol X here in his own very specific context, which stands apart from Stevens's by a considerable margin. But in a roundabout way his argument still manages to be enlightening. In his essay, Derrida illustrates "the becoming-theological of all discourse," the fact that at the moment of inscribing some hard-to-contain sign for a hard-to-express reality or experiential category, an "onto-theological reappropriation always remains possible"—even if Derrida in his own thinking explicitly refuses to posit the hyperessentiality on which all theology rests.[50] This insight applies to Stevens's text, too, and with a vengeance even. For the X that puts oppressive reality (or things, or perhaps words) under erasure also happens to be a common symbol for Christ (much as it additionally suggests the cross and crossbones associated with Christ's sacrifice through death). In one reading (the intuitive one), Stevens would certainly have us think ill of the tyranny of theology, the tyranny of what Parker calls the "ultimate apocalyptic Identity" and "shadowless Light" of Christ.[51] But readings here appear to be far beyond authorial control, and this happens also to be precisely what Stevens was experiencing around the time of composing "The Motive for Metaphor." To his utter dismay, he found himself being taken for

49. Jacques Derrida, "How to Avoid Speaking: Denials," 4.
50. Ibid., 6, 9.
51. Parker, "Motive for Metaphor," 78–79.

a mystic of sorts. Writing to Henry Church on November 10, 1942, Stevens reported on his chagrin:

> Shortly after I received your letter, a copy of THE CHIMERA came in and I noticed the advertisement based on the singular habits of St. Augustine. I loathe anything mystical and I particularly loathe mystical advertising, now that I have seen this specimen of it. But this is mild in comparison with a circular which the publisher sent out in which, after listing sundry eccentricities of Giotto and Duns Scotus and St. Augustine, he (or, rather, she) went on to say that NOTES TOWARD A SUPREME FICTION exhibited many symptoms of these. The thing horrified me, but there is nothing to do about it. I can only protest my innocence. (L 428)

Indeed, that is all he could do: protest his innocence. And that is all he would have been able to do in the case of a reading of "The Motive for Metaphor" that reverses the scales and argues that an interpretation of "X" as a positive emblem of a religious inclination is at least textually available. We should recall here how smoothly Northrop Frye was able to pass from a discussion of metaphor to "the transcendental and apocalyptic perspective of religion." Explicit authorial intentions do not manage to stop this sliding movement in the case of "The Motive for Metaphor" either. Metaphor and religion are of a piece to the extent that they both suppose an act of relating. Hence, if a religiously inspired reader wants to perform the essentially metaphorical operation of relating the religious desire for relation to the poetic desire for metaphor, there is for Stevens "nothing to do about it."

Clearly, the poem's ending entraps the reader in such a jungle of diametrical opposites that "The Motive for Metaphor" may be viewed as one of the prime examples of the almost unlimited dissemination of signification in Stevens's work. How far we are willing to extend those disseminations is for every reader to decide, and the pressure I have put on the interpretive process has been considerable. But we should at least be willing to admit that there is a good deal of irony to be found in the fact that "X," this "hardware of the uncanny,"[52] is also the Greek symbol for chiasmus and that this figure of speech traditionally embodies an enclosed totality. No interpretive closure and totality appear to be possible in this case. And this imperfection also reflects back, finally, on the title: "The Motive for Metaphor" offers a conspicuous instance of a text that exceeds authorial intentions and spreads

52. Fisher, *Intensest Rendezvous*, 126.

out into a variety of directions exactly at the point of trying to establish the motive for metaphor. Thus, it once more raises our awareness of how the category of metaphor exists under the aegis both of excess and of qualification: the ultimate X toward which the poem moves brings no closure but only an X-plosion of language and of signification. That the pieces cannot be collected to form a complete whole is not as crucial as the X-hilaration we derive from picking them up and assembling them in our own forever-changing ways of making sense. Poems like "The Motive for Metaphor" belong to a group of Stevens's writings that, in Maeder's words, "shows that the hope for metaphor is not to find new words, new illustrations, or new transfers; rather it lies in the changes that take place between a poem's point of departure and its point of arrival, the path a poem takes."[53] The transferential nature of metaphor-making, in other words, is actively displaced by Stevens onto the signification process itself, which must have the potential to keep on changing for as long as we dwell on it. These are the exhilarations of change that finally motivate the composition process for him, and the interpretation process for us.

Although "Thinking of a Relation between the Images of Metaphors" was probably written in the summer of 1945, it quite possibly germinated at the same time that Stevens was writing "The Motive for Metaphor." In a letter dated November 2, 1942, Stevens informed his private genealogical investigator, Lila James Roney, about the Pennsylvania area where his grandfather used to own a farm: "Neshaminy is a little place seven or eight miles from Doylestown. To the west of it lies the country through which the Perkiomen Creek runs. This creek, when I was a boy, was famous for its bass. It almost amounts to a genealogical fact that all his life long my father used to fish in Perkiomen for bass, and this can only mean that he did it as a boy" (SP 5). Given the appearance in the poem of Perkiomen, bass, and fishing, on the one hand, and the topic of metaphor, on the other, the first conception of "Thinking of a Relation" may well go back, then, to the same time as "The Motive for Metaphor."

A possible link between the two poems is provided also by the topic of identity, which in the earlier poem is implied in Stevens's happily changing self that is never quite itself. "Thinking of a Relation" experiments with the same topic, but this time pushes it to an extreme by trying to imagine a monolithic and monologous self that becomes almost identical with

53. Maeder, *Experimental Language*, 65.

its surroundings. This ostensibly good-humored poem consists of only eight couplets and opens innocently by painting a natural scene:

> The wood-doves are singing along the Perkiomen.
> The bass lie deep, still afraid of the Indians.
>
> (CP 356)

This is the American wilderness, with "Indians" still lurking in the bushes (as they indeed were in this part of Pennsylvania in the days of Stevens's father [SP 5]). Half facetiously, the speaker continues:

> In the one ear of the fisherman, who is all
> One ear, the wood-doves are singing a single song.

The scene immediately reminds us of the reductive experiment at the outset of "Metaphors of a Magnifico," where twenty men were reduced to a single man crossing a single bridge into a village. Here, by contrast, we have only a single man to start with, but he, too, is presented in a diminished and abstracted form. The nameless fisherman listens so reductively that he is not even all ears, as the expression goes, but simply "all / One ear." He listens in mono, not in stereo. He does not allow any ambiguity or polyphony or depth of perspective in what he hears, for to him the doves are all singing one song, in unison.

> The bass keep looking ahead, upstream, in one
> Direction, shrinking from the spit and splash
>
> Of waterish spears. The fisherman is all
> One eye, in which the dove resembles the dove.

Humorously, reductiveness lords it over the entire scene, since the bass also monomaniacally fix their eyes on a single target, and the fisherman now shows himself to be "all / One eye" as well, like a latter-day cyclops. The reductiveness is further enhanced by a remarkable contrast: the bass are said to be "shrinking from the spit and splash // Of waterish spears." This clause stands out from the rest of the text in at least two ways: first, by patently indulging in poetic mannerisms—using a triple *sp* alliteration reminiscent of Old English alliterative verse, augmented by several extra sibilants, an accumulative enjambment, and an irregularly spuming rhythm—and secondly, by self-consciously flaunting its metaphor, in a poem that precisely claims to present thinking on this subject. What the bass are shirking, it would appear, is a poeticized world of metaphor. The poem is set in a premodern world dominated by a teleological impulse and governed by uncomplicated perceptions. It is a world in which the fisherman believes himself able to cancel all difference until makeshift metaphors are killed and "the dove resembles" nothing but "the dove." It is a world we would expect Stevens to have left behind a long time ago, and so we are not surprised to find that the poem proceeds to break with reductive and totalizing gestures:

> There is one dove, one bass, one fisherman.
> Yet coo becomes rou-coo, rou-coo. How close
>
> To the unstated theme each variation comes . . .
> (CP 356–57)

Having condensed the poem's first half into a radically monistic, abstracted tableau of dove-bass-fisherman (somewhat on the analogy of man-bridge-village), the speaker seems to loosen his iron grip and to introduce a doubleness: the doves' single "coo" turns into the differential figure of an interval ("rou-coo"), which is itself repeated, thus suggesting a game of question-and-answer between different birds. There is an erotic component to this game, underscored by Stevens's much earlier use of the same French-derived onomatopoeic coinage in "Depression before Spring," where the "ki-ki-ri-ki" of the crowing cock "Brings no rou-cou, / No rou-cou-cou" (CP 63). By injecting an element of doubleness and difference, the "theme" must somehow remain "unstated," and all singing (not only the doves' but also the poet's) must turn into a "variation" upon that theme. Simultaneously, however, the birth of the double and of the act of doubling, which is the birth of metaphor and of metaphoricity, is also the birth of the possibility of approximation: it allows us to get wonderfully "close" to our themes. Once again, as in "Metaphors of a Magnifico," the suspension points may be read both as a sign of marveling and a sign of being stymied. If the poem were to end here, it would leave us with an amazed or wistfully sighing poet, depending on the tone we would prefer for coloring the exclamation. But the speaker takes a second throw, ending his poem unexpectedly as follows:

> In that one ear it might strike perfectly:
>
> State the disclosure. In that one eye the dove
> Might spring to sight and yet remain a dove.

> The fisherman might be the single man
> In whose breast, the dove, alighting, would grow still.
>
> (CP 357)

Though cautiously working in the hypothetical form, the speaker refuses to be thwarted by the treacherousness of trying to determine an identity. After all, no twenty different men, no social component needs to be reckoned with this time, just "the single man" in nature surrendering to the eye and ear, a single character who longs to get as close as is humanly possible to a sense of pristine identity. Even if the poem's opening couplets instilled in us a tonal uncertainty about the precise status of the speaker, who could have been ironizing the tableau and keeping his distance from it, we now recognize how strong Stevens's personal investment and his attachment to the fisherman's solitary endeavor really are. We even recognize a possible biographical inspiration in the characterization of the fisherman: having himself turned (partially) deaf in one ear as the probable result of childhood mastoiditis, Stevens had but one functioning ear left at the time of writing the poem.[54]

The single eye and ear thus become images not so much of reductiveness as of total concentration, evocations of a meditative state that seeks to suspend the stirrings of the self. Stevens very much wants his fisherman's language to "strike perfectly: / State the disclosure."[55] He is expressing his deep and continuing hope to hit upon a metaphor that does not falsify, where the relation between the images that make up the metaphor shades into literalness and self-identity: the dove must "spring to sight" by way of metaphor (much as the metaphor of springing itself) "and yet remain a dove." Perhaps such mediated immediacy is possible, Stevens muses, if not in the shared form of communication then at least for "the single man / In whose breast, the dove, alighting, would grow still." Inconspicuously, auxiliaries and grammatical mood have changed: Stevens "substitutes for the expected 'might' in the final line the far more conclusive 'would,' as the poem passes from the possible to the probable."[56] In doing so, he betrays the depth of his desire for a perfect poetic moment that would still the world, stop change, fix an identity. This aspect of desire also speaks from his concentration on the

---

54. Richardson, *Early Years*, 500–1, and *Later Years*, 403.
55. The image of a fisherman, the quest for a "disclosure," and the pun on "alighting" all belong to the same isotopy of revelation discussed in the previous chapter.
56. Helen Vendler, "The Qualified Assertions of Wallace Stevens," 164–65.

dove, traditionally associated with Venus and erotically connoted in several other poems like "The Dove in the Belly" (CP 366–67) and "The Dove in Spring" (OP 124–25).

The fantasy Stevens stages at the end of "Thinking of a Relation" wholly interiorizes the outer world, represented by the dove "alighting" in the poet's "breast," yet also lets that world flourish there and fill the fishing poet with a sense of growing power. That is what the concluding pun tells us. "To 'grow still,'" Eleanor Cook explains, "makes a double closure, as the dove grows quiet and also keeps on growing, which is how the A and B of po-etic metaphor should work."[57] In Stevens's more traditional fantasy here, the serendipity of striking a truly disclosing metaphor involves a fusion between tenor and vehicle into a single, expansively blossoming identity. Thus, "Thinking of a Relation between the Images of Metaphor" serves as a reminder that we should not underestimate the side of Stevens that was not always exhilarated by changes and polysemy and that strained for a more solid identity and a more static form of harmony. Of the three metaphor poems discussed in this chapter, "Thinking of a Relation" most clearly tells of Stevens's desire for unification. Strikingly, it is also the only one of the three that he suggested for inclusion in a volume of selected poems that was planned (though never produced) by his publisher, Knopf, in 1950.[58] Somehow, the septuagenarian Stevens, throwing a backward glance at his oeuvre, valued this little poem more than its two predecessors—contrary to so many of his later critics, for this is a neglected text in the canon of Stevens criticism.

To better understand the nature and strength of this predilection, we should step back finally and study what biographically lies behind this poem: a dissatisfaction with, and desire to escape from, the drudgery of an everyday working life; the wish to withdraw from the social environment into poetry and there to "grow still." That is what a letter to José Rodríguez Feo suggests. The letter was written shortly before Stevens composed "Thinking of a Re-lation" (which is one of a handful of poems he promised for Feo's literary magazine Orígenes). It deserves to be quoted at some length:

> To live in Cuba, to think a little in the morning and afterward to work in the garden for an hour or two, then to have lunch and to read all afternoon and then, with your wife or someone else's wife, fill the house with fresh roses,

57. Cook, Poetry, Word-Play, and Word-War, 179.
58. See Lensing, Poet's Growth, 282–85.

to play a little Berlioz (this is the current combination at home: Berlioz and roses) might very well create all manner of doubts after a week or two. But when you are a little older, and have your business or your job to look after, and when there is quite enough to worry about all the time, and when you don't have time to think and the weeds grow in the garden a good deal more savagely than you could ever have supposed, and you no longer read because it doesn't seem worth while, but you do at the end of the day play a record or two, that is something quite different. Reality is the great *fond*, and it is because it is that the purely literary amounts to so little. Moreover, in the world of actuality, in spite of all I have just said, one is always living a little out of it. There is a precious sentence in Henry James, for whom everyday life was not much more than the mere business of living, but, all the same, he separated himself from it. The sentence is . . .

> "To live *in* the world of creation—to get into it and stay in it—to frequent it and haunt it—to *think* intensely and fruitfully—to woo combinations and inspirations into being by a depth and continuity of attention and meditation—this is the only thing." (*L* 505–6)

Stevens is his usual hedging and qualifying self in this excerpt, and he indulges in quite a bit of projection, given the fact that his young Cuban friend (who was homosexual and unmarried) was actually "in a state of flux, if not anxiety, as he read and studied on his mother's sugar plantation."[59] But what is made clear by these words, at least, is the wish of a nearly sixty-six-year-old, busy insurance lawyer to go fishing all by himself in the Perkiomen (of poetry), and there "to *think* intensely and fruitfully—to woo combinations and inspirations into being by a depth and continuity of attention and meditation." Yet we may also hear, in one and the same gesture, the anxiety that such an escape might not satisfy him, that "the purely literary amounts to so little." This oscillation between, on the one hand, a love of imaginative concentration, play, and withdrawal into a world of creation and, on the other, an awareness of the limited value of these activities and an unwillingness to engage in any self-delusion about them extends beyond the particular historical moment recorded here. It remains one of the most important features of Stevens's poetic enterprise as a whole, both for himself and for his readers. To think about a relation between the images of metaphor, just like the dressing up of a magnifico in metaphors or the sketching of an autumnal aquarelle on the motive for metaphor, partakes of this plight. All these activities were at once "the only thing" *and* dangerous seductions that had the

---

59. Coyle and Filreis, introduction to *Secretaries of the Moon*, 2.

power to woo Stevens (and us) away from reality, that "indispensable ele-
ment of each metaphor" (*OP* 204). All these poems were the much-needed,
and just as much distrusted, pensive and imaginative distractions of a man
whose calling as a poet, sidetracked into a supplementary diversion, never
stopped filling him with ambivalent, yet no less urgent, feelings. We should
not complain, therefore, with Frye that "[Stevens's] conception of metaphor
is regrettably unclear" as much as we should remember some of the limits of
writing poetry.[60] The creation of metaphors, "the creation of resemblance by
the imagination" (*NA* 72), and the pondering of the workings of metaphor
are the poet's vocation and dedication, but they are also activities that may
amount to little in the light of "the great *fond*" of reality and of our need
to still our desire for tranquility and satisfaction "[m]erely in living as and
where we live" (*CP* 326).

---

60. Northrop Frye, "The Realistic Oriole: A Study of Wallace Stevens," 169.

Chapter 12

Poeticizing Epistemology

Is it possible to draw any conclusions from the last four chapters? Certainly I may corroborate what I announced at the outset of Part Two: that Stevens is a poet first and foremost, not a philosopher. And to the extent that his writings do have philosophical overtones, we have had ample opportunity to observe that they belong more to the realm of what Lacan wittily called *flousophie* than to the rigorously argumentative and discursive realm of philosophy in any strict sense.[1] But observations of this kind have become truistic at this point and hardly amount to a real conclusion. The relevant question is more difficult: Is it possible to draw valid conclusions from such diversity of detail, from such authorial and readerly attention to irreducible specificities and momentary inspirations? Can we jump from such painstaking analysis to unencumbered synthesis again? No doubt, *some* form of synthesis has to be reattempted and we should on the whole resist the seductive urge to denounce all synthetic moves because of the inevitable, systemic ways in which such moves smooth out and adulterate analytic findings. Yet we should also resist the easiness of synthetic gestures, particularly in the case of a poet like Wallace Stevens. In other words, the attempt to draw conclusions is one more of those impossible possible exercises whose (im)possibility is forcefully impressed on us by the very nature of Stevens's writings. For this is a poetry that offers an unusually treacherous admixture of specificity and generality, of particularity and universality—precisely the sort of admixture that defines the category of the literary in the eyes of many theorists.

---

1. Jacques Lacan, "Du sujet enfin en question," 233.

In an attempt at elucidating Derrida's puzzled and puzzling involvement with the interface between literature and philosophy, Derek Attridge argues that literature is that type of writing which stages the relationship between singularity and generality with haunting power and/or displays that relationship's unusual ability to give pleasure. Derrida's obsession, according to Attridge, has to do with "the puzzling yet productive relation between singularity and generality, a relation which for him is not merely a paradoxical coexistence but a structural interdependence. For if the literary text were absolutely singular each time we encountered it, it would have no access to the human world at all." In Derrida's words, "any work is singular in that it speaks singularly of both singularity and generality."[2] Stevens, as we know, had his own sense of this structural interdependence, for he compacted this idea into a more resistant formula—that of trying "by a peculiar speech to speak // The peculiar potency of the general" (CP 397).

In some respect, then, the deployment of philosophical generalities in critical comments on Stevens's poetry turns out to be unavoidable. This is what Kenneth Burke insisted on, in his previously quoted letter of November 1944 to Allen Tate, in which he asked rhetorically: "Is it not a bit ironical . . . to see a supposedly fairly relatively new poet like Stevens trying to explain his supposedly fairly relatively new esthetic by discovering the Kantian line-up somewhat more than 150 years late? I think you'll have to let more philosophy into your criticism, if only to avoid its coming in thus unnoticed, and naively." Philosophical concepts will always intrude on literary analyses, for, says Attridge, "in spite of literature's potential challenge to philosophy, literary studies are dominated by philosophical assumptions quite as much as philosophy is—perhaps even more so." Significantly, all the examples that Attridge proceeds to list turn out to be central to a critical discussion of Stevens as well. Stevens criticism, too, is full of "the rules of syllogistic reason, the ultimate priority of meaning over its mode of articulation, and such fundamental and absolute oppositions as the intelligible and the sensible, form and matter, subject and object, nature and culture, presence and absence."[3]

Synthetic gestures are themselves inscribed in Stevens's work. They cannot be escaped at the end of a string of close readings. Even a writer as

2. Attridge, "Derrida and the Questioning of Literature," 15; Derrida, " 'Strange Institution,' " 68.
3. Burke quoted in Filreis, *Actual World*, 97; Attridge, "Derrida and the Questioning of Literature," 3.

antiphilosophical as Nabokov acknowledged the place of generalization in literary criticism, though he did so with his own inimitably ironical brand of dismissiveness. "In reading," he liked to tell his students, "one should notice and fondle details. There is nothing wrong about the moonshine of generalization when it comes *after* the sunny trifles of the book have been lovingly collected."[4]

What kind of perspective on our finite human condition speaks to us from the ten poems I have closely looked at in the preceding four chapters? An ambivalent perspective, to be sure, one that strongly fluctuates and alternates, or that mixes positive and negative valorizations. It is a fluctuation, an alternation, a mixture that runs through the entire oeuvre and that has not been fundamentally affected by my choice of texts. The guises in which Stevens's attitude toward our human finitude comes dressed often appear to be captivatingly idiosyncratic, and many texts may have been highly responsive to the specificities of time and place, yet once we move on to the level of synthesis, we find that the generalizations we may distill from this handful of analyzed poems have their own legitimacy. They do so because almost all of these generalizations could have been arrived at on the basis of reading other poems (or parts of poems). This is what makes the particular choice of poems that I have made—a choice whose only criteria were the need to include texts from various stages of Stevens's writing life and the wish to avoid straying too far from the canon of central poems—ultimately a matter of striking indifference. Or to put it more positively: it allows the choice of poems to be in large part a personal one, motivated more by aesthetic and affective criteria than by philosophical necessity.

The nexus of perception, thought, and language that has been the object of study in the preceding chapters is deeply constitutive of our finite human condition and as such is often positively valued by Stevens. "The imperfect is our paradise" chants one of his most resounding poetic epigrams, and the idea is wittily expanded upon by affirming that "delight, / Since the imperfect is so hot in us, / Lies in flawed words and stubborn sounds" (CP 194). Stevens's celebration of the necessity of imperfection in "The Poems of Our Climate" naturally squares with a relativist and pragmatist acceptance of the idea (or experience) of incompletion in "The Motive for Metaphor"— an incompletion of both world and self that provokes our desire for "the

4. Vladimir Nabokov, *Lectures on Literature*, 1.

exhilarations of changes" (CP 288) and that motivates our drive for the invention of metaphor. To appreciate these exhilarations one must appreciate the many "parts" of our world that generate our incomplete and pragmatic "truths" (CP 242). This is the dominant idea of "Landscape with Boat," which invests strongly in an almost hedonistic world of the senses as the poem critiques an idealistic, fundamentalist art that abstracts itself too much from phenomenal reality. With "The Idea of Order at Key West" we have also read a paean to the formative and revelatory powers of art and language, as well as, more obliquely, to the autotelic aesthetic enchantment that music and "fragrant" words may bring (CP 130). "Bouquet of Roses in Sunlight" affirms our "sense" of reality as irreducibly resistant to the falseness of "the rhetorician's touch" (CP 431), and thus as an inalienably human limit to perception. And "The Plain Sense of Things" movingly demonstrates the power of the imagination to lift an old poet out of the doldrums by being "imagined as an inevitable knowledge, / Required, as a necessity requires" (CP 503). Together, all of these textual moments—even if I am forced to treat them reductively, betraying some of their complexities—show that much of Stevens's work manages to speak to our finite human condition with a humanistic wish for affirmation and a vitality, inventiveness, and resilience that continue to ennoble his poetry in the eyes of many readers. We do not generally think of Stevens as a man incapable of accepting the limitations imposed on us by the structure of reality, but rather as a man who extracts poetic enjoyment from them.

Still, against these many positive valorizations of the limitations that at one and the same time constrict and construct the human condition, we have also observed moments that were characterized by some form of *inability* to live with our finite condition. Those moments were most in evidence in "The Ultimate Poem Is Abstract," with its quietistic longing "to be / Complete, because at the middle, if only in sense," and the staged wish fulfillment that "in that enormous sense" we can finally come to "merely enjoy" (CP 430). We found additional traces of a more negatively valued finitude in "Thinking of a Relation between the Images of Metaphors," where a *reductio ad unum*, feeding into a nostalgia for unification and for the cancellation of all difference, prompts the fantasy of "one ear" in which Stevens's otherwise differential variations "might strike perfectly" (CP 357). "Metaphors of a Magnifico," in one possible reading, too, allowed us to observe a strong tendency to insist on reality as incommunicable—as ultimately impossible to represent dynamically in language. This tendency to seek out and court the aporiae of the relationship between reality and language is arguably one of the seductions least resisted by Stevens (and most responsible for the high esteem in which he is held by deconstructionists). To observe time and again how reality *an sich* is ultimately unreachable and unavailable in thought and writing, and to show how language, by its necessarily circumscriptive, approximative, and differential nature, never manages to fully overlap with the world of the senses on which it is grafted and to which it responds, is to continuously run the risk of falling into a safe epistemologizing habit and relying on a self-reflexive rhetorical gimmick. The many aporetic situations in Stevens, to the extent that they are willfully teased out by the poet rather than unintended textual effects, betray a lingering attachment to the ideals of fullness and totality and to the supremacy of logic and absolute thought categories.

But I have probably already gone too far in trying to synthesize what almost invariably proves to be heterogeneous, entangled, ambiguous, and ambivalent as the poems unfold to the cautiously reading eye and the diffidently listening ear. Poetry, like most art, is not good at promulgating ideas, nor at achieving consistency in them. It certainly is not a very fit medium for developing epistemological theories. What it is much better at is picking up notions of the sort systematically studied by epistemologists and embodying them in a context where these notions cut into other, less discursively organizable realms of thought and feeling. Stevens criticism is characteristically full of hesitation when it comes to assessing the importance of epistemological themes and perspectives in the poet's works. Even a relatively antagonistic outsider like Fredric Jameson can be seen, within one and the same essay, to chafe against Stevens's inveterate epistemologizing habit and to backtrack on at least two occasions by assuring us that he is only giving us the neutral facts and does not want to rush to condemn.[5]

Stevens's perception-thought-language nexus is not that of the epistemological textbook but that of a poet's variously invested daily experience. Even Derrida insists that "[l]ife is the nonrepresentable origin of representation,"[6] and in "The Noble Rider and the Sound of Words" Stevens is no less adamant about this. "The subject-matter of poetry," he assures us, "is not that 'collection of solid, static objects extended in space'" that would be sufficient for the theoretical epistemologist, "but the life that is lived in the scene that it composes; and so reality is not that external scene but the

5. Jameson, "Wallace Stevens," 12, 18.
6. Jacques Derrida, "The Theater of Cruelty and the Closure of Representation," 234.

life that is lived in it" (*NA* 25). "Perhaps more than any of his romantic ancestors," William W. Bevis comments upon this statement, "Stevens abstained from assigning value to object, subject, or their combination, except on a poem-by-poem basis."[7] What makes these poem-by-poem confrontations worth our while are precisely the several ways in which they exceed the narrowly epistemological in their attempts at weaving a richer, more subjective, more aesthetic, and more elusive texture. If we want to synthesize Stevens's views on the limits and interaction of perception, thought, and language, we finally need to identify those forms of excess, those poetic "disturbances" that cut through, complicate, and deflect the construction of neat little theories.

The first and not the least of these disturbances is the self-undercutting play of irony. If Stevens compulsively returned to the same epistemological conundrums to develop new poetic variations on them, he knew his game well enough to see the basic limitations of his enterprise. Professional critics working in an academic environment of theoretical sophistication are sometimes inclined to take his thought experiments more seriously than he did. The genre of criticism, with its demand for rational accountability, does not allow nearly as much playfulness and half-seriousness as the genre of poetry. When we read Richard Rorty's gibe at people obsessed with demonstrating "how the ineffable *could* be effed after all," we tend to be unsure whether we can afford to borrow this deflating and debunking style for our own supposedly serious theoretical work, even if we suspect that Stevens the pragmatic relativist and practitioner of bathos might have chuckled at the verbal play. Something similar applies to the many deconstructive ideas and practices Stevens's poetry anticipates: they are arguably there, but only in the form of "fast deconstruction." " 'Fast' deconstruction," David Bromwich argues in his critique of Paul de Man's career as a "slow" deconstructor, has "long been the extracurricular resort of clever or bored philosophers; as in William James's Hegelian revelation under the effects of laughing gas: 'What's mistake but a kind of take?' "[8] Such deconstruction, needless to add, has never been the prerogative of clever or bored philosophers alone: clever poets pretending to be bored philosophers may just as readily be expected to indulge in fast deconstructions, especially if they happen to be playful wits and rhetorical virtuosos.

7. Bevis, *Mind of Winter*, 9.
8. Richard Rorty, "Philosophy as a Kind of Writing: An Essay on Derrida," 151; David Bromwich, "Slow Deconstruction," 22.

One of the many forms Stevens's play takes is that of developing muted intertextual dialogues with other poets (especially in the romantic tradition), other thinkers (especially philosophers), and other artists (especially painters and musicians). We see this most clearly in a poem like "The Idea of Order at Key West," which can be held to make epistemological and language-philosophical statements only if we recognize the hybridity of these statements, which results from the poem's several other signifying levels. In the case of this poem, for instance, an implicit dialogue with romantic poetry proves to be just as important a writerly motive as the pursuit of a modern linguistic theory, and the same is true of the poem's meditations on the power and the effect of music and of art-making overall. These mixed poetic interests point to another common deflection of "straight" epistemological concerns in Stevens: we often find that what prompts his epistemological take on a subject is in fact the question of beauty, or questions of the nature of the aesthetic experience. These are questions that certainly depend on the nexus of perception, thought, and language with which we traditionally associate epistemology, but they just as obviously cannot be confused or conflated with narrowly epistemological issues. For one thing, they much more strongly bring into the game the dark field of the body, with its proper sensations and desires—a field that undercuts and shakes the predominance of the cerebrocentrism of classic epistemological discussions. It is this body also that calls for the *aesthetic embodiment* of ideas. We should remember the early aestheticist remark made by Stevens in his Harvard days (see page 154): "I like my philosophy smothered in beauty and not the opposite." Epistemological ideas and perspectives were entertained by Stevens for the purpose of writing poetry, and that purpose was to give pleasure by indulging in a play with rhetoric and structure, with the freshness of word-painting, with the rhythms and sounds of verbal music. Stevens's impulses were aestheticist first and foremost, and the gratification of the thinking mind was but one (important) component of the larger category of aesthetic satisfaction.

Aesthetic satisfaction, then, is another hybridizing factor that we must take account of in our understanding of Stevens's epistemological interests and attitudes, and so is desire. The latter transcends the merely physical need for aesthetic gratification, which may be subsumed under it. It also transcends the realm of the sexual and the libidinal, to which the concept is often reduced by Freudians. Desire in Stevens is a catchall category for sundry needs and (dis)satisfactions, many of them psychological and emotional in origin, as in the following epigram: "Poetry is an effort of a dissatisfied man to find satisfaction through words, occasionally of the dissatisfied thinker to find satisfaction through his emotions" (*OP* 191). Stevens's engagement with the perception of things is not born of simple theoretical interests or of an essentially scientific spirit, but of various types of desire. "Pink and white carnations—one desires / So much more than that," he characteristically sighs in "The Poems of Our Climate" (*CP* 193). "What is it he desires?" another poem asks, only to declare the answer out of bounds: "But this he cannot know, the man that thinks" (*CP* 188). Rational thought, Stevens often felt, cannot probe the deepest wellspring of our constitutive desires; it cannot reach either the fountain of our vitality and motivating energies or the source of our lack and disaffection.

Epistemological issues, with their inclination toward repetitiveness and sterility, repeatedly display their limited value in Stevens's poems. They often become secondary to a more psychological and existential plight: that of the endless self-assertiveness and obtrusiveness of the ego, that "evilly compounded, vital I" (*CP* 193) that on several occasions works to disrupt the equanimity Stevens would prefer for his more plainly propounding epistemological musings. This restive ego (or self, or mind, or consciousness: the categories are a tangle) often needs to be placated, or even, as Bevis suggests, temporarily surrendered in acts of tranquil meditation. The primary impetus on such occasions is psychological rather than epistemological, which is finally also the case whenever the issues of perception, thought, and language are viewed in the light of advancing old age and approaching death, as in "The Plain Sense of Things." There are many ways, in short, in which epistemological questions are deflected and hybridized in Stevens's writings, from the ironical and the ludic, the aesthetic and the physical, to the libidinal and the volitional, the psychological and the existential. A synthesis that fails to register these complications can offer only a lopsided portrait of the demands made, and the rewards procured, by this idiosyncratic body of work. And it will fail to do justice to the complexity of the factors that collectively constitute our human finitude.

Works Cited

Works by Wallace Stevens

The Collected Poems of Wallace Stevens. New York: Alfred A. Knopf, 1954.

Collected Poetry and Prose. Ed. Frank Kermode and Joan Richardson. New York: Library of America, 1997.

Letters of Wallace Stevens. Ed. Holly Stevens. New York: Alfred A. Knopf, 1966.

The Necessary Angel: Essays on Reality and the Imagination. New York: Vintage Books, 1951.

Opus Posthumous. Ed. Samuel French Morse. New York: Alfred A. Knopf, 1957.

Opus Posthumous. Revised, Enlarged, and Corrected Edition. Ed. Milton J. Bates. New York: Alfred A. Knopf, 1989.

The Palm at the End of the Mind: Selected Poems and a Play by Wallace Stevens. Ed. Holly Stevens. New York: Alfred A. Knopf, 1971.

Sur Plusieurs Beaux Sujects: Wallace Stevens' Commonplace Book. Ed. Milton J. Bates. Stanford: Stanford University Press, 1989.

Secretaries of the Moon: The Letters of Wallace Stevens & José Rodríguez Feo. Ed. Beverly Coyle and Alan Filreis. Durham: Duke University Press, 1986.

"Three Manuscript Endings for 'A Collect of Philosophy.'" In *Wallace Stevens: A Celebration*, ed. Frank Doggett and Robert Buttel, 50–56. Princeton: Princeton University Press, 1980.

For *Souvenirs and Prophecies*, see Stevens, Holly, below.

Other Works Cited

Abrams, M. H. *The Mirror and the Lamp: Romantic Theory and the Critical Tradition*. 1953. Reprint, Oxford: Oxford University Press, 1971.

Adams, Richard P. "Wallace Stevens and Schopenhauer's *The World as Will and Idea*." *Tulane Studies in English* 20 (1972): 135–68.

Altieri, Charles. *Painterly Abstraction in Modernist American Poetry: The Contemporaneity of Modernism*. Cambridge Studies in American Literature, vol. 37. Cambridge: Cambridge University Press, 1989.

———. "Wallace Stevens' Metaphors of Metaphor: Poetry as Theory." *American Poetry* 1:1 (fall 1983): 27–48.

———. "Why Stevens Must Be Abstract, or What a Poet Can Learn from Painting." In *Wallace Stevens: The Poetics of Modernism*, ed. Albert Gelpi, 86–118. Cambridge: Cambridge University Press, 1985.

Arensberg, Mary. "'A Curable Separation': Stevens and the Mythology of Gender." In *Wallace Stevens and the Feminine*, ed. Melita Schaum, 23–45. Tuscaloosa: University of Alabama Press, 1993.

———. Introduction to *The American Sublime*, ed. Mary Arensberg, 1–20. Albany: State University of New York Press, 1986.

Argyros, Alex. "The Residual Difference: Wallace Stevens and American Deconstruction." *New Orleans Review* 13:1 (spring 1986): 20–31.

Aristotle. *The Poetics*. In *Aristotle's Theory of Poetry and Fine Art, with a Critical Text and Translation of The Poetics*, 4th ed., by S. H. Butcher, 6–111. 1907. Reprint, New York: Dover Publications, 1951.

Attridge, Derek. "Derrida and the Questioning of Literature," introduction to *Acts of Literature*, by Jacques Derrida, ed. Derek Attridge, 1–29. New York: Routledge, 1992.

Axelrod, Steven Gould, and Helen Deese. "Wallace Stevens: The Critical Reception," introduction to *Critical Essays on Wallace Stevens*, ed. Steven Gould Axelrod and Helen Deese, 1–25. Boston: G. K. Hall, 1988.

Baeten, Brooke. "'Whose Spirit Is This?': Musings on the Woman Singer in 'The Idea of Order at Key West.'" *Wallace Stevens Journal* 24:1 (spring 2000): 24–36.

Bak, Saskia. "Visies op Mondriaan." *Ons Erfdeel* 37:1 (January-February 1994): 61–72.

Bakhtin, M. M. *The Dialogic Imagination: Four Essays*. Ed. Michael Holquist, trans. Caryl Emerson and Michael Holquist. 1981. Reprint, Austin: University of Texas Press, 1988.

Balakian, Anna. *The Fiction of the Poet: From Mallarmé to the Post-Symbolist Mode*. Princeton: Princeton University Press, 1992.

Barthes, Roland. *Empire of Signs*. Trans. Richard Howard. 1982. Reprint, New York: Noonday Press, 1989.

———. "Interview: A Conversation with Roland Barthes," interview by Stephen Heath. In *The Grain of the Voice: Interviews 1962–1980*, by Roland Barthes, trans. Linda Coverdale, 128–49. Reprint, Berkeley and Los Angeles: University of California Press, 1991.

Bates, Jennifer. "Stevens, Hegel, and the Palm at the End of the Mind." *Wallace Stevens Journal* 23:2 (fall 1999): 152–66.

Bates, Milton J. " 'The Emperor' and Its Clothes." In *Teaching Wallace Stevens: Practical Essays*, ed. John N. Serio and B. J. Leggett, 17–25. Knoxville: University of Tennessee Press, 1994.

———. Introduction to *Sur Plusieurs Beaux Sujects: Wallace Stevens' Commonplace Book*, ed. Milton J. Bates, 1–18. Stanford: Stanford University Press, 1989.

———. "Stevens' Books at the Huntington: An Annotated Checklist." *Wallace Stevens Journal* 2:3/4 (fall 1978): 45–61; 3:1/2 (spring 1979): 15–33; 3:3/4 (fall 1979): 70.

———. *Wallace Stevens: A Mythology of Self*. Berkeley and Los Angeles: University of California Press, 1985.

Beckett, Lucy. *Wallace Stevens*. 1974. Reprint, Cambridge: Cambridge University Press, 1977.

Beehler, Michael. "Kant and Stevens: The Dynamics of the Sublime and the Dynamics of Poetry." In *The American Sublime*, ed. Mary Arensberg, 131–52. Albany: State University of New York Press, 1986.

———. "Penelope's Experience: Teaching the Ethical Lessons of Wallace Stevens." In *Teaching Wallace Stevens: Practical Essays*, ed. John N. Serio and B. J. Leggett, 267–79. Knoxville: University of Tennessee Press, 1994.

———. "Stevens' Boundaries." *Wallace Stevens Journal* 7:3/4 (fall 1983): 99–107.

———. *T. S. Eliot, Wallace Stevens, and the Discourses of Difference*. Baton Rouge: Louisiana State University Press, 1987.

Bevis, William W. *Mind of Winter: Wallace Stevens, Meditation, and Literature*. Pittsburgh: University of Pittsburgh Press, 1988.

Biebuyck, Benjamin, and Jürgen Pieters. "Enkele bedenkingen bij het begrip 'intertekstualiteit.' " In *Stemmen in het magazijn: Intertekstualiteit in modernisme en postmodernisme*, ed. Koenraad Geldof and Bart Vervaeck,

13–37. ALW-cahier vol. 18. N.p.: Vlaamse Vereniging voor Algemene en Vergelijkende Literatuurwetenschap, 1997.

Blackmur, R. P. "Examples of Wallace Stevens." In *Language as Gesture: Essays in Poetry,* by R. P. Blackmur, 221–49. London: Allen and Unwin, 1954.

Bloom, Harold. *The Anxiety of Influence: A Theory of Poetry.* New York: Oxford University Press, 1973.

———. Interview by Imre Salusinszky. In *Criticism in Society: Interviews with Jacques Derrida, Northrop Frye, Harold Bloom, Geoffrey Hartman, Frank Kermode, Edward Said, Barbara Johnson, Frank Lentricchia, and J. Hillis Miller,* by Imre Salusinszky, 44–73. New York: Methuen, 1987.

———. Introduction to *Wallace Stevens,* ed. Harold Bloom, 1–13. New York: Chelsea House Publishers, 1985.

———. *Wallace Stevens: The Poems of Our Climate.* 1977. Reprint, Ithaca, N.Y.: Cornell University Press, 1987.

———. *The Western Canon: The Books and School of the Ages.* 1994. Reprint, London: Papermac, 1995.

Boehm, Rudolf. *Aan het einde van een tijdperk: Filosofisch-economische aantekeningen.* Weesp, Netherlands: Het Wereldvenster; Berchem, Belgium: EPO, 1984.

———. *Das Grundlegende und das Wesentliche—Zu Aristoteles' Abhandlung "Ueber das Sein und das Seiende" (Metaphysik Z).* The Hague: Martinus Nijhoff, 1965.

———. *Ideologie en ervaring: materialen voor een ideologiekritiek op fenomenologische grondslag.* Ed. Paul Willemarck and Lode Frederix. Gent, Belgium: Kritiek, 1984.

———. *Kritiek der grondslagen van onze tijd.* Trans. into Dutch by Willy Coolsaet. Baarn, Netherlands: Het Wereldvenster, 1977.

———. *Kritik der Grundlagen des Zeitalters.* The Hague: Martinus Nijhoff, 1974.

Booker, M. Keith. "'A War between the Mind and Sky': Bakhtin and Poetry, Stevens and Politics." *Wallace Stevens Journal* 14:1 (spring 1990): 71–85.

Bornstein, George. *Transformations of Romanticism in Yeats, Eliot, and Stevens.* Chicago: University of Chicago Press, 1976.

Borroff, Marie. *Language and the Poet: Verbal Artistry in Frost, Stevens, and Moore.* Chicago: University of Chicago Press, 1979.

———. "Making Sense of the Sleight-of-Hand Man." In *Teaching Wallace*

Stevens: Practical Essays, ed. John N. Serio and B. J. Leggett, 87–99. Knoxville: University of Tennessee Press, 1994.

———, ed. *Wallace Stevens: A Collection of Critical Essays*. Englewood Cliffs, N.J.: Prentice-Hall, 1963.

Bové, Paul A. *Destructive Poetics: Heidegger and Modern American Poetry*. New York: Columbia University Press, 1980.

Boyd, Brian. "Words, Works and Worlds in Joyce and Nabokov, or: Intertextuality, Intratextuality, Supratextuality, Infratextuality, Extratextuality and Autotextuality in Modernist and Prepostmodernist Narrative Discourse." *Cycnos* 12:2 (1995): 3–12.

Brazeau, Peter A. "'A Collect of Philosophy': The Difficulty of Finding What Would Suffice." In *Wallace Stevens: A Celebration*, ed. Frank Doggett and Robert Buttel, 46–49. Princeton: Princeton University Press, 1980.

———. *Parts of a World: Wallace Stevens Remembered*. New York: Random House, 1983.

Brecht, Bertolt. "Notizen zur Philosophie 1929–1941." In *Gesammelte Werke*, by Bertolt Brecht. Vol. 20, 125–78. 1967. Reprint, Frankfurt am Main: Suhrkamp Verlag, 1968.

Brogan, Jacqueline Vaught. "Introducing Wallace Stevens: Or, the Sheerly Playful and the Display of Theory in Stevens's Poetry." In *Teaching Wallace Stevens: Practical Essays*, ed. John N. Serio and B. J. Leggett, 51–62. Knoxville: University of Tennessee Press, 1994.

———. *Part of the Climate: American Cubist Poetry*. Berkeley and Los Angeles: University of California Press, 1991.

———. "'Sister of the Minotaur': Sexism and Stevens." *Wallace Stevens Journal* 12:2 (fall 1988): 102–18.

———. *Stevens and Simile: A Theory of Language*. Princeton: Princeton University Press, 1986.

———. "Wallace Stevens: Poems Against His Climate." *Wallace Stevens Journal* 11:2 (fall 1987): 75–93.

Bromwich, David. "Slow Deconstruction." *London Review of Books* 15:19 (October 7, 1993): 22–23.

———. "Stevens and the Idea of the Hero." *Raritan* 7:1 (summer 1987): 1–27.

Bruns, Gerald L. "Stevens without Epistemology." In *Wallace Stevens: The Poetics of Modernism*, ed. Albert Gelpi, 24–40. Cambridge: Cambridge University Press, 1985.

Burke, Edmund. *A Philosophical Enquiry into the Origin of Our Ideas of the Sublime and Beautiful.* 1759. Ed. J. T. Boulton. New York: Columbia University Press; London: Routledge & Kegan Paul, 1958.

Butler, Judith. *Bodies That Matter: On the Discursive Limits of "Sex."* New York: Routledge, 1993.

———. "The Nothing That Is: Wallace Stevens' Hegelian Affinities." In *Theorizing American Literature: Hegel, the Sign, and History*, ed. Bainard Cowan and Joseph G. Kronick, 269–87. Baton Rouge: Louisiana State University Press, 1991.

Campbell, P. Michael, and John Dolan. "Teaching Stevens's Poetry through Rhetorical Structure." In *Teaching Wallace Stevens: Practical Essays*, ed. John N. Serio and B. J. Leggett, 119–28. Knoxville: University of Tennessee Press, 1994.

Cleghorn, Angus. "Questioning the Composition of Romance in 'The Idea of Order at Key West.'" *Wallace Stevens Journal* 22:1 (spring 1998): 23–38.

———. *Wallace Stevens' Poetics: The Neglected Rhetoric.* New York: Palgrave, 2000.

Collini, Stefan. "Interpretation terminable and interminable," introduction to *Interpretation and Overinterpretation*, by Umberto Eco, with Richard Rorty, Jonathan Culler, and Christine Brooke-Rose, ed. Stefan Collini, 1–21. Cambridge: Cambridge University Press, 1992.

Cook, Eleanor. "The Poetics of Modern Punning: Wallace Stevens, Elizabeth Bishop, and Others." In *Against Coercion: Games Poets Play*, by Eleanor Cook, 172–86. Stanford: Stanford University Press, 1998.

———. *Poetry, Word-Play, and Word-War in Wallace Stevens.* Princeton: Princeton University Press, 1988.

———. "Wallace Stevens and the King James Bible." In *Against Coercion: Games Poets Play*, by Eleanor Cook, 128–38. Stanford: Stanford University Press, 1998.

Coolsaet, Willy. Translator's introduction to *Kritiek der grondslagen van onze tijd*, by Rudolf Boehm, trans. into Dutch by Willy Coolsaet, 9–14. Baarn, Netherlands: Het Wereldvenster, 1977.

Corrigan, Peter. *The Sociology of Consumption: An Introduction.* London: Sage, 1997.

Costello, Bonnie. "Effects of an Analogy: Wallace Stevens and Painting." In *Wallace Stevens: The Poetics of Modernism*, ed. Albert Gelpi, 65–85. Cambridge: Cambridge University Press, 1985.

————. "Wallace Stevens: The Adequacy of Landscape." *Wallace Stevens Journal* 17:2 (fall 1993): 203–18.

Coyle, Beverly, and Alan Filreis. Introduction to *Secretaries of the Moon: The Letters of Wallace Stevens & José Rodríguez Feo*, ed. Beverly Coyle and Alan Filreis, 1–31. Durham: Duke University Press, 1986.

Critchley, Simon. "The ancient quarrel." *Times Literary Supplement* 4,870 (August 2, 1996): 26.

Culler, Jonathan. *Framing the Sign: Criticism and Its Institutions*. Oxford: Blackwell, 1988.

————. Introduction to *Identity of the Literary Text*, ed. Mario J. Valdés and Owen Miller, 3–15. Toronto: University of Toronto Press, 1985.

————. *On Deconstruction: Theory and Criticism after Structuralism*. 1982. Reprint, London: Routledge & Kegan Paul, 1985.

Dale, Kathleen A. "Extensions: Beyond Resemblance and the Pleasure Principle in Wallace Stevens." *boundary 2* 4 (1975): 255–73.

DeLillo, Don. *Libra*. 1988. Reprint, London: Penguin, 1989.

de Man, Paul. *Blindness and Insight: Essays in the Rhetoric of Contemporary Criticism*. 2d rev. ed. London: Methuen, 1983.

————. "The Epistemology of Metaphor." *Critical Inquiry* 5:1 (autumn 1978): 13–30.

————. "Hypogram and Inscription." In *The Resistance to Theory*, by Paul de Man, 27–53. Theory and History of Literature, vol. 33. Manchester: Manchester University Press, 1986.

————. "Semiology and Rhetoric." In *Allegories of Reading: Figural Language in Rousseau, Nietzsche, Rilke, and Proust*, by Paul de Man, 3–19. New Haven: Yale University Press, 1979.

Dennett, Daniel C. *Kinds of Minds: Toward an Understanding of Consciousness*. [New York]: BasicBooks, 1996.

Derrida, Jacques. "Che cos'è la poesia?" Trans. Peggy Kamuf. In *A Derrida Reader: Between the Blinds*, ed. Peggy Kamuf, 221–37. New York: Columbia University Press, 1991.

————. "The Double Session." In *Dissemination*, by Jacques Derrida, trans. Barbara Johnson, 173–285. Chicago: University of Chicago Press, 1981.

————. "How to Avoid Speaking: Denials." Trans. Ken Frieden. In *Languages of the Unsayable: The Play of Negativity in Literature and Literary Theory*, ed. Sanford Budick and Wolfgang Iser, 3–70. Irvine Studies in the Humanities, vol. 3. New York: Columbia University Press, 1989.

————. *Positions*. Trans. Alan Bass. 1981. Reprint, London: Athlone Press, 1987.

————. "Signature Event Context." In *Margins of Philosophy*, by Jacques Derrida, trans. Alan Bass, 307–30. 1982. Reprint, Chicago: University of Chicago Press, 1986.

————. "The Supplement of Copula: Philosophy before Linguistics." In *Margins of Philosophy*, by Jacques Derrida, trans. Alan Bass, 175–205. 1982. Reprint, Chicago: University of Chicago Press, 1986.

————. "The Theater of Cruelty and the Closure of Representation." In *Writing and Difference*, by Jacques Derrida, trans. Alan Bass, 232–50. 1978. Reprint, London: Routledge & Kegan Paul, 1985.

————. " 'There Is No One Narcissism' (Autobiophotographies)." Interview by Didier Cahen, trans. Peggy Kamuf. In *Points . . . : Interviews, 1974–1994*, by Jacques Derrida, ed. Elisabeth Weber, 196–215. Stanford: Stanford University Press, 1995.

————. " 'This Strange Institution Called Literature': An Interview with Jacques Derrida." By Derek Attridge. In *Acts of Literature*, by Jacques Derrida, ed. Derek Attridge, 33–75. New York: Routledge, 1992.

————. "White Mythology: Metaphor in the Text of Philosophy." In *Margins of Philosophy*, by Jacques Derrida, trans. Alan Bass, 207–71. 1982. Reprint, Chicago: University of Chicago Press, 1986.

Dickie, Margaret. *Lyric Contingencies: Emily Dickinson and Wallace Stevens*. Philadelphia: University of Pennsylvania Press, 1991.

Dickinson, Emily. *The Poems of Emily Dickinson*. 3 vols. Ed. Thomas H. Johnson. Cambridge: Harvard University Press, Belknap Press, 1963.

Doggett, Frank. *Stevens' Poetry of Thought*. Baltimore: Johns Hopkins Press, 1966.

————. "This Invented World: Stevens' 'Notes toward a Supreme Fiction.' " In *The Act of the Mind: Essays on the Poetry of Wallace Stevens*, ed. Roy Harvey Pearce and J. Hillis Miller, 13–28. Baltimore: Johns Hopkins Press, 1965.

Doggett, Frank, and Robert Buttel, eds. *Wallace Stevens: A Celebration*. Princeton: Princeton University Press, 1980.

Doggett, Frank, and Dorothy Emerson. "About Stevens' Comments on Several Poems." In *The Motive for Metaphor: Essays on Modern Poetry*, ed. Francis C. Blessington and Guy Rotella, 26–36. Boston: Northeastern University Press, 1983.

————. "A Primer of Possibility for 'The Auroras of Autumn.' " *Wallace Stevens Journal* 13:1 (spring 1989): 53–66.

Donoghue, Denis. "The Book of Genius: Harold Bloom's agon and the uses of great literature." *Times Literary Supplement* 4,788 (January 6, 1995): 3–4.

Doyle, Charles. *Wallace Stevens: The Critical Heritage*. London: Routledge & Kegan Paul, 1985.

Eco, Umberto. *Interpretation and Overinterpretation*. With Richard Rorty, Jonathan Culler, and Christine Brooke-Rose. Ed. Stefan Collini. Cambridge: Cambridge University Press, 1992.

———. *The Limits of Interpretation*. 1990. Reprint, Bloomington: Indiana University Press, 1994.

———. *A Theory of Semiotics*. 1976. Reprint, Bloomington: Indiana University Press, 1979.

Edelman, Lee. *Homographesis: Essays in Gay Literary and Cultural Theory*. New York: Routledge, 1994.

———. *Transmemberment of Song: Hart Crane's Anatomies of Rhetoric and Desire*. Stanford: Stanford University Press, 1987.

Eder, Doris L. "A Review of Stevens Criticism to Date." *Twentieth Century Literature* 15 (April 1969): 3–18.

Eeckhout, Bart. "When Language Stops . . . Suspension Points in the Poetry of Hart Crane and Wallace Stevens." In *Semantics of Silences in Linguistics and Literature*, ed. Gudrun M. Grabher and Ulrike Jessner, 257–70. Heidelberg: Universitätsverlag C. Winter, 1996.

Eliot, T. S. *Collected Poems 1909–1962*. 1963. Reprint, San Diego: Harcourt Brace Jovanovich, n.d.

———. "The Metaphysical Poets." In *Selected Prose of T. S. Eliot*, ed. Frank Kermode, 59–67. 1975. Reprint, New York: Harcourt Brace Jovanovich; Farrar, Straus and Giroux, n.d.

Ellmann, Richard. "How Wallace Stevens Saw Himself." In *Wallace Stevens: A Celebration*, ed. Frank Doggett and Robert Buttel, 149–70. Princeton: Princeton University Press, 1980.

Emerson, Ralph Waldo. "Each and All." In *American Poetry: The Nineteenth Century. Volume One: Philip Freneau to Walt Whitman*, ed. John Hollander, 258–59. New York: Library of America, 1993.

———. "Experience." In *Ralph Waldo Emerson: Essays and Lectures*, ed. Joel Porte, 469–92. New York: Library of America, 1983.

———. *Nature*. In *Ralph Waldo Emerson: Essays and Lectures*, ed. Joel Porte, 5–49. New York: Library of America, 1983.

———. "Self-Reliance." In *Ralph Waldo Emerson: Essays and Lectures*, ed. Joel Porte, 257–82. New York: Library of America, 1983.

Endo, Paul. "Stevens and the Two Sublimes." *Wallace Stevens Journal* 19:1 (spring 1995): 36–50.

Ferry, Anne. *The Title to the Poem*. Stanford: Stanford University Press, 1996.

Filreis, Alan. *Modernism from Right to Left: Wallace Stevens, the Thirties, & Literary Radicalism*. Cambridge Studies in American Literature, vol. 79. Cambridge: Cambridge University Press, 1994.

———. *Wallace Stevens and the Actual World*. Princeton: Princeton University Press, 1991.

Fish, Stanley. *Is There a Text in This Class? The Authority of Interpretive Communities*. Cambridge: Harvard University Press, 1980.

Fisher, Barbara M. "Recollecting Holly." *Wallace Stevens Journal* 16:2 (fall 1992): 211–12.

———. Review of *Wallace Stevens and Literary Canons*, by John Timberman Newcomb. *Wallace Stevens Journal* 16:1 (spring 1992): 106–8.

———. *Wallace Stevens: The Intensest Rendezvous*. Charlottesville: University Press of Virginia, 1990.

Fletcher, Angus. Foreword to *Wallace Stevens: The Intensest Rendezvous*, by Barbara M. Fisher, ix–xix. Charlottesville: University Press of Virginia, 1990.

Fodor, Jerry. "Encounters with Trees." *London Review of Books* 17:8 (April 20, 1995): 10–11.

Freud, Sigmund. *The Future of an Illusion*. In vol. 21 of *The Standard Edition of the Complete Psychological Works of Sigmund Freud*, trans. under the general editorship of James Strachey et al., 3–56. 1961. Reprint, London: Hogarth Press, 1968.

Frye, Northrop. *Anatomy of Criticism: Four Essays*. 1957. Reprint, Princeton: Princeton University Press, 1990.

———. Interview by Imre Salusinszky. In *Criticism in Society: Interviews with Jacques Derrida, Northrop Frye, Harold Bloom, Geoffrey Hartman, Frank Kermode, Edward Said, Barbara Johnson, Frank Lentricchia, and J. Hillis Miller*, by Imre Salusinszky, 26–42. New York: Methuen, 1987.

———. "The Realistic Oriole: A Study of Wallace Stevens." In *Wallace Stevens: A Collection of Critical Essays*, ed. Marie Borroff, 161–76. Englewood Cliffs, N.J.: Prentice-Hall, 1963.

———. "Wallace Stevens and the Variation Form." In *Literary Theory & Structure: Essays in Honor of William K. Wimsatt*, ed. Frank Brady, John Palmer, and Martin Price, 395–414. New Haven: Yale University Press, 1973.

Gasché, Rodolphe. *Inventions of Difference: On Jacques Derrida*. Cambridge: Harvard University Press, 1994.

Gelpi, Albert. "Stevens and Williams: The Epistemology of Modernism." In *Wallace Stevens: The Poetics of Modernism*, ed. Albert Gelpi, 3–23. Cambridge: Cambridge University Press, 1985.

Gifford, Don, with Robert J. Seidman. Ulysses *Annotated*. 2d rev. ed. 1988. Reprint, Berkeley and Los Angeles: University of California Press, 1989.

Gilbert, Roger. *Walks in the World: Representation and Experience in Modern American Poetry*. Princeton: Princeton University Press, 1991.

Gilbert, Stuart. *James Joyce's* Ulysses: *A Study*. Rev. ed. 1952. Reprint, New York: Vintage Books, 1955.

Glaser, Elton. "Stevens at the Seminar Table." In *Teaching Wallace Stevens: Practical Essays*, ed. John N. Serio and B. J. Leggett, 63–73. Knoxville: University of Tennessee Press, 1994.

Goodman, Russell B. Introduction to *Pragmatism: A Contemporary Reader*, ed. Russell B. Goodman, 1–20. New York: Routledge, 1995.

Greene, Graham. "Graham Greene à l'écoute du monde," interview by Françoise Barthélémy. *Le Monde diplomatique* 412 (July 1988): 14.

Grey, Thomas C. *The Wallace Stevens Case: Law and the Practice of Poetry*. Cambridge: Harvard University Press, 1991.

Halliday, Mark. *Stevens and the Interpersonal*. Princeton: Princeton University Press, 1991.

Hartman, Geoffrey H. "The Poet's Politics." In *Beyond Formalism: Literary Essays 1958–1970*, by Geoffrey H. Hartman, 247–57. 1970. Reprint, New Haven: Yale University Press, 1971.

———. *Saving the Text: Literature/Derrida/Philosophy*. 1981. Reprint, Baltimore: Johns Hopkins University Press, 1985.

Hassan, Ihab. "The Culture of Postmodernism." *Theory, Culture & Society: Explorations in Critical Social Science* 2:3 (1985): 119–31.

———. "Imagination and Belief: Wallace Stevens and William James in Our Clime." *Wallace Stevens Journal* 10:1 (spring 1986): 3–8.

Heidegger, Martin. "The Origin of the Work of Art." In *Poetry, Language, Thought*, by Martin Heidegger, trans. Albert Hofstadter, 15–87. New York: Harper & Row, 1971.

———. "What Is Metaphysics?" Trans. David Farrell Krell. In *Basic Writings from* Being and Time *(1927) to* The Task of Thinking *(1964)*, by Martin Heidegger, ed. David Farrell Krell, 91–112. New York: Harper & Row, 1977.

Heinzelman, Kurt. "Williams and Stevens: The Vanishing-Point of Resemblance." In *WCW & Others: Essays on William Carlos Williams and His Association with Ezra Pound, Hilda Doolittle, Marcel Duchamp, Marianne Moore, Emanuel Romano, Wallace Stevens, and Louis Zukofsky*, ed. Dave Oliphant and Thomas Zigal, 85–113. Austin: Harry Ransom Humanities Research Center, 1985.

Hertz, David Michael. *Angels of Reality: Emersonian Unfoldings in Wright, Stevens, and Ives*. Carbondale: Southern Illinois University Press, 1993.

Hesla, David H. "Singing in Chaos: Wallace Stevens and Three or Four Ideas." *American Literature* 57:2 (May 1985): 240–62.

Hines, Thomas J. *The Later Poetry of Wallace Stevens: Phenomenological Parallels with Husserl and Heidegger*. Lewisburg, Pa.: Bucknell University Press, 1976.

Hollander, John. "The Sound of the Music of Music and Sound." In *Wallace Stevens: A Celebration*, ed. Frank Doggett and Robert Buttel, 235–55. Princeton: Princeton University Press, 1980.

Holmes, Barbara. *The Decomposer's Art: Ideas of Music in the Poetry of Wallace Stevens*. New Connections: Studies in Interdisciplinarity, vol. 1. New York: Peter Lang, 1990.

Holtzman, Harry, and Martin S. James, eds. *The New Art–The New Life: The Collected Writings of Piet Mondrian*. Boston: G. K. Hall, 1986.

Iser, Wolfgang. "Feigning in Fiction." In *Identity of the Literary Text*, ed. Mario J. Valdés and Owen Miller, 204–28. Toronto: University of Toronto Press, 1985.

James, William. *The Principles of Psychology*. Great Books of the Western World, vol. 53. Chicago: Encyclopaedia Britannica, 1952.

Jameson, Fredric. "Wallace Stevens." *New Orleans Review* 11:1 (spring 1984): 10–19.

Jarrell, Randall. "Reflections on Wallace Stevens." In *Poetry and the Age*, by Randall Jarrell, 124–36. London: Faber & Faber, 1955.

———. Review of *The Collected Poems of Wallace Stevens*. In *The Third Book of Criticism*, by Randall Jarrell, 55–73. London: Faber & Faber, 1975.

Jenkins, Lee Margaret. *Wallace Stevens: Rage for Order*. Brighton, U.K.: Sussex Academic Press, 2000.

Johnson, Barbara. *The Critical Difference: Essays in the Contemporary Rhetoric of Reading*. Baltimore: Johns Hopkins University Press, 1980.

Joyce, James. *Ulysses*. The Corrected Text. Ed. Hans Walter Gabler with

Wolfhard Steppe and Claus Melchior. Harmondsworth, U.K.: Penguin, in association with The Bodley Head, 1986.

Kamuf, Peggy. "Reading between the Blinds," introduction to *A Derrida Reader: Between the Blinds*, ed. Peggy Kamuf, xiii–xlii. New York: Columbia University Press, 1991.

Keats, John. *Letters of John Keats 1814–1821*. 2 vols. Ed. Hyder Edward Rollins. Cambridge: Harvard University Press, 1958.

Kenner, Hugh. *The Pound Era*. 1971. Reprint, London: Faber & Faber, 1975.

Kermode, Frank. *An Appetite for Poetry*. Cambridge: Harvard University Press, 1989.

———. "Dwelling Poetically in Connecticut." In *Wallace Stevens: A Celebration*, ed. Frank Doggett and Robert Buttel, 256–73. Princeton: Princeton University Press, 1980.

———. Interview by Imre Salusinszky. In *Criticism in Society: Interviews with Jacques Derrida, Northrop Frye, Harold Bloom, Geoffrey Hartman, Frank Kermode, Edward Said, Barbara Johnson, Frank Lentricchia, and J. Hillis Miller*, by Imre Salusinszky, 98–121. New York: Methuen, 1987.

———. Preface to 1989 edition of *Wallace Stevens*, by Frank Kermode, xi–xix. 1960. Reprint, London: Faber & Faber, 1989.

———. *The Sense of an Ending: Studies in the Theory of Fiction*. New York: Oxford University Press, 1967.

———. *Wallace Stevens*. 1960. Reprint, London: Faber & Faber, 1989.

Kern, Robert. *Orientalism, Modernism, and the American Poem*. Cambridge Studies in American Literature and Culture, vol. 97. Cambridge: Cambridge University Press, 1996.

King, Bruce. "Wallace Stevens' 'Metaphors of a Magnifico.'" *English Studies* 49:5 (October 1968): 450–52.

Kronick, Joseph G. "Large White Man Reading: Stevens' Genealogy of the Giant." *Wallace Stevens Journal* 7:3/4 (fall 1983): 89–98.

———. "Of Parents, Children, and Rabbis: Wallace Stevens and the Question of the Book." *boundary 2* 10:3 (spring 1982): 125–54.

Lacan, Jacques. "La Métaphore du Sujet." In *Écrits*, by Jacques Lacan, 889–92. Paris: Éditions du Seuil, 1966.

———. "Du sujet enfin en question." In *Écrits*, by Jacques Lacan, 229–36. Paris: Éditions du Seuil, 1966.

Lauter, Paul. "The Two Criticisms—or, Structure, Lingo, and Power in the Discourse of Academic Humanists." In *Canons and Contexts*, by Paul Lauter, 133–53. New York: Oxford University Press, 1991.

Leggett, B. J. *Early Stevens: The Nietzschean Intertext*. Durham: Duke University Press, 1992.

———. *Wallace Stevens and Poetic Theory: Conceiving the Supreme Fiction*. Chapel Hill: University of North Carolina Press, 1987.

Lensing, George S. "Stevens's Prosody." In *Teaching Wallace Stevens: Practical Essays*, ed. John N. Serio and B. J. Leggett, 100–18. Knoxville: University of Tennessee Press, 1994.

———. "Wallace Stevens and Stevens T. Mason: An Epistolary Exchange on Poetic Meaning." *Wallace Stevens Journal* 4:3/4 (fall 1980): 34–36.

———. *Wallace Stevens and the Seasons*. Baton Rouge: Louisiana State University Press, 2001.

———. *Wallace Stevens: A Poet's Growth*. 1986. Reprint, Baton Rouge: Louisiana State University Press, 1991.

———. "Wallace Stevens in England." In *Wallace Stevens: A Celebration*, ed. Frank Doggett and Robert Buttel, 130–48. Princeton: Princeton University Press, 1980.

Lentricchia, Frank. *After the New Criticism*. London: Athlone Press, 1980.

———. *Ariel and the Police: Michel Foucault, William James, Wallace Stevens*. Madison: University of Wisconsin Press, 1988.

———. *The Gaiety of Language: An Essay on the Radical Poetics of W. B. Yeats and Wallace Stevens*. Perspectives in Criticism, vol. 19. Berkeley and Los Angeles: University of California Press, 1968.

———. Interview by Imre Salusinszky. In *Criticism in Society: Interviews with Jacques Derrida, Northrop Frye, Harold Bloom, Geoffrey Hartman, Frank Kermode, Edward Said, Barbara Johnson, Frank Lentricchia, and J. Hillis Miller*, by Imre Salusinszky, 174–206. New York: Methuen, 1987.

———. *Modernist Quartet*. Cambridge: Cambridge University Press, 1994.

Leonard, James S., and Christine E. Wharton. *The Fluent Mundo: Wallace Stevens and the Structure of Reality*. Athens: University of Georgia Press, 1988.

Levin, Jonathan. *The Poetics of Transition: Emerson, Pragmatism, & American Literary Modernism*. Durham: Duke University Press, 1999.

Libby, Anthony. *Mythologies of Nothing: Mystical Death in American Poetry 1940–70*. Urbana: University of Illinois Press, 1984.

Litz, A. Walton. " 'Compass and Curriculum': Teaching Stevens among the Moderns." In *Teaching Wallace Stevens: Practical Essays*, ed. John N. Serio and B. J. Leggett, 235–41. Knoxville: University of Tennessee Press, 1994.

―――. *Introspective Voyager: The Poetic Development of Wallace Stevens*. New York: Oxford University Press, 1972.

Longenbach, James. "Hart Crane and T. S. Eliot: Poets in the Sacred Grove." *Denver Quarterly* 23:1 (summer 1988): 82–103.

―――. "The Idea of Disorder at Key West." *Raritan* 11:1 (summer 1991): 92–114.

―――. *Wallace Stevens: The Plain Sense of Things*. New York: Oxford University Press, 1991.

Macksey, Richard A. "The Climates of Wallace Stevens." In *The Act of the Mind: Essays on the Poetry of Wallace Stevens*, ed. Roy Harvey Pearce and J. Hillis Miller, 185–223. Baltimore: Johns Hopkins Press, 1965.

MacLeod, Glen G. "The Influence of Wallace Stevens on Contemporary Artists." *Wallace Stevens Journal* 20:2 (fall 1996): 139–80.

―――. *Wallace Stevens and Company: The* Harmonium *Years, 1913–1923*. Ann Arbor: UMI Research Press, 1983.

―――. *Wallace Stevens and Modern Art: From the Armory Show to Abstract Expressionism*. New Haven: Yale University Press, 1993.

―――, ed. "A Special Issue on Williams and Stevens." *William Carlos Williams Review* 18:2 (fall 1992).

Maeder, Beverly. *Wallace Stevens' Experimental Language: The Lion in the Lute*. London: Macmillan, 1999.

Mao, Douglas. *Solid Objects: Modernism and the Test of Production*. Princeton: Princeton University Press, 1998.

Mariani, Paul. *William Carlos Williams: A New World Naked*. 1981. Reprint, New York: W. W. Norton, 1990.

Marsh, Alec. "Stevens and Williams: The Economics of Metaphor." *William Carlos Williams Review* 18:2 (fall 1992): 37–49.

Masel, Carolyn. "Stevens and England: A Difficult Crossing." *Wallace Stevens Journal* 25:2 (fall 2001): 122–37.

Matterson, Stephen. "'The Whole Habit of the Mind': Stevens, Americanness, and the Use of Elsewhere." *Wallace Stevens Journal* 25:2 (fall 2001): 111–21.

McCann, Janet. *Wallace Stevens Revisited: "The Celestial Possible."* Twayne's United States Authors Series, no. 617. New York: Twayne Publishers; London: Prentice Hall International, 1995.

Melville, Herman. *Moby-Dick; or, The Whale*. Introduced by Andrew Delbanco, annotated by Tom Quirk. 1988. Reprint, New York: Penguin, 1992.

Merleau-Ponty, Maurice. "Cinq notes sur Claude Simon." *Esprit* 66 (June 1982): 64–66.

———. *Phenomenology of Perception.* Trans. Colin Smith. 1962. Reprint, Atlantic Highlands, N.J.: Humanities Press; London: Routledge, 1989.

Miller, J. Hillis. *Ariadne's Thread: Story Lines.* New Haven: Yale University Press, 1992.

———. "The Ethics of Topography: Stevens." In *Topographies,* by J. Hillis Miller, 255–90. Stanford: Stanford University Press, 1995.

———. "Impossible Metaphor: Stevens's 'The Red Fern' as Example." *Yale French Studies* 69 (1985): 150–62.

———. Interview by Imre Salusinszky. In *Criticism in Society: Interviews with Jacques Derrida, Northrop Frye, Harold Bloom, Geoffrey Hartman, Frank Kermode, Edward Said, Barbara Johnson, Frank Lentricchia, and J. Hillis Miller,* by Imre Salusinszky, 208–40. New York: Methuen, 1987.

———. *The Linguistic Moment: From Wordsworth to Stevens.* Princeton: Princeton University Press, 1985.

———. *Poets of Reality: Six Twentieth-Century Writers.* Cambridge: Harvard University Press, Belknap Press, 1965.

———. Preface to *Tropes, Parables, Performatives: Essays on Twentieth-Century Literature,* by J. Hillis Miller, vii–x. New York: Harvester Wheatsheaf, 1990.

———. "Prosopopoeia in Hardy and Stevens." In *Tropes, Parables, Performatives: Essays on Twentieth-Century Literature,* by J. Hillis Miller, 245–59. New York: Harvester Wheatsheaf, 1990.

———. "Stevens' Rock and Criticism as Cure." In *Wallace Stevens,* ed. Harold Bloom, 27–49. New York: Chelsea House Publishers, 1985.

———. "Theoretical and Atheoretical in Stevens." In *Wallace Stevens: A Celebration,* ed. Frank Doggett and Robert Buttel, 274–85. Princeton: Princeton University Press, 1980.

———. "When Is a Primitive Like an Orb?" In *Textual Analysis: Some Readers Reading,* ed. Mary Ann Caws, 167–81. New York: Modern Language Association of America, 1986.

———. "William Carlos Williams and Wallace Stevens." In *The Columbia Literary History of the United States,* ed. Emory Elliott, 972–92. New York: Columbia University Press, 1988.

Miller, Owen. "Intertextual Identity." In *Identity of the Literary Text,* ed. Mario J. Valdés and Owen Miller, 19–40. Toronto: University of Toronto Press, 1985.

————. Preface to *Identity of the Literary Text*, ed. Mario J. Valdés and Owen Miller, vii–xxi. Toronto: University of Toronto Press, 1985.

Mondriaan, Piet. "Natuurlijke en abstracte realiteit." *De Stijl* 2:9 (July 1919): 97–99.

————. "Neo-Plasticisme: De Woning—De Straat—De Stad." *i 10* 1:1 (1927): 12–18.

————. "De nieuwe beelding in de schilderkunst. IV. Beeldingsmiddel en compositie. (Vervolg)." *De Stijl* 1:4 (February 1918): 41–45.

————. "De nieuwe beelding in de schilderkunst. IV. De *redelijkheid* der nieuwe beelding." *De Stijl* 1:5 (March 1918): 49–54.

————. "De nieuwe beelding in de schilderkunst. VII. Van het natuurlijke tot het abstracte, d.i. van het onbepaalde tot het bepaalde. (I)." *De Stijl* 1:8 (June 1918): 88–91.

Morreel, Gert. " 'Cycloid Inclusiveness': The Striated Heteroglossia of Marianne Moore's 'Marriage.' " In *Exploring Feminine Space: Five Essays on Women's Writings*, ed. Marysa Demoor, 78–98. Gent, Belgium: Studia Germanica Gandensia, 1995.

M[orrison], B[ryce]. Review of *Debussy: Complete Piano Works*, performed by Walter Gieseking. *Gramophone* 74:877 (June 1996): 109, 114.

Morse, Samuel French. "A Sense of the Place." In *The Motive for Metaphor: Essays on Modern Poetry*, ed. Francis C. Blessington and Guy Rotella, 4–25. Boston: Northeastern University Press, 1983.

Moynihan, Robert. "Checklist: Second Purchase, Wallace Stevens Collection, Huntington Library." *Wallace Stevens Journal* 20:1 (spring 1996): 76–103.

Murry, John Middleton. "Metaphor." In *Countries of the Mind: Essays in Literary Criticism*, by John Middleton Murry, 1–16 of part 2, 1931. Reprint, London: Oxford University Press, 1937.

Nabokov, Vladimir. *Lectures on Literature*. Ed. Fredson Bowers. 1980. Reprint, San Diego: Harcourt Brace, Harvest/Bruccoli Clark, 1982.

Naylor, Paul Kenneth. " 'The Idea of It': Wallace Stevens and Edmund Husserl." *Wallace Stevens Journal* 12:1 (spring 1988): 44–55.

Newcomb, John Timberman. *Wallace Stevens and Literary Canons*. Jackson: University Press of Mississippi, 1992.

Nietzsche, Friedrich. *The Birth of Tragedy* and *The Genealogy of Morals*. Trans. Francis Golffing. 1956. Reprint, New York: Doubleday, Anchor Books, n.d.

————. *Götzen-Dämmerung oder Wie man mit dem Hammer philosophirt*. In pt. 6, vol. 3 of *Nietzsche Werke: Kritische Gesamtausgabe*, ed. Giorgio Colli and Mazzino Montinari, 49–157. Berlin: Walter de Gruyter, 1968.

———. "On Truth and Falsity in Their Extramoral Sense." Trans. Maximillian A. Mügge. In *Philosophical Writings*, by Friedrich Nietzsche, ed. Reinhold Grimm and Caroline Molina y Vedia, 87–99. New York: Continuum, 1995.

Norris, Christopher. *Deconstruction: Theory and Practice*. 1982. Reprint, London: Methuen, 1985.

———. *Derrida*. Cambridge: Harvard University Press, 1987.

O'Connor, William Van. *The Shaping Spirit: A Study of Wallace Stevens*. 1950. Reprint, New York: Russell & Russell, 1964.

Parker, Patricia A. "The Motive for Metaphor: Stevens and Derrida." *Wallace Stevens Journal* 7:3/4 (fall 1983): 76–88.

Pearce, Roy Harvey. *The Continuity of American Poetry*. Princeton: Princeton University Press, 1961.

———. "Toward Decreation: Stevens and the 'Theory of Poetry.'" In *Wallace Stevens: A Celebration*, ed. Frank Doggett and Robert Buttel, 286–307. Princeton: Princeton University Press, 1980.

Pearce, Roy Harvey, and J. Hillis Miller, eds. *The Act of the Mind: Essays on the Poetry of Wallace Stevens*. Baltimore: Johns Hopkins Press, 1965.

Perkins, David. *A History of Modern Poetry: Modernism and After*. Cambridge: Harvard University Press, Belknap Press, 1987.

Perloff, Marjorie. "Revolving in Crystal: The Supreme Fiction and the Impasse of Modernist Lyric." In *Wallace Stevens: The Poetics of Modernism*, ed. Albert Gelpi, 41–64. Cambridge: Cambridge University Press, 1985.

Pinker, Steven. *The Language Instinct: The New Science of Language and Mind*. 1994. Reprint, London: Penguin Books, 1995.

Poirier, Richard. *Poetry and Pragmatism*. London: Faber & Faber, 1992.

———. *The Renewal of Literature: Emersonian Reflections*. 1987. Reprint, New Haven: Yale University Press, 1988.

Quirk, Tom. *Bergson and American Culture: The Worlds of Willa Cather and Wallace Stevens*. Chapel Hill: University of North Carolina Press, 1990.

Rae, Patricia. *The Practical Muse: Pragmatist Poetics in Hulme, Pound, and Stevens*. Lewisburg, Pa.: Bucknell University Press, 1998.

Reddy, Srikanth. "'As He Starts the Human Tale': Strategies of Closure in Wallace Stevens." *Wallace Stevens Journal* 24:1 (spring 2000): 3–23.

Regueiro, Helen. "The Rejection of Metaphor." In *Wallace Stevens*, ed. Harold Bloom, 51–60. New York: Chelsea House Publishers, 1985.

Richardson, Joan. "Learning Stevens's Language: The Will & the Weather." In *Teaching Wallace Stevens: Practical Essays*, ed. John N. Serio and B. J. Leggett, 140–55. Knoxville: University of Tennessee Press, 1994.

———. *Wallace Stevens: The Early Years, 1879–1923*. New York: William Morrow, Beech Tree Books, 1986.

———. *Wallace Stevens: The Later Years, 1923–1955*. New York: William Morrow, Beech Tree Books, 1988.

Ricks, Christopher, ed. *Inventions of the March Hare: Poems 1909–1917 by T. S. Eliot*. London: Faber & Faber, 1996.

Riddel, Joseph N. *The Clairvoyant Eye: The Poetry and Poetics of Wallace Stevens*. 1965. Reprint, Baton Rouge: Louisiana State University Press, 1991.

———. "The Climate of Our Poems." *Wallace Stevens Journal* 7:3/4 (fall 1983): 59–75.

———. "The Contours of Stevens Criticism." 1964. In *The Act of the Mind: Essays on the Poetry of Wallace Stevens*, ed. Roy Harvey Pearce and J. Hillis Miller, 243–76. Baltimore: Johns Hopkins Press, 1965.

———. "Decentering the Image: The 'Project' of 'American' Poetics?" In *Textual Strategies: Perspectives in Post-Structuralist Criticism*, ed. Josué V. Harari, 322–58. 1979. Reprint, London: Methuen, 1980.

———. "Interpreting Stevens: An Essay on Poetry and Thinking." *boundary 2* 1:1 (fall 1972): 79–97.

———. "Metaphoric Staging: Stevens' Beginning Again of the 'End of the Book.'" In *Wallace Stevens: A Celebration*, ed. Frank Doggett and Robert Buttel, 308–38. Princeton: Princeton University Press, 1980.

———. "Postscript '90." In *The Clairvoyant Eye: The Poetry and Poetics of Wallace Stevens*, by Joseph N. Riddel, 279–89. 1965. Reprint, Baton Rouge: Louisiana State University Press, 1991.

———. "Wallace Stevens." In *A Survey of Research and Criticism since 1972*, vol. 2 of *Sixteen Modern American Authors*, ed. Jackson R. Bryer, 623–74. Durham: Duke University Press, 1990.

———. "Walt Whitman and Wallace Stevens." In *Wallace Stevens: A Collection of Critical Essays*, ed. Marie Borroff, 30–42. Englewood Cliffs, N.J.: Prentice-Hall, 1963.

Rieke, Alison. *The Senses of Nonsense*. Iowa City: University of Iowa Press, 1992.

———. "Wallace Stevens in the Classroom: 'More Truly and More Strange.'"

In *Teaching Wallace Stevens: Practical Essays*, ed. John N. Serio and B. J. Leggett, 129–39. Knoxville: University of Tennessee Press, 1994.

Rorty, Richard. "The Inspirational Value of Great Works of Literature." *Raritan* 16:1 (summer 1996): 8–17.

———. "Philosophy as a Kind of Writing: An Essay on Derrida." *New Literary History* 10:1 (autumn 1978): 141–60.

Rosenthal, M. L. *The Modern Poets: A Critical Introduction*. 1960. Reprint, New York: Oxford University Press, 1961.

Rosu, Anca. *The Metaphysics of Sound in Wallace Stevens*. Tuscaloosa: University of Alabama Press, 1995.

Ruppert, Jeanne. "Nature, Feeling, and Disclosure in the Poetry of Wallace Stevens." *Analecta Husserliana* 18 (1984): 75–88.

Said, Edward W. Interview by Imre Salusinszky. In *Criticism in Society: Interviews with Jacques Derrida, Northrop Frye, Harold Bloom, Geoffrey Hartman, Frank Kermode, Edward Said, Barbara Johnson, Frank Lentricchia, and J. Hillis Miller*, by Imre Salusinszky, 122–48. New York: Methuen, 1987.

———. *The World, the Text, and the Critic*. Cambridge: Harvard University Press, 1983.

Santos, Maria Irene Ramalho de Sousa. "The Woman in the Poem: Wallace Stevens, Ramon Fernandez, and Adrienne Rich." *Wallace Stevens Journal* 12:2 (fall 1988): 150–61.

Sawaya, Richard N. *The Scepticism and Animal Faith of Wallace Stevens*. New York: Garland, 1987.

Schaum, Melita. "Lyric Resistance: Views of the Political in the Poetics of Wallace Stevens and H. D." *Wallace Stevens Journal* 13:2 (fall 1989): 191–205.

———. *Wallace Stevens and the Critical Schools*. Foreword by John N. Serio. Tuscaloosa: University of Alabama Press, 1988.

Schleifer, Ronald. *Rhetoric and Death: The Language of Modernism and Postmodern Discourse Theory*. Urbana: University of Illinois Press, 1990.

Schulze, Robin Gail. "Teaching Wallace Stevens and Marianne Moore: The Search for an Open Mind." In *Teaching Wallace Stevens: Practical Essays*, ed. John N. Serio and B. J. Leggett, 179–91. Knoxville: University of Tennessee Press, 1994.

———. *The Web of Friendship: Marianne Moore and Wallace Stevens*. Ann Arbor: University of Michigan Press, 1995.

Schwarz, Daniel R. *Narrative and Representation in the Poetry of Wallace Stevens*. New York: St. Martin's Press, 1993.

———. *Reconfiguring Modernism: Explorations in the Relationship between Modern Art and Modern Literature*. London: Macmillan, 1997.

Serio, John N. *Wallace Stevens: An Annotated Secondary Bibliography*. Pittsburgh Series in Bibliography. Pittsburgh: University of Pittsburgh Press, 1994.

Serio, John N., and B. J. Leggett, eds. *Teaching Wallace Stevens: Practical Essays*. Tennessee Studies in Literature, vol. 35. Knoxville: University of Tennessee Press, 1994.

Sharpe, Tony. *Wallace Stevens: A Literary Life*. London: Macmillan, 2000.

Shaviro, Steven. " 'That Which Is Always Beginning': Stevens's Poetry of Affirmation." *PMLA* 100:2 (March 1985): 220–33.

Shibles, Warren A. *Metaphor: An Annotated Bibliography and History*. Whitewater, Wis.: Language Press, 1971.

Smith, Barbara Herrnstein. *Contingencies of Value: Alternative Perspectives for Critical Theory*. Cambridge: Harvard University Press, 1988.

Spivak, Gayatri Chakravorty. Translator's preface to *Of Grammatology*, by Jacques Derrida, ix–lxxxvii. Baltimore: Johns Hopkins University Press, 1976.

Springer, Mary Doyle. "The Feminine Principle in Stevens' Poetry: 'Esthétique du Mal.' " *Wallace Stevens Journal* 12:2 (fall 1988): 119–37.

———. "A Relativity of Angels: Wallace Stevens and Luce Irigaray." *Wallace Stevens Journal* 14:2 (fall 1990): 153–66.

Stegman, Michael O. "Checklist of Musical Compositions Relating to Stevens." *Wallace Stevens Journal* 16:2 (fall 1992): 196–204.

———. "Wallace Stevens and Music: A Discography of Stevens' Phonograph Record Collection." *Wallace Stevens Journal* 3:3/4 (fall 1979): 79–97.

Stevens, Holly. *Souvenirs and Prophecies: The Young Wallace Stevens*. New York: Alfred A. Knopf, 1977.

Still, Judith, and Michael Worton. Introduction to *Intertextuality: Theories and Practices*, ed. Michael Worton and Judith Still, 1–44. Manchester: Manchester University Press, 1990.

Strom, Martha Helen. "The Uneasy Friendship of William Carlos Williams and Wallace Stevens." *Journal of Modern Literature* 11 (July 1984): 291–98.

Suberchicot, Alain. *Treize façons de regarder Wallace Stevens: Une écriture de la présence*. Paris: L'Harmattan, 1998.

Tompkins, Robert R. "Stevens and Zen: The Boundless Reality of the Imagination." *Wallace Stevens Journal* 9:1 (spring 1985): 26–39.

Valdés, Mario J. "Conclusion: Concepts of Fixed and Variable Identity." In *Identity of the Literary Text*, ed. Mario J. Valdés and Owen Miller, 297–311. Toronto: University of Toronto Press, 1985.

Vendler, Helen. "Apollo's Harsher Songs." In *Part of Nature, Part of Us: Modern American Poets*, by Helen Vendler, 40–58. Cambridge: Harvard University Press, 1980.

———. "Dark and Deep." *London Review of Books* 18:13 (July 4, 1996): 3, 5–6.

———. *The Music of What Happens: Poems, Poets, Critics*. Cambridge: Harvard University Press, 1988.

———. "New Books on Wallace Stevens." *New England Quarterly* 59:4 (December 1986): 549–63.

———. *On Extended Wings: Wallace Stevens' Longer Poems*. Cambridge: Harvard University Press, 1969.

———. "The Qualified Assertions of Wallace Stevens." In *The Act of the Mind: Essays on the Poetry of Wallace Stevens*, ed. Roy Harvey Pearce and J. Hillis Miller, 163–78. Baltimore: Johns Hopkins Press, 1965.

———. "Stevens and Keats' 'To Autumn.'" In *Wallace Stevens: A Celebration*, ed. Frank Doggett and Robert Buttel, 171–95. Princeton: Princeton University Press, 1980.

———. "Wallace Stevens." In *The Columbia History of American Poetry*, ed. Jay Parini, 370–94. New York: Columbia University Press, 1993.

———. "Wallace Stevens." In *Voices & Visions: The Poet in America*, ed. Helen Vendler, 123–55. New York: Random House, 1987.

———. "Wallace Stevens: Teaching the Anthology Pieces." In *Teaching Wallace Stevens: Practical Essays*, ed. John N. Serio and B. J. Leggett, 3–16. Knoxville: University of Tennessee Press, 1994.

———. *Wallace Stevens: Words Chosen Out of Desire*. Knoxville: University of Tennessee Press, 1984.

———. "Writhing and Crawling and Leaping and Darting and Flattening and Stretching." *London Review of Books* 18:21 (October 31, 1996): 8–9.

Voros, Gyorgyi. *Notations of the Wild: Ecology in the Poetry of Wallace Stevens*. Iowa City: University of Iowa Press, 1997.

Walker, David. *The Transparent Lyric: Reading and Meaning in the Poetry of Stevens and Williams*. Princeton: Princeton University Press, 1984.

Walsh, Thomas F. *Concordance to the Poetry of Wallace Stevens*. University Park: Pennsylvania State University Press, 1963.

Weimann, Robert. "Textual Identity and Relationship: A Metacritical Excursion into History." In *Identity of the Literary Text*, ed. Mario J. Valdés and Owen Miller, 274–93. Toronto: University of Toronto Press, 1985.

Weston, Susan B. *Wallace Stevens: An Introduction to the Poetry*. New York: Columbia University Press, 1977.

Whiting, Anthony. *The Never-Resting Mind: Wallace Stevens' Romantic Irony*. Ann Arbor: University of Michigan Press, 1996.

Whitman, Walt. *Song of Myself*. In *Leaves of Grass*, by Walt Whitman, 188–247. New York: Library of America, Vintage Books, 1992.

Wilbur, Richard. "The Art of Poetry," interview by Ellesa Clay High and Helen McCloy Ellison. *Paris Review* 19 (winter 1977): 86–105.

———. "From Key West, Florida." *Wallace Stevens Journal* 3:3/4 (fall 1979): 140.

Willard, Abbie F. *Wallace Stevens: The Poet and His Critics*. Chicago: American Library Association, 1978.

Williams, Raymond. *Keywords: A Vocabulary of Culture and Society*. London: Fontana; Croom Helm, 1976.

Williams, William Carlos. *The Collected Later Poems of William Carlos Williams*. Rev. ed. New York: New Directions, 1963.

Wimsatt, W. K., and Monroe C. Beardsley. "The Intentional Fallacy." In *The Verbal Icon: Studies in the Meaning of Poetry*, by W. K. Wimsatt Jr., 3–18. Lexington: University of Kentucky Press, 1954.

Wood, Michael. "A Sort of Nobody." *London Review of Books* 18:9 (May 9, 1996): 11–12.

Wordsworth, William. *Lyrical Ballads, and Other Poems, 1797–1800*. Ed. James Butler and Karen Green. Ithaca: Cornell University Press, 1992.

Yingling, Thomas E. *Hart Crane and the Homosexual Text: New Thresholds, New Anatomies*. Chicago: University of Chicago Press, 1990.

Index

Abrams, M. H., 204–5
Adams, Richard P., 81–82, 110
Adorno, Theodor W., 76
Aesthetics, 2, 4, 20–21, 33, 44, 80, 88,
  92n78, 93, 97, 101–9, 112, 117, 120–21,
  123, 127–28, 130, 142, 155, 159, 174,
  177, 182, 186, 191, 227, 229, 264,
  267–69
Aiken, Conrad, 14n4, 208
Alain, 45
Alexander, Samuel, 45
Altieri, Charles, 161–63, 165
Ammons, A. R., 46n3, 107, 210
Aquinas, Thomas, 45, 83, 169n22
Arensberg, Mary, 90, 92n78
Argyros, Alex, 118n4, 222
Aristotle, 45, 83, 138, 178, 205, 231,
  236n13
Ashbery, John, 46n3
Attridge, Derek, 116, 263
Augustine, Saint, 254
Axelrod, Steven Gould, 33, 129

Bachelard, Gaston, 111
Baeten, Brooke, 224
Bakhtin, M. M., 40–41, 45
Balakian, Anna, 175n33
Barthes, Roland, 35–36, 43
Bate, W. Jackson, 47
Bates, Milton J., 33, 51, 97, 109, 129n29
Baudelaire, Charles, 46n3
Beckett, Lucy, 174
Beckett, Samuel, 213n16
Beehler, Michael, 198, 221
Beethoven, Ludwig van, 54n20
Benjamin, Walter, 102
Benveniste, Emile, 236n13
Bergson, Henri, 26, 45, 170n25

Berkeley, George, 45, 157, 228
Berlioz, Hector, 260
Bevis, William W., 32, 59, 64n17, 67–68,
  78–79, 84, 87, 92, 109, 147–48, 158,
  166, 170, 191–92, 195, 201–2, 267, 269
Bishop, Elizabeth, 210
Blackmur, R. P., 61, 67, 121
Blake, William, 45
Bloom, Harold, 16, 23–24, 43, 47–48, 51,
  55, 61n10, 63n15, 68–69, 77–78, 86,
  88, 90–91, 93, 97–98, 126, 128n29, 129,
  145n14, 201, 211–12, 220, 222, 247–48
Boehm, Rudolf, 3, 7, 83–85, 149, 236n13
Bonaventure, Saint, 45
Booker, M. Keith, 40–41
Bornstein, George, 101
Borroff, Marie, 33, 182n45, 238–39
Bourdieu, Pierre, 18
Bourget, Paul, 94n80
Boyd, Brian, 50–51
Brazeau, Peter A., 72, 105n94, 129n29,
  137–38, 173n28
Brecht, Bertolt, 9
Bremmer, H. P., 179n40
Brogan, Jacqueline Vaught, 151n21,
  164n12, 166
Broglie, Louis de, 45
Bromwich, David, 267
Bruno, Giordano, 45
Bruns, Gerald L., 40
Buddhism, 32, 64n17, 78, 81n51, 109, 202
Burke, Edmund, 92
Burke, Kenneth, 122, 158, 229, 247, 263
Butler, Judith, 4, 98, 110

Cage, John, 109
Campbell, P. Michael, 106, 161n5
Chaucer, Geoffrey, 15n5, 129

Permissions